SCHOOLING FOR TOMORROW
Directing Reforms to Issues That Count

SCHOOLING FOR TOMORROW
Directing Reforms to Issues That Count

Edited by
THOMAS J. SERGIOVANNI
JOHN H. MOORE
Trinity University
San Antonio, Texas

ALLYN AND BACON
Boston London Sydney Toronto

Library of Congress Cataloging-in-Publication Data

Schooling for tomorrow : directing reforms to issues that count /
    edited by Thomas J. Sergiovanni and John H. Moore.
        p.   cm.
    Includes bibliographies and index.
    ISBN 0-205-11690-6
    1. School improvement programs—United States.   2. School
management and organization—United States.   3. Education—United
States—Evaluation.   4. Education—United States—Aims and
objectives.   I. Sergiovanni, Thomas J.   II. Moore, John H.
LB2822.82.S374 1988   88-14530
371.2'00973—dc19   CIP

Printed in the United States of America

10 9 8 7 6 5 4 3 2   92 91 90 89

CONTENTS

PREFACE

The chapters that make up this book were written for the most part as background papers for presentation at a national conference on restructuring schooling. The conference was held at Trinity University in San Antonio, Texas, August 18–21, 1987. Funded by a grant from the Southwestern Bell Foundation, with assistance from the Brackenridge Foundation of San Antonio, the "Bell Conference" brought together teachers, school administrators, representatives from the foundations, teacher unions, professional administrator associations, state departments of education, policy specialists, and academic and political leaders to consider new strategies that could redirect reform initiatives. The goal was to consider issues and directions that would not only work for today but also be sufficiently self-sustaining to carry the school improvement process well into the twenty-first century. Reforms directed to tomorrow's schools must not rely on external forces and pressures but need to be institutionalized as part of the culture of schooling.

Schooling in America is frequently an arena for conflict, and the decade of the 1980s has earned a niche in history on this score. The words "school reform" seem to be on everyone's lips, but the array of proposed solutions leaves the impression that everyone is talking and no one is listening. The players include newcomers such as governors, state legislators, and state boards of education, as well as veterans from the foundations, academia, the business community, the scientific community, and professional associations that represent the various educational constituencies. The debate has been lively; the number of reports on public education issued since 1983 is unprecedented in the history of American education. A special literature has even emerged—studies and commentaries that provide seemingly endless analysis of what the reports do and don't say, who agrees with whom, what values are at stake or ignored, whose interests are served by what report, and so on.

Disagreements are a way of life within our political system; conflict is its engine. This is the nature of democracy. However, there is a fundamental distinction between disagreements related to the theme of the nation's basic values, on the one hand, and disagreements over how these values are to be realized in policies and institutions, on the other. The philosopher's shorthand is to refer to these as ends values and means values, respectively. Unresolved conflict over ends values leads to a nation divided and ultimately imperiled. Conflict over means values, by contrast, can generate alternative perspectives that lead to better courses of action.

On the surface, the great school debates of the 1980s seem to be over ends values, and the political interests that are at stake appear to be totally at odds. However, although the differences are real and the conflicts are hard-fought, it is means values rather than ends values that are being contested. The issues have to do with identifying the key leverage points needed to bring about school improvement. Will the schools' ills be cured by raising requirements for graduation, providing merit pay for teachers, extending the school day, increasing the professional status of teachers, empowering principals, mandating teacher evaluation, developing testing programs to monitor progress better, or some combination of these and other remedies?

It would be naive to assume that all stakeholders in education hold identical ends values. Parents want the schools to provide students with personal attention and an equal opportunity to succeed. Business, by contrast, wants the schools to produce a workforce that will enable it to compete better with the world's Hondas and Hyundais. The military wants research laboratories to churn out better weapons systems and believes that this effort is connected to what goes on in eighth grade classrooms. Some academics and intellectuals urge the schools to adopt an academic focus designed to pass on civilization's knowledge imperatives, believing these to be the keys to tomorrow's survival. It is unlikely, however, that any of these interest groups would choose one of the values represented to the total exclusion of the others. The values of equity, efficiency, and excellence are interdependent. When in balance, each nurtures the other; excessive attention to one upsets the balance, endangering the others. The neglect of any of these values ultimately results in the neglect of all.

It will make a difference how the nation decides to pursue the values of equity, efficiency, and excellence in reforming schools. Some school improvement perspectives and directions count more than others; some leverage points are more powerful than others; and some changes are more efficacious than others.

This book is about better means to school improvement. Much has been accomplished by early reform efforts, but the chapters of this book point future efforts in a new direction, which the contributors believe has a better chance of changing what counts most in the end—day-by-day teaching practices and learning experiences in America's classrooms. The proposals offered by contributors have a pragmatic bent. Rational management systems and theoretical treatises about what needs to be done to promote school excellence, if they do not take into account the realities of the workplace, do not count very much in bringing about sustained improvements in our schools.

ACKNOWLEDGMENTS

The editors would like to thank the Southwestern Bell Foundation and the Brackenridge Foundation of San Antonio, Texas, for their generous support. The conference was held as part of the program of the Brackenridge Forum for the Enhancement of Teaching. Thanks are extended as well to the teachers who serve on the Brackenridge Forum: Jo Ann Garcia, Gail Helt, Jimmie R. Jones, L. D. Naegelin, Nancy Patterson, Carmen Pettit, David Plylar, Patricia Ramirez, Rose Ellen Ranson, Shirley Rich, Kristine Riemann, Carol Ann Smith, Sharon Spencer, Linda Swanson, and Michelle Wallish. Ernest L. Boyer, Susan J. Rosenholtz, and Arthur Wise participated in the Forum as associates. Theodore R. Sizer and Linda McNeil served as consultants to the Forum.

A very special acknowledgment goes to Ronald K. Calgaard, president of Trinity University. His steadfast commitment to the improvement of elementary and secondary schools serves as a model for all of higher education.

Trinity graduate student Kathy Krnavek served as conference coordinator, and Cathy Penshorn assisted with the editing of the book. Most important, the editors' deepest appreciation is extended to the conference participants whose chapters make up the book and to those who attended the conference, for their challenging and insightful participation.

Thomas J. Sergiovanni
John H. Moore

CONTRIBUTING AUTHORS

SAMUEL B. BACHARACH is Professor of Organizational Behavior in the New York State School of Industrial Labor Relations at Cornell University and a Senior Consultant at Organizational Analysis and Practice, Inc. He has published many scholarly articles, most recently "The Generation of Practical Theory: Schools as Political Organizations," which appeared in the *Handbook of Organizational Behavior* (1987). He is co-author of "Power and Politics in Organizations" (1980), *Bargaining: Power Tactics and Outcomes* (1981), and an edited volume entitled *Organizational Behavior in Schools and School Districts* (1981).

ROLAND S. BARTH is Co-Director of the Principals' Center at Harvard University. He is now at work developing a National Network of Principals' Centers. Barth joined the faculty at Harvard after a distinguished career as a principal. He is a consultant to schools and a frequent contributor to professional literature. His publications include *Run School Run* (1980), "Writing About Practice" (1982), and "The Professional Development of Principals" (1984).

RONALD S. BRANDT is Executive Editor of the Association for Supervision and Curriculum Development, responsible for *Educational Leadership* and other ASCD publications. The author of numerous articles, Dr. Brandt was Associate Superintendent for Instruction for the Lincoln, Nebraska, Public Schools from 1970 to 1978. He has also been a teacher of English and social studies, junior high school principal, staff member of a regional educational laboratory, and director of staff development for the Minneapolis Public Schools. In the 1960s he taught in a teacher training college in Nigeria.

REBECCA CANNING is Vice Chair of the State Board of Education of Texas and chair of the board's long-range planning committee, which developed the current four-year plan for public education in Texas. She also addresses public policy and services as a member of the Texas Health and Human Services Coordinating Council and the Executive Board of the United Way of Texas. She is a former superintendent of a Texas Youth Commission institution for abused and neglected children and youth.

DAVID L. CLARK is William Clay Parrish, Jr. Professor of Education in the Curry School of Education, University of Virginia. He has also served as Professor at Ohio State University and Indiana University. For a number of years, he was Dean of the School of Education at Indiana. His research studies and publications have included work in organizational theory, policy studies, teacher education, and the change process in education.

SHARON CONLEY is Assistant Professor of Education Foundations and Administration in the School of Education at the University of Arizona. She received her Ph.D. from the University of Michigan in 1983. Her research interests are primarily centered on the application of theories of organizational behavior to the study of schools. Her recent articles have appeared in such journals as *Teachers College Record, Sociology of Work and Occupations, The Journal of Personnel Evaluation in Education*, and *Phi Delta Kappan*.

LARRY CUBAN is Professor of Education and Associate Dean for Academic and Student Affairs at Stanford University. He has initiated an ongoing superintendents' roundtable for school superintendents in Santa Clara County to discuss policy issues and currently heads the Stanford/Schools Collaborative. Dr. Cuban's books include *Teachers and Machines: The Use of Classroom Technology Since 1920* (1986); *How Teachers Taught, 1890–1980* (1984); and *Urban School Chiefs Under Fire* (1976). *The Managerial Imperative: The Practice of Leadership in Schools* was published in 1987.

HOWARD GARDNER is Professor of Education and Co-Director of Project Zero at Harvard University, Professor of Neurology at the Boston University School of Medicine, and Research Psychologist at the Boston Veterans Administration Medical Center. A developmental psychologist by training, he has focused his research on the development and breakdown of human symbol-using capacities, with a particular emphasis on artistic cognition. Among his books are *Frames of Mind: The Theory of Multiple Intelligences* (1983), *Art, Mind, and Brain: A Cognitive Approach to Creativity* (1982), and *The Mind's New Science: A History of the Cognitive Revolution* (1985).

MICHAEL W. KIRST is the Chair of Administration and Policy Analysis in the School of Education at Stanford. He has had an extensive career in government, including positions as President of the California State Board of Education, Staff Director of the U.S. Senate Subcommittee on Manpower and Poverty, and Associate Director of the White House Fellows. His recent books include *Who Controls Our Schools?* and *Schools in Conflict*. Professor Kirst is Co-Director of Policy Analysis for California Education.

JUDITH E. LANIER is Professor of Teacher Education, Dean of the College of Education, and Acting Assistant Provost at Michigan State University. A former elementary and junior high school teacher, she was founding Co-Director of the Institute for Research on Teaching at MSU and the first Vice-President of the American Educational Research Association's Division on Teaching and Teacher Education. Lanier now serves as President and Executive Board Chair for the Holmes Group, a consortium of research universities dedicated to program development and research on the problems of teacher education and school learning. She also serves on the National Board for Professional Teaching Standards and its planning group, and has been a member of the Carnegie Forum's Task Force on Teaching as a Profession. Her recent publications include primary authorship of the Holmes Group's report, *Tomorrow's Teachers,* and a chapter on teacher education in the third edition of the *Handbook for Research on Teaching.*

REUBEN R. McDANIEL, JR. is Jesse H. Jones Professor of Management at the University of Texas, Austin. An expert in business policy analysis, he has conducted a number of public policy studies in Texas, including work for the Department of Human Resources and the Department of Public Welfare. Among his many publications are *Organization: An Information Systems Perspective* (1979) and "Exploiting Information Technologies to Design More Effective Organizations" (1986). His work reflects an interest in various kinds of professional organizations, including schools and universities, hospitals, and engineering enterprises.

JUDITH M. MELOY is in the Office of Research and Evaluation, Connecticut State Department of Education, Hartford, Connecticut. Before this appointment, she was at Indiana University-Purdue University, Indianapolis, researching leadership and the change process in schools and colleges. In 1986, she received a Ph.D. in higher education and educational research from Indiana University.

DOUGLAS E. MITCHELL is Professor of Education at the University of California, Riverside. His research emphasizes policy and the impact of policy on the educational system. Dr. Mitchell's books and publications include *Work Orientation and Job Performance: The Cultural Basis of Teaching Rewards and Incentives* (1987), *The Impact of California's Legislative Policy on Public School Performance* (1980), and *Shaping Legislative Decisions: Education Policy and the Social Sciences* (1981).

JOHN H. MOORE is Norine R. Murchison Professor of Education at Trinity University. He joined the Trinity University faculty in 1968 and has been Chairman of the Department of Education since 1973. He has served on the Texas State Board of Education Commission on Standards for the Teaching Profession, the Texas Association of Colleges for Teacher Education, the San Antonio Teacher Education Advisory Center, the Association for Supervision and Curriculum Development, the National Commission on Supervision, and the Alamo Area Association for Supervision and Curriculum Development. His scholarship interests are in the area of education policy, and he has been active in the educational reform movement in Texas. He has testified before numerous state legislative groups and the Select Committee on Public Education in Texas, regarding matters related to teacher education. In December 1985, Moore served as a participant in the Bi-National Symposium on Educational Reform, held in the People's Republic of China. He is Director of the Brackenridge Forum for the Enhancement of Teaching.

A. HARRY PASSOW is Jacob H. Schiff Professor of Education at Teachers College, Columbia University. He is also a Senior Researcher at the ERIC Clearinghouse on Urban Education. His many publications include *Reforming Schools in the 1980s: A Critical Review of the National Reports* (1984) and *Secondary Education Reform: Retrospect and Prospect* (1976). His interests include education of the gifted, urban education, school reform, and curriculum development. He is currently President of the World Council on Gifted and Talented Children, Inc.

DAVID H. PLYLAR is a fellow of the Brackenridge Forum for the Enhancement of Teaching and a social studies and math teacher at Harlandale High School in San Antonio. With 22 years experience in education, he has taught all grades from 7 through 12. He served for four years as Vice Principal at a junior high school and was Director of an alternative school for two years.

ROSE E. RANSON is a fellow of the Brackenridge Forum for the Enhancement of Teaching, Chair of the English department, and an English teacher at Alamo Heights High School in San Antonio. She is a member of the National Council of Teachers of English, the Texas Joint Council of Teachers of English, the San Antonio Area Council of Teachers of English, the Conference of Secondary School English Department Chairpersons, and local and state teachers associations.

PHILLIP SCHLECHTY is the Executive Director of the Jefferson County Public Schools and of Gheens Professional Development Academy and Professor of Educational Administration at the University of Louisville. Schlechty has published numerous books and articles on topics related to school reform and has received the AERA Professional Service Award and the AFT Quest Citation Award. He serves on the Board of Directors of the Kentucky Education Foundation, the AACTE Commission on National Certification, the Editorial Advisory Board of *Instructor Magazine*, and the Advisory Board of the National Center for Research on Teacher Education.

DONALD A. SCHÖN is Ford Professor of Urban Studies and Education, Department of Urban Studies and Planning, Massachusetts Institute of Technology. He has worked as a researcher and practitioner on problems of technological innovation, organizational learning, and professional effectiveness. In 1970, he was invited to deliver the Reith Lectures on the BBC. His books include *Theory in Practice: Increasing Professional Effectiveness* (1974) and *Organizational Learning: A Theory of Action Perspective* (1978), both with Chris Argyris; *The Reflective Practitioner* (1983); and *Educating the Reflective Practitioner* (1987).

MICHAEL W. SEDLAK is Associate Professor of Teacher Education and Senior Researcher, Institute for Research on Teaching, Michigan State University. He is a historian of education and has published widely in the fields of youth policy, the evolution of the teaching profession and professional education, and the history of educational reform. His major books include *Education in the United States: An Interpretive History* (1976), with Robert L. Church, and the award-winning *Selling Students Short: Classroom Bargains and Academic Reform in the American High School* (1986), with Christopher Wheeler, Diana Pullin, and Philip Cusick.

THOMAS J. SERGIOVANNI is Lillian Radford Professor of Education at Trinity University, San Antonio, Texas. For nineteen years, he was Professor of Education Administration and Supervision at the University of Illinois, Urbana-Champagne. In recent years, his work has focused on the use of scientific knowledge in practice and in developing models of management and leadership that fit better the context of practice. Recent books include *Leadership and Organizational Culture*, edited with John E. Corbally (1984); *Educational Governance and Administration*, with Martin Burlingame, Fred Coombs, and Paul Thurston (2nd ed., 1987); *The Principalship a Reflective Practice Perspective* (1987); and *Supervision: Human Perspectives*, with Robert J. Starratt (1988). Dr. Sergiovanni is an Associate with the Brackenridge Forum for the Enhancement of Teaching.

LEE S. SHULMAN is Professor of Education and Professor of Psychology at Stanford University. He was previously Professor of Educational Psychology and Medical Education at Michigan State University, serving as a member of that faculty from 1963 to 1982. His recent research has consisted of long-term case studies of individuals who are participating in teacher education programs or are in their first year of teaching. Shulman is currently working on the development of new approaches to the assessment of knowledge and skill in teaching. A member of the National Academy of Education, Shulman is past President of the American Educational Research Association. His writings include *Handbook of Teaching and Policy* (1983) and numerous articles for the *Harvard Educational Review* and *Educational Researcher*.

KENNETH A. SIROTNIK is currently Research Professor in the College of Education at the University of Washington. He has participated as a senior member of many educational research teams, including the nationally recognized A Study of Schooling. His publications range widely over many topics, including measurement, statistics and evaluation, computer technology, educational policy, change, and school improvement. His most recent co-edited book, *Critical Perspectives on the Organization and Improvement of Schooling*, reflects a long-standing commitment to reconceptualizing and reconstructing inquiry and method in the context of educational practice.

KARL E. WEICK is the Rensis Likert Collegiate Professor of Organizational Behavior and Psychology at the University of Michigan. Prior to this appointment, he held the Hawkins & Company Centennial Chair in Business Administration at the University of Texas at Austin. He has been on the faculties of Purdue University, the University of Minnesota, and Cornell University. He is a former editor of *Administrative Science Quarterly* and has served on the editorial boards of several other journals. In 1986 he received the Distinguished Career award of the Academy of Management, of which he is a Fellow. His publications include *The Social Psychology of Organizing* (revised edition, 1979) and the co-authored *Managerial Behavior, Performance and Effectiveness* (1970). He is working on topics such as how people make sense of confusing events, the effects of stress on thinking and imagination, self-fulfilling prophecies, substitutes for rationality, and managing high-risk systems.

ARTHUR E. WISE is director of the RAND Corporation's Center for the Study of the Teaching Profession in Washington, D.C. The Center conducts research on policies that affect teachers and teaching and helps design, implement, and evaluate reform efforts. Among his publications are *Rich Schools, Poor Schools: The Promise of Equal Educational Opportunity,* the 1968 book that conceived the idea for such school finance reform lawsuits as *Serrano, Rodriguez,* and *Robinson.* A 1979 book, *Legislated Learning,* critically examined some of the effects of government regulation on the American classroom and foreshadowed the emergence of teacher professionalism.

SCHOOLING FOR TOMORROW
Directing Reforms to Issues That Count

CHAPTER 1

What Really Counts
in Improving Schools?

THOMAS J. SERGIOVANNI
Trinity University

The principal walks into Barbara's class to observe her teaching as part of a mandated teacher evaluation program. The evaluation will be based on a performance measurement system composed of lists of behaviorally anchored indicators that are purported to make up good teaching. The principal's task is to observe Barbara's teaching, keeping a record of the indicators she displays. Barbara manages to display nearly all of the required indicators, earning a high score that warrants a rating of excellent. During her previous observation, Barbara displayed only a few of the required indicators; the principal considers the improvement in her score to be a sign that Barbara's teaching is getting better.

INDICATORS AND THE REAL THING

Some would conclude from the incident described above that school reforms are working. Before that judgment can be made, however, the indicators of school reform must be distinguished from the real thing. The two are often confused, resulting in an illusion of success. They are the same only if the reforms reach into America's schools and classrooms and influence, as planned, what principals and teachers believe, think, and do and what happens to students and learning. Those who evaluate the efficacy of school reform initiatives need to be concerned not only with what people seem to be doing but also with what is actually hap-

1

pening. An efficacious school reform initiative is one that produces the desired effects on a sustained basis.

When the principal leaves the classroom, Barbara breathes a sigh of relief. After the first round of evaluations, Barbara and some other teachers got together to figure out how they might best teach in order to get higher scores. They discussed, for example, the types of lessons that would enable them to show the most indicators to an evaluator. They talked about the best ways to get students ready to participate in the lesson in a manner that would elicit higher evaluation scores. Now that the evaluation is over, Barbara feels relieved. She is ready to go back to teach the way she likes and thinks best.

The story of Barbara illustrates a reality that must be faced by those who seek to improve our schools. America's schools are loosely connected in a management sense but tightly connected in a cultural sense. What matters most are the norms of the work group and individuals' beliefs, values, patterns of socialization, convictions, and commitments. Management systems and related patterns of control, which are easily circumvented, are less important. The theories that often drive school improvement efforts are based on the opposite premise: They give too much attention to managerially oriented systems of control and not enough to the human factors associated with increased performance.

It is not enough for reformers to have good ideas for improving schools and to work hard in getting these ideas implemented. The implementation process itself is key. The mandated evaluation system Barbara faces, for example, might make sense from a pedagogical point of view; the processes used to implement the system might (on paper anyway) win high marks for technical soundness and management rigor. Nonetheless, the intended reform has not proved efficacious. This approach to school improvement reinforces the old adage: The more things change, the more they stay the same.[1] Mandates for improvement from the state and other sources have their place, and competent management systems for implementing changes remain important. However, school reformers must have not only sound proposals but also efficacious strategies for school improvement.

PITCHING AND SURFING VIEWS OF SCHOOLING

Unanticipated negative consequences often plague school improvement efforts. The neophyte in matters of school improvement may conclude that desired effects can be detected by measuring discrete school outcomes, but experienced school improvement practitioners understand that the effects of any change are multiple and often contradictory. Every gain in one dimension has consequences in another—often more evasive—dimension. Sustained school improvement has not been achieved if test score gains are accompanied by increased dropout rates, if close monitoring of teaching is accompanied by faltering morale, or if there is concentration on a few teaching objectives that can be easily measured at the expense of more important objectives that are difficult to measure.

Schooling is a complex affair; it resembles surfing more than it does pitching.[2] When school improvement initiatives are based on the pitching metaphor, schooling is viewed as a simple process of delivering teaching (the ball) to specific targets (the strike zone). Pitches that miss the zone are declared balls and therefore don't count in the final score. To increase the likelihood that strikes will be thrown, the emphasis is on monitoring and refining the delivery system.

The surfing metaphor describes more accurately how schools work and principals and teachers think and act. The idea is to ride the wave of the pattern as it unfolds, adjusting to shifting circumstances. The pattern is made up of goals and circumstances that must be handled in a balanced way. Like surfing, schooling is difficult to monitor and improve from a distance; it must be observed and coached up close. Crucial to success in surfing are the successive, interrelated decisions the surfer makes as he or she responds to unique and ever-changing situations. Improvement efforts, therefore, are not designed to program what the surfer does but rather to inform the instincts and decisions he or she makes.

School improvement experts often favor the pitching metaphor for schooling, because it is easier to deal with. Rules and regulations, for example, can influence how the pitching game is played more easily than they can the surfing game. Policies and initiatives, however, should not be chosen for how they look but for how they work; targets and goals should not be chosen because they are easy to deal with but because they are important. On this count, it is better to have an approximate answer to the right question (though the answer may be vague and difficult to implement) than an exact answer to the wrong question.[3]

There is a sense of urgency in these comments. America's resources are not unlimited; other areas of concern compete with education for attention. More limited, perhaps, than time or money is the public's attention span. Public attention is now focused on the quality of education, so the time is right for action. How long this interest will sustain itself is anybody's guess, but once attention shifts, it is likely that unfulfilled school improvement initiatives will remain that way for some time. Now is the time to concentrate efforts on the key leverage points for school improvement that count the most in the long run.

In thinking about refocusing reform efforts, it may be helpful to differentiate between first and second levels of change. The first level changes how things look on the outside, and the second how things work on the inside. Sometimes it is hard to get second-level changes without attending to the first, but changes that do not include the second level are illusions. To be satisfied with illusion is to confuse the indicators of school improvement with the real thing. The standards and rules, procedures and protocols that have been introduced in recent years are examples of first-level changes. They represent the high ground of school reform. Emphasizing second-level change means focusing on the everyday life of schools and teachers, students and learning.

STATED POLICY AND POLICY IN USE

Within education, too much emphasis is given to the policy development process and not enough to the embodiment of policy in professional practice. The classical literature in administration and public policy makes a fairly clear distinction between policy development and use in practice, but a more realistic view of the policy process is to distinguish between *policy as stated* and *policy in use*. Policy in use refers to policy that is created as guidelines are interpreted, mandated characteristics are weighed, different priorities are assigned, action theories are applied, and ideas come to life in the form of decisions by superintendents, principals, and teachers. In schooling, the line between policy and professional practice is fragile, and separation of the two is unrealistic.

Policy created in use is the policy that is felt by principals, teachers, and students as schooling takes place. It results from the interpretation of policy statements in a loosely connected world. This is a conclusion reached by Michael Lipsky in his development of the theory of "street-level bureaucracy"[4] and by Crowson and Porter-Gehrie in their application of this concept to the study of urban principals.[5] Crowson and Porter-Gehrie found that though principals were constrained by a variety of mandates, rules, and regulations, they exercised a great deal of discretion within this structure. This discretion resulted not only in the flexible use of mandates and procedures but also in the creation of circumstances and rules *in use* that put principals at the heart of the policymaking process. They created the policies felt by teachers and students. Crowson and Porter-Gehrie conclude that the structure of power in schools is in many ways more "decentralized and fragmented" than "centralized and monolithic," despite the views of those who seek to reform these schools.[6] Similar conclusions about "looseness" and discretion have been reached by others.[7]

BEYOND EXPECTED PERFORMANCE

When school improvement efforts are based on the "managerially tight, culturally loose" premise, the most that can be hoped for is to bring the system up to par where it has fallen behind and keep it at par otherwise. Barbara, for example, will do what the system requires when she has to respond. However, since she is responding to forces outside of herself, her efforts will probably be limited to giving "a fair day's work for a fair day's pay." The principal and the evaluation system represent formidable sources of authority to which she has to respond, and she responds as would any *subordinate*. It is not likely that Barbara will go beyond this minimum effort to consistent and self-sustaining outstanding performance. Outstanding performance is rarely given by subordinates responding to authority; it is a quality associated with one's beliefs and commitments.

As Bernard Bass points out in his groundbreaking study of leadership and performance, performance beyond expectation is a function of people believing in what they are doing, recognizing its importance and value, and finding meaning and significance in work.[8] Experts in motivation would agree. Sustained quality performance that exceeds the ordinary cannot be compelled; it is a function of one's higher-order needs and wants.[9] In many schools through the country, performance did slip below par. The regulations, mandates, programs, and systems of the high ground of school reform were proper responses to this problem. However, if the nation wants more than par, if it aspires to excellence, school improvement efforts will need to focus on the "inside" of schooling, teaching, and learning.

CLOSE TO THE CLASSROOM

Given the culturally tight and managerially loose nature of schooling, the interaction between stated policy and policy in use, and the reality that sustained performance beyond expectations comes from inner forces and the felt motivation of principals and teachers, it is clear that the key leverage points for improving America's schools are those that are close to the classroom.

Getting the real thing when it comes to school improvement will require that a new balance be struck among those who have a stake. The states must continue to provide strong leadership and push for school improvement on a variety of fronts. They need to be firm in their resolve to make things better and unwavering in setting high standards and insisting on accountability. They also need to provide the resources, the encouragement, and the help that will make things happen in the local schools. Within this framework of accountability and help, schools, principals, and teachers must be empowered to function in ways that make sense to them.

Empowerment is not the same thing as acknowledging the *de facto* discretion that already exists in the system. It is a deliberate effort to provide principals and teachers with the room, right, responsibility, and resources to make sensible decisions and informed professional judgments that reflect their circumstances. Sometimes empowerment is confused with laissez-faire management, in which people are free to do whatever pleases them. With empowerment, one must be given responsibility to decide while at the same time accepting responsibility to achieve. Empowerment and accountability are therefore inseparable; empowerment has meaning only when it is linked to purposes and intents.

Is teaching to emerge as an independent profession, beholden only to the norms of what the profession believes to be best practice, or a civil service profession, where discretion is more bounded? Most of those who advocate professionalism in teaching have the latter mind. In a civil service profession, the practitioner has discretion over the "hows" but not the "whats." Standards of best practice, for example, emerge from ethical and technical deliberations, from one's university training, and from being socialized into one's profession. In education, such standards might include issues of how the curriculum is best arranged and taught in given situations, how classrooms are to be organized, how students are to be evaluated, who gets promoted, and what constitutes a good course in history. On these and similar questions, teachers and principals (as "principal teachers") should rightly decide.

The "whats" of schooling, by contrast, have to do with issues of purpose, the substance of schooling, and broad outcomes. Within our political system, the "whats" are appropriately decided by the policy process in response to the wishes of the people, directly and through government. Teachers and principals participate in this process, of course, but as citizens rather than as professionals. The profession of teaching should rightly be held accountable to these "whats," but only if the profession is given responsibility for deciding the "hows." In the absence of this discretion, one must look to where decisions are actually made in order to place accountability properly.

Much of today's talk about empowerment may well be misdirected. Empowering teachers, for example, is too narrow a focus; more emphasis needs to be given to empowering the school site. After all, principals, parents, and teachers at the school level count the most in determining whether quality schooling will take place. It is necessary to find strategies, directives, hopes, and visions that can bring these three critical groups of players together in a shared commitment and common direction.

Empowerment focused on the school is an important dimension of the school improvement formula, but empowerment will remain an empty slogan unless it is understood more fully. In the current school reform discussion, for example, too much emphasis is given to the rights of the various participants involved. What are the rights of the states, the parents, the school districts, the principal, the teacher, and the students? As Allan Bloom points out, the opposite of right is not wrong but *duty.*[10] The question of duty is essential in any discussion of empowerment. With every right given to any of the schools' stakeholders, a corresponding duty must be established. It may be time to suspend our discussion of rights until our declared obligations and commitments catch up. When the rights and responsibilities sides of the ledger are in balance for any group, any subsequent increase of rights is followed by a corresponding acceptance of responsibility. As Bloom points out, "From our knowledge of our rights flows our acceptance of the duties of the community that protects them."[11] The test of leadership for those involved in present school improvement efforts will be in finding ways to expand both rights and responsibilities throughout the educational system.

NOTES

1. Many similar tales can be told. Some teachers teach narrowly and obsessively to tests in order to get high student scores; some students take "easy" courses to maintain extracurricular eligibility; some students are reclassified by principals so as to make them exempt from rules; teachers and principals often reach various kinds of accommodation as reform policies are transformed into "policies in use."

2. Thomas J. Sergiovanni, "Will We Ever Have a True Profession?" *Educational Leadership 44* (8), 1987, pp. 44–49.

3. Richard Rose, "Disciplined Research and Undisciplined Problems," in Carol H. Weiss, ed., *Using Social Research in Public Policy Making* (Lexington, Mass.: Lexington Books, 1977), p. 23.

4. Michael Lipsky, "Toward a Theory of Street-level Bureaucracy," in Willis D. Hawley et al., eds., *Theoretical Perspectives on Urban Politics* (Englewood Cliffs, N.J.: Prentice-Hall, 1976), pp. 196–213.

5. Robert L. Crowson and Cynthia Porter-Gehrie, "The Discretionary Behavior of Principals in Large-City Schools," *Educational Administration Quarterly 16* (1), 1980, pp. 45–69.

6. Ibid.

7. See, for example, Karl Weick, "Educational Organizations as Loosely Coupled Systems," *Administrative Science Quarterly 21*, 1976, pp. 1–19; Seymour Sarason, *The Culture of the School and the Problem of Change* (Boston: Allyn and Bacon, 1971).

8. Bernard Bass, *Leadership and Performance Beyond Expectation* (New York: The Free Press, 1985). This theme is extended in Chapter 10 of this book, "The Leadership Needed for Quality Schooling."

9. See, for example, Abraham Maslow, "A Theory of Human Motivation," *Psychological Review 50* (2), 1943, pp. 370–396; Thomas J. Sergiovanni, "Factors Which Affect Satisfaction and Dissatisfaction of Teachers," *Journal of Educational Administration 5* (1), 1966, pp. 66–82; and J. R. Hackman and Greg Oldham, *Work Redesign* (Reading, Mass.: Addison-Wesley, 1980).

10. Allan Bloom, *The Closing of the American Mind* (New York: Simon and Schuster, 1987).

11. Ibid., p. 166.

IMPROVING THE BASIS
OF SCHOOL REFORM

Part I provides an examination of the present basis for school improvement and suggests some new directions that hold promise for producing more efficacious strategies. In Chapter 2, "Present and Future Directions in School Reform," A. Harry Passow summarizes and evaluates reform efforts since the appearance of *A Nation at Risk* in 1983. He notes that the early reports presented their findings "eloquently and persuasively and were successful in stimulating responses and action from the public and policymakers." He then provides a thoughtful analysis of subsequent reform through 1986.

This first wave, he observes, concentrated on low-cost and high-visibility activities that included rules and regulations, mandates, and requirements designed to toughen up the curriculum and raise standards for teachers and teaching. He cautions against retreating from the progress made during this period or dismissing these early approaches to school reform as being superficial. Passow points out, nonetheless, that this early effort may well have yielded all that it could in bringing about improvements. Significant improvements in the future, his analysis suggests, would require a shift in focus to such issues as the school site, parents and teachers, the day-by-day curriculum students experience, teaching, and learning.

Using the metaphor of a second wave, Passow provides a penetrating analysis of a series of reports that have appeared since 1986 that point the way toward this new emphasis. In his estimation, the going will not be easy. Passow raises many questions that will need to be resolved. Will the curriculum reforms now being advocated prepare Americans for the twenty-first century? Does the nation really want to achieve the twin goals of equity and excellence, beyond the level of rhetoric? Can equity and excellence be achieved without making significant changes in the nature and structure of schooling? Indeed, will the ways in which educators have thought about curriculum strategies and school improvement in the past century be appropriate for the next? Passow is optimistic, albeit cautiously, about the future direction of educational reform and the agenda of the second wave that now seems to be replacing that of the first.

In Chapter 3, Douglas Mitchell takes up the problem of developing standards for evaluating the effectiveness of school reform initiatives. He believes that any particular view of what is effective or not effective will depend, in part, on the perspective one brings to this task. Pragmatists, for example, are interested in whether the policies that are proposed will work or not. Moralists, by contrast, are interested in whether the policies proposed are good or not. Conservatives want to know whether the policies proposed are needed or not. Finally, rationalists are interested in whether the policies will actually change the schools or not. He argues that these different perspectives need to be understood and brought together into a better, more integrated analysis.

Mitchell then examines the tensions that exist among four public values that have characterized the educational scene since the beginning of this republic: the values of efficiency, equality, excellence, and freedom of choice. In his view, it is important that reform efforts strike a balance among these competing values. Mitchell then proposes a set of criteria that can be used in evaluating the appropriateness and efficacy of school reform efforts. The criteria are framed as six key questions that need to be addressed whenever school reform efforts are evaluated. Is the reform responsive to all legitimate interests? Does the reform support the integrity of the school system? Does the reform provide needed incentives for implementation? Is the reform integrated into the overall policy system? Is the reform economically feasible? Finally, is the reform politically feasible? He believes that the criteria provide a basic framework that can be shared by policymakers and policy implementers.

In Chapter 4, Michael W. Kirst notes that the traditional balance in state and local control has shifted to more state centralization over the last 25 years. He points out that the centralization of testing, curriculum, and accountability has narrowed the discretionary decision prerogatives of local policymakers and teachers; if continued at its present pace, this trend may have negative consequences for school effectiveness.

Kirst attributes the shift of control from the local to the state level to a loss of confidence by state officials in local decisionmaking and local boards, the decreased use of categorical aid to the schools, state funding patterns and formulas, the increase in the prominence and power of competing pressure groups, and the recent spate of state reform bills. In his analysis, the reform bills themselves are symptomatic of the larger issues at stake and need to be understood accordingly.

Though recognizing the importance of a strong state presence in governing schools and of viable and legitimate systems of accountability, Kirst speculates as to whether the balance of control has been upset in such a way that school effectiveness is now being compromised. He notes, for example, that excessive state control contradicts the importance of such values as teacher professionalism and teacher autonomy. The findings of research into effective schools point out the importance of local school site autonomy. Kirst believes that a more sensitive balance among state and local interests needs to be developed. This balance will require some correction in the present state of affairs. To that end, he believes that attention needs to be given to rebuilding and restoring school boards and to developing systems of accountability that protect the state's interest without compromising teacher autonomy and professionalism and the needs of local schools and school districts.

In Chapter 5, Kenneth A. Sirotnik makes an important distinction between conceiving of the school as the unit of change or basis for change and the school as the *center* of change. Despite an impressive array of research findings and a long history of advocacy in the literature of educational change, only recently have those interested in school improvement taken seriously the idea that educators in schools must become empowered agents in their own school improvement processes.

Sirotnik then proceeds to develop a series of compelling arguments in support of beginning and ending school improvement efforts with the school itself. One strand of argument, for example, based on what is known about the nature of scientific knowledge, deals with how school improvement research should take place. He believes that if the goal of school improvement is to help teachers and principals reflect better on their practice, the extent to which present strategies support this goal may have to be reexamined. He points out that unless reflection is present, increased performance and quality schooling will remain evasive goals. Reflective practice, in his estimation, is most likely to occur when the school itself is viewed as the center of change.

Sirotnik then moves to the literature on organizational theory and management practice, assessing their effects on the behavior of people at work. He notes that all theories and approaches to management are not equal. Not only are some more likely to promote reflective practice and improved performance; others actually are regressive. The most promising theories and practices, he asserts, are those that promote local initiative, create meaning and significance where it counts the most, and bond people together in a common covenant in support of school purposes.

Sirotnik concludes his analysis by suggesting that the school itself can by no means bring about the needed changes. As the center of improvement, the school becomes the setting and the arena for a variety of others (from the universities and state departments, for example) to work together. He proposes a model of collaborative inquiry centered in the school as an important key to improvement. In his words, "What school reform needs is a long-term commitment to the hard business of inquiry and educational reconstruction where the agenda for reform resides—in schools."

CHAPTER 2

Present & Future Directions in School Reform

A. HARRY PASSOW
Teachers College, Columbia University

At a White House press conference in April 1983, with President Ronald Reagan at the podium, the National Commission on Excellence in Education (NCEE) released its report titled *A Nation at Risk: The Imperative for Educational Reform*. This ushered in what has since become known as "the year of the educational reform reports."[1] By the end of that year, the Education Commission of the States observed:

> Hardly a month has passed without the release of a major report by a prestigious group of citizens concerned about the nature of American education. And sprinkled between the major releases have been dozens of state task force reports, interim studies and articles about school renewal, effective schools, business-related partnerships or ways to meet the educational needs of a rapidly changing society.[2]

Although *A Nation at Risk* put it most forcefully and dramatically, a theme common to almost all the reports was the clear warning that American education was deteriorating seriously and that the nation's very future was threatened by the erosion of its educational foundations: "Our once unchallenged preeminence in commerce, industry, science, and technological innovations is being overtaken by competitors throughout the world."[3] This equation of the failure of America's schools with a declining economy and weakened national security triggered the current reform movement.

The charge to the National Commission on Excellence in Education included the mandate that "it do all other things needed to define the

13

problems of and the barriers to attaining greater levels of excellence in American education."[4] The commission's report, *A Nation at Risk*, declared that the "educational foundations of our society are presently being eroded by a rising tide of mediocrity that threatens our very future as a nation and a people."[5] The report listed thirteen "educational dimensions of risk" that the commission viewed as indicators of a serious crisis in education, including poor achievement test scores, declines in both enrollments and achievement in science and mathematics courses, the high costs to business and the military for providing remedial and training programs, unacceptable levels of functional illiteracy found among American children and adults, and poor performance of America's students on comparative studies of educational achievement. The NCEE list did not exhaust the list of crisis indicators, of course, and other reform reports extended and detailed the problems of America and its schools.

For the most part, the reports present their "findings" eloquently and persuasively, aiming to stimulate response and action from the public and policymakers. They have been successful to a large extent. While this was hardly the first time that schools have been criticized and blamed for some failing in American society—reform reports have appeared regularly since the famed Report of the Committee of Ten in 1893[6]—the spate of reports issued in 1983–1984 resulted in an unprecedented outpouring of activities at the federal, state, and local levels. The nation was equally alarmed by Russia's orbiting of Sputnik in October 1957, and the passage of the National Defense Education Act (NDEA) of 1958 certainly contributed to what became known as "The Era of Curriculum Innovation," when dozens of projects were undertaken to strengthen curricula and teaching, especially in the areas of science, mathematics, and foreign languages. However, the frenetic efforts that followed the launching of Sputnik cannot be compared to the reform efforts of the 1980s. Even a decade earlier (1973–1974), at least a dozen reports also proclaimed the shortcomings of America's secondary schools and proposed policy and program changes that would have dramatically affected schools and other youth-serving agencies, had they been implemented. However, the reform reports of the 1970s provoked little legislative or regulatory change and were largely ignored by the public, as well as by many educators. (They are, incidentally, almost completely ignored in the reform reports of the 1980s.)

In May 1984, the Department of Education's description of the response to the studies issued during the year since the release of *A Nation at Risk* (*A Nation Responds: Recent Efforts to Improve Education*) began as follows: "During that year, deep public concern about the Nation's future created a tidal wave of school reform which promises to renew American education."[7] It was a year, the department asserted with some possible hyperbole, in which:

- The ethic of excellence reasserted its strength as a beacon for American education and a measure of progress.
- Several major studies on American secondary schools appeared, some of them in preparation for years.
- Professional educators seized the opportunity to make improvements in school practice.
- Consensus developed over the imperative to close . . . "the alarming gap between school achievement and the task to be accomplished."
- The nation's governors exerted their leadership, and were supported by legislatures across the country in enacting and funding comprehensive school reform packages.
- Corporate leaders enlisted in the struggle to improve education.
- The American public, after years of dissatisfaction, reaffirmed its faith in American schools, listed education high among its concerns about the national agenda, and supported tax increases tied to improving educational quality.[8]

A Nation Responds quite correctly noted that "these efforts [were] not narrow in origin, focus, support, or goals. The diversity of task forces at work on education around the country—task forces including citizens, parents, students, teachers, administrators, business and community leaders, and elected and appointed public officials—[was] evidence of the scope."[9] The Department of Education talked about the "extraordinary array of initiatives under discussion and underway" as being impressive. The Education Commission of the States estimated that well over 300 state-level task forces were working on some aspect of school reform, with governors, legislators and state education departments all vying for leadership. National educational organizations issued interpretative materials about the study reports, together with their own agendas for reform. The National Education Association, the American Federation of Teachers, and their local and state affiliates joined the reform movement. Many local school districts acknowledged the need for reform, some checking their own performance against the recommendations of the national reports, and undertook local reforms. Corporations and businesses became more visibly involved in efforts to improve education. A year or so after publication of the major report, the media and the public still seemed interested in and concerned about "educational excellence" and what needed to be done to achieve it.

THE FIRST WAVE OF REFORM REPORTS OF THE 1980s

Although the reports differed in terms of their focus, methods of inquiry, data bases (if any), and recommendations, there were a number of common themes and similarities in emphasis. Educational excellence needed to be promoted (the rising tide of mediocrity had to be reversed), educational standards had to be raised, and public confidence in the quality of American education had to be rebuilt. Briefly, these common themes included:

- The need to attain the twin goals of excellence and equity.
- The need to clarify educational goals, unburdening schools from responsibilities they cannot or should not fulfill.
- The need to develop a common core curriculum (not unlike the standard college-bound curriculum) with few or no electives, little or no curricular differentiation, but only pedagogical differentiation.
- The need to eliminate tracking programs so that students could tackle the common core courses in a common curriculum in different ways.
- The need for major changes in vocational education—in the student populations served, the curricula provided, and the sites of such education if offered.
- The need for education to teach about technology, including computer literacy, and to become involved in the technological revolution.
- The need to "increase both the duration and intensity of academic learning," lengthening the school day and school year.
- The need to recruit, train, and retain more academically able teachers, to improve the quality of teaching, and to upgrade the professional working life of teachers.
- The need to redefine the principal's role and put the "principal squarely in charge of educational quality in each school."
- The need to forge new partnerships between corporations, business, and the schools.[10]

The term "excellence" became the shibboleth of the reform movement. Excellence came to mean "higher standards," which were defined as tougher academic requirements, reduction or elimination of electives (especially "soft subjects"), more mathematics and science, more homework, more tests, tighter disciplines, and longer school days and school years. As Pipho put it, "Suddenly the parade was moving under the unifying banners of more rigorous standards for students and more recognition and higher standards for teachers."[11] Finn described the "efforts to improve educational quality [as] universalistic, scholiocentric, and cognitive. They unabashedly assume that everyone can and should learn the same things, at least up to a point, and that point should be the same for everyone in a school, a community, or an entire state."[12]

With this perception of reform, together with the traditional view of education as a "state function," in the early stages of the reform movement,

> states approached the perceived need for change with sweeping legislative mandates. In some states these were single laws (though some ran as long as 100 pages); in other states reform packages consisted of many bills enacted at the same time. . . .
> Meanwhile state boards of regents and state boards of education

were also mandating changes. But, since these changes often consisted of altering rules and regulations, they were formulated slowly, over a period of months. . . .[13]

By December 1986, in the fourth year of reform, a survey by the Education Commission of the States noted that if state reform activity is reduced to its least common denominator, there are two unifying themes: "more rigorous academic standards for students and more recognition and higher standards for teachers."[14] As for changes affecting student standards,

- 45 states and the District of Columbia have altered their reported requirements for earning a standard high school diploma, and these changes have universally been increases in required courses.
- 34 states and the District of Columbia had minimum requirements in 1980 and have added to that number.
- Mathematics requirements were increased in 42 states. . . .
- 34 states changed their science requirements.
- 18 states modified their language arts requirements.
- Social studies requirements were changed in 26 states.
- Physical education and health requirements changed in 14 states.
- Computer literacy is now a requirement in six states.
- [As for the National Commission on Educational Excellence's "Five New Basics,"] 15 states meet the English guideline; 10 clearly meet the science recommendation; 15 meet the social studies guideline; none meet the foreign language requirement; and six states require some kind of computer science.
- School attendance age has been changed in 15 states. Six have added years at the end of mandatory schooling; six start students younger; three do both.
- Six states increased the length of the school year; seven states decreased it.
- The length of the school day has not undergone a major shift.[15]

As for changes affecting standards and compensation for teachers, the ECS study found that "most states have been actively reassessing the structure of the teaching profession, including such matters as the requirements for certifying teachers, ways of recognizing and compensating good teachers, and ways of introducing the concept of career ladders into the teaching profession."[16] In fact, it is in the changes regarding teachers and teaching that the "second wave of reform" is emerging.

As one of the more active states involved in educational reform and one whose reform activities have been studied more than many others, California provides some insights into the "educational reform movement." California's Senate Bill 813 provided the legislative authority for school reform. In its report, *Conditions of Education in California, 1985–86,* the Policy Analysis for California Education (PACE) group identified what it called structural changes brought about by educational reform—creation of model curriculum standards, increased enrollment in academic courses, longer days (six periods in every high school) and longer school years (180 days), participation in the Mentor Teacher Program, certification of administrators in skills for teacher evaluation, creation of new administrator training centers, development of additional and more rigorous state assessment tests, and publication of 28 quality indicators for each local school district. . . .[17]

In its analysis for 1986–1987, PACE observed that these structural changes could be made relatively straightforwardly—the state could easily expand the number of mathematics and science courses required, for example—but "determining the content of those courses, selecting adequate textbooks, purchasing appropriate materials, recruiting qualified teachers, training teachers in the necessary skills, changing the district policies and school structures to nurture the teaching of those courses, and ensuring that new courses produced improved student learning is a long-term complicated process, the existence and success of which are not assured by structural changes alone."[18] PACE concluded that in order to achieve full and effective implementation of the goals of reform—"better curriculum, improved teaching, successful schools, and rising student knowledge and ability to think—requires changes in teachers' attitudes and skills, in administrators' expertise, and in school organization and culture, all of which are difficult, time consuming to produce, and dependent upon local enthusiasm, commitment and effort."[19] In sum, PACE argued that if change were to take place, the locus of action and responsibility must now shift from the state level to the local level. PACE observed that although the state could "*initiate and nurture these processes, it cannot mandate their outcomes. . . . the state now depends upon actions of those at the local level, persons who actually manage and deliver educational services to students, to implement the hopes of educational reform and improvement*" (emphasis added).[20]

New York State's Regents Action Plan represents an effort at comprehensive educational reform through the regulatory route of the State Education Department. Planning actually began in 1982, before the publication of the reform reports. In 1983, the draft of the first Action Plan was reviewed at ten regional conferences throughout the state. On the basis of the review, a Revised Action Plan was prepared and approved by the Board of Regents in March 1984.[21] In November 1984, a new *Part 100 of the Commissioner's Regulations* was issued to go into effect on September 1, 1985 after a phase-in between 1984 and 1985. The Part 100 regulations spelled out in great detail new elementary and secondary school program and course requirements, new state and local diploma requirements, and a Comprehensive Assessment Report process involving each school district; it recommended the use of state syllabi where those were available.[22] In addition, the Action Plan launched a program to strengthen pupil performance by strengthening teaching. A number of state initiatives dealt with recruitment and preservice education, teacher certification, staff development, improving the conditions of teaching, teacher recognition, evaluation of teaching personnel, and professional discipline.

Because of the recognized significance, scope, and cost of the Action Plan, the Board of Regents approved an evaluation plan, which mandated that the Department collect data regarding the extent to which the plan was being implemented and whether it was "having intended effects on pupils, professional personnel, and school districts, particularly those school districts which have a history of below standard achievement," so that mid-course corrections or changes could be made by the Regents in state policies and activities.[23] The first annual report, issued in October 1986, addressed forty-eight questions and provided data on the Action Plan's impact on students, professional personnel, school buildings, school districts, the State Education Department, and state financial assistance. The report concluded, "While there are indications that the implementation is well under way and that certain desired effects are beginning to be achieved, it is too early to draw any conclusions and definitive answers to the questions."[24] In the meantime, New York State's schools and school districts are involved in various ways of phasing in required programmatic and structural changes as required by the Part 100 regulations. In all probability, further formative evaluation studies will lead to the same conclusions as PACE's regarding the importance of "those at the local level, persons who actually manage and deliver educational services. . . ."[25]

In an essay titled "A History of School Reform in New York State: Implications for Today's Policy Makers," Kelly and Seller observed:

> In the past, school reform has been noticeably unsuccessful when it has focused on social, political, and economic issues the school could not and may never have been able to resolve. On the other hand, when the reform focused on exposing students to specific curricula or requiring minimal academic standards, it has been able to effect change. The reforms of the 1980s may not be able to make the United States technologically superior to Japan, but may improve what schools try to teach students.[26]

A Fall 1985 survey by Kemmerer and Wagner of state educational reform actions (it is at the state level that most such studies are done) led to the conclusion:

> Generally, the states have concentrated on low cost, high visibility activities. A relatively large number of states have adopted new curriculum guides, raised teacher certification standards, and established

grant and loan programs for teacher education. Initiatives receiving limited or no state support include proposals to promote parental involvement in the schools, to expand local school development, to improve teacher training programs, to keep more talented individuals in teaching, and to find new ways to meet the needs of students less interested or gifted in academics than average. Importantly, these latter initiatives tend to be ones likely to produce significant improvements in student performance.[27]

THE SECOND WAVE OF REFORM REPORTS OF THE 1980s

The past two years have witnessed the issuance of what can be considered a "second wave of reform reports." Among this crop of reports, those of the Holmes Group (*Tomorrow's Teachers: A Report to the Holmes Group*) and the Carnegie Forum on Education and the Economy (*A Nation Prepared: Teachers for the 21st Century*) have been most widely discussed.[28] *What Next? More Leverage for Teachers*, a publication of the Educational Commission of the States, discussed redefining the teaching profession and enlarging "teacher empowerment" as the next step in educational reform.[29] All three reports are concerned with bringing about changes in teachers and their preparation and in the conditions of teaching.

First Lessons: A Report on Elementary Education in America was described by its author, Secretary of Education William Bennett, as the first major report on elementary education since 1953. His conclusion—surprising to many readers—was that "America's elementary education is not menaced by a 'rising tide of mediocrity.' It is, overall, in pretty good shape. By some measures, elementary schools are doing better now than they have in years. Yet elementary education in the United States could do better still."[30] Ernest Boyer, president of the Carnegie Foundation for the Advancement of Teaching and author of the 1983 reform report titled *High School: A Report on Secondary Education in America*, issued a report of a study on *College: The Undergraduate Experience in America*, described the undergraduate institution as a "troubled institution," and made a number of recommendations for reform of that institution.[31]

With *First Lessons* and *College: The Undergraduate Experience in America*, the reform reports moved the reform downward and upward from the secondary school focus of most of the first wave's reports. The National Governors' Association's publication, *Time for Results: The Governors' 1991 Report on Education* consisted of the reports of seven task forces that dealt with what Governor Lamar Alexander called "the seven toughest questions that can be asked about education in the U.S.A., questions which *must* be answered if there are to be better schools."[32]

A Nation at Risk asserted that "not enough of the academically able students are being attracted to teaching; that teacher preparation programs need substantial improvement; that the professional working life of teachers is on the whole unacceptable; and that a serious shortage exists in key fields."[33] The National Commission's recommendations, many of which were echoed in subsequent reports, were aimed at improving the preparation of teachers and making teaching "a more rewarding and respected profession." These recommendations, which deal with the selection and preparation of teachers, inducements for recruiting more able students into teaching, in-service continuing education for teachers, appropriate compensation, career ladders, master teachers, and employment of qualified individuals without pedagogical training, have all been the focus of many state legislative and regulatory activities. Yet the Holmes Group, the Carnegie Forum and the Educational Commission of the States reports all argue, as did the PACE survey, that classroom teachers play a critical role in educational reform as the "persons who actually manage and deliver educational services to students."

All three reports are concerned with the standards for entry into teaching, especially during times of teacher shortage; the nature of teacher preparation, particularly at the undergraduate level; the working conditions of teachers; and the recognition and rewards of teaching. The five goals set by the Holmes Group for its members (membership number increased from the original 14 to 123) were to strengthen the liberal arts foundation of teachers; to change the structure of the teaching profession so as to recognize differences in teachers' knowledge, skills, and commitment; to raise the standards of entry into the profession; to strengthen the connections between the schools of education and the schools; and to make schools better places, in which teachers can work and learn. The Holmes Group members are now engaged in efforts to attain these goals *within their own institutions*, working with other faculties of the university, with school districts, and with state departments and state legislatures. The reforms of the Holmes Group consortium are still in the very early stages.

The Carnegie Forum noted that the reform efforts of the last decade have involved "many courageous actions . . . and much of value has been achieved," but that many of the best teachers now staffing schools "are immensely frustrated—to the point of cynicism."[34] The report argues that many of these teachers see little change in matters that directly affect teaching and learning, increasing rigidity in the bureaucratic structure within which they work, and their opportunities for exercising professional judgment more and more limited. Increasingly, *"they believe that teachers are being made to pay the price for reform, and many do not believe that the current conception of reform will lead to real gains for students."*[35] (Emphasis added.) What is needed, the Carnegie Forum report asserts, is a "fundamental redesign that will make it possible for those who would reform from the outside and those who would do so from the inside [to] make common cause."[36]

The Carnegie Forum's suggestions for redesigning and restructuring the schools include the following:

- Create a National Board for Professional Teaching Standards to establish standards for what teachers need to know and be able to do.
- Restructure schools to provide a professional environment for teaching, freeing teachers to decide how best to meet state and local goals for children but holding them accountable for student progress.
- Restructure the teaching force, creating a category of "Lead Teachers" who have demonstrated ability to provide leadership in redesigning schools and helping colleagues uphold high standards of learning and teaching.
- Require a bachelor's degree in the arts and science as a prerequisite for the professional study of teaching.
- Design a new graduate school professional curriculum leading to a Master in Teaching degree based on systematic knowledge of teaching together with school internships and residencies.
- Mobilize national resources to prepare minority youth for teaching careers.
- Relate incentives for teachers to schoolwide performance and provide the staff, services, and technology essential to teacher productivity.
- Make teachers' salaries and career opportunities competitive with other professions.[37]

Both the Holmes Group and the Carnegie Forum's Task Force on Teaching as a Profession have a number of common themes and proposals that view teachers as the key to educational reform and school renewal. Both see a need for dramatic changes in teacher education programs, for significant changes in the conditions of teaching, and for the professionalization of teaching, including better salaries and career opportunities. Both propose differentiated staffing that takes into account "differences in knowledge, skill and commitment" among teachers. Both speak of greater empowerment of teachers, giving teachers greater control over the teaching-learning process, yet holding teachers to greater accountability for student achievement. Both are concerned with developing links or partnerships between universities and schools, both for teacher education and for school improvement. Neither the Holmes Group nor the Carnegie Forum Task Force discusses a role for the federal government in bringing about the changes recommended; this is an interesting comment on the shift in focus, away from the federal role as perceived during the past two or three decades, in dealing with what is surely a national problem. Both argue that a shift is needed beyond the first wave of reform, which, to a large extent, involved legislation, regulation, and mandates mainly at the state level, to be implemented at the local or district level—a shift to change in the structure and nature of teaching and the conditions of teaching as the keystone of reform.

In the chairman's summary in *Time for Results: The Governors' 1991 Report on Education* (issued in August 1986), Governor Lamar Alexander wrote, "The Governors are ready to provide the leadership needed to get results on the hard issues that confront the better schools movement. We are ready to lead the second wave of reform in American public education."[38] Speaking for his gubernatorial colleagues, Alexander tied better education to better jobs, as did *A Nation at Risk:* "To meet stiff competition from workers in the rest of the world, we must educate ourselves and our children as we never have before."[39]

Time for Results presented the reports and recommendations of seven task forces, each headed by a governor and each dealing with one of what the governors believed were the seven "toughest questions" that could be asked about education—the hard issues that confront the reform movement—so that the governors could lead the second wave of reform. These were questions dealing with teaching, leadership and management, parent involvement and choice, readiness, technology, school facilities, and college quality.[40] Over a period of twelve months, the governors held hearings around the country; spoke with "hundreds of parents, students, decision makers [unspecified], and scholars," and received written suggestions and testimony from more than a thousand individuals and groups. The recommendations of the governors' task forces range across the whole spectrum of schooling. Among those that attracted Alexander's attention were:

- Now is the time to work out a fair, affordable Career Ladder salary system that recognizes real differences in function, competence, and performance of teachers.
- States should create leadership programs for school leaders.
- Parents should have more choice in the *public* schools their children attend.
- The nation—and the states and local districts—need report cards about results, about what students know and can do.
- School districts and schools that don't make the grade should be declared bankrupt, taken over by the state, and reorganized.
- It makes no sense to keep closed half a year the school buildings in which America has invested a quarter of a trillion dollars while we are undereducated and overcrowded.
- States should work with four- and five-year-olds from poor families to help them get ready for school and decrease the chances that they will drop out later.
- Better use of technologies through proper planning and training for use of videodiscs, computers, and robotics is an important way to give teachers more time to teach.
- States should insist that colleges assess what students actually learn while in college.[41]

The common thread in all of the reports and recommendations, Alexander declared, was that the governors were "ready for some old-fashioned horse-trading. We'll regulate less, if schools and school districts will produce better results."[42] However, Governor Alexander did not want to be misunderstood: "We're not ready to bargain away minimum standards that some states are now setting. But we have learned that real excellence can't be imposed from the distance. *Governors* don't create excellent schools; *communities*—local school leaders, teachers, parents, and citizens—do."[43] *Time for Results* indicates the governors' continued interest in reform and the assignment of education to a high priority. The recommendations of the Governors' Association task forces deal primarily with aspects of education and schooling, many of which were the focus of the first wave of reform, which understandably are "legislatable" and for which schools can be held accountable on an improved "report card."

The "results" theme was repeated by Secretary of Education William Bennett in an April 1987 speech to the nation's education writers. Bennett declared that "achievement, assessment, and accountability, all adding up to results; these are the fundamental principles of educational reform."[44] Specifically, Bennett asserted:

> *Fundamentally, education reform is a matter of improved results.* It aims directly at bringing about measurable improvements in the knowledge and skills of American students. Education reform looks first to output, not input. . . . It means emphasizing the achievement of students—holding high expectations and setting correspondingly high standards. Reform also means emphasizing the achievement of teachers and principals . . . [who] should be paid and promoted according to their performance. . . . *Second, emphasizing results means emphasizing assessment.* . . . *Finally, emphasizing results means emphasizing accountability, not bureaucracy.*[45]

Bennett also believed that his principles of achievement, assessment and accountability were under heavy assault—more and more states were retreating from reform, and many reforms that had been previously enacted were now in danger. Ever since *A Nation at Risk* was issued, Bennett argued, "there has been entrenched and determined opposition to reform" from the "educational establishment" (a group apparently needing no specification), with its special interests and its belief that reform requires lots of money.[46] Bennett described this as "polite extortion. This most durable and persistent lament is nothing short of hijacking education reform and holding it for ransom."[47] Bennett's view was naturally denied by the "educational establishment," and it seemed to draw few supporters. Even the Governors' Association report had implied that they were willing to pay for school reform, if only "results" were forthcoming.

There is, however, a growing concern among educators that by leg-islating and mandating specific reforms and increasing the extent to which schools and teachers would be held accountable for student achievement—prime elements of the first wave of reform—the goals of the second wave were being made more difficult or even impossible to achieve. A case study by McNeil on the impact of reform on the teachers in a magnet school in a Texas district is informative in this regard. As McNeil put it, while many teachers in the district were "truncating their personal knowledge in order to control student behavior and elicit mini-mal student compliance," the magnet school teachers enjoyed an atypical autonomy of method and content design.[48] At the beginning of the study, McNeil found the magnet school "a refreshing field experience," in which the "sameness across classrooms" was missing and a pervasive enthusiasm resulted from a "mandate to deviate from state and local regulation." However, in connection with statewide reform efforts, two management policy shifts—the implementation of a new assessment program for students and the creation of a state-level instrument for as-sessing teaching methods, which became known as "teacher assess-ment"—the curriculum content and methods of teaching in the district were directly affected.

The new policies, McNeil found, contributed to the "fragmentation of teachers, curricula and teaching." Reforms that were meant to up-grade the quality of curriculum and teaching had a reverse effect: "by applying standardized, reductive formulas to content and pedagogy, [the reforms] undermine the integration of teacher, student and subject; they unintentionally (or so one hopes) set in motion a de-skilling note present in the pre-reform days of the magnet school."[49] As a result of a situation in which prespecified curriculum is taught and on which a pro-ficiency test is based, teachers reported "a real loss of power and in some ways a loss of face," as well as a "further distancing of the teacher as a person and as subject matter expert from the discourse of the class-room."[50] Instead of viewing the student assessment program as an effort to bring equity of educational quality to the district's children, the teach-ers viewed it as taking away their chief areas of discretion and authority and reducing their professional teaching role. Thus, McNeil argues, it is

> very easy for accountability to co-opt curriculum, to control it in the name of affirming and even improving it. . . . To affirm professional teaching, to support the "lived" curriculum will indeed call for major structural changes. They must be weighed not against their facility to link objectives to numbers but against their tendencies to foster inte-gration, not de-skilling and fragmenting, of teacher knowledge, skill and practice. The second-wave reforms will be structurally much more difficult to envision, much less put into place, if the first wave of reforms is permitted institutionalization, especially at the national level.[51]

Both the Holmes Group and the Carnegie Forum Task Force on Teaching are concerned with questions of attracting and retaining competent people to teaching, in part by transforming the teacher's work environment. Do the principles of "achievement, assessment and accountability" contribute to or conflict with the creation of conditions conducive to better teaching and learning? Can a teaching profession be created ready and capable of assuming the new powers and responsibilities for redesigning schools for the future? Theodore Sizer believes that many reformers "confuse standardization with standards, and in the process sap the morale of the ablest teachers and principals who well know that children have to be schooled flexibly, even individually. We trivialize the process of learning by oversimplifying it; and by the oversimplification represented by mandated standard practice, we lessen the potential of teachers. . . ."[52]

Sedlak and his colleagues see "the present standards-raising movement, although backed by serious and well-intended people" as basically flawed: "Reformers have attempted to change public education from the top down with mandates to address a particular problem; with rules, procedures, and standards generated to facilitate goal attainment; and with monitoring and evaluation to assess progress. What has been missing has been an appreciation of how such programs would actually affect the daily lives of students and teachers."[53] Ravitch has observed "that educational reform movements have taken teachers for granted and treated them as classroom furniture rather than as thinking, possibly disputatious human beings."[54] Shanker suggests that reformers have only tinkered around the edges of the current system. What is needed, he contends, is "a revolution, a radical departure from the way we structure our schools and think about teaching. . . . The professional ideals that draw women and men into teaching—intensive and individual work with students, personal intellectual challenge, cooperation with colleagues, and control over one's work, to name a few—are everywhere thwarted. . . . It is essential that teachers have the opportunity to become full professionals with the same challenges, responsibilities, and rewards as other professionals in our society."[55]

There can be little question that the first wave of reform of the 1980s has resulted in greater state control of education and the enactment of the kinds of changes PACE described as "structural changes" in the schools. How much and what kind of improvements have occurred as a consequence of these reform efforts is uncertain. While the nature and substance of a "second wave of reform" are perceived differently by different groups, the recognition that a second wave is currently underway suggests that the goals of the reformers have not been fully attained and that if school reforms are to be realized, reform by legislation, regulation, and mandate are not sufficient.

Three years after *A Nation at Risk,* Pipho noted that one could come to contrary conclusions: the reform movement was nearly dead, or the movement was alive and thriving.[56] On the "nearly dead" side, he pointed to such "facts" as state legislatures enacting fewer omnibus reform bills, the economy forcing some states to abandon or curtail reform, legislators being disappointed in so few changes having actually occurred in the classroom, new coalitions beginning to work against changes in the governance and basic structure of the schools, and many of the politicians who had led the reform effort leaving office. On the "alive and thriving" side, Pipho cited the unparalleled activity of state legislatures and boards of education, the continuing interest of state policy leaders in reform, the recognition that state assistance is needed for implementation at the local level, the acknowledgment that many of the things that could be enacted by law and regulation have been, the realization that the assimilation of changes into the classroom and building are much slower and more complex, and the recognition that a different and better balance is required between state and local control.

In a sense, the nature and quantity of reform activities of the past three or four years are clear. What is only now beginning to develop is a better idea of what the outcomes of these reforms have been. One possible prototype is the Policy Analysis for California Education (PACE) project's annual *Conditions of Education in California,* which presents a compilation and an analysis of California's educational performance and a "judgment regarding the dynamic interplay of economic, demographic, social and policy conditions surrounding California's elementary and secondary schools."[57] Several states are collecting benchmark data as a basis for assessing the impact of school in the future. In June 1987, Hechinger reported that in schools across the nation, the indications are that test scores have improved, especially in the basic skills. He notes, however, that the validity of many of the tests remains open to question: "In general, while the minimal competency tests administered to students, and in some cases to teachers, has multiplied, little progress has been made in reforming the tests themselves. And when tests are written hastily in response to legislative mandates, their quality may have actually declined."[58]

FUTURE DIRECTIONS IN SCHOOL REFORM

The present situation with regard to educational reform brings a number of questions to mind. What, for example, if the governors, legislators, and state departments of education raise academic standards, increase graduation requirements, raise teacher salaries, enact career ladder programs, set "no pass, no play" rules, and all of the other things they have been busily engaged in during the past few years and then either lose interest in education or find that "the results"—higher test scores in the basic skills—are not forthcoming? How long can the themes of "a crisis in education" and the "pursuit of excellence" sustain the present reform efforts? What if it is recognized that the essentials of the reforms proposed by Adler, Boyer, Goodlad, and Sizer, for example, cannot be implemented by fiat and require sustained efforts at the individual school building level—something that each of these reformers has already initiated in different ways? How to deal with the differences among the recommendations of the various reports? What if such problems as those of dropouts, minorities, and the disadvantaged are not resolved by raising requirements and standards? Does interest in a particular educational problem really have a maximum of a seven-year life cycle, as some educational observers believe?

Reflecting on the four years of reform since the publication of the spate of reports in 1983–1984, it is clear that although there have been many "crises" in education and calls for reform before, the nature and magnitude of reform activities is unprecedented. What has been and is being "reformed" is still being debated. As William Chance put it recently:

> Following the heat of the summer, it is difficult to measure the effects of a storm, and so it is with all of this. The reforms are seen both as significant and superficial. Skepticism over their relevance, precision, and persistence underlies metaphorical references to band-aids, furniture rearrangements and additional costs of paint. [One] analyst argues that "if the reforms do not affect who is teaching and what is going on in the classroom, they can hardly be considered reforms . . . improvement, maybe, but to call it reform is to misuse the vocabulary."[59]

Ongoing analyses and critiques of the reform reports have ranged far and wide. There are those who argue that the "really significant problems" of school and society are not addressed by current reform activities—among them such problems as educational equity, quality of education, goals, disadvantaged and special populations, and preparing for the future. Some critics maintain that the top-down approach, with legislative and regulatory mandates, detailed rules, standards and requirements, monitoring and assessment processes, can bring about only limited changes—many of which have already been or are being effected by the states. As the PACE group pointed out, the state can initiate and encourage change and provide some of the resources needed, but the state cannot mandate desired outcomes. It must rely on the local school and the school district to actually implement change. It is in affecting what goes on in the classroom that reform efforts appear to be most problematic, and the focus of reform seems now to be shifting slowly in that direction.

In thinking about the future directions in school reform, more attention will have to be paid to the context of education and schooling, to what is being reformed, and to how reform is effected or implemented.

Introducing its plan for 1986–1990, the Texas Education Board noted: "In preparing this Long-Range Plan, the Board has been acutely aware that the environment in which students grow up and learn in Texas is changing dramatically. Demographic and economic changes will affect the composition of the state's classrooms, support for education, and what children need to learn. A Long-Range Plan must take into account this new environment."[60]

It is not in Texas alone that these changes are being considered. In *Time for Results,* Governor Alexander comments on

> how huge changes in the structure of America, its families and population, make our crusade for better schools even harder. In 1985, just 7 percent of our households had a working father, a mother who stayed home and two or more children. Of all the children born in 1983, 50 percent will live with one parent before reaching age 18. We are told that by the year 2000, approximately one-third of our population will be "minority." Already more than half the students in many of the nation's largest public schools are non-white, and this percentage is certain to increase.[61]

A decade ago, the California Commission for Reform of Intermediate and Secondary Education cited what it called "alarming statistics" concerning the "unstable social climate" in which children and youth are being raised: divorce rate, poor voting record, alcoholism, suicide, drug abuse, child abuse, venereal disease, dropouts, and, lastly, dropping achievement test scores. These are conditions, the RISE Commission observed, "which stem largely from society's inability to find effective solutions to the problems it created."[62] The consequence is that "young people now are confronted with confusing and complicated social problems and turmoil that earlier generations never encountered. These situations have a profound effect on today's youth and upon the attitudes and performance of young people in and out of school."[63]

Other changes have an impact on education and schooling. Each year more than a million teenagers become pregnant, and 400,000 end their pregnancies by abortion. A sizable proportion of high school students work. Approximately three-quarters of the graduating seniors report working, many of them as much as 20–30 hours per week. The number of students "at risk" has increased. The dropout problem, especially among minority and poor youth, has not diminished, and the unemployment rate for dropouts is three times that of high school graduates. The educational gap between the advantaged and the disadvantaged seems not to have narrowed. The schools are regularly criticized for poor performance and contributing to illiteracy—cultural, scientific, economic, aesthetic, civic, technological, and other varieties. Illiteracy in the sense of not being able to read or write now constitutes only one of the many kinds of illiteracy that afflict Americans today.

Society continues to change, and the context of schooling is changing as well. The children in schools today are similar in many ways and different in others from those of even a generation ago. Teachers and teaching are similar and different as well. There have been profound changes in the students, the families and communities from which they come, and the schools they attend. In schools, the changes involve authority, power, and interpersonal and professional relationships, as well as the instructional processes, resources, and climate. Even the perception of schools and schooling is different. Both adversarial and cooperative relationships between students and faculty, faculty and administration, schools and parents/communities have increased.

There are those who argue that these changes in the context of schooling and the nature of schools are irrelevant—simply a way for educators to avoid fulfilling their responsibilities. Others argue that to ignore these changes is to fail to deal with the realities affecting the processes and outcomes of education and schooling, thus impeding reform efforts in the long run. What is clearly erroneous is the notion that we need only return to the programs and practices of yesteryear to regain our excellence. There are few who do not agree that we must "return to the basics," but there are many who question whether the "basics" of today are identical with those of the past. As the 1990s appear just ahead, society and its needs have changed; the contexts of schools and schooling have changed. The question is how and to what extent these changes have occurred and how they should impact on thinking about education and schooling both within and outside the place called school.

The reform reports of the 1980s reopened a broad range of philosophical, political, and educational issues. Adler, for example, argues that John Dewey's revolutionary message "was that a democratic society must provide equal educational opportunity not only by giving all its children the same quantity of public education—the same number of years in school—but also by making sure to give them all, with no exceptions, the same quality of education." [64] To achieve this same quality, Adler proposes that there be the same objectives for all and the same curriculum for all. Even more strongly, Chance asserts that "throughout its modern existence the practice of public education has mocked its grandest ideal: *Universal Education*. While providing *schooling* to the masses, in practice the program has limited *education* . . . for most American's *education* was never there." [65] Chance views the imposition of common standards by states as profoundly important: "[S]tates are mandating the coterminous presence of excellence *and* equity by imposing academic requirements that must be met by *all* students, Black and

White, sparkling and dull. In doing so, they move the system toward its fundamental goal of Universal Education *for the first time ever.*"[66] Although presented with axiomatic conviction, Chance's arguments raise a number of issues as to whether the school system had, in fact, operated on an assumption that most children cannot learn and whether by setting requirements and standards that all children must fulfill, the states can "bring the derogated dimension—intellectualism—to parity."[67] Were the schools ever "the engines of progress, productivity and prosperity" which the Carnegie Forum Task Force on Teaching believes they must "once again" become, or were they not?[68]

In *A Nation at Risk,* the National Commission on Excellence in Education defined excellence at the level of the individual learner as meaning "performing on the boundary of individual ability in ways that test and push back personal limits, in school and in the workplace," with the school or college setting high expectations and goals for all learners and trying in every way to help students reach them.[69] Will extending the course requirements in basic subjects, toughening standards, eliminating curricular differentiation and choice produce individual excellence? Can the present thrust of reform, with its emphasis on academic goals of mastery of basic skills and fundamental processes and on intellectual development, contribute to schools achieving other goals—social, civic, cultural, personal, and vocational? What kinds of reforms will educate creative, productive individuals who are also concerned with morality and social responsibility?

These few questions are intended to suggest that issues concerning *what* is to be reformed are still unresolved and will come into better focus as we move into the next stage. The curricular and instructional agendas for reform are constantly being reviewed and revised. For example, in June 1987, the New York State Board of Regents approved a K–12 Curriculum Guide on AIDS to supplement the K–12 health syllabus, adding AIDS instruction to the basics/essentials for its students. As with all curriculum reform, there are issues concerning content and processes to be taught and learned, equal access to knowledge, resources to be used, standards to be achieved, and ways of monitoring progress.

Despite the assertions or implications of most reform reports, American schools exhibit considerable diversity along all dimensions of schooling and education—ecology, climate, nature and quality of personnel, nature and quality of instruction, resources, organization and structure, school/climate interactions and relationships, and so on. Some schools seem to be constantly engaged in a process of self-renewal, while others never really begin. Some schools and districts seem to go through the motions of reform and renewal, but others can document change and improvement.

Few of the reform reports addressed questions of implementation.

The National Science Board Commission described specific roles and functions for governmental agencies, private corporations and foundations, the states, and local groups as part of its action plan to improve science, mathematics, and technology, but its plan has brought little or no action, possibly because of a $1.5 billion federal price tag. Adler, Boyer, Goodlad, and Sizer have all undertaken programs involving consortia of individual buildings to implement the essentials of reforms they have recommended. Few of the reform writers apply the findings from the research and inquiry into the processes of change and innovation of the past two decades. Few explore the complexities of school governance—particularly at the state, district, and building levels—as this affects program implementation and reform. Goodlad points out that

> mandating ways to improve pupil achievement is at best futile and at worst dangerous, especially as we come to know more about such phenomena. And then, when we consider the probability that achievement test scores tell us hardly anything about the quality of education anyway, for legislators and other policymakers to preoccupy themselves with how to increase them begins to look silly.[70]

From their review of research, Lieberman and Rosenholtz concluded that just as the major barrier to change in the school is the culture of that school—its school organization and "regularities" that govern the way things happen—the major bridge to improvement and change is that same culture. "Years of imposed innovations—to be implemented every September 1st—have taught teachers that they will not be given assistance, support, or time to implement it, whatever the idea."[71] Yet, as Finn put it, reformers "have chosen, for the most part, to work through [the] system primarily by yanking and shoving and regulating and tempting the people and the institutions that compose it to operate differently."[72]

Thus, there have been two conflicting trends in recent years. On the one hand, there has been a shift from local control to increased state centralization, a growing legalization of the educational process, and an increase in the state's monitoring and accounting activity. On the other hand, there has been a recognition of the need for local district involvement in all aspects of reform and the school improvement process—staff development, curriculum development, instructional strategies, materials and supplies, new technologies, and governance. What has happened in the past three years, Goodlad notes, has been

> a remarkable turnaround regarding teachers' roles in school improvement. . . . Careful analyses of a perceived narrowing in the scope of their decision making prior to 1983 went almost unnoticed in the policy arena. . . . Is it overly cynical to suggest that those who confidently invaded the culture of the school and the ecology of the system as a

whole in order to put things right began to realize the complexity of the problems and the political wisdom of transferring the improvement to teachers?[73]

During the flood of reform reports in the 1970s, one of the common themes was that schools, especially high schools, were dinosaur-like, unchanging, and unresponsive to the changing conditions. Addressing secondary school principals in February 1975, the U.S. Commissioner of Education at the time, Terrel H. Bell, described the two basic challenges facing secondary education as the need for restructuring schools "to accommodate young people who are more mature, more capable of responsibility, more willing to begin the transition to adulthood than any recent generation" and the need "to get back in touch with the community and its many institutions than can and should contribute to the education of the young."[74] A 1976 report of the National Panel on High Schools and Adolescent Education declared that "the high school is increasingly ill-matched to many, possibly a growing majority, of its present adolescent population who are either too old or too mature to live under the routine controls and strictures of a large high school without serious disturbances to them and to the school."[75] There is little evidence that the policies and recommendations of the reform reports of the 1970s were implemented to any extent, yet the reports of the 1980s criticize schools as if the dramatic proposals for change had actually occurred. The reports of a decade ago are completely ignored in the reports of the 1980s.

The first wave of reform reports in the 1980s caught the attention of policymakers and the public in ways and to an extent that were unprecedented. Not even the launching of Sputnik, which led to passage of the National Defense Education Act of 1958 and sparked dozens of curriculum projects and teacher education programs, set off a comparable flurry of study, legislative and regulatory activity at the state and district levels. As early as December 1984, the Department of Education identified some twenty recommendations found in the various reports, surveyed state education departments to ascertain which had been or were being enacted by their legislatures, and issued a chart comparing state efforts. There was no attempt to assess the quality of the reforms.

Three years later, there appears to be a growing consensus that a second wave of reform is needed: one that focuses on "teachers, their world, and their work as the starting points for improving school." In a discussion of Peters and Waterman's *In Search of Excellence*, which described "the extraordinary energy exerted above and beyond the call of duty when the worker . . . is given even a modicum of apparent control over his or her destiny," Cross observed that with few exceptions, the reform reports recommend greater external control, regulation, and accountability, and that this is what has been happening.[76] She concludes, somewhat pessimistically:

> The curriculum will be tidied up, goals will be articulated, standard-
> ized tests will control transitions from one level of schooling to an-
> other, prospective teachers will study a core of common learnings, and
> the teacher education curriculum will be restructured to include cer-
> tain experiences in specified sequences. There is not much evidence
> that the current mania for tidiness will produce orderly schools in
> which students and teachers pursue learning with the contagious en-
> thusiasm that is so essential to excellence.[77]

On the basis of reflections on the present directions in school reform, it seems reasonable to believe that the direction reform will now
take will be based on a recognition that "full and effective implementation of the goals of education reform . . . requires changes in teachers'
attitudes and skills, in administrators' expertise, and in school organization and culture," as a PACE report put it.[78] Moreover, there appears to
be some recognition, as Louis put it, that

> under the right circumstances, change orchestrated at the school level
> has a significant chance of making a difference. . . . Our best bet for
> improving schools lies not with fine-tuning state reforms (although
> some of these are, of course, necessary) but with stimulating individ-
> ual schools to change and providing them with appropriate assistance.
> A number of studies suggest that both process assistance (help in
> guiding the school's progress through the change programs) and spe-
> cialized training (to provide staff with new skills) is needed to imple-
> ment significant change.[79]

The plan of the Carnegie Forum's Task Force on Teaching as a Profession is undoubtedly the boldest and most comprehensive proposal to
appear in the second wave of reform, aiming at changing the attitudes,
skills and performance of the teaching force and the conditions of teaching as essential for attaining reform. The task force tackled the focal elements of school improvement in calling for restructuring the schools to
provide a professional environment, restructuring the nature of the
teaching force, revising the recruitment, education, and induction of
teachers, making salaries and career opportunities market-competitive,
relating incentive to schoolwide performance, and providing the technology, services, and staff needed for teacher productivity. However,
implementation of still another national committee report is not likely to
be any easier than implementation of its predecessors. A group has already been convened to plan for a National Board for Professional
Teaching Standards, which will "define what teachers need to know and
be able to do" and create "rigorous, valid assessments to see that certified teachers do meet those standards." As past reform efforts have

consistently demonstrated, it will not be easy to get states, local school districts, and institutions of higher education to become involved in planning, decisionmaking, and policy-setting. In some ways, the Holmes Group task is easier in that those higher education institutions are aiming to reform themselves. While they cannot do so by themselves and require the involvement of state departments of education and local school districts, the focus of change is on the teacher-educating institutions.

The Carnegie Forum Task Force and other reform groups recognize "the crucial function of the teacher" and the difficult, complex task of bringing about the changes they are aiming for. They propose that the teaching force in place and the teachers coming onto that force both be changed. The Task Force quite correctly asserts "that real reform cannot be accomplished despite teachers. It will only come with their active participation."[80] Moreover, the Task Force acknowledges that "growing number of disadvantaged students—from low income families, non-English speaking backgrounds and single parent households"—require "more help than conventional teacher ratios permit" and more sophisticated, knowledgeable, committed teachers who understand the special needs of these students.[81] Restructuring the teaching force and the conditions of teaching is a formidable task. The Carnegie Forum Task Force is optimistic, believing that there is a growing awareness that fundamental changes in the structure of schools and teaching are needed for further progress and that the conditions are such that dramatic change may be easier to achieve than incremental change. While awareness of these changes and their potential is growing, whether the conditions for dramatic change exist, still remains to be seen.

For some time now, especially as a result of the studies of school improvement over the past two to three decades, there has been recognition that the key unit for change is the individual school. The individual school, however, functions in a broader context of a district and a state. As Goodlad notes, "For a school to become the key unit for educational change requires a substantially different stance at the district level than now exists," and that new stance "is for the district [and the state] to encourage the individual school to come up with *its* plan based on its *own* analysis of that school's problems." Not only must the district and state encourage school-based analysis and planning; it must also provide guidance and support for the process. Goodlad has argued,

> Cosmetic changes can be legislated and mandated; the ways children and youth acquire knowledge and ways of knowing cannot. These depend on the knowledge and creativity of teachers. Better preparation of principals and teachers along with help and time for designing programs *at the site*, are necessary ingredients of school improvement. This message is at best only at the rhetorical level of acceptance at policymakers seeking to improve schooling. Unless it becomes a guid-

ing principle of action as well as faith, little more than peripheral changes in the central curricular and instructional functioning of schools is likely to occur.[82]

This is the quandary the nation faces in predicting future directions in educational reform. Reformers *know* that they must restructure the teaching force and the conditions under which learning and teaching take place, and they *know* that this restructuring is most likely to succeed if they focus on the individual school for reform within the broader context in which that school functions. However, thousands of building units and school districts and 52-plus states control schools and schooling. Can they implement the fundamental reforms that are currently being advocated, even assuming that those are the "right" reforms?

Sizer and his colleagues are attempting to implement the reforms they advocate through a Coalition of Essential Schools, which includes some forty schools, ten of which are in a core group with which the staff works intensively. The Association for Supervision and Curriculum Development is working with a network of schools to bring about reform. Adler has undertaken a project to implement his *Paideia Proposal*, and Boyer has a group of schools exploring implementation of the reforms advocated in *High School*. There are other groups actively engaged with schools and school systems, but altogether they represent a small fraction of America's schools. There are schools and school districts that are engaged in self-renewal efforts. Will their successes and failures be disseminated in ways that will have a broader impact on the nation's schools? Will state and district policymakers provide the leadership, the guidance, and the support needed for the on-site staff development and school restructuring that are necessary for real improvement in schools across the country? Will the new knowledge bases and pedagogical strategies needed to deal with the changes in students, the contexts of their schooling, and the societies from which they come be generated— in ways that will provide guidance for policymakers and practitioners? Will the growing trends toward state-level centralization and accountability prevent or facilitate the kinds of individual building unit changes that a consensus seems to think is needed? How long can the current climate, which has made education a "hot item," be sustained? Will the curriculum reforms advocated by current reformers really prepare Americans for the twenty-first century? Do the schools and society really want to achieve the twin goals of equity and excellence beyond the level of rhetoric? Can the schools achieve equity and excellence without significant changes in the nature and structure of society? Do we have or are we generating the knowledge that will enable our schools to graduate the vast majority of students (with all their differences and similarities) with the knowledge, skills, insights, attitudes, commitments, motivations, and concerns that will enable them to live successfully in the next century? Will the curriculum, strategies, and services of the past century be appropriate for the next?

That educators, policymakers, and the public are even asking questions like these suggests that we can be cautiously optimistic about future directions of educational reform. In the second wave of reform of the 1980s, the emphasis on pedagogy, curriculum, teachers as professionals, school governance and structure, and the process of school improvement gives reason for cautious optimism.

NOTES

1. National Commission on Excellence in Education, *A Nation at Risk: The Imperative for Educational Reform* (Washington, D.C.: U.S. Government Printing Office, 1983).

2. Education Commission of the States, Task Force on Education for Economic Growth, *Action for Excellence* (Denver, Colo.: Education Commission for the States, 1983), p. 1.

3. National Commission on Excellence in Education, op. cit., p. 5.

4. Ibid., p. 1.

5. Ibid., p. 5.

6. Committee on Secondary School Studies, *Report of the Committee on Secondary School Studies* (Washington, D.C.: U.S. Government Printing Office, 1893).

7. Department of Education, *A Nation Responds: Recent Efforts to Improve Education* (Washington, D.C.: U.S. Government Printing Office, 1984), p. 11.

8. Ibid.

9. Ibid., p. 15.

10. A. Harry Passow, *Reforming Schools in the 1980s: A Critical Review of the National Reports* (New York: ERIC Clearinghouse on Urban Education, 1984), pp. 37–81.

11. Chris Pipho, "States Move Closer to Reality," *Phi Delta Kappan 68*, December 1986, p. K1.

12. Chester E. Finn, Jr., "The Drive for Educational Excellence: Moving Toward a Public Consensus," *Change 15*, April 1983, p. 16.

13. Pipho, op. cit., p. K2.

14. Ibid., p. K5.

15. Ibid., pp. K5–K6.

16. Ibid., p. K6.

17. PACE (Policy Analysis for California Education), *Conditions of Education in California, 1986–87* (Berkeley, Calif.: Policy Analysis for California Education, 1986), p. 3.

18. Ibid.

19. Ibid.

20. Ibid.

21. New York State Education Department, *New York State Board of Regents Proposed Action Plan to Improve Elementary and Secondary Education Results in New York* (Albany, N.Y.: State Education Department, 1984).

22. New York State Education Department, *New Part 100 of the Commissioner's Regulations* (Albany, N.Y.: State Education Department, 1984).

23. New York State Education Department Office of Elementary, Secondary, and Continuing Education, *Evaluation of the Implementation of the Regents Action Plan: Annual Report* (Albany, N.Y.: State Education Department, 1986), p. 1.

24. Ibid., p. 161.

25. PACE, op. cit., p. 3.

26. Gail P. Kelly and Maxine S. Seller, "A History of School Reform in New York State: Implications for Today's Policy Makers," in *National Education Reform and New York State: A Report Card* (Albany, N.Y.: State University of New York, Fall 1985), p. 102.

27. Frances Kemmerer and Alan P. Wagner, "A Report Card: Education Reform in the States," in *National Education Reform and New York State: A Report Card* (Albany, N.Y.: State University of New York, Fall 1985), p. 1.

28. The Holmes Group, *Tomorrow's Teachers* (East Lansing, Mich.: The Holmes Group, 1986). Carnegie Forum on Education and the Economy Task Force on Teaching as a Profession, *A Nation Prepared: Teachers for the 21st Century* (New York: Carnegie Forum on Education and the Economy, 1986).

29. Education Commission of the States, *What Next? More Leverage for Teachers* (Denver, Colo.: Education Commission of the States, 1986).

30. William J. Bennett, *First Lessons: A Report on Elementary Education* (Washington, D.C.: U.S. Government Printing Office, 1986), p. 1.

31. Ernest L. Boyer, *High School: A Report on Secondary Education in America* (New York: Harper and Row, 1983). Ernest L. Boyer, *College: The Undergraduate Experience in America* (New York: Harper and Row, 1987).

32. National Governors' Association Center for Policy Research and Analysis, *Time for Results: The Governors: 1991 Report on Education* (Washington, D.C.: National Governors' Association, 1986), p. 2.

33. National Commission on Excellence in Education, op. cit., p. 22.

34. Carnegie Forum on Education and the Economy Task Force, op. cit., p. 26.

35. Ibid.

36. Ibid.

37. Ibid., pp. 35–41.

38. Lamar Alexander, "Chairman's Summary," in *National Governors' Association*, op. cit., p. 7.

39. Ibid., p. 5.

40. Ibid., p. 2.

41. Ibid., p. 3.

42. Ibid.

43. Ibid., p. 4.

44. William J. Bennett, "Is the Education Reform Movement Being Hijacked?" (paper presented to the 40th Anniversary National Seminar of the Education Writers Association in San Francisco, April 5, 1987), p. 3.

45. Ibid., pp. 2–3.

46. Ibid., p. 7.

47. Ibid., p. 1.

48. Linda M. McNeil, "The Cooptation of the Curriculum" (paper presented at the Annual Meeting of the American Educational Research Association, April, 1987), p. 4.

49. Ibid., pp. 6–7.

50. Ibid., p. 7.

51. Ibid., p. 29.

52. Theodore R. Sizer, "Common Sense," *Educational Leadership 42*, March 1985, p. 23.

53. Michael W. Sedlak, Christopher W. Wheeler, Diana C. Pullin, and Philip A. Cusick, *Selling Students Short: Classroom Bargains and Academic Reform in the American High School* (New York: Teachers College Press, 1986), p. 185.

54. Diane Ravitch, *The Schools We Deserve* (New York: Basic Books, 1985), p. 19.

55. Albert Shanker, "Teachers Must Take Charge," *Educational Leadership 44*, September 1986, p. 12.

56. Pipho, op. cit., pp. K6–K7.

57. PACE, op. cit., p. 1.

58. Fred M. Hechinger, "Final Grade: Modest Gains," *New York Times*, vol. 136, June 16, 1987, p. C8.

59. William Chance, ". . . the best of educations." *Reforming America's Public Schools in the 1980s* (Washington, D.C.: John D. and Catherine T. MacArthur Foundation, 1986), p. 2.

60. Texas Education Agency, *1986–1990: Long-Range Plan of the State Board of Education for Texas Public School Education* (Austin, Tex.: Texas Education Agency, 1987), p. 2.

61. Alexander, op. cit., p. 6.

62. California Commission for Reform of Intermediate and Secondary Education, *The RISE Report* (Sacramento, Calif.: California State Department of Education, 1975), p. xii.

63. Ibid., p. xi.

64. Mortimer Adler, *The Paideia Proposal: An Educational Manifesto* (New York: Macmillan, 1982), p. 4.

65. Chance, op. cit., p. ii.
66. Ibid.
67. Ibid.
68. Carnegie Forum on Education and the Economy, op. cit., p. 2.
69. National Commission on Excellence in Education, op. cit.
70. John I. Goodlad, "Structure, Process and Agenda," in John I. Goodlad, ed., *The Ecology of School Renewal*, Part I, 86th Yearbook of the National Society for the Study of Education (Chicago: University of Chicago Press, 1987), p. 9.
71. Ann Lieberman and Susan Rosenholtz, "The Road to School Improvement: Barriers and Bridges," in *The Ecology of School Renewal*, op. cit., p. 94.
72. Chester E. Finn, Jr., "We Can Shape Our Destiny," *Educational Leadership 44*, September 1986, p. 4.
73. John I. Goodlad, "Toward a Healthy Ecosystem," in *The Ecology of School Renewal*, op. cit., p. 215.
74. Terrell H. Bell, "The Principal's Chair: The Pivotal Seat in Secondary Education" (address to Conference of National Association of Secondary School Principals in Las Vegas, Nevada, February 10, 1975).
75. John H. Martin, chairman, National Panel on High School and Adolescent Education, *The Education of Adolescents* (Washington, D.C.: U.S. Government Printing Office, 1974), p. 37.
76. K. Patricia Cross, "The Rising Tide of School Reform Reports," *Phi Delta Kappan 66*, November 1984, p. 69.
77. Ibid., p. 170.
78. PACE, op. cit., p. 3.
79. Karen Seashore Louis, "Reforming Secondary Schools: A Critique and an Agenda for Administrators," *Educational Leadership 44*, September 1986, p. 34.
80. Carnegie Forum on Education and the Economy, op. cit., p. 26.
81. Ibid., p. 32.
82. Nelson Quinby, "Improving the Place Called School: A Conversation with John Goodlad," *Educational Leadership 42*, March 1985, p. 19.

CHAPTER 3

Measuring Up: Standards for Evaluating School Reform

DOUGLAS E. MITCHELL

University of California, Riverside

Measuring the effects of school reform is a bit like negotiating an arms agreement. In the abstract, everyone thinks it's a great idea and wants it to move forward quickly. Once assessment begins, however, people quickly realize that defining issues and specifying the questions to be asked largely controls the outcome of the process. All too easily, therefore, the abstract agreement dissolves and arguments over the assessment procedures and evaluation criteria ensue. If everyone could agree on exactly what school reform policies are expected to accomplish, and if everyone shared the same values and beliefs about the nature and value of schooling, this chapter would be easy to write.

Quite obviously, this is not the case. School reforms are inspired by divergent conceptions of education. They are often brought into existence by extended and sometimes serious social conflict. Not infrequently, in fact, reform proposals are intentionally misrepresented by their advocates in an attempt to blunt criticism or attach strong public sentiments to their own private interests.

The principal advocates of most reform policies tend to have little patience with the measurement of results. They fear that objective assessment will vitiate commitment to the reform ideology, excusing lapses in attention, or encourage disinterested observation at the expense of dedication to the cause of reform. That is not to say, of course, that reform advocates are not interested in measuring the performance of schools. They are very much interested in measurement—primarily, however, to document school system shortcomings and failures, not to assess the wisdom of recently enacted or yet untried proposals for change.

All this means that assessment is itself caught up in the process of school reform. What is to be assessed, how it is to be measured, and what meanings are to be attached to school performance data are all questions that influence the politics of reform adoption and implementation. Hence these basic assessment questions are inextricably linked to the reform process itself.

For those who are responsible for implementing school reform, assessment has a very different meaning. Proving that proposed or adopted reforms improve overall school performance justifies budget requests. Showing which particular program or policy elements have the most dramatic effects helps to focus attention and organize implementation efforts. At the same time, showing that some policies have limited impact or unexpected side effects provides a rationale for resisting centralization of authority or protecting traditional modes of practice.

It is to be expected, therefore, that zealous reform advocates will want this chapter to emphasize assessment of school performance. They will be looking for ways of critically appraising the targets of reform and will be wary of discussions about how to measure the worth of their own reform proposals. By contrast, policymakers and school staff members primarily concerned with reform implementation are likely to prefer an approach that looks less at current school practice and more at the characteristic effects of specific reform policies.

Hence, it is appropriate to begin by describing the audiences to whom this chapter is addressed. While radical reformers will not be particularly well served by the framework presented here, the analysis developed below is one that can be shared by a broad range of policymakers and school leaders. It examines the basic issues involved in assessing the floodtide of school reform proposals adopted in the wake of *A Nation at Risk* in 1983.[1] Four alternative motives or purposes for reform assessment are identified. The role of reform in establishing support for some public values at the expense of others is reviewed. The question of how various reforms tap underlying structural control mechanisms in order to influence school performance is briefly examined. Finally, a set of six political criteria, to be used in assessing the legitimacy and value of particular reforms, is presented.

One obvious dimension of policy evaluation will not be addressed in this chapter. There will be no analysis of the problems of reliability and validity in data collection and analysis. These are significant problems, of course, but they have been treated extensively by others and, in my judgment, are subordinate to the larger political and social questions addressed here. While technical problems of data collection and analysis will always limit our ability to know exactly what effect a particular reform policy has produced, the establishment of suitable evaluation criteria depends much more on our understanding of public values and our assumptions about how to control school operations than on the accuracy of measurement or sophistication of analysis.

THE PURPOSE OF ASSESSMENT:
WHY MEASURE THE REFORMS?

Evaluation of school program and policy reform serves many different social purposes. As described below, four of the most important could be labeled the pragmatic, the moral, the conservative, and the rational. The development of assessment questions, the collection of data, and the interpretation of findings are all influenced by which of these basic purposes is being used to organize the evaluation process. Analysts embracing different purposes tend to develop very different ways of establishing criteria and weighing available evidence regarding the adequacy and usefulness of specific reforms.

The Pragmatist's Question: Does the Policy Work?

The pragmatist asks of educational reform: "Does it work?" This pragmatic interest in policy assessment is grounded on the assumption that most school failures result from the failure of educators effectively to pursue straightforward, commonly accepted, and morally righteous goals and objectives. Pragmatic reforms arise when people recognize the differences between effective and ineffective programs. Pragmatists see the purpose of reform as the enhancement of program performance within the existing educational system.

Pragmatists emphasize the differences between policy and practice. They insist that the acid test of good policy is its ability to facilitate or force improved practice. Lt. Colonel Oliver North is probably the nation's best known pragmatist. The "can do" mentality expressed in his testimony before Congress is an archetype of pragmatic concern with implementation. Public agencies exist to "get the job done," and reform proposals are evaluated according to the degree to which they ensure this result. While most pragmatists do not share his belief that it is proper to ignore or subvert policies if they interfere with the performance of assigned tasks, they do tend to share his frustration and impatience with bureaucratic red tape and the cautious, "play it safe" attitude nurtured in most public agencies.

Evaluation measurement, for the pragmatist, is focused on assessing the relative effects of various implementation mechanisms on the attainment of specific policy goals. For a reform to "measure up," it must improve the efficiency and effectiveness of the system.

The Moralist's Question: Is the Policy Good?

In sharp contrast with the pragmatic approach to evaluation, moralists want to know: "Is the policy good?" Moralists see the world as a place where goals are not shared and where disagreement, rather than lack of motivation, is responsible for failure. For them, program effectiveness is eroded more by disagreement over the legitimacy of competing social goals or the appropriateness of various means for achieving them than by the tendency of policy systems to interfere with practice. From this perspective, reform is important as a vehicle for releasing energy and mobilizing effort. Good reforms tap basic beliefs and inspire individuals to dedicate themselves to the fulfillment of lofty purposes.

Moral idealism is strong in the educational community. It enables teachers to work for wages significantly below those paid for comparably trained workers in other industries. It is also a popular perspective among reformers and public officials. Federal education policy under the Reagan Administration is a good example of this moralist tone; energy in this administration is sharply focused on the righteousness of specific educational techniques and the moral purposes of schooling.

The assessment of school reform, for the moralist, begins with the articulation of values. Measurement is concentrated on the extent to which various reforms succeed in supporting positive values and reducing the danger that inappropriate values will be tolerated or given public support.

The Conservative's Question: Is the Policy Necessary?

While pragmatists and moralists tend to be polar opposites in their approach to policy assessment, they both differ from the conservatives, who ask of school reform: "Is this policy really necessary?" Policy, as the conservative critic sees it, is all too often driven by the self-interest of bureaucratic officials seeking to expand their own resources or political power. Conservatives approach governmental action with the view that it should be kept to a minimum and prevented from unduly interfering with private initiative and action. Reform is generally equated with reduction in public expenditure, relaxation of governmental regulation, or privatization of organizational control.

When it comes to the measurement of educational reform, the conservatives are most likely to ask for some form of cost-benefit analysis. Moreover, the benefit side of the equation is likely to emphasize student achievement gains or returns to the larger society, rather than reduced workloads or more attractive working conditions for school personnel. Until a cost-benefit advantage is demonstrated, conservatives will tend either to endorse the status quo or to opt for a reduction in public investment in education.

The Rationalist's Question: Does the Policy Improve Performance?

Rationalists tend to evaluate school reform skeptically, asking: "Does this policy actually change school performance?" For the rationalist, good policy is the result of a strong knowledge base and insightful analysis of alternative ways to shape organizational behavior and support high performance. School reform is seen as rearranging the conditions under which educators work, the incentives that motivate their actions, or the organizational and policy structures that define and shape their responsibilities. Evaluation is a matter of finding out how effective the changes have been.

When measuring the effects of reform, rationalists adopt the view expressed by Albert Einstein: To understand a thing truly, you must try to change it. That is, they are inclined to approach policy evaluation as a series of "before and after" measurements of system performance. Policies need to be tried in order for their effects to be known. Hence the rationalists frequently support pilot programs and encourage adoption of "sunset" laws to ensure that ineffective programs are discontinued.

Measuring Up #1: Assessing Reform within and across Perspectives

Conflict over both the methods of assessing school reform and the creation of standards for evaluating its impact are almost inevitable when observers have contrasting views of the rationale for reform. The pragmatist's demand for results (and studied disinterest in deeper value questions) strikes the moralist as an outrageous disregard for essential human qualities. Similarly, the conservative's penchant for limiting all governmental action frustrates the rationalist's desire to improve schooling through carefully documented but often expensive educational programs. The pragmatist's disregard for established procedures offends the conservative's belief that proper procedures are essential in defining the criteria for good decisionmaking. The moralist, viewed as dangerous and uncontrollable by the rationalist, finds the rationalist's willingness to experiment with other people's lives offensive.

Assessment of recent school reform efforts can only stimulate conflict and controversy if the contrasting views separating pragmatic, moralist, conservative, and rational reformers are not taken into account. Before the results of any reform assessment can be broadly accepted, all four of these perspectives will need to be considered and addressed.

TWO CONCEPTIONS OF THE SUBSTANTIVE CONTENT
OF SCHOOL REFORM

Bringing the various motives for reform assessment into focus makes it possible to undertake the difficult task of analyzing the impact of specific reform policies on the overall character and operation of the school system. This process is made complex by the fact that success must be measured in terms of both the *direction* of change and its *magnitude*. There is a basic dilemma with regard to direction: Political consensus on the aims of reform is frequently lacking. One reformer's breakthrough to high performance is often viewed by others as a threat to basic social values. Hence, the establishment of evaluation criteria requires a clear understanding of the underlying educational policy *values*. Only when these values are clearly framed can standards of assessment be developed.

When it comes to assessing the magnitude of policy impact, another evaluation dilemma emerges. Control over school performance is not a unidimensional process; there are a number of different control mechanisms available to policymakers. It is the aggregate effect of the entire set, not the impact of a single control mechanism, that must be assessed. To measure the extent of impact, therefore, we need to know how *structural control* over school performance is created. Only as the control system is described and analyzed will it be possible to assess clearly the effect of particular reform policies.

The problems of competing public values and multiple control structures are explored in the next two sections of this chapter in order to lay a foundation for the development of more specific assessment criteria in the final section.

REFORM AS A DECLARATION OF VALUES AND GOALS

Competing public values play a critical role in shaping and reshaping the educational reform process. Herbert Kaufman identified three core values in American public policy:

1. Ensuring service *quality* by creating a politically neutral and technically competent cadre of public servants
2. Providing for *efficiency* in the delivery of services by establishing strong executive leaders charged with organization and coordination of the service agencies
3. Guaranteeing *equality* of access to the service system by creating broad-based democratic governance mechanisms to oversee the service delivery agencies.[2]

A fourth value should be added to Kaufman's list. Public policy in America has always been sensitive to the goal of:

4. Maintaining freedom of *choice* by securing protection and personal liberty for all citizens

Since this fourth core value was given constitutional status in the Bill of Rights, it tends to get less direct attention in statutory law and administrative regulations. Nevertheless, it remains a core value and a constant source of pressure for reform.

As Kaufman noted, these core values exist in constant tension. Policy reforms inevitably favor some at the expense of others. Hence, before any particular reform can be evaluated, it is necessary to identify which values it is intended to enhance and to assess how much its implementation compromises the others.

Setting standards for the assessment of current school reform efforts will be facilitated by pausing for a moment to clarify the meaning of each of the four primary public policy values and explore the ways in which each value is linked to particular reform strategies.

Efficiency of School Service Delivery

Efficiency considerations dominated most educational reform efforts during the first half of this century. Americans have had an intense love-hate relationship with efficiency as a public value since the founding of the republic. The cruel efficiencies of totalitarian government have been recognized and feared. At the same time, the productive efficiency of American business and industry are just as frequently cited as the models of public service programs. Whether attention is given to economic inefficiency or social disorganization, Americans have always worried that liberty and democracy could make us vulnerable to decadence or invasion. Thus Americans have always worried about how to secure a stable social order and a viable economy—defining both in terms of efficient delivery of services and closely held lines of authoritative control.

Thomas Hobbes raised the issue of social order and efficiency to the level of theoretical principle when he declared that governments are needed to create a social order—without which life becomes, "brutish, short and ugly."[3] For Hobbes, the arbitrariness of efficient governmental authority was a small price to pay for the resulting security and order that supports civilized life.

Although Hobbes was the originator of the proposition that governmental efficiency was a basic public value, the American experience lies closer to the economic efficiency concepts developed in Frederick Taylor's *Scientific Management*.[4] As Callahan notes, a "cult of efficiency," growing out of the industrial revolution, defined the reform agenda for more than three decades.[5] In recent years, calls for stronger disciplinary policies for students and teachers are revitalizing the Hobbesian argument. Some elements of the new conservatism in America are giving new life to his authoritarian concept of governmental efficiency.

In education, efficiency has often been presented as the self-evident rationale for cost-cutting and tax reduction. However, it has also been advanced as the underlying reason for strengthening the office of the superintendent of schools, the transfer of control over school programs and personnel certification to state agencies, and the consolidation and reorganization of school districts. In its most recent incarnation, efficiency has been advanced as the reason for taxpayer revolts against education funding and as a primary objective for introducing computers and other new technologies into the public schools.

Equality of Educational Opportunity

The very first "self-evident" truth set forth in the Declaration of Independence is that "all men are created equal." Nevertheless, Americans have had enormous difficulty embodying this core value in public programs and policies. It took the Civil War to extend citizenship equity to black Americans, and a prolonged and aggressive civil rights protest movement was necessary to turn formal citizenship rights into reasonably equitable access to transportation and public accommodations, voting rights, and equal access to public schooling. It is fair to say, however, that equity has remained a vital public value, which can be powerfully invoked as the basis for proposing and enacting basic policy and program reforms.

It was Karl Marx who framed the problem of equity for modern political theory.[6] He argued that inequalities in society are a governmental responsibility because they are the result of an inevitable dynamic of private social relationships. In private society, Marx argued, there is a steady accumulation of wealth and privilege in the hands of one social class at the expense of others. This unequal distribution of private wealth produces a clash of class interests that continuously threatens the stability of the state. Marx reasoned that revolutionary warfare would be the inevitable result of this process. Thus, he concluded, government must intercede in private relationships, preventing the accumulation of wealth by one social group and providing all citizens with an opportunity to share equitably in the benefits of economic productivity and the privileges of full citizenship.

The Marxist vision of inevitable revolution by disenfranchised groups against the privileged classes has not come to fruition, of course, but it has been halted primarily by political leaders who understood his argument and acted to keep private wealth from producing the most egregious of the inequities Marx described.

In education, equity has been used to motivate reforms at two distinct levels. First, schools have been pressured to ensure that equality of educational opportunity is provided to all children, within and among schools. Intervention at this level began with litigation over the rights of minority children to attend desegregated schools (symbolized in the *Brown* v. *Board of Education* decisions by the Supreme Court in 1953 and 1954). It was extended to cover inequalities of school finance, affirmative action in hiring, fair representation of minority group members in curriculum materials, and scrutiny of the issue of fairness in testing student progress. The need for repeated judicial intervention to produce equal access to public education is a sad commentary on the failure of American institutions to embody the basic principles of equity—and a confirmation of Marx's belief that privileged classes would not easily give up social advantages.

On a second level, a more aggressive concept of equity has been used to argue that schools should provide remedial services for disadvantaged children and special education services for the handicapped. These services are provided in order to secure greater equity in society, after these children leave the school. The argument has been that the schools are not responsible only for providing services impartially to all clients. Rather the schools are seen in this context as society's equaliz*ing* agency—overcoming the natural tendency for private social relationships to create and perpetuate inequalities among groups and classes. This second equity argument has been used to support the development of Headstart, special education programs and services, economic opportunity fellowships for higher education, and a wide variety of other compensatory and remedial programs.

Excellence in School Performance

Educational quality or excellence has been an important public value throughout the history of public education. Even during the period when the industrial "cult of efficiency" controlled most policy decisions, advocates of a progressive, "child centered" curriculum were effectively placing this value onto the policymaking agenda.[7] Concern for quality has been a uniquely powerful source of reform pressure during the 1980s. Indeed, over the last decade, the issue of educational quality has largely replaced the equity agenda of the 1960s and 1970s in most policymaking arenas. Today's quality debates focus primarily on setting standards for students and teachers, providing new school programs, and expanding resources. In his early discussion of basic public values, Kaufman identified quality improvement with support for the development of "neutral technical competence" among staff members in agencies responsible for delivering public services.[8] In education, this competence was first supported through tenure and certification laws for teachers, and later through the development of a broad array of staff specialists in child development, curriculum subject matter, and instructional pedagogy. Today it is being expressed in reforms aimed at the "professionalization" of teaching and the creation of career ladders or incentive pay systems for differential compensation of staff members who perform well.

In political theory, the view that government is the best agency for providing some services to citizens was classically formulated in Rousseau's *Social Contract*.[9] In Rousseau's framework, good governments improve the quality of life for all citizens. Indeed, citizens join together in collective action just because they can achieve, through government, goals that they would be incapable of reaching through private actions. Thus citizens have a contractual relationship with the state: Quality services and improved life opportunities are to be provided in exchange for reduced personal liberties.

Freedom of Choice as the Ultimate Value

Liberty or freedom of choice is arguably the most basic of all American public values. The nation's founders passionately believed that good government is defined by its ability to establish and preserve freedom of choice for its citizens. They believed that revolution against established governments can be justified by a showing that it has deprived citizens of liberty without just cause. This was the bedrock of the classical liberalism formulated by John Locke and John Stuart Mill.[10] It was summed up in Thomas Jefferson's oft-quoted aphorism, "that government governs best that governs least."[11]

As a public value, choice is difficult to pursue through positive governmental action. Liberty is the default condition in a liberal state. Positive statements of public policy tend to reduce rather than expand individual liberties. The maximum in individual liberty exists when the statutes are silent.

Nevertheless, choice has emerged as a critical issue in recent education policy debates. A substantial number of observers believe that schools have become overly rigid in organizational structure and are unnecessarily interfering with the liberties of families and children. For a variety of reasons, expansion of client and public choice in education has become the litmus test of good policy for some public officials. The most prominent and controversial of recent strategies to expand choice include educational vouchers, tuition tax credits, open enrollment plans, support for private schools, and other strategies to allow families and children to choose among schools and educational programs. Many strategies for choice expansion are less dramatic, and less controversial, however: development of alternative schools and school programs, citizen participation in program planning, and decentralization of budget and management decisions.

Measuring Up #2: Assessing a Reform in Public Values

Competition among the basic values of efficiency, equity, quality and choice in the reform of public education is basic to the American culture and system of government. This does not mean that one value should win and the others lose. Quite to the contrary, the real test of school reform adequacy is whether these core public values are being held in the proper tension. Are all four values receiving enough attention, but not so much as to destroy legitimate concern with the others?

A recent study of the value orientations of state-level policymakers in six states provides three lessons about the competition among these core public values.[12] First, policymakers find it relatively easy to identify their own value biases. They are comfortable explaining, in vivid language, the public values that serve to guide their own policy choices, and they are able to explain in what ways their own views differ from those of other key policymakers. Second, value preferences are translated into support for specific educational programs and policy decisions. While many people are frustrated at the failure of public schools to respond promptly and energetically to new policy initiatives, state-level policymakers are able to identify policy strategies commensurate with their values and have succeeded in enacting a wide (albeit sometimes inconsistent and confusing) array of policies aimed at strengthening their value commitments. Third, recent public insistence on improved educational quality has been adopted so wholeheartedly by many policymakers that they may give too much attention to this value, thus threatening long-term damage to policies needed to guarantee equity, efficiency, and choice.

REFORM AS STRUCTURAL CONTROL

Competition among basic public values is not the only way to look at school reform. For some purposes, in fact, it is much more important to analyze the *structure* than to understand the intent of education policy changes. While they are motivated by value commitments, reform policies do not influence school performance through the good intentions of their advocates, but by creating or reshaping basic mechanisms of control. When reform is viewed structurally, it is conceptualized as a matter of supporting, guiding, or constraining schools by altering the specific forces that limit options and reward particular forms of action.

Sometimes the structural constraints actually produced by a reform are quite different from those originally intended. Generally, of course, reformers intend to generate a particular set of structural constraints—providing funding for specific services, mandating the use of particular tests or textbooks, limiting the options of students and local educators in specified ways. In actual practice, however, the constraints experienced by school people can be very different from those originally contemplated by the policymakers. Budget categories may be too broad (allowing funds to be spent in unexpected ways) or too narrow (making it impossible to pay for the intended services). Textbooks intended to guarantee the availability of high-quality instructional materials may go unused because they are pedagogically inappropriate for some students.

Generally speaking, neither the advocates of reform nor their critics undertake a thorough structural analysis. This is largely due to the fact that systematic study of the structural character of schools and of the policy options available to change them is very much in its infancy. Recent research has begun to demonstrate, however, that policymakers at all governmental levels have a fairly well-defined and rather limited repertoire of instruments at their disposal for trying to guide, support or control school performance. A recent study of policymaking in six states found that virtually all state policy initiatives rely on one or more of seven basic structural mechanisms for environmental control.[13] It is appropriate to review these seven mechanisms and to examine how they could be measured in order to assess the impact of various school reforms.

Finance and Governance

Finance and governance are the most basic structural elements in the public school system. Without fiscal resources and an organizational structure with the legal authority to receive and spend them, schools literally do not exist.

Finance policy is the most widely recognized target of structural reform in the schools. Sometimes reform in this domain is directed primarily at changing the total amount of money being allocated to education. During the 1970s and early 1980s, for example, taxpayer revolts across the country curtailed revenues for all state and local governments, forcing policymakers to reduce real-dollar school expenditures rather dramatically. Together with rapid declines in federal support, these reductions captured and held the attention of a very large portion of the education community. They dramatically reduced the purchasing power of teacher salaries and forced reorganization and school closings in many districts.

Increasing the total amount of money being provided to the schools became a high priority concern in the years immediately following release of *A Nation at Risk* in 1983. Driven largely by a desire to improve quality, total expenditures for education have risen rapidly since then, but in most states the new resources are accompanied by intense pressure for other changes in the schools.

While the total amount of money made available to the schools is critical, school finance policy is structurally very complex and can be used to pursue many different reform goals. A wide variety of fiscal control mechanisms are available for use in encouraging equal access to schooling, efficient use of resources, or greater flexibility and choice at the lowest levels of the school system. Quality considerations are explicitly reinforced when performance criteria are attached to the distribution of funds.

In addition to expenditure and revenue equalization policies (usually mandated by the courts), finance reform is most obviously linked to equity values through the creation of categorically funded remediation and enrichment programs. Beyond raising overall spending, quality is reinforced with such mechanisms as textbook financing and incentive pay for teachers. Efficiency is the primary motive behind uniform accounting systems and funding activities that encourage economies of scale (for example, transportation funding to encourage consolidation of small districts). Proposed voucher and tuition tax credit schemes are ways of using finance policy to enhance choice.

It is not always clear what values are at stake in particular finance policy changes. Moreover, the intentions of those who propose or adopt particular policy changes are not always the best measure of their actual effect. Thus, when reform assessment is being undertaken, it is important to isolate and assess the actual consequences of change.

The structuring of *school governance*—a system for determining attendance boundaries for schools and districts and for allocating decisionmaking authority among the various interested parties at each level of government—has been the object of reform throughout the history of public education. In an earlier era, district reorganization and consolidation was seen as a basic target for reforms motivated by efficiency considerations. More recently, equity considerations have driven reorganization of school attendance boundaries. When equity is teamed with choice, magnet schools and educational vouchers gain support. Reformers concerned primarily with raising the quality of educational services tend to concentrate on shifting authority among various groups. During the period when unions were being organized, teachers were seen as the most likely advocates of increased school quality. More recently, school administrators are gaining in credibility as the advocates of excellence.

Personnel Training and Certification

The third basic structure in education is the staff. Personnel training, certification, employment, evaluation, and continued professional development are the central targets of the most recent wave of structural reforms. A wide variety of structural changes in the school personnel system have been proposed or attempted. They range from radically restructured teacher salary systems to extensive redefinition of work responsibilities. Some policies are aimed at "repopulating" the teaching work force (either by bringing brighter, more able new teachers into the work force or by "weeding out" those who are not performing adequately).

Other reforms give little attention to changing the membership of the work force but concentrate instead on trying to improve the skill level and/or the motivation of those who currently hold teaching jobs. Many reform efforts see teacher performance as an individual matter and concentrate on evaluating or encouraging individual teachers. Others see the problem in group or organizational terms and seek to enhance the impact of teacher work groups or create collaborative work settings.

Whether any of the floodtide of recent staff structure reforms will be successful depends, to a substantial degree, on the extent to which they are compatible with the way teaching and learning activities are organized in the schools. They are doomed to failure if they are incompatible with the systems of school finance and governance within which they are embedded. Success will be only modest if personnel changes are not supported by changes in the school program, student assessment system, curriculum materials, and even school facilities development.

Program Definition and Student Assessment

Closely connected with day-to-day school operations are the core structures of program definition and student assessment. *Program definition* policies specify *how long* children are in school, *what* subjects they study while they are there, *how* these students will be approached, and *who* their classmates will be. Recent program definition reforms have concentrated largely on requiring *more:* more hours in the day, more days in the year, more subjects to be covered, more homework, and more tightly specified requirements for promotion and graduation.

Student assessment reforms have also been widely adopted. At the individual level, standardized tests have been increasingly rejected as vehicles for controlling student assignment to special school programs. Curiously, however, just as the courts have been banning standardized tests as instruments for placing children in special programs, states have been radically expanding and elaborating new test systems aimed at evaluating school performance, holding teachers accountable, and controlling promotion and graduation. Legally, we may be headed for a serious crisis: Tests that are declared inadequate for assessing individual student problems are being relied on as instruments for controlling school performance and staff rewards.

Curriculum Materials and School Facilities

Development and adoption of *curriculum materials* and controlling the development and maintenance of *school facilities* complete the list of basic structural control mechanisms available to policymakers. Changes in these last two basic structures generally proceed more slowly than those in the other structural elements. Text materials can be modified more quickly than buildings, but the lag between new development of instructional content or pedagogical concepts and the full incorporation of those concepts throughout any given school curriculum is at least a decade or more. Nevertheless, policymakers can substantially alter teaching behavior by revising curricula or redesigning the school plant. Research suggests that state adoption of textbooks is probably the most powerful tool available for shaping the content of public school instruction. Also, the creation of suburban "shopping mall high schools" played a significant role in facilitating and supporting program fragmentation and isolation in secondary schools.

Measuring Up #3: Assessing Change in Environmental Control

Technical assessment of the consequences that follow the adoption of a discrete change in any one of the seven basic structural control systems is a manageable, if complex, social science task. The problem becomes more difficult when several changes are made simultaneously, and it becomes exceedingly complex when several different control structures are being modified at the same time. When multiple changes in control are to be examined from divergent value perspectives, with different underlying purposes in mind, the problem becomes technically impossible. Thus, while awareness of the ways in which reform policies are affecting each control mechanism is of great importance, it cannot hope to produce clear and broadly endorsed assessments of the legitimacy or actual impact of large-scale reform efforts. The best that can be hoped for is that knowledge of structural change will become well incorporated into the political processes of policy formation and refinement.

POLITICAL CRITERIA FOR ASSESSING SCHOOL REFORM

The foregoing discussion provided a framework for interpreting the effects of school reform. All school reforms, it has been argued, can be assessed in terms of

1. The purposes and assumptions used to frame evaluation questions
2. The public values embodied in the reform policies adopted
3. The structural mechanisms used to shape school system behavior

While these concepts provide a framework for measuring and interpreting the consequences of reform activities, they do not fully specify *criteria* for evaluating whether a particular reform has been, on balance, helpful or harmful to the educational system. Hence, this final section describes somewhat more precisely a few basic standards to be applied once the purposes of reform, its effects on public values, and the mechanisms used in its implementation have been examined.

Before particular criteria are described, it should be noted that setting standards for evaluation of any program or policy is always the most controversial part of an assessment process. Implicit in any set of standards is a set of normative judgments about the essence of good government. Criteria can be made simple and straightforward only if we oversimplify our vision of government. Radical libertarians (some would say anarchists), for example, place the value of personal choice above all other public values and thus reject all programs aimed at "promoting the general welfare" as improper exercises of governmental authority. Similarly, efficiency enthusiasts can ignore the need for high-quality services and can cut and squeeze governmental spending without limit. In the give and take of pragmatic politics, however, such single-mindedness cannot be sustained. Criteria need to be developed that will produce an acceptable *balance* among the competing public values, not the unlimited pursuit of a single value.

Similarly, when reviewing the domains of environmental control incorporated into various reforms, criteria could be developed by assigning absolute responsibility for control in each domain to a particular governmental level or agency. However, in the real world of complex organizations and cross-cutting political interests, authority over each of the seven basic domains of school system control will have to be shared—among local, state and federal decisionmakers; between lay political interests and professional technical concerns; and between organized interest groups and the unorganized interests of school clients and the public at large.

The criteria for successful reform must combine a substantive *technical* interest in the seven structural control systems used to shape school performance with a *political* assessment of whether various public values and reform purposes are being adequately expressed.

Six critera can, I believe, integrate the questions of value balance, structural control, and evaluation purposes. These criteria can be framed as six key questions to be addressed whenever school reform efforts are being evaluated.

1. Is the Reform Responsive to All Legitimate Interests?

This criterion examines the linkage between reform and tensions among basic social values. It asks simply whether the reform in question was developed through a democratic process. Democratic decision making does not, of course ensure technical adequacy. The role of democratic governance is to ensure that divergent assumptions and competing values have a reasonable chance to influence the goals and processes of reform. There are no technical processes for deciding which values should be embodied in any public service program. Legitimate policy goals can only be identified through democratic decision processes.

Whether or not a particular reform meets this criterion can be assessed either *procedurally* or *substantively*. Procedurally, a reform meets the test of responsiveness to legitimate interests if all stakeholders have had a chance to participate (either directly or through effective representation) in the development and adoption of the reform programs.

Substantively, reforms are legitimately democratic if a full assessment of their impact on school operations and outcomes indicates that legitimate stakeholders equitably share in high-quality services that are efficiently delivered and do not needlessly undermine freedom of choice. If some interested groups have not been able to participate in the development of a reform, it is still appropriate to argue that all have been substantively represented if the resulting policy produces an appropriate balance among the four basic public values for all parties.

To apply this criterion, the legitimate stakeholders in public education must be identified, an analysis made of their participation in the policymaking process, and the impact of the reform in question assessed. While the relative importance of various stakeholder groups will vary from reform to reform, the following will almost always be on the list:

1. *Students* are entitled to fair treatment and high-quality educational services.
2. *Families* have an interest in the care and keeping of their children and an investment interest in the long-term value of the educational services provided.
3. *Teachers* have an interest in working conditions and a body of expertise that should be respected in the development of school programs and teaching duties.
4. *School administrators* have an interest in the overall integrity of the school organization and a legitimate interest in the development and protection of authority sufficient to realize that integrity.
5. *Local school district citizens* have a fiscal interest in the schools and a set of social and political interests in the nature of the educational services provided.
6. *State governments* have a constitutional responsibility for creating and sustaining the schools and an increasingly lively set of economic development and political interests in the quality and efficiency of school operations.
7. *The national civic community* has an interest in the moral, political, social, and economic goals of education, especially with regard to economic development and strengthening of the civic culture.
8. *Corporations, universities, and the military* are the principal consumers of educational output and have a legitimate interest in the number and quality of high school graduates; this concern gives rise to a strong but imprecise interest in the overall functioning of the school system.

2. Does the Reform Support the Integrity of the School System?

The second criterion focuses on the way reform policies handle the seven structural control mechanisms. Once the criterion of democratic representation of values has been met, the question becomes: "Do the reforms contribute to the development of an overall integrity in the school system, or do they largely disrupt operations, institutionalize inequities, create inefficiencies, or needlessly interfere with freedom of choice?" This question is not easily answered, but it is perhaps the most important one facing policymakers today. Whenever substantial reforms are adopted, at least some individuals will be made uncomfortable and will find their work more risky or demanding. Naturally, they will believe that the reforms are interfering with school operations and reducing, rather than increasing, their overall effectiveness. Often these feelings will be wholly self-serving, reflecting the problem of adjusting to new expectations rather than actual interference with productive work. At times, of course, such complaints will be wholly justified. Reform efforts can easily be so ill-conceived or poorly implemented as to become sources of poor performance rather than a means of improving the schools. It is not enough, therefore, merely to assess changes in opinion when trying to evaluate the impact of reform on overall school operations.

To meet the criterion of support for the overall integrity of the school system, reform efforts will need to assess how the seven structural control mechanisms are used to support teaching and learning (the basic business of the schools) and facilitate cooperation and integration in complex organizations (the universal form of schooling in America). In both of these areas, important advances in knowledge have been made during the last several years. It is gradually becoming evident that oversimplified behavioristic learning psychologies that emphasize reinforcement-based learning do not give adequate attention to problem solving and other higher-level thinking skills. Hence behavioristic distribution of fiscal incentives or behavioristic assumptions embodied in curriculum materials should be viewed with suspicion.

Recent work on organizational cultures has led to a better understanding of how to secure high performance from individual workers and productivity from the overall system. Setting high standards for individual workers and concentrating on the employment of productive technologies within the organization are not enough, however. High-performance systems have to find ways of motivating individuals, providing them with a sense of excitement and enjoyment as well as with performance targets and accountability standards. Moreover, organizational performance depends very heavily on stability—on the maintenance of standards over long periods of time and the willingness to stick

with new programs long enough to ensure that everyone really understands how they are expected to work. Too rapid change is the enemy of
high productivity rather than a means for its achievement.

3. Does the Reform Provide Needed Incentives for Implementation?

When it comes to improving school performance, reform programs
need to generate both "screens" and "magnets." That is, they must both
set forth clear standards for the performance of individuals or organizational units and provide suitable rewards for those who accept the challenge and meet the new standards. There are two key considerations to
be kept in mind, however, when evaluating the way reform programs
distribute rewards. First, educators are generally quite sensitive to the
availability of intrinsic psychological rewards, such as a sense of participation in a valued enterprise or deriving a sense of accomplishment
from their work. Like everyone else, they are interested in money and
public status, but education is still, at root, a moral enterprise. All of the
key participants in the schools—administrators, teachers and students—
face a rapid and debilitating depletion of their psychic energies if they do
not feel good about the programs and processes in which they are engaged. It is virtually impossible to overcome the negative consequences
of alienation, guilt, and anxiety through the distribution of salary increases or other material rewards.

The second critical point to keep in mind in assessing the incentives
for reform implementation is that rewards distributed exclusively to individuals on the basis of competitive evaluations of their performance
tend to produce isolation and alienation rather than reinforcing the cooperation that is so essential to good school performance. Moreover, as
studies of cooperative learning techniques have begun to demonstrate, it
is not necessary to use individual competition to identify high performance in the school system. Cooperative group behavior can be rewarded, and this can produce very powerful changes in the climate and
character of the organization's activities.

4. Is the Reform Integrated into the Overall Policy System?

It is not enough for school reforms to attend to specfic values or particular mechanisms of structural control individually. School performance depends on the aggregate effect of the full range of policies, not
just the latest mandate for change. States can use personnel system reform to enhance teacher professionalism by adopting career ladder programs, reforming teacher training, or mandating teacher involvement in
program planning. If, however, these policies are accompanied by continued support for teacher participation in school governance through
narrow, industrial union approaches to labor relations or the demean-

ing practice of subjecting teachers to highly publicized and narrowly constructed literacy tests, professionalization will be doomed to failure. Similarly, if economic incentives are increased to attract more able young people into the profession, while building construction and other working conditions are neglected, there is little reason to expect more able candidates to seek entry or remain in the teaching work force for very long.

5. Is the Reform Economically Feasible?

This criterion is very straightforward in concept, but it is often devilishly hard to apply in practice. There is virtually unanimous agreement that reforms should produce benefits worth their economic costs, but it is extraordinarily hard to assess the costs and the benefits of most school reforms. The marketplace principle used in private sector service delivery begs the question of cost-benefit analysis in education. In a market environment, products or services are presumed to be worth their cost if individual consumers agree to purchase them at the going market price. Public services, however, are developed in just those areas where ordinary market forces cannot be counted on to establish a positive cost-benefit ratio. Hence, the willingness of individuals to pay for education is not a suitable measure of its social benefit. Improving efficiency so that costs are reduced without loss of service is easy to justify, but it is also rare. In other areas of reform, it remains for the political system to place an economic value on school services that increase equality of opportunity, enhance choice, or expand the overall quality and level of education. What is the dollar value of creating equal opportunity structures for handicapped children? Or expanding the number of course and program options? These questions can only be answered politically. A reform assessment process can only be expected to isolate the costs and describe the trade-offs.

Economic feasibility analysis can also be used to examine trade-offs among the various control mechanisms. In dollar terms, governance reform tends to be relatively cheap, and building changes expensive. In value terms, however, the worth of contributions made by each to the realization of specfic goals cannot be determined through economic analysis.

6. Is the Reform Politically Feasible?

Like economic benefit, the question of political feasibility for any particular reform is conceptually simple. Could the same results be achieved with less disruption, anxiety, and alienation? Then the reform should not be adopted. Will both lay citizens and education professionals come to see the reform as a positive contribution to the quality of life in the schools? If not, the reform cannot be politically sustained and will be constantly subjected to resistance, neglect, or subversion.

Like assessment of economic benefit, however, analysis of the political feasibility of a reform is difficult to gauge. What timeframe should be used? Ideas that are very unpopular at one time can gain support and eventually become the cornerstone of support for public education; witness the broad-based support for compulsory schooling for all children. Ideas that look very promising during development and adoption may prove disastrously unpalatable when it comes time for implementation; witness the support for new science and math curricula under the National Defense Education Act.

It is appropriate, nevertheless, for reforms to be assessed by asking whether they have given proper weight to the disruptive consequences of their implementation and the level of support they generate from all groups involved in the educational system. The level of political support for shifting from one public value to another is relatively easy to gauge; the development of political support across the seven control structures is more difficult to assess. Determining when and why testing reform should be used rather than personnel or governance change is important, but not always easy.

CONCLUSION

This chapter has explored three dimensions of the problem of developing standards for assessing school reform policies. First, assessment motives differ sharply depending on whether one takes a pragmatic, moralist, conservative, or rationalist approach to the problem. Second, four competing public values (efficiency, equity, quality, and choice) control the development of criteria for identification of legitimate and effective school reforms. Finally, policymakers have at their disposal a limited repertoire of seven basic structural control elements. These provide the basis for measuring actual impact.

With these three dimensions of the assessment problem in mind, six specific criteria for the assessment of reform activities were developed. These criteria certainly are not exhaustive, but they do provide a basic framework that can be shared by both policymakers and policy implementors.

NOTES

1. National Commission on Excellence in Education, *A Nation at Risk: The Imperative for Educational Reform* (Washington, D.C.: U.S. Government Printing Office, 1983).

2. Herbert Kaufman, "Emerging Conflicts in the Doctrines of Public Administration," *American Political Science Review* 50 (4), 1956, pp. 1057–1073.

3. Thomas Hobbes, *Leviathan* (C. B. Macpherson, ed.) (Harmondsworth, U.K.: Penguin, 1986).

4. Frederick Taylor, *Scientific Management* (New York: Harper & Brothers, 1911).

5. Raymond Callahan, *Education and the Cult of Efficiency* (Chicago: University of Chicago Press, 1962).

6. Karl Marx, *Karl Marx: The Essential Writings* (Frederick L. Bender, ed.) (Boulder, Colo.: Westview Press, 1986). See also Karl Marx, *Early Writings* (T. B. Bottomore, trans. and ed.) (New York: McGraw-Hill, 1964).

7. Diane Ravitch, *The Troubled Crusade: American Education, 1945–1980* (New York: Basic Books, 1983).

8. Herbert Kaufman, op. cit.

9. Jean Jacques Rousseau, *The Social Contract* (Maurice Cranston, trans.) (Harmondsworth, U.K.: Penguin, 1968).

10. John Stuart Mill, *On Liberty* (David Spitz, ed.) (New York: Norton, 1975). See also John Locke, *The Second Treatise of Government* (Thomas P. Peardon, ed.) (New York: Liberal Arts Press, 1954).

11. Thomas Jefferson, *Writings/Thomas Jefferson* (New York: Viking Press, 1984).

12. Douglas E. Mitchell, Frederick M. Wirt, and Catherine Marshall, "Alternative State Policy Mechanisms for Pursuing Educational Quality, Equity, Efficiency and Choice Goals" (Final Report to the United States Department of Education, Office of Educational Research and Improvement under grant number NIE-G-83-0138, University of California, Riverside).

13. Ibid.

CHAPTER 4

Who Should Control the Schools? Reassessing Current Policies

MICHAEL W. KIRST

Stanford University

This chapter will analyze the changing balance in who controls the schools. The basic thesis is that local authorities have slowly been losing decisionmaking power to the states. Within the local district, the school sites have lost ground, while the central offices have gained. For example, the curricular and staff development authority of local schools and classrooms have gravitated toward central district staff and state testing programs.

There are some sound and justifiable reasons for this trend, including concern for academic standards, but the shift in control has progressed such that it is time to reassess which level of education should control what. This can only be done by understanding why higher levels have lost confidence in the policymaking capacity and the results produced by the lower levels.

Consequently, the chapter begins with an overview of recent governance trends and the underlying reasons for central control. It then moves to the particular case of increased state and district control of instructional policy and the resulting impact on teacher autonomy and professionalism.

The problems of local school boards are highlighted in the next section, because school boards are the key legal unit of local governance. The chapter concludes with some alternatives for rethinking the balance of control. The final sections address sorting out the responsibilities of each level, including such issues as flexible funds for school improvement and teacher professionalism, with its attendant relationship to increased teacher decisionmaking influence at the school and classroom level. Ways of trading state regulations for local school outcome incentives are suggested. The chapter is written based on a belief that the state should establish core values and curriculum, but more local flexibility is needed to adapt school policies to varied needs and utilize the staff ability at the school level. Parent choice as a control mechanism is not addressed here because of limits on length.

A partial framework for this paper is "institutional choice."[1] One of the crucial policy decisions is the choice of a decisionmaker. For example, courts have been reluctant to delegate civil rights protection to local school districts in Mississippi. Another type of institutional choice is whether to place various functions in the hands of markets (for example, vouchers) or politics (for example, school board elections). The recent state reform movement has included institutional choice to enhance the curricular and testing role of state government.

Clune stresses that two general characteristics of available institutions are important: agreement on substantive goals and capacity to achieve those goals. Substantive goals are crucial because of the need to ensure support for a policy. Courts may be more enthusiastic about civil rights than school boards, but support must be buttressed by capacity. Courts cannot run school districts. The method of choosing institutions can be called "comparative institutional advantage" and begins with criticism of a particular institution.

> Since no decision maker is perfect, the distrust directed at one decision maker must be carefully weighed against the advantages of that decision maker and both the advantages and disadvantages of alternative decision makers. In other words, although the logic of institutional choice typically begins with distrust, distrust itself proves nothing in the absence of a superior alternative. . . . The logic of comparative institutional advantage also implies the futility of seeking perfect, or ideal, implementation of a policy. . . . The real world offers a "least worst choice" of imperfect institutions. . . .[2]

A problem with institutional choice analyses is the tendency to confuse predictive with normative applications. In education, predictive connections concerning outcomes from institutional choice are often unclear. For example, how much state control of curriculum will lead to how much decline in teacher professionalism? How does client control through vouchers lead to increased learning? The *rate* of substitution is equally unclear. At what point does increased federal influence in education lead to a decline in the state role? It is possible to avoid a zero-sum situation through various win-win scenarios, such as a state standardized curriculum that helps teachers communicate higher-order thinking and does not interfere with teacher professionalism or autonomy. In sum, institutional choice is complex, uncertain, and subject to continual political change.

Americans have made some important choices about the formal legal powers of the various institutions governing education. The provision of schooling is a power reserved to the states in the U.S. Constitution. The courts support the right of a state government to abolish any school district or to take over its management and dismiss local officials. Despite the legal primacy of the state government, important decision-making power has traditionally been delegated by states to local school district officials. In the early years of the republic, Americans feared distant government; they wanted important decisions made close to home. The doctrine of local control of public schools occupies a long and revered place in American political ideology. It was once heralded as a minor "branch of theology," but recent events have transformed the historic essence of local control of education. There follows a historical analysis of the balance of control.

THE LOSS OF CONFIDENCE IN LOCAL AUTHORITIES

Concern about the quality of American education has virtually exploded in the past few years. This period of national interest in education has been characterized by an intense response on the part of the states, which threatens to shift control of education in ways that may conflict with teacher autonomy and local flexibility.

- Tougher high school graduation requirements have been approved in 48 states.
- Textbooks, tests, and curricula have been revised and aligned through state policy.
- State policies toward teachers have been overhauled to upgrade qualifications, create career ladders, provide incentives, and revamp evaluation.

Since 1984, states have boosted school aid by more than 25% after inflation.[3] Much of this funding has resulted from state omnibus bills containing up to eighty separate reforms.

The most striking feature of state/local relations in the last ten years has been the growth in state control over education. Several decades ago, local education organizations of administrators, teachers, and school board members set the state policy agenda. Today, the organizations of professional educators and the local school organizations are making only marginal suggestions for change in state initiatives, which are shaped by governors, legislators, chief state school officers, and businesses. Under the Reagan Administration, the federal role has been restricted to the bully pulpit and sponsorship of small pilot programs.

These trends promise a restructuring of state and local relations that will cede even more control of education to the states. Some of this loss of local discretion is deserved, but it can become excessive if current trends continue. The evolving state/local relationship will include an enormous range of variation in the aggressiveness with which states take control. The highly aggressive states include California and Florida; among the least aggressive states are New Hampshire and Colorado.

The recent spurt in state activity comes on top of the steady growth in state control throughout the 1970s, when states began to get involved in such matters as accountability, school finance reform, categorical programs, school improvement efforts, minimum competency testing, and civil rights regulations. However, it was not until the 1980s that state governments provided the majority of the current operating funds for education. State contributions now exceed local expenditures by 6%.

The recent spate of reports on the state of education nationwide is indicative of a loss of confidence in the ability of local authorities to provide high-quality education. States are concerned about economic competition, and state legislatures have therefore felt compelled to step in and preempt local discretion. State actions have been directed at the heart of the instructional process in order to upgrade the qualifications of the basic U.S. labor force.

The loss of confidence in local authorities has progressed over many years. In the mid-1960s, federal and state authorities contended that local schools were not "accountable." This charge was made despite the fact that there are about 100,000 local school board members elected for three- or four-year terms, on a staggered basis. The accountability movement spawned new systems of teacher education, budget controls, and state testing. In the 1960s and early 1970s, federal and state authorities began categorical programs to earmark funds for target groups that were neglected or underrepresented in local politics. California ended up with forty-five distinct federal and state categorical programs for such areas as handicapped, disadvantaged, gifted, and limited English-speaking children. States also earmarked more funding categories for "special needs" such as vocational education and rural schools.

The mid-1970s was the height of the school finance reform movement, which demonstrated that local property tax bases were inherently unequal. States assumed more of the burden of financing, and more state control followed the new state dollars. The mid-1970s was also the peak of new court regulations on local schools, indicating that schools could not be trusted to guarantee student rights or due process. Increased legislative attention to local education expanded state education codes, and lawsuits directed at local authorities multiplied.

Discontent with local academic standards led states to prescribe stricter, more uniform standards for teachers and students. Starting in the 1970s, with minimum competency tests, this trend accelerated after the 1980–1982 recession. Yet the literature on effective schools suggests that the most important changes take place when those responsible for each school are given more responsibility rather than less. While centralization may be better for naval units, steel mills, and state highway departments, the literature on effective schools suggests that it is more important that principals, teachers, students, and parents at each school have "a shared moral order."

Why is the current wave of state influence taking a centralized course?[4] Basically, state governments do not believe that local authorities pay sufficient attention to curriculum quality, teacher evaluation, and academic standards. Higher statewide standards do appear to be consistent with some parts of the literature on effective schools. For instance, higher standards can be used to foster clear instructional objectives and specify the content and outcomes of schooling. However, new state curricula that specify the grade level at which particular math concepts must be learned (as the Texas proposal does) create rigid timetables that might destroy the kind of flexible school climate that usually characterizes effective schools. There is also conflict between state centralization and the teacher autonomy that enhances teacher professionalism.

SCHOOL GOVERNANCE IN THE 1990s—EVERYBODY AND NOBODY IN CHARGE

In my view, local school district autonomy will continue to shrink unless measures are taken to restore confidence in local authorities and increase their policymaking capacity. The increased reliance on nonlocal funding will continue to shift power away from the district. Specifically, local administrators and boards will have less say in setting the policy agenda and controlling decision outcomes. The local superintendent and administrative staff often act as a reactive force, trying to juggle diverse and changing coalitions across different issues and levels of government. Many school reforms disappeared without a trace, but others left organizational additions that could be easily monitored and created a constituency. Part of the legacy of the prior era was a tremendous growth in specialized functions of the school, including administrative specialists in vocational education, driver education, nutrition, health, and remedial reading. Many of these new structural layers diluted the influence of the superintendent and the local board. These specialists were paid by federal or state categorical programs and were insulated from the superintendent's influence by the requirements of higher levels of government. Their allegiance was often to the higher levels of education governance rather than to the local community.

FIGURE 4-1
Trends in educational governance, 1950–1987.

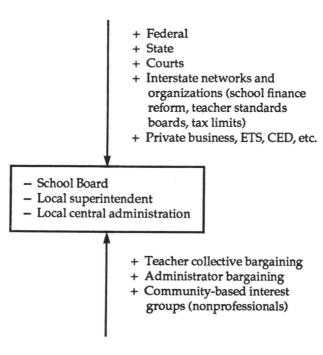

+ Federal
+ State
+ Courts
+ Interstate networks and
  organizations (school finance
  reform, teacher standards
  boards, tax limits)
+ Private business, ETS, CED, etc.

– School Board
– Local superintendent
– Local central administration

+ Teacher collective bargaining
+ Administrator bargaining
+ Community-based interest
  groups (nonprofessionals)

+ *Increasing influence*
– *Decreasing influence*

The discretionary decision zone of the local superintendents and the boards has become squeezed progressively into a smaller and smaller area during the last two decades. This trend must be arrested and reversed. I see nothing to reverse these trends in the late 1980s (see Figure 4-1). From the top, local discretion has been squeezed by the growth of the federal government, the state government, and the courts. There has also been an increase in the influence of private interest groups and professional "reformers" such as the Ford Foundation and the Carnegie Foundation. Interstate organizations, such as the Education Commission of the States, and nationally oriented organizations like the Council for Exceptional Children increased their role. Superintendents and local boards found their decision space squeezed from the bottom by such forces as the growth of local collective bargaining contracts reinforced by national teacher organizations. A study by the Rand Corporation documents the incursion of teacher organizations into education policy.

In the 1960s, growing local interest groups often resulted from nationwide social movements oriented toward such issues as civil rights, women's roles, students' rights, ethnic self-determination, and bilingual education. These nonlocal social movements spawned local interest groups that began agitating for changes in local operating procedures. They advocated such changes as suspension of students and curriculum differentiation. Traditional parent groups such as PTA and AAUW, which generally support local school authorities, became less influential.

As the 1970s came, forces such as economics and demography reduced local decisionmaking authority even further. The declining population of students and spreading resistance to increased school taxes further constrained local initiative and options. In many states, the end of the 1970s brought a period of disillusionment with professionals in general and educators in particular. In the 1980s, interventions from above have focused on curricular and teacher issues. A key trend was the centralization of decisions about curricular content in central district offices, with a consequent loss of local autonomy (see Figure 4-2).

The accountability concept, for example, originated largely from federal, state, and court sources but had major impact on local decisions. Due process requirements and competency-based graduation mandates are also good examples. Social movements in the 1970s differed from those of the nineteenth century. A century ago, reformers such as Horace Mann were interested in building up institutions like the

FIGURE 4-2
Trends in educational governance, 1980–1987.

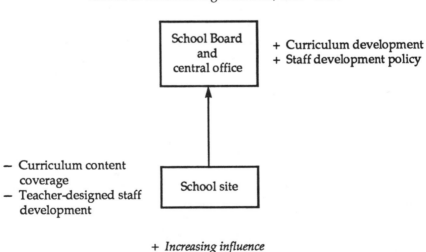

+ *Increasing influence*
− *Decreasing influence*

schools; now, many social movements question these public institutions and try to make them more responsive to forces outside the local administrative structure. Some would even assert that these social movements are helping fragment school decisionmaking in such a way that local citizens cannot influence local school policy. The newspapers reflect violence, drug use, and declining test scores as the predominant state of public education, further encouraging federal and state interventions.

In California, this situation has become so serious that schools suffer from shock and overload. The issue becomes how much change and agitation an institution can take and continue to respond to its local clients and voters. Californians are also confronted with numerous initiatives such as Proposition 13, vouchers, and spending limits. Local citizens go to the local school board and superintendent, expecting redress of their problems, and find the necessary decisionmaking power is not there. The impression grows that no one is "in charge" of public education.

All of this does not mean that local authorities are helpless; rather, it means that they cannot control their agenda or structure most of the decision outcomes as they could in the past. The local superintendent must deal with shifting coalitions at various government levels to gain a marginal advantage for a brief period. Policy items on the local board agenda are increasingly generated by external forces (federal, state, and courts) or are reactions to proposals from local interest groups, including teachers. The era of the local administrative chief has passed, with profound consequences. The state-based reform strategy discussed above will intensify these trends, favoring nonlocal influences on education policy.

It is simplisitic to label this changing governance structure as "centralization." There is no single central control point, but rather a fragmented "elevated oligopoly." From the local school board perspective, the latter term refers to higher authorities (federal, state, courts), outside interests (ETS and the Council for Exceptional Children), local internal interests (Vocational Education Coordinator), and other local agencies, such as police and health authorities, that have an impact on education. The shift of influence to higher levels has not resulted in a commensurate loss of influence for local interest groups. The parents of handicapped and bilingual students have considerably more impact in local settings than they did twenty-five years ago.

Recent state reforms have often been based on local citizens' desires.[5] In California, a new state superintendent was elected on a reform platform. In most other states, governors, legislators, and elected politicians led the charge for higher academic standards. Citizen voter preferences are as decentralized a mandate as one gets in a democracy, so the issue is not so much centralization in policy influence, as the progressive loss of local school board and administrative decisionmaking power. Projecting the current trends twenty years into the future, the threat of minimized local discretion becomes more dramatic.

CURRICULUM INFLUENCE AT THE STATE LEVEL

State initiatives in the curricular area are a good example of the potential impact on teacher's authority. They also raise significant concerns about the potential conflict between teacher autonomy and state accountability. The new state focus is on curriculum quality and the appropriate capabilities of teachers to teach a curriculum that includes critical thinking and higher-order skills. Moreover, new state and local curricular policies reinforce and interact with each other to expand the potential impact on teachers.

Traditionally, states have left academic curriculum content specification largely to local discretion, satisfied to specify a few required course titles and issue advisory curricular frameworks for local consideration.[6] States did respond to lobbies outside traditional academic subjects by specifying courses in driver training, physical education, vocational education, and health. Even in the most centralized states, the appropriate role was thought to be the establishment of minimum standards rather than the quality concerns that now dominate state agendas. The same sort of policy activists who spearheaded the interstate diffusion of such 1970s "reforms" as school finance equalization and minimum competency testing for high school graduates have now turned their efforts to academic curriculum as a prime domain for new state policies. New techniques such as statewide curriculum alignment of tests, texts, frameworks, and accreditation are providing the reformers with methods that can significantly affect local policy and classroom content. The traditional subject-matter organizations of educators (math, English, and the like) and major education lobbies (NEA, AASA) are mostly in a reactive mode as the state reformers conceive new curricular policies. The subject-matter organizations were outlobbied in the past by advocates of "new" subject areas who sought a place in the curriculum for physical education, driver training, and vocational education; they are now displaced by the "reformers."[7]

Why the States Feel They Must Be More Involved in Academic Standards

The more aggressive state academic role is a direct result of highly critical analyses of local education standards, exemplified by *A Nation At Risk*. States have developed major economic development strategies and see education as a crucial component for economic growth and international competition. State politicians became alarmed by allegations that American school achievement lagged behind that of other nations and was a major cause of our inability to compete in a world economy. Governors and legislators were impressed by the arguments that local school officials had permitted academic standards to drop and were inattentive to the need for higher-order skills and a more complex curriculum. Local school policymakers seemed to be overemphasizing the basics such as rote math and simplistic reading exercises. Future economic competition with rivals such as Japan and Germany was considered to require a more adaptable work force, with a breadth and depth of educational background that local officials seemed unable to provide.

State Techniques for Control

Margaret Goertz has prepared a matrix of instruments that states use to influence local academic standards and overcome local resistance to state imposed curriculum.[8] (See Figure 4-3.) She distinguishes

FIGURE 4-3
Types of State Educational Standards.

   I. Performance standards
      A. Student test scores
      B. Teacher test scores
      C. Grading policy
      D. Observation of performance
  II. Program standards
      A. Curriculum:
         Range and level of courses available
         Curriculum guides
         Instructional materials
         Availability of academic, college prep, general
            education, vocational curriculum
         Availability of special programs (special education, compensatory education, etc.)
      B. Time in School
         Number of days, class periods, length of day
      C. Class size
      D. Staff/student ratio
      E. Type of staff
 III. Behavior standards
      A. Attendance
      B. Discipline
      C. Homework
      D. Extracurricular participation

Adapted from Margaret E. Goertz, *State Educational Standards* (Princeton, N.J.: Educational Testing Service, 1986). Reproduced by permission.

state (1) *performance standards* that measure an individual's performance through tested achievement and observations, (2) *program standards* that include curricular requirements, program specifications, and other requirements affecting time in school, class size, and staffing, and (3) *behavior standards* that include attendance requirements, disciplinary codes, homework, and so on.

Her fifty-state survey shows dramatic increases from 1983 to 1986 in state specification and influence in all these types of standards. A closer analysis, however, reveals that the 1983–1986 reform wave only accelerated a state policy trend that began over fifteen years before in such areas as compensatory and special education. The 1983–1986 state initiatives focused on the core academic subjects rather than special services for target groups.

The scope of state activity is very wide, but the effectiveness of state influence upon local practice has often been questioned. Some educators think it is quite potent, while others feel that "loose coupling" between state and local organizations leads to more symbolic compliance. Curricular alignment is one concept states are using to control local curriculum more tightly and overcome the local capacity to thwart implementation of state policies. California is a particularly good example of the techniques for such alignment, as presented in Figure 4-4. The key is to have the same curricular content emphasized and covered across the state: curricular frameworks, tests, textbook adoption criteria, accreditation standards, content expectations for university entrance, and criteria for teacher evaluation. The identical content coverage must be a thread woven through all of these state policy instruments. Local control advocates are appropriately concerned about such a strategy. Before 1984, major state curricular policy instruments were disconnected, shooting off in different directions. One unit devised state tests without much consultation or content integration with the state textbook division. The curricular frameworks were nominally coordinated with state texts, but not carefully embedded in the state criteria sent out to potential publishers for bids. The 1987 California approach relies, however, on state curricular controls that do not exist in more locally oriented states such as Colorado or New Hampshire. A major component of the 1983–1986 reforms was to encourage central offices to recentralize the curriculum. Unpublished research in six states by Clune and Fuhrman demonstrates that this district centralization has taken place and that school sites have lost curricular flexibility.

A major concern for future research is whether these increased state initiatives change the teaching context and, if so, how such state impact enhances or detracts from teacher autonomy and professionalism. A teaching context analysis should provide substantial information on whether state and local reform initiatives have created a conflict between accountability and teacher discretion.

FIGURE 4-4
California curriculum alignment.

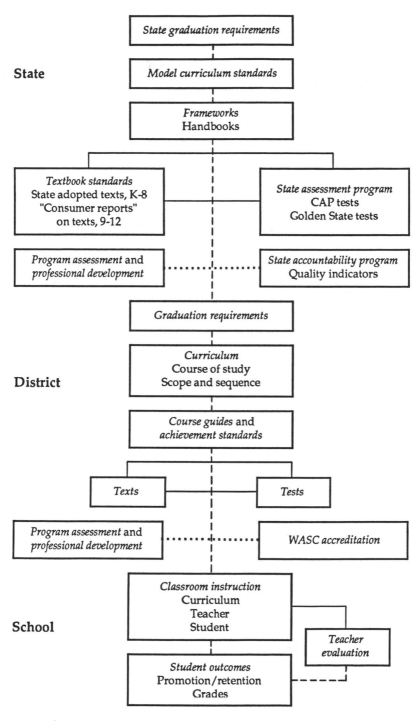

Source: Beverly B. Carter, School of Education, Stanford University.

THE SPECIAL PROBLEMS OF LOCAL SCHOOL BOARDS

School boards have been subjected to an unprecedented attack during the 1980s. A top federal official, Chester Finn, called them a "dinosaur left over from the agrarian past," and Albert Shanker, President of the American Federation of Teachers, called for a major overhaul modeled on hospital boards, which meet less than once a month. In 1986, the National Governors Association recommended state takeover and direct operation of school districts that failed repeatedly to educate children. In a 1986 national poll, school board members expressed strong concern about the intrusion of state control into local policymaking as a result of the recent state reform movement. State policymakers, at the start of the reform era in 1983, contended that local boards were neglecting academic standards, curriculum policy, and teacher evaluation. The major 1983–1984 national reports barely mentioned school boards.

Many political observers believe the school board is in trouble and needs help. A national study by the Institute for Educational Leadership (IEL) found very strong local support for the concept of a local school board as an institutional buffer from state and professional administrative control.[9] School boards are deeply embedded in American political culture and appear to be here to stay, but the public does not necessarily support the school board in its own local community, rarely turns out for school board elections in greater numbers than 10–15% of the eligible electorate, and knows very little about the role and function of school boards. Based on the IEL study, Neal Peirce asks, "If the school board's popular constituency misperceives their role and doesn't care enough to exercise its franchise in their selection, how fully or forcefully will the boards ever be able to function?"

School Board Study Findings

In 1986, IEL conducted a national survey and nine metropolitan case studies of the status of school boards. These findings are congruent with other school board research.

1. There is strong support for maintaining the basic institutional role and structure of the school board. School boards are in trouble. As grass-roots institutions they confront a basic paradox. The study found strong support among community leaders, parents, local citizens, and educators for preserving school boards to keep schools close to the people, but there is widespread public ignorance of their established roles and functions. There appears to be deep public apathy and indifference, as reflected in the difficulty of attracting quality candidates to serve as board members in many communities and in the abysmally low voter turnout for board elections. This civic ignorance bodes even greater trouble for school boards in the future, as student populations become more diverse and creative leadership more necessary. Systematic efforts to promote greater understanding of the important role of school boards must be initiated in communities throughout the country.

2. Board members are increasingly perceived as representing special interests, and the trusteeship notion of service in which board members represent the entire community has been less prominent in recent years. Board members, educators, and the public say that divisiveness and the problem of building a cohesive board from disparate members, many with single constituencies or issues, are major factors affecting board effectiveness and community perceptions.

3. Boards, particularly in urban areas, have become more representative of the diversity in their communities and often include leaders from disparate constituencies within the larger community. This is positive in terms of diverse populations gaining access to board service. However, when board members are not from traditional community leadership and power structures, they lack easy and influential access to civic, political, and economic decisionmakers.

4. Local boards and their members have only sporadic interaction with general government and tend to be isolated from mainstream community political structures. There is very little systematic communication between school system governance and general government, despite the fact that increasing numbers of students have learning problems associated with nonschool factors. These include poor housing, lack of family support and resources, and limited employment opportunities. In addition, when interaction between the school system and general government does exist, it often takes place only through the superintendent. Fiscally dependent boards, which must interact with town/municipal government bodies, are frequently mired in adversarial relationships. Some urban community leaders believe it may be time to rethink the nonpartisan nature of school board elections. Perhaps election to the board through the mainstream political party structures is an issue worthy of debate in some communities. The majority of boards in the United States are nonpartisan.

5. Board members are seriously concerned about the growing intrusiveness of the states as the reform movement evolves. Boards feel they are largely reacting to state proposals rather than initiating their own. The governors, legislators, and chief state school officers have more media visibility and want to intervene more. Local board events are local media stories, while statewide reforms get more coverage.

6. Board members continue to grapple with tensions over necessarily gray areas between a board's policymaking and the superintendent's administrative responsibilities. In the districts in which

board–superintendent relationships are good, little attention is paid
to this dichotomy. However, some school boards, particularly in larger
heterogeneous districts, have or wish they could have staff that served
board members directly. There appears to be less willingness in these
districts to rely on the superintendent and administrators to "staff"
the board.

7. The need for school board education and development is generally recognized, but too often it is merely informational and episodic. There is minimal access to or involvement in developmental
skills-building. Too little attention is given to development of working
relationships among board members and to development of boards as
corporate bodies. Boards that recognize the need for such development
have retreats and goal-setting meetings, evaluate their performance, and
provide for oversight of the implementation of their policies. Such boards
appear to have a greater sense of effectiveness.

**8. Urban, suburban, rural, and small-town boards alike find more
commonalities than differences among the challenges to their effectiveness.** These include:

- Public apathy
- Lack of public understanding of the role of boards
- Poor relationships with state policymakers
- Need for board strategies to evaluate board effectiveness
- Lack of time and operating structures to focus on education
- Difficulty in becoming a board rather than a collection of individuals
- Improving teaching in the framework of collective bargaining
- The amount of time boards invest in their work as against satisfaction with accomplishments and ability to determine their own priorities

At the end of this chapter, I will suggest several policies to improve the
effectiveness of school boards.

RETHINKING THE BALANCE OF CONTROL

This chapter has argued that:

- The total array of influences on school policy has tended to narrow the discretionary decision space of local policymakers and teachers over the past twenty-five years.
- The traditional balance in state and local control has shifted to more state centralization over the past twenty-five years.
- The centralization of testing, curriculum, and instructional policy at the state and district level is narrowing teacher autonomy in the classroom. If carried to extremes, this centralization could threaten

- movements to enhance teacher professionalism, such as the Carnegie and National Governors Association's recommendations.[10]
- This shift in control can be attributed to several sequential but interacting forces, including (1) a loss of confidence by higher authorities in local decisionmakers, including school boards, (2) the increased use of categorical grants, (3) changes in state funding patterns to enhance equity and place limits on local spending, (4) increasing involvement of legislation and lawsuits in the education process, (5) the tendency of the 1983–1987 omnibus state reform bills to centralize more authority than they decentralize.
- There appears to be nothing significant that will reverse these trends; it is likely that they will continue for a number of years.
- The current challenge is to rethink the institutional choices by analyzing the purposes and mission of the schools and sorting out which level has the best capacity to serve the students. The federal or state role, for example, is often crucial when redistributive policies are needed—for example, in the areas of civil rights and school finance. Local politics preclude local substantive agreement with many policies that cause radical redistribution of resources. This task can be broken down into (1) state versus local central office; (2) central office versus school site; (3) influence *within* the school site.

The task begins with an analysis of the relationship between control and effective schools. What is the relationship between centralization and effective schools? Answering this question can give an empirical basis for recommending changes in the current pattern of control.

Effective Schools and Control

Some researchers see an inherent tension between a strong state and central district role and the flexibility needed for effective schools. Others believe that centralized and standardized policies can make more schools effective. Effective schools policies have been translated by central district offices into a standardized curriculum for schools, with content restricted largely to test outcomes. A view of schools as complex institutions, however, is linked to the positive "school climate" stressed in effective schools research. Michael Cohen expresses this climate as follows:

> The norms and values which characterize the school community, and which unite individual members of the organization into a more cohesive identity, pertain both to the academic function of the school, as well as to the nature of the day-to-day interactions and social relations among staff and students. . . . However, . . . community in schools is dependent upon . . . creation of a moral order, which entails respect for authority, genuine and pervasive caring about individuals, respect for their feelings and attitudes, mutual trust, and the consistent enforcement of norms which define and delimit acceptable

behavior. . . . The importance of a shared moral order should not be underestimated, for it can be traced to several fundamental properties of schools. . . . [The] schools cannot rely simply on coercive power to bring about order. Rather, schools are normative organizations, which must rely on the internalization of goals, the legitimate use of authority, and the manipulation of symbols, as means of controlling and directing the behavior of participants. . . .[11]

Much of the literature on effective schools suggests that the most important changes are assisted by increased school site responsibility. Research stresses the importance of developing a "shared moral order." Chester Finn observes:

> The point is subtle but powerful. Effective schools are more akin to secular counterparts of religious communities than they are like army brigades, bank branches, or factory units. They share a belief structure, a value system, a consensual rather than hierarchical governance system, an enormous amount of psychic and emotional "investment" by participants, and a set of common goals and convictions that blur the boundaries between the private and organizational lives of their participants. Schools may not be the only public sector enterprises with these characteristics, but the others are apt to be elite, idiosyncratic and perhaps transitory enterprises—the White House staff, NASA's Apollo team, the military's "special forces"—rather than numerous, permanent, "ordinary" institutions. . . . Bluntly stated, the existence—but rarity—of such "effective schools" itself tends to confute the doctrine of essential uniformity, for it means that the schools in a given system or state are apt to be similar with respect to relatively superficial matters but dissimilar along dimensions that matter more; yet the inertial autonomy of schools qua schools also means that efforts to make ineffective schools more closely resemble effective schools in the ways that matter most are certain to be very difficult and quite likely to meet with little success. Moreover, policymakers seeking greater uniformity must be terribly careful lest they "level downward" through well-intentioned efforts that wind up sapping the vitality of the most effective schools rather than invigorating the others.[12]

Higher educational standards appear consistent with the effective schools research in terms of clear curricular objectives and the establishment of specific cues on preferred instructional content and outcomes. However, the new state tests used in Texas specify the grade level in which particular math concepts must be covered. This rigid instructional timetable could shatter the inner-directed climate that effective schools display. Again, Finn expresses it well:

> The truly vexing paradox is that in seeking to overcome inertial autonomy by "tightening the couplings" in school systems—by replacing those elastic bands that allowed some schools to lag behind with steel

bars meant to get them all moving at the same speed, as the public seems to demand and as the doctrine of essential uniformity would seem to dictate—policymakers would derail the very cars that had gotten themselves balanced on the tracks by allocating their loads and resources in proportion to their own capacities.[13]

One way to reconcile these problems is for the state or district to emphasize desired outcomes in very broad terms without prescribing curricula or procedures in detail. State education agencies (SEAs) and LEAs should encourage schools to be different except for some common core of skills and knowledge. The teachers at each school site can develop a "teamwork approach" that emphasizes shared educational goals. SEA and LEA policymakers cannot order schools to be "effective," but norms and standards must somehow be internalized at the building level. How to do this very well is not known, but the current all-out push in many states for detailed control and methods (for example, a required number of minutes of writing) may not yield optimal results.

The same problems arise when one considers school effectiveness plans of local school districts. Usually, the central district office prescribes standard tests, curriculum guides, and even textbooks. This "curricular alignment" holds some promise for improving standardized test scores, but what will it do to existing distinctive and unusually positive school climates? While school site autonomy has helped a few outstanding schools to find their own best strategy, many other schools have been free to continue their poor performance.

In the current climate of crisis and "unilateral educational disarmament," there is a rush to mandate these new effectiveness-oriented "reforms." However, the California and Florida approaches are not attempting these changes in a systematic or interrelated fashion, with a clear perspective on their impact. Rather, various legislators have their favorite ideas, which are added to the statute with a staple gun. Missing from these action plans is what drives classroom teaching performance:

> To have a direct sustained impact on student performance and teaching practice would require either structural changes in the conditions of teaching, a great deal of on-site cooperative work with teachers, school site program planning and implementation, or some imaginative combination of these. . . . The assumptions about improving high school academic performance through external mandates or legislative fiat . . . miss the mark of providing a solid conceptual foundation for improvement policies.[14]

In sum, the literature on effective schools suggests a mix of top-down and bottom-up controls in education. There is no one best system to be imposed from the top, but it is unlikely that bottom-up initiative alone will turn an ineffective school around. Overall, however, the literature provides a warning concerning excessive centralization either at the state or central office level. The relationship between the state and local levels in school improvement will be discussed next.

The Philosophical Rationale for Maintaining a Strong Local Role

The initial sections of this chapter diagnosed the drift toward state control. Coombs provides four reasons why the local role in education policy needs to be maintained and strengthened in some states where it has declined precipitously:[15]

1. The public supports more local influence and less influence for the federal and state governments.
2. Local school district decisions tend to be more democratic in several important ways than decisions made at higher levels of government.
3. The functional tension between state and local policymakers results in policy that is better adapted to diverse local contexts.
4. Further erosion of the local role would run the risk of causing diminishing public support for the public schools.

In support of the first point, Coombs cites the following 1986 Gallup poll data:

	Level of government		
Should have:	*Federal government*	*State government*	*Local School Board*
More influence	26%	45%	57%
Less influence	53	32	17
Same as now	12	16	17
Don't know	9	7	9

The biggest loser in this public referendum is the federal government, but note that local school board influence is preferred much more often than state government. The 1986 Gallup Poll also contains data suggesting that the public is no less reluctant to increase local property taxes than other broad-based taxes. Public dissatisfaction with the property tax peaked in the late 1970s and now has dissipated. Odden analyzed the dramatic 25% real increase in spending for education from 1983 to 1986 and concluded that one of the "secrets" of education reform funding has been the significant role played by the property tax.

> The big news at the local level is this large overall [property tax] increase that, nationwide, nearly matches the rise in state revenues and actually exceeds big state rises in several reform states, such as Florida, Texas, and Virginia, where the state rise has received national attention. Despite national swings in sources of funding for schools, the

property tax remains a robust revenue provider, even in the education reform era.[16]

Advantages of Local School Policymaking

There are numerous and conflicting positions on how well school politics meets the democratic ideal. The issue here is whether school politics is more democratic than control by federal or state authorities. Most citizens have a greater opportunity and more chance of influencing policy in their local district than of influencing policymakers or administrators at the federal or state level. Local school policymakers serve fewer constituents than state officials and are much closer geographically as well as psychologically. It can be time-consuming and difficult to get to the state capital.

Local school board elections provide a means of influencing local policymakers that is much more direct than the same number of citizens' influence on a state legislator representing many areas. In the nation's thousands of small school districts, a significant proportion of the community knows at least one school board member. Local media provide better information and can capture the attention of citizens more effectively than reports from a distant state capital. All of this is not meant to claim that local school politics approaches the democratic ideal. Indeed, a Gallup poll revealed that 36% of a national sample of citizens knew "very little" or "nothing" about their local public schools. Nevertheless, local school officials are better able to anticipate the zone of tolerance that local school constituencies permit than are state policymakers.

Most states are too large and diverse for uniform policies to be effective in all areas. As Coombs puts it, in one policy area after another, there exists "nested policy in which the states provide the general contours and the local districts fill in with more specified policies."[17] The "functional tension" tends to provide more appropriate and adaptable policies than statewide specification. There are large areas, however, like civil rights and equal opportunity, where local flexibility must be greatly restricted. Most states, for example, have prescribed teacher certification requirements but leave hiring and compensation issues to local districts.

The final argument for enhancing local discretion is based on the linkage between political efficacy and public support of schools: Citizens will participate in politics more if they believe that they can have an impact upon policies. The local level offers the best opportunity for efficiency; therefore, a diminution in local efficacy will lead to less overall citizen participation in education policy. Coombs states:

> . . . a person is more likely to communicate his or her policy preference to officials when he or she perceives the probable impact of the

communication on policy to be high. . . . If local government decision making enhances citizen participation in school politics, it follows that citizen confidence in, and support of, the public school system are apt to be strengthened as well.[18]

The reasoning is that people's satisfaction with the outcomes of collective decisions will be greater if they have participated in making those decisions. Consequently, less local control leads to more citizen dissatisfaction. In California, for example, local parents are told that the school board is too constrained to remedy their grievances. The citizen is referred to a state office or in some cases a court order. This may lead to alienation from the local public school.

SOME PRINCIPLES OF SCHOOL GOVERNANCE

In the process of rethinking the balance of state and local control, it will be useful to keep several "ideal" principles in mind. What follows is not a comprehensive set of governance principles but rather serves illustrative purposes.[19]

- An ideal system retains decisions at the lowest governmental level unless there is a compelling reason regarding equity, liberty, or efficiency to elevate the issue.
- An ideal system permits clear and reciprocal communication, from state policy makers to instructional personnel. Clear communication will enable the state to implement its policies with a minimum of inefficiency and, in turn, to receive opinions and information from those directly connected with schooling about needed alterations and reforms.
- An ideal system eliminates unnecessary duplication of education services and ensures performance accountability.
- An ideal system protects the state's overall interests while simultaneously soliciting and implementing reasonable preferences of local clients.
- An ideal system is neither so large as to invite formation of impermeable and insensitive bureaucracies nor so small as to jeopardize equality of educational opportunity or risk absurd diseconomies of scale.
- An ideal system balances public control over one of its most important institutions (schools) with the autonomy of education professionals.
- An ideal system is sufficiently stable as to encourage and maintain client and employee allegiance while simultaneously containing appropriate flexibility, so as to accommodate inevitable changes in social and economic conditions over time.
- An ideal system possesses mechanisms for self-assessment and adjustment, so as to sustain its utility and vitality.

SCHOOL IMPROVEMENT AS A FIRST STEP

One technique for providing more local flexibility has been state policies that encourage local initiative, such as California's School Improvement Program (SIP). This program may provide the most encouraging example of a new model of school governance. Part of AB 65 in 1977, it was designed in part to combine categorical programs in a comprehensive school site plan through a school site council. In a major break with prior categorical approaches, SIP provided discretionary money to school sites (about $100 per average daily attendance), rather than a grant tied to specific state purposes. The funding is for neither basic maintenance nor categorical projects. Instead, SIP supports an individual school's assessment of its own priority needs and implementation of a program to address them. The fundamental concept is that the school and its local community, rather than the district or state, should take primary responsibility for setting local improvement objectives.

There are two key components of SIP: the school site council and the program review. The school site council is composed of parents, staff, and students (in secondary schools). The council governs the way SIP funds are used in schools. The council prepares a review of the school program and develops a plan for improvement that combines categorical funds with SIP's flexible allocation.

The program review is an assessment of a school's School Improvement Program, conducted by a consortium of local educators from outside the district. The review is structured by the program quality review criteria promulgated by the state department of education. Several research reports reveal that the program quality review criteria determine what is addressed in a school's improvement program.

While SIP's key planning elements remain, the Honig administration has revamped the program to emphasize curriculum improvement, core academic program, and redesign of programs for special populations to reinforce and complement the general education program of schools. In addition, state department program advisories have urged local districts to use SIP funds to provide support needed to engage in a continuing change and improvement process—training, staff development, coaching, curriculum materials and supplies, new technologies—rather than restricting all funds for permanent staff such as teacher aides. Moreover, the program quality review criteria recently have been changed to focus attention on the substance and quality of a school's curriculum and to require that categorical programs provide services that reinforce that curriculum program. In short, SIP is now conceived as an implementation vehicle for improving local schools, with Senate Bill 813 providing the content and focus for those improvement efforts.

RECOMMENDED CHANGES IN OTHER STATE POLICIES

States can take additional actions other than SIP to provide more local flexibility.

1. Many state education codes have grown incrementally and include outmoded and needless local restrictions. States should appoint a task force to review their codes and cut out unnecessary and outmoded regulations.
2. States should increase their use of waiver policies whereby the state board can waive any part of the education code for justifiable reasons. Districts can petition for exemptions from the state code, and the burden of proof should be on the state to justify why the waiver can not be granted.
3. States should remove limits on local revenue raising that preclude local election increases or should establish a passing requirement of no more than a majority. Some states establish ceilings on locally voted revenue regardless of local sentiment, and others require a two-thirds majority for tax increases.
4. States should pass or enforce laws that require full state funding of mandated programs or activities that must be carried out at the local level. Some states prohibit local revenue increases and then mandate local expenditures without any state reimbursement. Obviously, this leads to much less local discretion.
5. States should provide model curricula to local districts and use state tests to assess whether a limited common core of knowledge has been covered locally. States should *not* specify the pace at which teachers should present content or define all the details of local curriculum.
6. States should review the aggregate and cumulative effect of their policies upon teacher autonomy and professionalism. It is not any single regulation that is crucial, but the totality of the state role.
7. States should create blue-ribbon commissions that review the trends and balance in the governance of education and make recommendations that pertain to the particular state's context.

STRENGTHENING LOCAL SCHOOL BOARDS

In a preceding section, some major problems with school board effectiveness were discussed, as well as the strong public commitment to the concept of a local board. Confidence in the local board must be rebuilt if there is to be any reversal of the trend toward state centralization. Clearly, the issue is how to strengthen the school board rather than to eliminate or diminish its role. The following recommendations meet many of the criticisms in the prior section.[20]

1. An effective board leads the community in matters of public education, seeking and responding to many forms of participation by the community.
2. An effective board exercises continuing oversight of education programs and their management, draws information for this purpose from many sources, and knows enough to ask the right questions.
3. An effective board, in consultation with its superintendent, works out and periodically reaffirms the separate areas of administrative and policy responsibilities and determines how these separations will be maintained.
4. An effective board establishes policy to govern its own policymaking and policy oversight responsibilities, including explicit budget provisions to support those activities.
5. An effective board invests in its own development, using diverse approaches that address the needs of individual board members and the board as a whole.
6. An effective board establishes procedures for selecting and evaluating the superintendent. It also has procedures for evaluating itself.
7. An effective board collaborates with other boards through its statewide school boards association and other appropriate groups to influence state policy and the state leadership's way of meeting the needs of local schools.

RETHINKING THE BALANCE BETWEEN THE CENTRAL DISTRICT OFFICE AND THE SCHOOL SITE

Many U.S. school districts are very small; the distance between the central district office and the school site is minimal. However, in districts of more than 15,000 students, greater problems arise as to who should control education within the local context. Central offices must perform certain functions: establishing the length of school days, raising and allocating revenue, planning for enrollment, reporting to state and federal authorities, and providing such programs as special education and staff development. Most central offices go beyond this minimal role and specify a great deal of what must go on at the school site. Central collective bargaining procedures also create uniform central standards.

There are several criteria for deciding what should be done centrally and what should be done at the site. This is a matter of philosophy in such respects as the desirability of a common core curriculum or one's willingness to take risks with school-site decisionmaking. My own views have changed over the past decade to favor more curricular centralization, because of concern about academic standards, but there are also questions of feasibility. Can each local school site faculty create a coherent English curriculum or rethink the need to embed critical thinking in the social studies curriculum? Many of these tasks are best completed through a committee of teachers and staff from many schools, coordinated by the central office.

The main arguments for moving decisions to the school site probably do not involve economics or cost effectiveness. The functions still must be performed at some level. Levin posits several advantages for school site decentralization:[21]

1. District policies are typically made in a uniform fashion that ignores the enormous variety of student needs and characteristics at various schools.
2. Teachers and school-based educators may not accept responsibility for educational outcomes that they did not establish.
3. The teaching talent at the school district level is underutilized because of centralized control that permits teachers to make too few decisions.

There are several mechanisms for devolving control from the district to the school site. School site budgeting provides large unrestricted funds to school sites, which decide the mix of resources utilized. Personnel decisions can be returned to the site, but they are rarely returned entirely. Most of the school site governance schemes include a site council. The council membership is often embroiled in controversy because of such difficult issues as teacher majority, the appropriate role of the principal, and representation by lay persons. There is no one best system, but given the analysis at the outset of this chapter, I favor more school site flexibility.

The recent proposals of the Carnegie Forum stress more teacher influence *within the school*, through such devices as lead teachers, and peer review. So far, other than isolated cases in Toledo, Ohio and Dade County, Florida, little has been done about these suggestions. A key question is whether teachers should be the main influence on what is taught and how to teach it. The literature on effective schools stresses the principal as an instructional leader and benign dictator. This is a very different concept from a school site council controlled by a teacher majority. In the mid-1970s, I advocated that there be a majority of lay persons on school site councils, but this concept conflicts with the Carnegie notion of building a "true teaching profession" through larger spheres of teacher autonomy. It is unclear what school site governance arrangement is optimal; more experimentation is needed. Like most other issues in this chapter, this is more a matter of conflicting values and philosophy than of technical feasibility. This conflict is indeed the essence of politics. The political implications were expressed precisely by Schattschneider:

> All forms of political organization have a bias in favor of the exploitation of some kinds of conflict and the suppression of others because organization is the mobilization of bias. Some issues are organized into politics while others are organized out.[22]

The key to the changes that I recommend will be the creation and sustenance of an influential political constituency, which is not clearly defined or evident at this juncture. School restructuring and political devolution can have a romantic aura but have not been translated into a mobilized constituency. Changes in who controls the schools evolve incrementally over long periods of time and rarely emerge as a major "crisis" that can create new constituencies and coalitions. The locally based organizations of school boards and superintendents are a potential start, but other allies are uncertain. Many teacher organizations have been uncertain about restructuring and devolution. The major political actors at the state level have not been as responsive to decentralization as they have been to academic excellence. Teacher professionalism and restructuring lack power as emotional political symbols.

At the outset, the chapter stressed the need to restore confidence in educators as a prerequisite for reversing the trend of control. School boards are important to this goal, but perhaps the most important development would be a dramatic rise in the public's confidence in teachers. A national teacher standards board would be a crucial part of this, but it will take a concerted effort over a long period of time.

NOTES

1. The institutional choice analysis is derived from William Clune, *Institutional Choice as a Theoretical Framework*, published by the Center for Policy Research in Education, Rutgers University, 1987.

2. Ibid., pp. 4–5. For an overview of who controls the schools, see Fred Wirt and Michael Kirst, *Schools in Conflict* (Berkeley: McCutchan, 1982).

3. See Allan Odden, "The Economics of Financing Educational Excellence," paper presented to the 1987 Annual Meeting of AERA, Washington, D.C., April 1987.

4. For an expansion on this theme, see Lorraine M. McDonnell and Susan Fuhrman, "The Political Context of School Reform," in Van D. Mueller and Mary McKeown, eds., *The Fiscal, Legal, and Political Aspects of State Reform of Elementary and Secondary Education* (Cambridge, Mass.: Ballinger, 1986).

5. See William Chance, *The Best of Educations: Reforming American Public Schools in the 1980s* (Chicago: MacArthur Foundation, 1986).

6. Herbert M. Kliebard, *The Struggle for the American Curriculum: 1893–1958* (Boston: Routledge & Kegan Paul, 1986).

7. See William Boyd, "The Politics of Curriculum Change and Stability," *Educational Researcher* (February 1979), p. 14.

8. Margaret E. Goertz, *State Educational Standards* (Princeton, N.J.: Educational Testing Service, 1986).

9. Jacqueline Danzberger, Michael Kirst, Michael Usdan, Luvern Cunningham, and Lelah Carrol, *Improving Grass Roots Leadership* (Washington: Institute for Educational Leadership, 1986). The writer acknowledges the help of Jacqueline Danzberger in drafting the school board sections of this chapter.

10. See Task Force on Teaching as a Profession, *A Nation Prepared: Teachers for the 21st Century* (New York: Carnegie Corporation, May 1986) and the National Governors Association, *Time for Results* (Washington, D.C.: 1986), pp. 29–48.

11. Michael Cohen, *Instructional Management in Effective Schools* (Washington, D.C.: National Institute of Education, 1983), p. 8.

12. Chester Finn, "Toward Strategic Independence: Policy Considerations for Enhancing School Effectiveness," paper prepared for the National Institute of Education, 1983, p. 7.

13. Ibid., p. 7.

14. Larry Cuban, "Corporate Involvement in Public Schools," *Teachers College Record* 85 (2), Winter 1983, p. 195.

15. Fred S. Coombs, "The Effects of Increased State Control on Local School District Governance," paper presented to the 1987 Annual Meeting of the AERA, Washington, D.C., April 1987.

16. Odden, op. cit., p. 8.

17. Coombs, op. cit., p. 15. For more discussion of this view, see William L. Boyd, "Public Education's Last Hurrah: Schizophrenia, Amnesia, and Ignorance in School Politics," paper presented to Annual Meeting of APSA, Washington, D.C., August 1986.

18. Coombs, op. cit., p. 8.

19. These principles were provided by James W. Guthrie of the University of California, Berkeley, before the California Commission on School Management and Governance, 1985.

20. Recommendations from Danzberger et al. The author was one of the co-authors of this book.

21. Henry M. Levin, "Finance and Governance Implications of School Based Decisions" (unpublished paper, 1987).

22. E. Schattschneider, *The Semisovereign People* (New York: Holt, Rinehart, and Winston, 1960), p. 71. For a popular version of this concept applied to schools, see Michael W. Kirst, *Who Controls Our Schools* (New York: W. H. Freeman, 1984).

CHAPTER 5

The School as the Center of Change

KENNETH A. SIROTNIK

University of Washington

There are over 2.6 million of them in our nation's public elementary and secondary schools. Together, they constitute over 67% of the 3.9 million staff of all types employed by the local education agencies across the nation. They make up 98% of the total educational staff serving and supporting districts and schools.[1]

Who are they? They are the *educators*—teachers, principals and other administrators, special educators, counselors, librarians, and aides—who staff the public school system at the building level. They are the people who spend their work days behind the walls of schools and doors of classrooms, educating the nation's children. Classroom teachers alone—nearly 2.2 million of them—account for over 26 billion teacher–student contact hours each academic year in public elementary and secondary schools across the nation.[2] Clearly, what goes on in those classrooms is much the same as what went on a generation ago, and a generation before that, regardless of national commission reports, state reform movements, or even directives from local educational agencies.[3]

That the centers for educational change and school improvement are anywhere else than in the nation's schools would be a difficult proposition to defend in light of these statistics. In my experience, I have encountered very few educators who were willing to argue that change was centered in committee rooms in the District of Columbia, in state departments of education, in school districts, or departments of education in universities and colleges. Yet the history of attempts to effect school reform suggests otherwise; these attempts have, by and large, been top-down exercises, intervention strategies fashioned in the tradition of Frederick Winslow Taylor's principles of scientific management.[4] The "time and motion" studies of the turn of the century have become the research, development, diffusion, adoption, implementation, and evaluation studies of modern times.

It has only been recently—the last several years, really—that an alternative paradigm for improving schools has been taken seriously in the reform proposals and actions of educational agencies. After a long history of advocacy in the literature on educational change,[5] the idea that educators in schools must become empowered agents in their own school improvement processes is finally coming into favor. The trend toward building-based decisionmaking in many districts and schools, although a bit short of the liberating experience some have advocated, is certainly a step in this direction.

The purpose of this chapter is to celebrate the coming out of a good idea—that the power to effect significant educational change is, indeed, in the hands of educators in schools. Yet, although I will construct an argument for schools as the centers of educational change, they certainly are not alone in their efforts. I have deliberately avoided terminology like "the school as the *unit* of change" or "the school as the *basis* of change," in order to avoid the impression that all our eggs for educational change and school improvement are in the baskets of school buildings. To say that something is at the center implies a good deal around it. Ignoring the impact (for better or worse) of district, county, and state educational agencies, educational consultants and change facilitators, colleges of education, and parent and other community groups would be professing ignorance of the *ecological* dynamics surrounding the public schooling of children and youth and the problems of accountability and responsibility that go with it.[6] However, if schools and what goes on inside them are not at the center of the educational ecology, then current efforts toward change and improvement are horribly misguided. My choice of terminology—the school as the *center* of change—should therefore be obvious and the implications clear.

However, the force of the obvious argument is not always compelling. Just the fact that the educational work force is concentrated overwhelmingly in schools, and the day-to-day action in terms of educational delivery takes place in these buildings, does not convince everyone that schools should be the center of change. Part of the problem arises because of two meanings of the word "center," both of which I intend in my choice of the term. Nearly all educators would probably agree that the school should be the *focal point* or target of educational change and improvement efforts. Not all educators seem to agree, however, that the school should be the *place* for inquiry and reflective practice—the place for critical thinking, dialogue, decisionmaking, action-taking, and evaluation in educational change and improvement efforts.[7]

I will argue in this chapter that schools are both the objects and arenas of educational improvement and change, notwithstanding the crucial importance of the educational resources and constituencies surrounding schools. The most compelling strand of my argument, I believe, is epistemological in nature, having to do with the claims of legitimacy made for how knowledge is generated and acted upon. However, two other strands—which I will label the *organizational* and the *experiential*—deserve emphasis as well and represent the more typical arguments put forth by others for centering on schools. Put simply, to understand the dynamics of school-based change, one must understand the structure and function of schools as organizations. Moreover, to estimate the potential and likelihood of school-based change, one must review the "successes," "failures," and lessons learned from the change efforts of the past.

Whatever their relative appeal in constructing the argument, all three strands—the epistemological, organizational, and experiential—complement one another and together support the thesis that the school is the center of change. Furthermore, and perhaps most importantly, these several strands of the argument coalesce around the same conditions for professional activity in schools—the kinds of attitudes people need to share, the kinds of behaviors they need to engage in, and the kinds of working conditions that need to be nurtured and sustained. After exploring the thesis of schools as centers of change through considerations of epistemology, organizational theory, and empirical experience, I will end with some implications of the thesis for school practice.

THE EPISTEMOLOGICAL STRAND

Those who seek to make changes (and, it is hoped, improvements) in schools usually claim either implicitly or explicitly some sort of knowledge base to support their efforts. These claims can run the gamut from divine inspiration and mystical intervention to empirically based explanations, understanding, or critiques. My interest is in the latter types of claims. My use of the term "empirical" is intended to be very general in nature, covering the sorts of explanations derived from experimental, quasi-experimental, and correlational studies in the tradition of the scientific or hypothetico-deductive methods; the sorts of interpretations derived from the more exploratory and naturalistic methods of case study and participant observation; and the sorts of action-oriented analyses derived from dialectical critiques of the ideological content in extant knowledge and practices. I wish to discuss these several traditions of producing and using knowledge in terms of how we have thought conventionally, and how we might think alternatively, about making changes and improvements in schools.

Perhaps the predominant world view of knowledge and the utilization of knowledge in educational change stems directly from what has been labeled the "positivist" and "post-positivist" tradition in scientific research. Actually, there are several "world views" embedded in this tradition, but their differences are less important than their similarities for present purposes.[8] Essentially, knowers see themselves as separated from what is to be known. Many educational researchers, for example, see themselves as separated from the objects of their study; they attempt to accumulate empirical evidence in support of law-like relationships between variables, much as a classical physicist might accumulate evidence to support the equation $d=(\frac{1}{2})gt^2$ and, thus, a theory explaining the behavior of falling objects.

The educational researcher is also interested in explaining behavioral phenomena, like the rise and fall of achievement test scores, for example. However, instead of relatively easy and straightforward variables to measure, like distance and time, the educational researcher has variables like self-concept, achievement, intelligence, academically engaged learning time, principal leadership, and school effectiveness. Instead of nearly error-free and highly valid measurements and nearly perfect and replicable equations, the educational researcher has error-prone measurements of questionable validity and statistical guesses of approximate relationships that are typically weak and difficult to replicate from one case to the next.

This is not to suggest that appropriately contextualized interpretations of empirical research programs have no heuristic value for informing both theory and practice. When constructs are not overly interpreted, when results are considered tentative, when the sociopolitical context of the times is taken into account, when values and practical interests are recognized as intrinsic parts of the action in human affairs, then bodies of educational research—like the studies on teacher behavior, methods of teaching and learning in specific subject areas, classroom organization and management, teacher education, cognitive development, and school effectiveness—can be brought to bear usefully on programs of school improvement and change. As Cronbach concluded over a decade ago,

> Social scientists are rightly proud of the discipline we draw from the natural-science side of our ancestry. Scientific discipline is what we uniquely add to the time-honored ways of studying man. Too narrow an identification with science, however, has fixed our eyes upon an inappropriate goal. The goal of our work . . . is not to amass generalizations atop which a theoretical tower can someday be erected. . . .

> The special task of the social scientist in each generation is to pin down the contemporary facts. Beyond that, he shares with the humanistic scholar and the artist in the effort to gain insight into contemporary relationships, and to realign the culture's view of man with present realities. To know man as he is is no mean aspiration.[9]

These conclusions are remarkably parallel in content and sentiment to the philosophically based analysis of the behavioral sciences by Abraham Kaplan a decade earlier, when the R&D bandwagon was just beginning to gather momentum:

> Many behavioral scientists, I am afraid, look to methodology as a source of salvation. . . . There are indeed techniques to be mastered, and their resources and limitations are to be thoroughly explored. But these techniques are specific to their subject-matters, or to distinctive problems, and the norms governing their use derive from the contexts of their application, not from general principles of methodology. . . . The work of the behavioral scientist might well become methodologically sounder if only he did not try so hard to be so scientific![10]

Unfortunately, this more pragmatic and contextualized interpretation of empirical inquiry has not really become part of the practical wisdom of the research, development, dissemination, and evaluation community. Soltis, for example, laments that "there [still] seems to be a basic common agreement . . . that educational research must be empirical, objective, and value free—'scientific' in the positivist's sense."[11] This parochial interpretation of traditional scientific method has spawned a number of false dichotomies or dogmas of inquiry—objectivity versus subjectivity, fact versus value, quantity versus quality, basic research versus applied research, and so forth—that have been the subject of on-again-off-again debate in the educational research community.

Perhaps the most insidious of these dogmas is the presumed split between research and practice that John Dewey spent a lifetime trying to repair. The damage is still with us, and it becomes particularly apparent when the dominant view of educational change and school improvement—R, D, D, and E—is critically appraised.[12] This linear model of "research, development, diffusion, and evaluation" essentially pits experts against practitioners. Those "in the know" are the scholars that generate the research and the experts that package and disseminate the findings in usable form and evaluate the use of these packages in practice. Those "in need of knowing" are the practitioners, the workers in schools, the consumers of new knowledge once it is appropriately distilled into in-service programs. School-based educators are seen as deficient in one or more skill areas and in need of retraining, rather than as professionals who reflect upon their work and upon ways in which they might do their work better. Schools are seen as places in disrepair and in need of fixing, rather than as messy social systems in the process of evolution.

Changing schools, then, becomes a process of programmatic intervention and installation—of applying the remedies of research to the ills of
practice. The school is an *object* to be changed, not a *center of change*—
developing knowledge and informing agendas of action happen some-
where else (in research universities, R & D centers, and district offices, for
example), not as an ongoing part of professional life in schools.

To those researchers, developers, and change agents who are feeling unjustly berated by this barrage of criticism, I apologize. They might
well complain that I have oversimplified the RDD&E process and that
people do not really think and behave in these ways. I can only share
with them some twenty years of working in and around universities,
districts, and schools and my overwhelming impression that this "oversimplified" world view of research and practice is as alive and well today
as it was in the latter half of the 1960s. I have seen superintendents literally hand over lists of "independent" and "dependent" variables to their
principals with exhortations to achieve the expected cause-effect relationship. "Apply the principles of school effectiveness (principal leadership, high expectations, safe and orderly environment, etc.) and raise
the standardized test scores in your school!" I have commiserated with
teachers who spend three in-service days per academic year learning
new techniques and 177 classroom days teaching in the same old conditions and circumstances of schooling. I have argued with colleagues in
research universities who insist that the "science" of educational inquiry
can and must be separated from the "folklore" of educational practice.
In case any of us doubts the certainty of science, one can always consult
Goodwin Watson's *What Psychology Can We Trust?* or, if something more
contemporary is preferred, the U.S. Department of Education's *What
Works*.[13]

Major adjustments in epistemology are required to realize the potential for improvement and change in today's schools. These include
not only more modest, realistic, and philosophically sound interpretations of research in the tradition just described, but also an accepting of
additional perspectives on knowledge and action as legitimate inquiry—
perspectives that lead directly to schools as centers of change. Inquiry in
the phenomenological tradition offers one of the necessary adjustments.
Phenomenology puts the knower back in touch with what might be
known; through the various methods of, and approaches to, observation and case study—ethnography, ethnomethodology, symbolic interactionism, analytic induction, grounded theory, and so on—the researcher interprets the "text" of daily living, much as a historian might
interpret the written texts of the past.[14] This *hermeneutic* approach to
generating knowledge relies heavily upon the accumulation of interpretations of what people say and do in social settings (for example,
schools) and the meanings they attribute to their words and deeds.[15] In

effect, phenomenologists attempt to get as close as possible to peoples' interpretations of their own worlds.

One method of "getting close" is through *participant observation*, where the researcher plays a more active part, over a substantial period of time, in the events and activities of the people and social systems under study. Through formal and informal data collection—structured interviews and casual conversations; systematic and anecdotal observations; records, lists, materials, and other archival documents; daily journals and records of critical incidents; interpretive summaries—the "thick" descriptions and analytical interpretations can be constructed of schooling phenomena (such as leadership dynamics, learning climate, and hidden or implicit curriculum) that are not possible using the correlational and experimental methods of the more positivist traditions.[16] Instead of *explanations* based upon statistical associations between operationally defined constructs, *interpretations* are drawn directly from actual circumstances, events, behaviors, and expressed sentiments as played out daily by people in the context of their work.[17] Although less rigorous and systematic, the ordinary ways in which people construct personal meaning and working knowledge in the context of organizational life resemble very closely the methods of phenomenological inquiry. Studies of the bases upon which teachers, for example, make instructional decisions consistently find that personal knowledge and experience are much more powerful influences on teachers' interpretations and understanding of their work than is knowledge generated by others outside the realm of these experiences.[18]

This is not to suggest, however, that personal knowledge is necessarily better or worse than knowledge generated in other ways; rather, it is to suggest that the working knowledge of teachers is legitimate and something to be reckoned with. In effect, there are nearly two and a half million "participant observers" in charge of public school classrooms, operating on a reservoir of both exceptional and conventional wisdom. The trick is to tap into the exceptional and break through the conventional. By providing teachers real opportunities to consider, critique, modify, and adapt the best that research has to offer in the context of their day-to-day work and their personal and collective teaching experiences, changing conventional practice becomes a possibility.

Consider, for example, the difficult issues of homogeneous versus heterogeneous grouping and managing individual differences in ability for instructional purposes in schools and classrooms. Suppose it is argued that the conventional wisdom of the relatively enduring stratifications and social sorting of kids into "groups" (at the elementary level) and "tracks" (at the secondary level) is misguided and promotes neither equity nor excellence in schooling. Suppose, further, that there are possible alternative practices that have enjoyed some empirical validation through research and development efforts—cooperative learning and peer tutoring methods, for example. How, then, would epistemological predispositions condition the way one might think about and engage in the process of changing grouping practices in schools and classrooms?

Restricting inquiry and knowledge utilization in the RDD&E tradition would place educators in schools in the position of consumers. One or another brand of cooperative learning strategy would be advocated, packaged, and dispensed in the usual in-service manner. Teachers would presumably receive the new knowledge and transfer it to their classroom practices, perhaps with the help of consultants or LEA resources, to the extent provided. Schools may be targets of change, but they are not centers of change; educators in schools are, in essence, passive recipients of fix-up routines designed to repair the machinery. Ideally, the more standardized and "teacher-proof" the routine, the more likely it is that educators in schools can replicate the intended outcomes.

Alternatively, admitting the phenomenological perspective into the domain of legitimate knowledge, schools can become centers of inquiry *activity*. Rather than focusing on implementing solutions (such as a cooperative learning technique), the focus is turned toward the problem itself (such as instructional management of individual differences), and educators can become actively engaged in reflective behavior. What does one do now to handle differences in students' readiness to learn new skills? Why does one use particular instructional practices? What experiences has one had to suggest that these practices are or are not productive? What other instructional practices are possible? Assuming cooperative learning might be one of these, what strategies are currently being advocated? (At this point in the inquiry, an "in-service" or a field visit would be particularly useful.) To what extent are these strategies adaptable to the situation at hand? What revisions and modifications can be made, if necessary, to make it worthwhile to pilot test some alternative practices? What is one learning from these new experiences— ways to further refine and improve the cooperative learning practices or, perhaps, the need to rethink the whole grouping issue? In effect, I am outlining, here, an inquiry scenario that puts educators into the *center* of a knowledge generating and using process. I am not suggesting that schools somehow become mini-R&D centers, but rather that any hope of significant and sustained educational change will need to recognize the personal nature of knowledge and the need for the significant involvement of educators in developing their own understanding.[19]

However, such an adjustment in epistemology is not enough. The most problematic aspect of knowledge generated and packaged in the more popular "scientific" tradition is not its reductionist and decontextualized character, but its pretense of value-free, objective science. A popular text on research methods, for example, states that "scientific problems are not moral and ethical questions"[20] and that value statements implying "shoulds" or "oughts" are "metaphysical [statements] that cannot be tested. . . . This does not mean that scientists would necessarily spurn such statements, say they are not true, or claim they are meaningless. It simply means that *as scientists* they are not concerned with them."[21]

As a scientist, I am concerned with them, metaphysically and methodologically. I find no comfort in being relieved from my responsibilities as a valuing human being in a society of human beings, conducting inquiries with the hope of bettering the human condition (educational practice, for example). If, for example, I conducted some of the recent school effectiveness research, I would be ethically and morally bound to acknowledge my choice of outcome indicator—my explicit or implicit decision to value a narrowly defined range of basic skills as operationalized in standardized test scores as a criterion against which "school effectiveness" would be judged. Likewise, in doing conventional studies of time on task or academically engaged learning time, I would need to warn educators who might place higher value on interpersonal communication skills, critical thinking, student decisionmaking, and so forth, that my findings were again limited to different student outcomes. In fact, were I to have conducted my studies using alternative criteria, I might have identified alternative teaching practices (such as role play and simulation or student discussion) that would tend to conflict with those (such as teacher-led, direct instructional strategies) that correlated with typical measures of basic skills.[22]

Inquiry is not value-free.[23] As Grene concludes in her analysis of the relationship between knower and known, "[t]here is . . . no intelligible discourse independently of evaluation. Appraisal underlies all speech, and therefore all knowledge."[24] Moreover, as Grene goes on to argue, since "knowing is essentially a kind of doing, and human doing is always value-bound, then knowledge is so as well."[25] This represents another significant adjustment of the knowledge paradigms in both the positivist and phenomenological traditions. Inquiry is no longer something that is necessarily done first and then assembled for use. Knowledge generated in human action has purpose, and with purpose come values and human interests. There is little to be gained, therefore, in the expectation that knowledge will be utilized without the concomitant expectation that values and human interests need to be explicit in the knowledge-generating process.

I have already anticipated this idea of knowing in action in my discussion above of the phenomenological tradition and the stretching of this tradition to include educators as participant observers in their own program of school-based inquiry and change. I deliberately chose the homogeneous grouping and tracking issues precisely because of their ideological content and not-too-subtle implications for the educational interests of some at the expense of others.[26] Not many other specific educational issues can generate debate (and anger) more quickly than discussions of the merits and demerits of the tracking and homogeneous grouping research and practices. My hope was that as readers followed my little scenario above of teachers developing their own knowledge base around alternative practices (such as cooperative learning strategies), they would become increasingly uncomfortable due to unstated assumptions and biases; for what is missing from that scenario is the explicit consideration of meritocratic and democratic values and human interests in educational practice. Moreover, I used phrases that concealed some value-laden constructs that have traditionally structured the way many have interpreted and measured human potential. I referred, for example, to "managing individual differences in *ability* for instructional purposes," a phrase consistent with (1) ascribing the characteristic of fixed intellectual potential to each student and then (2) assigning students to instructional groups or tracks based upon such measures as "intelligence quotients" or "scholastic aptitude." Later, I used the phrase "student differences in readiness to learn new skills," wherein the term "readiness" is intended to suggest not *if students can learn* but *when (and under what conditions) students will learn.*[27]

This chapter, of course, is not about tracking, grouping, time on task, or school effectiveness. I have simply used those issues to illustrate the point that knowledge, whatever the particular method(s) for creating and using it, is always situated in a human context of beliefs, values, and interests. This is to suggest again the importance of contextualizing both extant and new knowledge *where the action is* in social settings—*schools*, for example. It is necessary, therefore, to accommodate both the ideological content of inquiry and the active engagement of people in the process of inquiry. Digging into the normative nature of inquiry requires more than generating associations between measured constructs and more than generating interpretations of communicated human experience; it requires the systematic and rigorous *critique* of explanations and understandings—a deliberately and critically reflective stance with respect to all knowledge.

This critical-dialectical perspective on producing and using knowledge represents the second major challenge to traditional research and development.[28] It represents, as well, a challenge to what might appear as relatively benign understandings that are inferred from the careful studies of ethnographers, participant observers, and the like. Through the process of rational discourse, critical-dialectical methods require of those to whom knowledge and action matter most that they tease out tacit beliefs, values, and human interests—both their own and those embedded in the production of knowledge in the first place. The idea of producing knowledge one place and then installing it for use in another place is an alien concept in the world of critical inquiry. Regardless of where and how knowledge is generated, critical-dialectical methods demand that it be "re-known" in the context of values-based human activity—a concept of critical knowing in action or a "critical phenomenology," if you will. As Van Manen puts it, this is the process of "linking ways of knowing with ways of being practical."[29]

Once again, we are led to the importance of schools as centers of change. We are led to the idea of making the ordinary ways that working knowledge is already accumulated and used by educators in schools much more systematic and rigorous. Practice becomes the subject of deliberate reflection; values, beliefs and human interests are resurrected from individual and collective subconsciousness; and the best of extant knowledge can be reviewed critically for use in the context of these inquiry activities.

This requires building upon the reflective practice suggested earlier for educators as participant observers in their own schools. For a number of years, my colleagues and I have been attempting to combine competing epistemological perspectives into a working synthesis that capitalizes upon what we argue are productive tensions between the several ways of knowing. This process of *critical inquiry* is oriented toward developing a working consensus and agendas for action. Critical inquiry requires that participants, as individuals and groups, maintain a self-conscious stance with respect to all types of knowledge—that they deliberately engage dialectically in the process of knowing, through a series of generic questions designed to keep the discourse alive, informed, and values-based.[30]

First, the participants in a critical inquiry must continually remind themselves that the problems they face have a current and historical context, and that the problems—using time effectively, staff communication, grouping students for instruction, and the like—must be situated in these contexts in order to be understood. "What are we doing now?" "How did it come to be that way?" These are questions that help frame this discussion.

Second, to be *critical*, the inquiry must demand of participants that they confront the political reality of significant educational issues and that they recognize and contend with embedded values and human interests.[31] The question to be addressed here is "Whose interests are (and are not) being served by the ways things are?"

Third, a program of critical inquiry demands of participants that their inquiry be *informed* and that knowledge of all types be brought to bear upon issues under discussion. This includes the results of research studies (correlational, experimental, ethnographic, participant-observational, and so on) typically reported in books, journals, and occasional and technical reports from educational research projects; the educational innovations in curriculum and instruction, and organizational leadership and development that are typically disseminated by consultants and through workshops; the results of studies done by LEAs; the experiential accounts of the participants themselves; and so forth. Moreover, information can be purposely generated in the context of the inquiry through the use of surveys, interviews, observations (teachers observing one another at work, for example), and document reviews such as curriculum plans, textbooks, and evaluation instruments. The question to keep in mind here is "What information and knowledge do we have (or need to get) that bear upon the issues?"

Finally, participants must continually remind themselves that all is not talk; notwithstanding the omnipresent ambiguity in educational organizations like schools, actions can and must be taken, reviewed, revised, retaken, and reviewed again. The questions to ask at every opportunity are "Is this the way we want things to be?" and "What are we going to do about all this?" A program of critical inquiry never really ends; it is, indeed, the process of school renewal and change.[32]

Understand that I am not suggesting that only educators in schools can participate in the inquiry—district staff, university-based educators, educational consultants, parents, and students are all viable participants in the discourse. I am suggesting, however, that only the schools are the centers of change—not legislative offices, districts or service centers, R&D centers, colleges of education, or professional development centers. These are all valuable *resources*, but given the epistemological considerations discussed thus far, knowledge and practice come together only through human discourse and action in the organizational context, not simply through better training programs for individuals, teacher-proof curricula, or meta-interpretations of the various and sundry educational research studies. The center for the discourse suggested by the above questions, therefore, can be located nowhere else but in schools.

THE ORGANIZATIONAL STRAND

Since I believe that I have already presented the most compelling strand of the argument for schools as centers of change, I will not dwell too long on these next two supporting strands. Clearly, there is an extensive and distinguished literature on organizational theory and practice concerning the structure and function of organizations and the implications thereof for the behavior of people in organizations.[33] Much of this literature has been translated directly for educational organizations (public schools in particular), often in the context of educational administration.[34] Interestingly, the development of "world views" regarding what constitute appropriate theoretical frames through which to view organizational practice parallels in most respects the several paradigmatic traditions of legitimate knowledge reviewed above.

The industrial revolution and the turn of the century heralded the attempts to establish order, rationality, and a scientific base for organizational structure, decisionmaking, and work. Between the scientific management principles offered by writers such as Taylor and the hierarchical, bureaucratic structure envisioned by Weber, the foundation was set for a rational, linear, machine-like view of organizational development that persists to this day.[35] This view tends to be characterized by top-down decisionmaking and accountability structures, the search for and use of technological solutions to human problems, and the monitoring of work through the use of quality control indicators.

It did not take long for this view to be swallowed hook, line, and sinker by educators (in universities, districts, and schools) and educational reformers (wherever located). The "school as a factory" metaphor, for example, was launched early on by Ellwood Cubberley, in one of the first of a long line of books on educational administration:

> Our schools are, in a sense, factories in which the raw products (children) are to be shaped and fashioned into products. . . . The specifications for manufacturing come from the demands of twentieth-century civilization, and it is the business of the school to build its pupils according to the specifications laid down. This demands good tools, specialized machinery, continuous measurement of production to see if it is according to specifications, the elimination of waste in manufacture, and a large variety in the output.[36]

Although the metaphor is more subtle at times, one can still find it shaping the way people think about schooling today:

> Education Is California's Growth Industry. . . . The conditions are right for California's public education system . . . to become, in the vernacular of the private sector, the hot new industry of the 1980s and 1990s. The resources are there. . . . These children are California's greatest natural resource. [Schools are] the key supplier[s] to every public and private sector. . . . [Their] product—educated people—will shape our entire society.[37]

One can clearly see parochial interpretations of the positivist tradition at work in these metaphors and resultant organizational practices. Local educational agencies have been particularly eager to adopt "new" management schemes that were invented (and that are on their way to being discarded) in the private sector—SOPs (standard operating procedures), MBO (management by objectives), PERT (program evaluation review technique), and the like. Much of the macro-level educational research that has been conducted follows the same model of production line and input-process-output—the raw materials of schooling (input characteristics of the community, students, teachers), the machinery of schooling (organizational processes and instructional practices), and the quality control indexes of schooling (achievement test score outcomes).[38] Changing and improving organizations, then, is the equivalent of good management and the application of research-based technology. When the machinery of a school is out of whack, change (or retrain) the personnel, using the best available know-how. In effect, manipulate the manipulable inputs and processes to effect the desired outcomes.

Partly as a reaction to the robotic flavor of scientific management, the human relations view of organizations and organizational life gained momentum with the early work of people like Chester Barnard and Elton Mayo, followed in more contemporary versions by theorists such as Argyris and McGregor.[39] The argument was that people have needs as individuals and as members of groups; an organization, no matter how well managed, will not be effective unless the personal and interpersonal domains of human behavior are cared for. The predominate view of organizations, however, remained mostly unchanged; they were still regarded as relatively closed social systems with management, worker, and production functions—if you could just get people feeling good about themselves and their workplace, then the satisfied employees would produce better products.

Critics of the human relations movement have noted—rightly, I believe—that organizational conflict is not something that can be eliminated through sensitivity training and the other organizational development devices that flourished during the application phases of human relations theory. "Differences in economic structure and power positions cannot be communicated away," as Etzioni has noted.[40] The idea of "communication" in organizational development terms, of course, bears little resemblance to the idea of "communicative competence" in the critical-dialectical traditions discussed above.[41] In the former, people are "trained" to relate to one another, to become conscious of their own hang-ups, and to find ways of diminishing (if not eliminating) conflict within the existing parameters of the organization. In the latter, people continually struggle not only with interpersonal relations but with the very structures and conditions within which they work—conflicts in values and human interests are the very substance of the discourse. From the human relations perspective, then, schools would be more like centers of therapy than centers of change.

Both the narrow scientific management and human relations views of organizations (schools included) have given way to alternative conceptions of organizations and organizational life. School districts and schools, for example, are not closed systems; they interact continuously with their sociopolitical environments at the local, state, and national levels. Complex organizations like districts and schools are often combinations of formal and informal structures and functions, personal and interpersonal dynamics, and political conflicts between special interest groups. These organizations, to a noticeable extent, develop a mini-culture of their own, consisting of many of the usual features that define cultures—norms, roles, expectations, symbols, rituals and ceremonies, explanations about why things are the way they are (myths), conventional behaviors that maintain conventional wisdom, and so on.[42]

One of these "cultural regularities"[43] is organizational ambiguity.[44] The idea that all goals are specified in advance and acted upon systematically as planned is just another one of the organizational myths. March has argued persuasively that although organizations are not without overarching purposes, specific goals and objectives, rather than directing action, usually become obvious through action.[45] He suggests that the conventional and linear ways that people think they are supposed to use to make sense out of organizational life must be turned upside-down—that is, treating "goals as hypotheses . . . intuition as real . . . hypocrisy as transition . . . memory as an enemy . . . [and] experience as a theory" is much more in line with the ways people ordinarily develop working knowledge.[46]

This shifting of world view regarding organizations and behavior within organizations mirrors the shift to the phenomenological concepts and methods discussed previously. It puts the organization and the people within the organization back into the picture with respect to how the place functions and changes. Weick captures this epistemological shift well in the context of organizational life:

> People commonly assert, "I'll believe it when I see it." This bit of wisdom probably should be turned on its ear so that it approximates more closely the ways in which people actually act: "I'll see it when I believe it."[47]

These statements, of course, suggest an even greater shift in organizational theory and change than Weick probably had in mind. For at the heart of beliefs (and their dispositions toward action—their attitudes) are *values*—fundamental standards for moral judgments, personal and social conduct, and human existence.[48] Thus, in any discussion of values in a sociopolitical context, human interests and ideologies are implicit. Attitudes toward using cooperative learning techniques in classrooms, for example, are conditioned by beliefs regarding the appropriateness of tracking and homogeneous versus heterogeneous classes, which, in turn, are rooted in values concerning the nature of freedom, justice, and serving the educational interests of some at the expense of others.

Paralleling the shift to critical-dialectical perspectives in knowledge production and utilization, there has been a growing movement in organizational theory (and particularly in the theory of school administration) that has challenged the prevailing wisdom of the scientific management, human relations, and open systems cultural perspectives.[49] Although admitting that organizations can be characterized in part by features from each of these perspectives, the critical view of organizations challenges the very conditions and power relationships that define organizational structure and function.

For example, the view of organizations as cultures has given rise to a kind of "management by symbols" concept of organizational change. Ouchi's *Theory Z* suggests that companies develop a culture around a central organizational philosophy while at the same time promoting non-token participative management at all levels of leadership within the organization.[50] Schools and schooling, of course, may be a bit more complicated. Meyer and Rowan suggest a rather elaborate culture of schooling that is held together through the tight coupling of symbols and ceremonies at the levels of administrator accountability and the loose coupling of administration, teachers, and teaching behind classroom doors.[51] These conceptions of organizations, although clearly placing them in the center of the action for change, offer little in the way of change strategy other than trying to manipulate symbols, roles, norms, expectations, and the other features that make up the complex of organizational culture.

A critical perspective of organizations, on the other hand, like its epistemological counterpart, is the catalyst for action. It is concerned primarily with trying to change the organization in the process of trying to understand it—the concept of praxis. In his seminal paper on the dialectical view of organizations, Benson summed up the argument thusly:

> A dialectical analysis of organizations . . . should be concerned with conditions under which people may reconstruct organizations and establish social formations in which continuous reconstruction is possible. This provides guidance regarding the selection of research questions. Some important issues are the humanization of work processes, the development of systems of participation (self-management), the discovery of alternatives to bureaucracy, the removal of systems of dominance, the provision for the utilization of expert knowledge without creating technocratic elites, removing the resistance of organizations to more rational arrangements. . . . These are, of course, difficult problems and the task is complicated by the possibility that contradictions will develop between them, for example, creating rational systems may undermine self-management.

Thus, the prospect is for a continuous process of reconstruction.[52] This leads once again to the organization—the school—as the center of change. It does not lead one to see the school naively as isolated from its sociopolitical context, able to engage in miraculous self-renewing activities without district, community, state, and federal support. It does, however, lead to where the day-to-day action is, to where, with the proper motivation and support, the prevailing conditions and circumstances in schools can be challenged constructively within the context of competing values and human interests.

THE EXPERIENTIAL STRAND

Up to this point, my argument has been largely conceptual in nature, although I have alluded to studies based upon observations of how people ordinarily go about making sense of their work. Consider, for the record, what the history of attempts to make fundamental changes in schools has to add to the argument.

Perhaps the most comprehensive foray into the successes and failures of major educational innovations and change strategies was the series of change agent studies conducted by the Rand Corporation. Nearly 400 local and national federally funded projects were reviewed from the standpoints of initiation, implementation, and continuity. Berman and McLaughlin finally concluded that the findings

> reveal inconsistent and generally disappointing results. Despite considerable innovative activity on the part of local school districts, the evidence suggests that: No class of existing educational treatments has been found that consistently leads to improved student outcomes. . . . "Successful" projects have difficulty sustaining their success over a number of years. . . . [They] are not disseminated automatically or easily, and their "replication" in new sites usually falls short of their performance in the original sites.[53]

Strategies found by the researchers to be particularly ineffective included the use of "outside consultants . . . packaged management approaches . . . one-shot, preimplementation training . . . pay for training . . . formal evaluation . . . [and] comprehensive [overly ambitious] projects."[54] A constellation of strategies found to be more promising included "concrete, teacher-specific, and extended training; classroom assistance from project or district staff; teacher observation of similar projects in other classrooms, schools, or districts; regular project meetings that focused on practical problems; teacher participation in project decisions; local materials development; [and] principal participation in training."[55] The phrase "mutual adaptation" was coined by the researchers to indicate the two-way nature of the more successful innovations—that is, the willingness of educators in schools and districts to bend in accordance with project requirements and the flexibility of project staff to modify project requirements in accordance with the exigencies of schooling.

In short, as the arguments in the preceding two sections have suggested, people who live and work in complex organizations like schools need to be thoroughly involved in their own improvement efforts, if significant and enduring organizational change is the purpose one has in mind. Not surprisingly, the same conclusion is reinforced by the experiences of the many educators in universities and schools who have engaged in what has been variously labeled as action, interactive, or collaborative research. The Golden Rule of collaborative research is "Do with others as you would have them do with you." After reviewing a number of such efforts between university- and school-based educators, Tikunoff and Ward have delineated clearly the principles and characteristics of collaborative research.[56]

> (1) researchers and practitioners work together at all phases of the inquiry process; (2) the research effort focuses on "real world" as well as theoretical problems; (3) mutual growth and respect occur among all participants; and (4) attention is given to both research and implementation issues from the beginning of the inquiry process.

The outcomes that tend to characterize collaborative research efforts are:

> (1) . . . collaboration promotes investigating and understanding the complexity of the instructional process and the context in which instruction occurs; (2) . . . [results] appear to be more robust and externally valid; (3) teachers perceive the findings . . . to be more immediately useful . . . ; (4) teachers . . . utilize the data collection procedures and processes for investigating their own instructional problems; and (5) all participants obtain new insights and understandings about their own and other participants' roles in education.

These principles and characteristics, of course, overlap considerably with the critical inquiry paradigm that I outlined in the first section. It is good news, indeed, that implications from a philosophy of knowing-in-action correspond with the experiences of the more successful efforts in changing and improving practices in schools. But these efforts are not without problems; by their very nature they conflict with many of the cultural regularities of schooling and the ordinary ways in which educators have tried to bring about change. For these reasons, my colleagues and I recognized through our own trials and tribulations that the collaborative paradigm outlined above had to be shifted in accord with a more critical perspective on organizations and organizational change.[57] In effect, a fifth item must be added to the list of principles: Attention is given through critical discourse to the beliefs, values, and human interests that invariably interact with the process of generating and using knowledge.

CONCLUSION

Any of these several strands—preferably, the combined strength of all three—support the conclusion that schools are not only the targets of educational improvement but are, indeed, the centers for educational change. As centers for educational change, I have argued, they must be centers of inquiry. By this I am not suggesting that schools compete with colleges, universities, and research centers. I am suggesting that educators in schools, using all the collaborative help they can get, become their own change agents and active and critical consumers of their own and others' knowledge in the context of their own practices and the changing of these practices.

Two decades ago, Robert Schaefer delivered the ninth John Dewey lecture, entitled "The School as a Center of Inquiry."[58] I have only two misgivings regarding this work, which I consider, on the whole, to be among the finest statements of the thesis that I have tried to argue for here. My first misgiving is his choice of title—I wish he had used another so that I could have considered it for my own. *The school as a center of inquiry* really embodies the whole idea of the target, locus, and process of educational change and school improvement.

My second concern relates to Schaefer's vision of what inquiring schools might look like—how they might be structured, staffed, and operationalized. He and I are in clear agreement that the present conditions and circumstances of schools could not be more antithetical to centers of inquiry and change if they had been so planned from the outset. The isolation of educators (both teachers and administrators) from one another, the lockstep chopping up of the instructional day into isomorphic relationship with subject matters, the indiscriminate allocation of untenable student–teacher ratios, the almost nonexistent time for genuine reflective practice, and the lack of commensurate rewards given the nature of the job are among the worst of these conditions and circumstances. This dismal picture is perhaps no more vividly portrayed than by Sizer's description of Horace—his dreams of becoming a teacher and his compromises having become one.[59]

As clear as it is that schools are the centers of change, it is also evident that they must be significantly altered if they are to function as centers of inquiry. Releasing teachers and administrators for significant periods of time from instructional and routine duties in order to engage in the kind of critical inquiry suggested above is the primary focus of this reconstruction. Reorganizing and integrating the curriculum, more efficient use of human resources, time, and technology, and eleven-month appointments of educators are among the more obvious ideas with which to experiment.[60]

Yet what would be the nature of the inquiry, and who would be doing it? Here is where Schaefer and I part company. I am not convinced that it is either necessary or sufficient that schools, as centers of inquiry and change, must be connected to universities and be inhabited by an elite corps of trained "researcher-teachers" or "scholar-teachers" in order for the school to become the renewing organization that we envision.[61] All my experience working with educators in schools suggests that there already exists an enormous reservoir of talent just waiting for the dam to burst.[62] Being playful with ideas, being inventive and creative, being reflective with respect to one's practice,[63] are not matters that require an advanced degree or an invasion of consultants with titles after their names. I have personally encountered as many (perhaps more) nonreflective theoreticians in colleges and universities as I have nonreflective practitioners in districts and schools. Critical inquiry is not only a process, but also an attitude, based upon strongly held beliefs and values beyond those ordinarily fostered in research universities, that requires leadership and nurturance in a hospitable organizational environment. The leadership can come from any source—parents, teachers, principals, district staff, university staff—so long as the principles of collaborative and critical inquiry are taken seriously. I am not suggesting, therefore, that collaborations or partnerships between schools and universities are of little or no use. Indeed, they have enormous catalytic potential for the kind of school transformations (and, I should add, concomitant reconstruction of colleges of education as well) that are clearly necessary.[64] (Surely, teacher education programs will need to participate in these transformations and prepare and socialize new educators accordingly.)

The conference for which this chapter was prepared was based on the pleasantly optimistic hope for a *new* wave of more thoughtful and constructive school reform. The "first" wave of the early 1980s that drenched the public schools would appear to be receding from our educational shorelines save for a backwash directed at institutions of higher education, and particularly at liberal arts and teacher education programs. Of course, there have been many "first" waves. Each time, they break in a crash of symbols and ceremonies, leaving residual effects in schools and classrooms that are scarcely more than ripples. Pomp and circumstance gets played out at the federal and state levels—calls for "back to the basics," tougher accountability standards, minor salary increases for teachers, and the like—as though the conditions, practices, and people in schools were only flotsam and jetsam in the swell.

I am not too sanguine about waves—they usually end up taking away more than they bring. What school reform needs is a long-term commitment to the hard business of inquiry and educational reconstruction where the agenda for reform resides—in schools. The school is the obvious place where educators can come together to deal with tough issues and good ideas in the context of practice. The school is the place where critical inquiry is not just an armchair dialectic, but a paradigm of knowing and reknowing in the context of action. Schools are not only places for teaching critical thinking; they are also places for thinking critically about teaching.

In attempting, therefore, to sustain whatever is left that is positive in this decade of educational reform, it must not be forgotten where the ultimate power to change is and always has been—in the heads, hands, and hearts of the educators who work in our schools. True reform must go where the action is.

NOTES

1. W. Vance Grant and Thomas D. Snyder, *Digest of Education Statistics, 1985–86* (Washington, D.C.: Office of Educational Research and Improvement, U.S. Department of Education, 1987). See Table 47, p. 52.

2. Ibid., p. 52, Table 39. The estimate assumes 4 instructional hours per day, 180 instructional days per year, and 17.1 pupils per teacher, using average daily attendance figures.

3. Larry Cuban, *How Teachers Taught: Constancy and Change in American Classrooms, 1890–1980* (New York: Longman, 1984); John I. Goodlad, M. Francis Klein et al., *Behind the Classroom Door* (Worthington, Ohio: Jones, 1970); Philip W. Jackson, *Life in Classrooms* (New York: Holt, Rinehart & Winston, 1968); Kenneth A. Sirotnik, "What You See Is What You Get: Consistency, Persistency, and Mediocrity in Classrooms," *Harvard Educational Review* 53, 1983, pp. 16–31.

4. Frederick W. Taylor, *The Principles of Scientific Management* (New York: Harper & Row, 1911).

5. See, for example Mary M. Bentzen et al., *Changing Schools: The Magic Feather Principle* (New York: McGraw-Hill, 1974); John I. Goodlad, "The Individual School and its Principal: Key Setting and Key Person in Educational Leadership," *Educational Leadership 13*, 1955, pp. 2–6; John I. Goodlad, *The Dynamics of Educational Change* (New York: McGraw-Hill, 1975); Bruce R. Joyce, Richard H. Hersh, and Michael McKibbin, *The Structure of School Improvement* (New York: Longman, 1983); and Robert J. Schaefer, *The School as a Center of Inquiry* (New York: Harper & Row, 1967). Another intimately related line of supporting research and practice, one I will not attempt to review here, can be found in the work on social ecologies. For example, see Roger G. Barker, *Ecological Psychology: Concepts and Methods for Studying the Environment of Human Behavior* (Stanford, Calif.: Stanford University Press, 1968) and Paul V. Gump, "The Behavior Setting: A Promising Unit for Environmental Designers," *Landscape Architecture 61*, 1971, pp. 130–134.

6. Goodlad, *The Dynamics of Educational Change;* John I. Goodlad, ed., *The Ecology of School Renewal,* 1987 Yearbook, Part I, National Society for the Study of Education (Chicago: University of Chicago Press, 1987); Seymour Sarason, *The Culture of the School and the Problem of Change* (Boston: Allyn and Bacon, 1971 and 1982).

7. For an expanded treatment of this discussion, see Kenneth A. Sirotnik and Jeannie Oakes, "Critical Inquiry for School Renewal: Liberating Theory and Practice," in Kenneth A. Sirotnik and Jeannie Oakes, eds., *Critical Perspectives on the Organization and Improvement of Schooling* (Boston: Kluwer-Nijhoff, 1986). See also similar discussions by Ann and Harold Berlak, *Dilemmas of Schooling: Teaching and Social Change* (London: Methuen, 1981); and Eric Bredo and Walter Feinberg, eds., *Knowledge and Values in Social and Educational Research* (Philadelphia: Temple University Press, 1982).

8. D. C. Phillips, "After the Wake: Postpositivistic Educational Thought," *Educational Researcher 12* (5), 1983, pp. 4–12. See also the response in the same issue by Elliot W. Eisner, "Anastasia Might Still be Alive, But the Monarchy is Dead," pp. 13–24.

9. Lee J. Cronbach, "Beyond the Two Disciplines of Scientific Psychology," *American Psychologist 30,* 1975, p. 126.

10. Abraham Kaplan, *The Conduct of Inquiry: Methodology for Behavioral Science* (San Francisco: Chandler Publishing, 1964), p. 406.

11. Jonas F. Soltis, "On the Nature of Educational Research," *Educational Researcher 13* (10), 1984, p. 6.

12. See the Rand change agent studies by Paul Berman and Milbrey Wallin McLaughlin, *Federal Programs Supporting Educational Change, Vol. VIII* (Santa Monica, Calif.: The Rand Corporation, 1978). For other commentaries on, critiques of, and alternatives to the RDD&E model, see, for example, Eleanor Farrar, John DeSanctis, and David Cohen, "The Lawn Party: The Evolution of Federal Programs in Local Settings," *Teachers College Record 82,* 1980, pp. 77–100; Michael Fullan, *The Meaning of Educational Change* (New York: Teachers College Press, 1982); Goodlad, *Dynamics of Educational Change*; Joyce, Hersh, and McKibbin, *The Structure of School Improvement*; Ann Lieberman, ed., *Rethinking School Improvement: Research, Craft, and Concept* (New York: Teachers College Press, 1986); Sarason, *The Culture of the School*; and Arthur Wise, "Why Educational Policies Often Fail: The Hyperrationalization Hypothesis," *Journal of Curriculum Studies 9,* 1977, pp. 43–57.

13. Goodwin Watson, *What Psychology Can We Trust?* (New York: Bureau of Publications, Teachers College, 1961); *What Works: Research about Teaching and Learning* (Washington, D.C.: United States Department of Education, 1986).

14. A sampler of readings in this area includes Herbert Blumer, *Symbolic Interactionism: Perspective and Method* (Englewood Cliffs, N.J.: Prentice-Hall, 1969); William J. Filstead, ed., *Qualitative Methodology: Firsthand Involvement with the Social World* (Chicago: Markham, 1970); Harold Garfinkel, *Studies in Ethnomethodology* (Englewood Cliffs, N.J.: Prentice-Hall, 1967); Barney G. Glaser and Anselm L. Strauss, *The Discovery of Grounded Theory: Strategies for Qualitative Research* (Chicago: Aldine, 1967); Elliot G. Mischler, "Meaning in Context: Is There Any Other Kind?," *Harvard Educational Review 49,* 1979, pp. 1–19; and George Spindler, *Doing the Ethnography of Schooling: Educational Anthropology in Action* (New York: Holt, Rinehart & Winston, 1982).

15. See, for example, Roger Jehenson, "A Phenomenological Approach to the Study of the Formal Organization" in George Psathas, ed., *Phenomenological Sociology: Issues and Applications* (New York: Wiley, 1973); Paul Ricoeur, "The Model of the Text," *Social Research 38,* 1971, pp. 529–555; and Charles Taylor, "Interpretation and the Sciences of Man," *Review of Metaphysics 25,* 1971, pp. 3–34.

16. See Clifford Geertz, *The Interpretation of Culture* (New York: Basic Books, 1973).

17. See the discussion by David P. Ericson and Frederick S. Ellett, "Interpretation, Understanding, and Educational Research," *Teachers College Record 83,* 1982, pp. 479–513.

18. A number of researchers and observers of life in schools and classrooms have noted the ways in which practitioners construct and act upon personal knowledge. For example, see Donald W. Dorr-Bremme, "Assessing Students: Teacher's Routine Practices and Reasoning," *Evaluation Comment 6* (4), 1983; Mary M. Kennedy, *Working Knowledge and Other Essays* (Cambridge, Mass.: Huron Institute, 1982); Dan C. Lortie, *Schoolteacher: A Sociological Study* (Chicago: University of Chicago Press, 1975); Robert MacKay, "How Teachers Know: A Case of Epistemological Conflict," *Sociology of Education 51,* 1978, pp. 177–187; and Willard Waller, *The Sociology of Teaching* (New York: Wiley, 1932). For a more general argument, see Donald A. Schön, *The Reflective Practitioner: How Professionals Think in Action* (New York: Basic Books, 1983).

19. The example I have chosen comes from first-hand experience with an effort to integrate cooperative learning into an elementary school curriculum using a sequence of inquiry not unlike that described here. See Sydney H. Farivar, "Developing and Implementing a Cooperative Learning Program in a Middle Elementary Classroom," unpublished doctoral dissertation (Los Angeles: University of California, 1985).

20. Fred N. Kerlinger, *Foundations of Behavioral Research* (New York: Holt, Rinehart & Winston, 1986), pp. 20–21.

21. Ibid., p. 5.

22. For a review of the school effectiveness research, see Stewart C. Purkey and Marshall S. Smith, "Effective Schools: A Review," *The Elementary School Journal 4,* 1983, pp. 427–452. The research on time on task has been reviewed by Barak Victor Rosenshine, "Academic Engaged Time, Content Covered, and Direct Instruction," *Journal of Education 160,* 1978, pp. 38–66.

23. I realize that the argument supporting this statement will not be fully developed here. Many have attempted to do so, however, and a partial list of sources, in addition to those noted in note 7, is as follows: Michael W. Apple, "The Process and Ideology of Valuing in Educational Settings" in Michael W. Apple, Michael J. Subkoviak, and Henry S. Lufler, Jr., eds., *Educational Evaluation* (Berkeley, Calif.: McCutchan, 1974); Richard J. Bernstein, *The Restructuring of Social and Political Theory* (Philadelphia: University of Pennsylvania Press, 1978); Fred R. Dallmayr and Thomas A. McCarthy, eds., *Understanding and Social Inquiry* (South Bend, Ind.: University of Notre Dame Press, 1977); Henry A. Giroux, *Ideology, Culture & the Process of Schooling* (Philadelphia: Temple University Press, 1981); and Max Van Manen, "An Exploration of Alternative Research Orientations in Social Education," *Theory and Research in Social Education 3*, 1975, pp. 1–28.

24. Marjorie Grene, *The Knower and the Known* (New York: Basic Books, 1966), p. 172.

25. Ibid., p. 179.

26. Jeannie Oakes, *Keeping Track: How Schools Structure Inequality* (New Haven, Conn.: Yale University Press, 1985).

27. Discussions of the ideological content and of sloppiness in the historical use of constructs like intelligence, ability, and potential can be found in Howard Gardner, *Frames of Mind: The Theory of Multiple Intelligences* (New York: Basic Books, 1983); Stephen Jay Gould, *The Mismeasure of Man* (New York: W. W. Norton, 1981); and Israel Scheffler, *Of Human Potential: An Essay in the Philosophy of Education* (Boston: Routledge & Kegan Paul, 1985).

28. I have been influenced most in this area by two writers: Jurgen Habermas, particularly his books *Knowledge and Human Interests* (Boston: Beacon Press, 1971) and *Communication and the Evolution of Society* (Boston: Beacon Press, 1979), and Paulo Freire, particularly his books *Education for Critical Consciousness* (New York: Continuum, 1973) and *Pedagogy of the Oppressed* (New York: Continuum, 1970).

29. Max Van Manen, "Linking Ways of Knowing With Ways of Being Practical," *Curriculum Inquiry 6*, 1977, pp. 205–228.

30. Paul E. Heckman, Jeannie Oakes, and Kenneth A. Sirotnik, "Expanding the concepts of renewal and change," *Educational Leadership 40*, 1983, pp. 26–32; Sirotnik and Oakes, *Critical Inquiry for School Renewal;* and Kenneth A. Sirotnik, "Evaluation in the Ecology of Schooling: The Process of School Renewal," in Goodlad, ed., *The Ecology of School Renewal.*

31. I hope readers understand that the term "critical" is being used here in the epistemological sense intended—dialectical and constructive, not polemical and destructive.

32. Sirotnik, "Evaluation in the Ecology of Schooling."

33. Good overviews can be found in Lee G. Bolman and Terrence E. Deal, *Modern Approaches to Understanding and Managing Organizations* (San Francisco: Jossey-Bass, 1984) and W. Richard Scott, *Organizations: Rational, Natural and Open Systems* (Englewood Cliffs, N.J.: Prentice-Hall, 1981).

34. See, for example, E. Mark Hanson, *Educational Administration and Organizational Behavior* (Boston: Allyn & Bacon, 1985); Wayne K. Hoy and Cecil G. Miskel, *Educational Administration: Theory, Research, and Practice* (New York: Random House, 1987); Richard A. Schmuck et al., *The 2nd Handbook of Organization Development in Schools* (Palo Alto, Calif.: Mayfield, 1977). See also the alternative perspectives in the collection by Thomas J. Sergiovanni and John E. Corbally, eds., *Leadership and Organizational Culture: New Perspectives on Administrative Theory and Practice* (Urbana, Ill., and Chicago: University of Illinois Press, 1984).

35. Taylor, *The Principles of Scientific Management;* Max Weber, *The Theory of Social and Economic Organizations* (New York: Free Press, 1947). For a seminal critique of scientific management and its impact upon education, see Raymond E. Callahan, *Education and the Cult of Efficiency* (Chicago: University of Chicago Press, 1962).

36. Ellwood P. Cubberley, *Public School Administration* (Boston: Houghton Mifflin, 1916), p. 338.

37. *Who Will Teach Our Children: A Strategy for Improving California's Schools* (Sacramento, Calif.: California Commission on the Teaching Profession, 1985).

38. See the review by Naftaly S. Glasman and I. Biniaminov, "Input-Output Analyses of Schools," *Review of Educational Research 51*, 1982, pp. 509–539. The most notable ex-

ample, of course, is the report by James S. Coleman et al., *Equality of Educational Opportunity* (Washington, D.C.: U.S. Government Printing Office, 1966).

39. Chester I. Barnard, *The Functions of the Executive* (Cambridge, Mass.: Harvard University Press, 1938); Elton Mayo, *The Social Problems of an Industrial Civilization* (Boston: Graduate School of Business Administration, Harvard University, 1945); Chris Argyris, *Personality and the Organization* (New York: Harper & Row, 1957); Douglas McGregor, *The Human Side of Enterprise* (New York: McGraw-Hill, 1960).

40. Amitai Etzioni, *Modern Organizations* (Englewood Cliffs, N.J.: Prentice-Hall, 1964), p. 44.

41. Contrast group communication strategies presented in Schmuck et al., *The 2nd Handbook of Organization Development*, for example, with those advocated by Habermas, *Communication and the Evolution of Society* and Freire, *Education for Critical Consciousness*.

42. Terrence E. Deal and Allan Kennedy, *Corporate Cultures* (Reading, Mass.: Addison-Wesley, 1982). Examples of work pertaining specifically to schools are Christopher J. Hurn, *The Limits and Possibilities of Schooling* (Boston: Allyn & Bacon, 1978); Lortie, *Schoolteacher*; Sarason, *The Culture of the School*; and Waller, *The Sociology of Teaching*.

43. Sarason, *The Culture of the School*, Chapter 6.

44. James G. March and Johan P. Olsen, *Ambiguity and Choice in Organizations* (Oslo, Norway: Universitetsförlaget, 1976).

45. James G. March, "Model Bias in Social Action," *Review of Educational Research 42*, 1972, pp. 413–429.

46. Ibid., pp. 426–427.

47. Karl E. Weick, *The Social Psychology of Organizing* (New York: Random House, 1979), pp. 134–135.

48. Milton Rokeach, *Beliefs, Attitudes, and Values* (San Francisco: Jossey-Bass, 1970).

49. Examples are Richard J. Bates, "Toward a Critical Practice of Educational Administration," in Sergiovanni and Corbally, eds., *Leadership and Organizational Culture*; J. Kenneth Benson, "Organizations: A Dialectical View," *Administrative Science Quarterly 22*, 1977, pp. 1–21; William Foster, *Paradigms and Promises: New Approaches to Educational Administration* (New York: Prometheus Books, 1987); Thomas B. Greenfield, "Organization Theory as Ideology," *Curriculum Inquiry 9*, 1979, pp. 97–112.

50. William Ouchi, *Theory Z* (Reading, Mass.: Addison-Wesley, 1981). See also the accounts of Thomas J. Peters and Robert H. Waterman, Jr., *In Search of Excellence* (New York: Harper & Row, 1982).

51. John W. Meyer and Brian Rowan, "The Structure of Educational Organizations," in M. W. Meyer et al., eds., *Studies on Environments and Organizations* (San Francisco: Jossey-Bass, 1978).

52. Benson, "Organizations: A Dialectical View," pp. 18–19.

53. Berman and McLaughlin, *Federal Programs Supporting Change, Vol. VIII*, pp. 1–2.

54. Ibid., pp. 27–28.

55. Ibid., p. 34.

56. William J. Tikunoff and Beatrice A. Ward, "Collaborative Research on Teaching," *The Elementary School Journal 83*, 1983, pp. 466–467.

57. Jeannie Oakes, Sharon Hare, and Kenneth A. Sirotnik, "Collaborative Inquiry: A Congenial Paradigm in a Cantankerous World," *Teachers College Record 87*, 1986, pp. 545–561.

58. Schaefer, *The School as a Center of Inquiry*.

59. Theodore R. Sizer, *Horace's Compromise: The Dilemma of the American High School* (Boston: Houghton Mifflin, 1984).

60. See, for example, the ideas suggested by John I. Goodlad, *A Place Called School: Prospects for the Future* (New York: McGraw-Hill, 1984).

61. Schaefer, *The School as a Center of Inquiry*, pp. 75–77.

62. ". . . our data indicate that teachers rise to challenges," concluded Berman and McLaughlin, *Federal Programs, Vol. VIII*, p. 25. Anyone who doubts this might wish to read the article by Lynn Olson, "Study Groups Giving Committed Teachers the Chance to Reflect, Share, and Learn," *Education Week* (June 3, 1987).

63. In Schön's *The Reflective Practitioner*, we have as good a summary as any of what reflective practice can be: "When someone reflects-in-action, he becomes a researcher in

the practice context. He is not dependent on the categories of established theory and technique, but constructs a new theory of the unique case. . . . he does not keep means and ends separate, but defines them interactively as he frames a problematic situation. . . . He does not separate thinking from doing. . . . Because his experimenting is a kind of action, implementation is built into his inquiry" (p. 68). The program of critical inquiry suggested here adds the critical-dialectical component to reflection-in-action and demands that it be not only an individual process but also a group process.

64. Kenneth A. Sirotnik and John I. Goodlad, eds., *School-University Partnerships in Action: Concepts, Cases, and Concerns* (New York: Teachers College Press, 1988).

PART II

TEACHERS & LEARNERS: THE CORNERSTONE OF REFORM

Teachers and learners are at the heart of the school improvement process. Efficacious school reforms are those which influence what teachers and learners do on a sustained basis. "If reforms don't influence what's going on in the classroom, they can hardly be considered reforms." You've heard such truisms before, but they are worth repeating. One of the problems with truisms is that their common acceptance invites complacency. Despite the fanfare of school reform in recent years, a closer look reveals that reformers have yet to become serious about directing reforms to teachers and learners in a way that counts. This topic is of sufficient importance to command exclusive attention in a book on school improvement. Part II of this book provides a more selective look by examining four critical themes: teacher efficacy, the balance between common and specialized learnings, the dimensions of quality schooling, and reflective practice in teaching.

The basic premise of Chapter 6 is that quality schooling and teacher efficacy are inextricably linked. Judith Lanier and Michael Sedlak provide a compelling and sometimes biting argument in support of this premise. The message for policy developers is clear. Efforts to improve quality that ignore the issue of teacher efficacy will not have efficacious results. Striving for improvements in quality by enhancing teacher efficacy is a cost-effective and powerful strategy.

Lanier and Sedlak begin by providing a tougher, more intellectually rigorous, and more demanding vision of quality schooling than that which now drives school improvement efforts. They point out that many teachers lack the requisite professional knowledge essential for their conception of schooling to become a reality. Even where knowledge is present, teachers are hamstrung by institutional constraints and are unable to use it. Teacher efficacy refers to the extent to which teachers have sufficient power to teach to that vision. This power will come from two sources: better preparation on the one hand and an empowered work context on the other. To Lanier and Sedlak, "teacher knowledge is at the core of teacher efficacy. Even if America's teachers were suddenly free from institutional constraints, much of the same teaching and learning that we want to change would continue." Arguing that not just any knowledge will do, they then provide an analysis of the kind of knowledge needed for teacher efficacy.

In Chapter 7, Howard Gardner proposes a theory of knowledge development and curriculum organization that challenges conventional thinking. He seeks a new balance between specialized and comprehensive knowledge. In contrast to the present "cone" conceptions of knowledge organization (where students are provided with increasing specialized knowledge as their academic careers progress), Gardner proposes a "wave" conception, with undulations beginning with general knowledge and alternating with specialized. In his words, "I envision a broad oscillation over these seven-year periods, with early childhood and adolescence featuring more generalized concerns, middle childhood and early adulthood calling for relative specialization."

Gardner's speculations stem in part from insights he gleans from his own theory of multiple intelligence and from those of others involved in contemporary cognitive-scientific work.

Getting serious about improving teaching requires applying to teachers what is known about how to optimize learning conditions for students. From this simple premise, Lee Shulman, in Chapter 8, provides a compelling case for emphasizing collaboration in teacher education. Teachers may teach alone but need to learn together.

Shulman does not find convincing the evidence in support of our present practices of teaching in college classrooms and in-service workshops, nor the belief that teachers can learn alone on the job as they accumulate experience. He argues that teachers improve when they have an opportunity to reflect on their teaching under coaching conditions, with teacher and supervisor colleagues. It is also important that the learning content and setting be context-specific and practical. The fruits of reflection are higher-order teaching and enhanced student performance.

The argument in favor of context specificity and collaboration stems in part from the limits of human rationality. To overcome these limits, Shulman maintains, teachers must "construct conceptions or definitions of situations rather than passively accept what is presented to them. . . .

Humans are rational only when acting together; since individual reasoning is so limited, men and women find opportunities to work jointly on important problems, achieving through joint effort what individual reason and capacity could never accomplish." These premises lead Shulman to propose a number of changes in pre-service and in-service preparation, including the development of visible and invisible "colleges" of teachers as forums for learning. He draws parallels with medicine and other professions where such colleges represent the intrastructure for developing and communicating theoretical and practical knowledge.

How one understands professional knowledge makes a difference. In Chapter 9, Donald A. Schön points out that public confidence in our professions has eroded in recent years, as a result of failures on the part of some of our most prestigious professional establishments to live up to the expectations of the public. This accusation rings too familiar with respect to the educational establishment. Schön attributes part of the disillusionment with the professions to the way professionals are prepared. He maintains that preparation seems not to fit the context and the realities of professional practice.

Schön then provides an analysis of the epistemology of professional practice that has traditionally dominated the thinking and writing about the professions and has shaped the nature of preparation programs. He points out that traditional conceptions stem from the positivistic tradition, where rigor is valued over relevance and precision over accuracy. Rationalistic conceptions of stability and order for the context of practice are assumed, but in reality this context is dynamic, ambiguous, and ill-defined. Schön provides a detailed critique of the mismatch between professional knowledge and the context and problems of professional practice. He believes that improvement will result from adopting an alternative view of professional knowledge. Under the rubric "reflection-in-action," Schön describes how this new conception of professional knowledge should be construed. To him, professional knowledge is created in use as professionals practice. Formal training, therefore, should provide scientific principles and modes of analysis that help professionals reflect better in practice and make more informed decisions. Schön concludes his chapter by examining the relationship between conceptions of school knowledge and reflection-in-action. He proposes the concept of reflective teaching as the ideal to which pre-service and in-service teacher education programs should attend.

CHAPTER 6

Teacher Efficacy & Quality Schooling

JUDITH E. LANIER

MICHAEL W. SEDLAK
Michigan State University

There has emerged a portrait of school learning that is unflattering to an enterprise as widely supported as schooling in the United States. Analysts of this unflattering condition have agreed that teachers are central to the solution and must become responsible for a renaissance in school learning. However, the situation is confounded by a classic "Catch-22." Many teachers lack the requisite professional knowledge essential to the responsibility, yet those who do possess such knowledge remain so hamstrung by institutional and contextual constraints that they are unable to use it. The alleviation of *both* the knowledge constraints and the contextual constraints are essential to attacking the student learning problems that now characterize schools.

Teacher efficacy—the empowering knowledge and opportunity for participation in the reconstruction of schools—is the means of transforming student learning from task-completion to understanding; from ritualized hoop-jumping to acquiring meaning and social value. Teacher efficacy is the means of transforming our nation's much-criticized educational institutions into quality schools. We first discuss changes that are needed for quality school learning and then the implications of our conception for efficacious teaching.

QUALITY SCHOOLING

The claim that quality schooling cannot be obtained without teacher efficacy calls for clarification of the value-laden meanings many people attribute to these terms. Since our reasoning is premised on the view that quality schooling would lead to efficacious learning—and would therefore differ considerably from the schooling we know today—we begin by addressing this difference. The difference highlights America's need to replace today's often vacuous and obfuscated school learning with more meaningful intellectual development.

The problem is that school learning has taken on a special life of its own, with a unique set of purposes and rituals. Its character does little to enhance students' abilities to think and reason independently or to prepare them for citizenship in a democratic society. The value of contemporary school learning does not lie in empowering students for constructive mental action. Rather, the value of most school learning lies in moving students through school, helping them stockpile a variety of credits and credentials—happy faces drawn on worksheets, teachers' smiles, grades, grade placements, class rankings, diplomas, letters of recommendation, degrees, and advanced degrees. School learning consists of learning to complete assigned tasks in order to gain access to some anticipated higher level of schooling. The intellectual engagement that most students demonstrate is primarily with a process—going through rituals with friends and colleagues—instead of acquiring knowledge and skills that broaden understanding, intellectual competence, and commitment to the sustenance and continued development of a good society.

Nor does the value of school learning ordinarily lie in its contribution to a better life. Even though most citizens, parents, and children themselves invest heavily in the educational enterprise because of its presumed contribution to making good lives, most learning in schools contributes little to this ambition. School learning is severed from learning and living outside of school.

School Learning as Trivial Work and Wasted Effort

Young people engaged in the chore of becoming students, of trying to understand and adjust to the purposes of schooling as learned from their teachers, elders, and friends, come to trivialize learning. They become accustomed to turning the empowering potential of intellectual competence into the superficiality of school learning.

The trivialization of valuable knowledge, habits of mind, and skills into school learning has been one of the greatest failures of our efforts to educate effectively. It has not gone entirely unnoticed, but virtually all efforts to address it, including some current reform initiatives, have been redirected in ways that have ultimately reinforced and aggravated the problem. By continually substituting surrogates for real learning, the process of trivialization continues, and it perpetuates the distinction between learning in school and learning out of school.[1]

Without question, John Dewey erred when he assumed that the costs of students adapting to the dominant pattern of school learning were widely evident: "I do not suppose any great argument is needed to prove that breach of continuity between learning within and without the school is the great cause in education of wasted power and misdirected effort."[2] The costs have not been evident to everyone. Many of Dewey's followers drew conclusions from his observations about the nature of learning in school that led to disastrous experiments; Dewey himself criticized the misapplication of his concern with engaging students.[3] However, except for an occasional naive and dramatic flourish, thoughtful progressives were committed to empowering students through school learning and rejected the superficial learning that they found everywhere. Despite some of their excesses, they offered a critique of school learning that remains penetrating. Scholars today may be avoiding much of the vocabulary of the progressive critique (some perhaps intentionally, to avoid the taint by association), but the observations and aspirations of many modern educational leaders are consonant with those of their predecessors. They are contributing to a broad awareness of the dangers and limitations of perpetuating trivial school learning.

For the past decade, scholars have repeatedly highlighted the depth of educational passivity and disengagement among students in our high schools and upper elementary grades.[4] We now know that such behavior is not simply characteristic of urban secondary schools. It is not a problem common only to schools on reservations or in the midst of rural poverty. Disengagement, passivity, and a conception of school progress as the accumulation of credits, scores, or credentials characterize learning even in the best schools of our most privileged suburban communities, where nine graduates out of ten go on to respected institutions of higher education. It characterizes learners in the elementary grades, junior colleges, and many advanced graduate and professional programs. It is simply the way America's young people have learned to go to school. As David Cohen observes, "teaching is telling, learning is accumulating, and knowledge is facts."[5]

Some scholars account for this pattern of school learning by focusing on the impact of our competing purposes for formal education.[6] Some see the educational system as one component in an elaborate credentials market, where individuals attempt to discern the value of different credentials and then gauge the investment required to obtain them. They adjust their behavior in credentialing institutions so as to acquire the certificates assumed to be of value. Because of anticipation that the credentials will be exchanged for desired goods, credentialist aspirations come to shape the nature of student participation in educational institutions. Students come to comply superficially with required procedures. This sort of motivation partially explains the extent of disengagement and passivity.

The scholarship that speaks to these problems is vivid and painful. It is troubling to realize that a major obstacle to improving education lies in one of the underlying purposes for schooling itself, but the problem is real. Much of the trivialized learning that occurs in school is rooted in the shifting value of educational credentials, over which schools and educational leaders have admittedly modest control.

Recently, other scholars have begun to reveal the ways in which the schooling process itself contributes to and reinforces passive, disengaged school learning. Cognitive psychologists, in particular, have focused their attention on the distinctions between learning in and out of school. Their portrait of school learning is just as troubling as that presented by anthropologists and sociologists, but the psychologists have exposed its roots in traditional teaching practice. If the dismal quality of school learning is attributable entirely to the ebb and flow of the credentials market, then it is difficult to identify and exploit opportunities to improve things. However, if a significant part of the difficulty is pedagogical in the broadest sense (that is, rooted in teaching practice and the curriculum), then there are familiar and reasonable grounds from which to approach the problem.[7] The problem of trivial learning can then be addressed directly through pedagogical intervention.

School Learning Diminished by the Common-Sense Lore on Basic Skills

There is now broad professional consensus that the U.S. educational system leaves higher-order reasoning or thinking skills relatively undeveloped. The 1981 National Assessment of Educational Progress in reading and literature indicated that the majority of nine- to seventeen-year-old students "show little ability to analyze or evaluate a passage, drawing on portions of the text as evidence to support their judgments."[8] The National Assessment reported in 1985 that only 5% of students, even at age seventeen, "have advanced reading skills and strategies."[9] Similarly, students apparently fail to develop the ability to improve their own writing by restructuring, correcting errors, and revising their drafts. Students spend very little time writing in school, and homework assignments rarely include thoughtful writing assignments. Most of the "writing" that students do involves verbatim copying from textbooks.[10]

Mathematics is no better. Although many students possess rudimentary computational skills in mathematics, they do not have the quantitative reasoning and problem-solving skills essential to applying those skills in different contexts.[11] As recently as 1987, mathematics learning comparisons from the International Educational Achievement projects showed that the United States (1) was among the lowest of all advanced industrialized countries taking part in the study, (2) was lower than its own record of a decade earlier, and (3) was near the mean on computation but well below the mean in noncomputational areas such as word problems.[12]

Part of the problem lies in the traditional view of basic learning and its relationship to higher-order cognitive skills. The common-sense notion that basic skills are themselves empowering pervades U.S. society. It is widely believed that knowing how to cipher, an example of a celebrated rudimentary skill, is valuable either to further achievement in school or to achieving independence and self-reliance outside of school. School districts customarily respond to critiques of deteriorating higher-order cognitive skills by emphasizing that all students must learn basic skills first—then they can be given the opportunity to respond to more challenging expectations and materials. It is revealing that exceptions to this general rule are found in schools and school districts that reverse these experiences for their "gifted and talented" students.

Running contrary to this common-sense assumption is the professional knowledge that basic skills by themselves are not empowering as educational ends. For example, it does not empower a child to remain uninvited or excluded from quantitative reasoning or conceptual and textual interpretation for years and years, until he or she has learned to add and subtract. It is quantitative reasoning, and the ability to apply such complex cognitive skills to problems in a variety of contexts, that is empowering. Educational systems do children no favors by restricting their access to opportunities to develop such abilities, in the interest of requiring them first to master "basic skills."[13]

This conventional response, according to an increasing volume of scholarship, is part of the problem. As Devaney and Sykes argue,

> the very system we have in place to efficiently teach basic skills in the early grades may work to hinder the acquisition of higher order skills in the later grades. Tests and instructional methods in the elementary grades concentrate almost exclusively on applying rules in order to read, to write, and to do arithmetic. And assessment tests relentlessly for these things. *Students consequently become "addicted" to the basics and develop little capacity or inclination later on to engage in tasks requiring real reasoning.*[14]

Although it is essential that all students acquire basic skills, contemporary practice rests on the faulty assumption that students should learn basic skills *first*, before encountering academic work that demands more complex intellectual skills. This deceptively simple notion about teaching and learning is simply wrong.

Through all sorts of mechanisms, including minimum competency tests and text selection procedures, school districts have encouraged (sometimes forced) teachers to focus their attention on basic skill development, regardless of the children's age or social development. Such encouragement is based upon the assumption that students need rudimentary, foundational skills in reading, writing, and arithmetic computation before their learning can progress effectively. It is thought that without the ability, for example, to understand the meaning of individual words, or the mechanics of writing such as punctuation and subject–verb agreement, and the rules of addition, subtraction, multiplication, and division, students will be unable to succeed as they continue through school. By concentrating attention and resources on basic skill acquisition at the expense of higher-order cognitive growth, many schools inadvertently enforce a self-defeating notion of learning—one that "emphasizes isolated skills, recall of factual knowledge and conceptual knowledge, and the ability to execute rotely learned procedures."[15]

Allan Collins and his colleagues have constructed one of the most scathing indictments of this tradition of school learning. Even in the best of cases, they argue, when students acquire accurate factual content and appropriate concepts, "the conceptual and problem-solving knowledge acquired in school remains unintegrated and largely inert, unavailable for use in many realistic problem contexts."[16] Most students, they agree, "do not understand the need, let alone have the skills, for assessing a new problem, generating and evaluating different approaches to solving it, deriving new information about the problem," or relating new understanding to "known processes, concepts and facts."[17] Students routinely fail to develop the ability to apply the factual knowledge or rudimentary conceptual understanding that they acquire in school; they are unable to make use of them—indeed, to understand that they might be made use of—outside of school.

It is instructive to examine evidence from basic instruction in the fundamental areas of mathematics and the language arts. Although basic computational abilities are increasingly developed in arithmetic classes, the predominant pattern of instruction at the elementary level is characterized, according to Romberg and Carpenter, by "extensive teacher-directed explanation and questioning followed by student seatwork on paper-and-pencil assignments."[18] Such an emphasis is flawed, they claim, because mathematics becomes divorced from science and other disciplines in which it plays an integral part. As a result, students inevitably conceive of mathematics simply as the acquisition of specific isolated skills and facts and fail to understand and acquire the ability to reason quantitatively and apply mathematical concepts in other contexts. It poses an additional problem, because it assumes that knowledge acquisition consists exclusively of absorbing concepts and facts in one's memory bank for later use. This view of learning is terribly misinformed. Students do not simply absorb accurately what they are told or read, but rather are always reconstructing what they learn in relation to what they already know. The traditional approach, therefore, fails to capitalize on the rich, informal, evolving mathematical understanding that students bring to their math classes.[19]

Romberg and Carpenter, drawing on the work of Clark and Yinger, also point out that language arts teachers are rarely concerned with the meaningfulness or integration of assigned activities.[20] The Report of the Commission on Reading, *Becoming a Nation of Readers*, corroborates the conclusion that teachers fail to integrate reading, writing, and subject-matter instruction and devote little time to helping students learn strategies for extracting and organizing critical information from texts. The report reminded its readers of one study in which "only 45 minutes of comprehension instruction, not counting time spent asking and answering questions, were found during almost 18,000 minutes of observation in reading and social studies periods in 39 classrooms in 14 school districts."[21] Students often bring home as many as 1000 workbook pages and skill sheets completed during their reading periods over the course of an academic year; such seatwork activities rarely require students to draw conclusions or develop their higher-order cognitive abilities.[22]

The literacy problem in the United States during the late twentieth century is not rooted in widespread failure to acquire basic reading skills; almost all students are able to identify words by the sixth or seventh grade. Although some high school students continue to have trouble decoding, reports over the past generation indicate a level of general mastery of word identification processes. It is the higher-order skills and strategies that they fail to acquire—abilities that they are unlikely to gain from leisure-reading activities.[23]

The traditional view that identified "learning to read with the subskills of recognizing and pronouncing words and with the activities of scanning text and saying it aloud"[24] is an inadequate definition of literacy today. Students will not learn to comprehend by learning one skill, adding a second, and continuing in a linear fashion until they develop the ability to think critically about texts.

Besides those who have exposed the confused and dysfunctional relationship between basic and higher learning, others have added to the critique of school learning. Devaney and Sykes have outlined two central corollary problems. First, school learning tends to rely on well-structured problems and fails to develop skills in responding to more realistic "ill-structured" problems. Drawing on the work of Frederiksen, Devaney and Sykes observe that problems in classrooms are customarily "clearly presented with all the information needed and with an appropriate algorithm available that guarantees a correct answer, such as long division, areas of triangles, Ohm's law, and linear equations." In real life, however, many of the problems people face are "ill-structured."[25]

> Schools seldom require students to solve such fuzzy problems—problems that are not clearly stated, where the needed information is not all available, there is no algorithm, and there may not be a single answer that can be demonstrated to be correct.[26]

Second, constant exposure to basic, rudimentary learning encourages students to devise strategies to reduce uncertainties and present their teachers with correct answers. As long as right answers alone are valued, students will "invent faulty procedures for solving problems that often go undetected by teachers and tests."[27]

Students will also rely heavily on "memorizing strategies" to accomplish their school tasks. They exhibit glaring discontinuities between what "they are able to state about a field and what they actually do in solving problems. In all cases they are not likely to understand what they are being taught."[28] Both of these problems suggest further limitations of traditional school learning and its inability to empower students outside of the teacher-guided classroom context.

This growing critique of the nature of school learning and the concomitant necessity of empowering students are gradually building broad acceptance of vintage professional knowledge. Lauren Resnick's recent admonitions are well grounded in earlier understanding of the ways school learning was routinely trivialized and made virtually unusable outside of school. In one of his most powerful essays, John Dewey called attention to the tendency of children in school to acquire "outward" forms of methods without the capacity to put them to "genuinely educative use."[29] As every teacher knows, he wrote, "children have an inner and outer attention." The child's inner attention focuses the mind on the matter at hand; in contemporary language, inner attention is similar to active engagement. External attention, in contrast, is given to a book or a teacher "as an independent object." Children, Dewey observed, "acquire great dexterity in exhibiting in conventional and expected ways the *form* of attention to school work, while reserving the inner play of their own thoughts, images, and emotions for subjects that are more important to them."[30]

In other words, teachers are able to get students to conform with procedures without engaging them in any genuine way. Teachers who accept and emphasize the obligation to manage their classrooms, Dewey observed, almost inevitably "make supreme the matter of external attention."[31] The "inherent tendency" for the teacher is to adapt his or her methods "in relation to the outward rather than the inner mode of attention."[32] Participating in this sort of relationship over several years has a deleterious effect on children's learning. "Unconsciously, but none the less surely, the student comes to believe in certain 'methods' of learning, and hence of teaching which are somehow especially appropriate to the school—which somehow have their particular residence and application there."[33] Dewey's astute observations foreshadowed those of others who have called attention to the "gamesmanship" character of school learning.[34]

However, quality schools must go beyond simple recognition of the flawed nature of most school learning, and they must go beyond mere derogatory labeling. Quality schools must rid themselves of the teaching and testing policies and practices that encourage the now well-understood problems of trivial learning. Easier to identify and disparage than to eradicate, the problems pose an extraordinary challenge to educators seeking quality schooling through improved learning.

Quality Schooling Must Emphasize Meaningful Subject Matter Learning

In contrast to the limitations of decontextualized and unapplicable learning in school, a number of contemporary scholars have designed and tested strategies that strengthen higher-order cognitive and basic skills simultaneously. Collins and his colleagues reported a series of illuminating efforts to reject traditional patterns of school learning that have contributed to the inability of students to apply or use their skills in other contexts.[35] These studies share a commitment to altering the conceptual understanding of students toward school tasks, particularly in reading, writing, and mathematics.

Brown and Palinscar, for example, have improved students' reading abilities dramatically by changing the orientation of children toward reading in school. Under the new conception, students "recognize that reading requires constructive activities such as formulating questions and making summaries and predictions, as well as evaluative ones such as analyzing and clarifying the points of difficulty in the text."[36] Similarly, Berieter and Scardamalia developed in children "an entirely new view of the writing process" by devising activities that helped students to apply and utilize their skills. Schoenfeld worked with students to change their "control strategies and belief systems" in such a way that they developed "a fundamentally new understanding of mathematics." All three projects incorporated activities that were designed "to change the children's assumptions about the nature of expert problem-solving," so that they could begin to assume responsibility for learning on their own and for applying their skills outside of specific assignments posed by their teachers.[37]

As such scholars have begun to develop imaginative strategies for strengthening advanced cognitive skills, it is important to recognize that they have abandoned the traditional view of rigidly sequenced learning from basic to higher-order thinking. They have demonstrated the effectiveness of integrating both types of learning. In doing so, they have exposed the problems associated with maintaining a false separation between basic and higher-order skill development. They hold promise for empowered learning in school settings. They provide the scaffolding that students need to exploit knowledge, to begin to think independently, and to apply their learning outside of the context of specific school assignments.

However, these impressive efforts to overcome the limitations of traditional school learning by strengthening higher-order cognitive skills will not achieve broad and enduring success until meaningful opportunities for students to apply their subject-matter learning are found and regularly engaged. Just as increased professional understanding indicates that it is not enough for teachers to know their subjects, it is equally clear that teachers knowing their subjects and how to present them effectively does not guarantee empowered learning.

Quality Schooling Must Emphasize the Civic Ends of American Education

In addition to changing the depth and actual value of subject-matter knowledge per se, schools and teachers cannot overlook their larger societal responsibilities. Preparing each new generation for effective participation in a democratic way of life is an equally important educational obligation. Public education in America cannot afford to emphasize powerful thinking in the absence of concern for the civic ends of intellectual competence. It is therefore fortunate that the demands for higher-order knowledge and skills and effective democratization of our citizenry are not only mutually compatible but complementary.

These demands are complementary because effective civic education emphasizes the development of critical discourse, just as higher-level learning emphasizes the development of critical thinking. They are complementary because effective civic education demands active and interactive reasoning on issues that require mental operations of a problem-finding and problem-solving nature—important ingredients for meaningful subject-matter learning. They are complementary because effective civic education affords schools the opportunity to relate important aspects of otherwise separated school subjects to one another and to the world of learning outside of school. Also, they are complementary because effective civic learning provides the breadth and social reality needed to counterbalance the more specialized, technical dimensions of disciplinary study by itself. Such a balance is essential if schools are to meet their societal obligation of helping young citizens learn to address questions of purpose and morality in a democratic republic.

Effective, responsible democratic participation requires two things. First, it cannot occur without the active engagement of its citizens in the determination of community affairs. It does not matter if the community is the neighborhood, the city, the state, the region, or the nation. What matters is the intellectual disposition and opportunity of people to participate actively in the continuing construction and reconstruction of a good society. "Democracy," as political scientist Mary Dietz has recently argued, "gives us a conception of ourselves as 'speakers of words and doers of deeds' mutually participating in the public realm." This vision of democracy, she continued, can flourish only with a sense of "democratic citizenship" that

> is a practice unlike any other; it has a distinctive set of relations, virtues, and principles all its own. Its relation is that of civic peers; its guiding virtue is mutual respect; its primary principle is the "positive liberty" of democracy and self-government, not simply the "negative liberty" of noninterference.

It does not simply expect toleration of the actions of others but demands that "all matters relating to the community are undertaken as 'the people's affair.'"[38]

This ideal, of course, is especially challenging—just as its realization is imperative—in a nation of great diversity, where cultural, ethnic, and religious groups are understandably inclined and too often encouraged to put their short-term self-interest before the long-term interests of the community. That is why, beyond active engagement, a democratic polity also requires citizens who are capable of understanding and valuing its members, both individually and collectively—including those of the past as well as those of the present and the future. "The democratic vision," according to Dietz, "does not legitimize the pursuit of every separate, individual interest or the transformation of private into public virtues." Rather, "democracy is the form of politics that brings people together as citizens. Indeed, the power of democracy rests in its capacity to transform the individual as teacher, trader, corporate executive, child, sibling, worker, artist, friend, or mother into a special sort of political being, a citizen among other citizens."[39] Citizens in a democracy must be predisposed to consider the complex array of trade-offs involved in social decisions—when to place public interests ahead of private goals, and vice versa—and they must be able to analyze them critically and weigh them fairly. This quality of democratic responsibility is as important as the capacity and enthusiasm for active participation, for it raises the polity above single-issue politics and narrow motives of self-interest alone.

In other words, democracy requires the development of a civic identity that goes beyond individuals caring "simply" for themselves and others. It requires learning the capacities and values of statesmanship and the ability and predisposition to make decisions from an informed, caring, and courageous perspective.

The emerging conception of higher-order school learning combined with preparation for citizenship gives continuity to intellectual empowerment as the overarching purpose of quality education. Just as higher-order cognitive processes require opportunities to integrate and apply various kinds of knowledge and skills, so preparation for citizenship requires close association with real communities. Part of the problem with the present tradition of school learning is that it is rooted in the general isolation of schools from their surrounding communities. As things stand, even if students did acquire higher-level knowledge and skills in school, they would have little opportunity to put their intellectual competence to constructive use outside of school. Beyond reading about it in textbooks, few students have any real opportunity to learn about community as it relates to citizenship in a nation committed to democratic ideals and principles. Quality schooling simply cannot be detached from the communities of which it is a part; many schools must become better connected with their communities.

To make academic learning meaningful and to prepare students for democratic citizenship, school learning must become a part of, instead of apart from, community life. As Schwab argued, "community can be learned," and "human learning is a communal enterprise."

> The propensities that constitute community are learned only as we undergo with others the processes through which we learn other things. Meanwhile, the support, communication, and example that make it possible to learn these things become accessible and acceptable to us only as our propensities toward community develop.[40]

Community is essential for individual as well as social health. Contrary to much popular sociology, Schwab argues, "individuality can arise only in society, only through community." A sense of individual identity is developed and tested not through introspection, but by "affecting others" through our growing capabilities and through involvement with others, in their problems, in the common culture. The nation's vital democratic social institutions and our values of justice through the law, liberty, equality, and fairness depend upon commitment to and participation in community.

Schwab and others argue that "community is threatened with extinction in America." Although work involves other people, they are too often seen as "competitors or henchmen, superiors or subordinates, not as fellow human beings." Community has been stunted, many believe, by social and geographic mobility, accelerating urbanism, and what Schwab called the "systematic inculcation of limits to community," such as racial or class prejudice and ethnic stereotyping.[41]

Schools remain one of the few institutions that have potential for strengthening America's sense of community. This vision has stirred educational and civic leaders for more than a century, as different generations have felt the absence of community in their own way. Schools as "learning communities" would develop cherished values more effectively than do workbook exercises, quizzes in civics or social studies, or an annual 30-minute lecture by a representative from the Society for the Prevention of Cruelty to Animals on kindness to all living things. Learning communities are characterized by a quality of engagement and participation that is unfamiliar in many institutions today. They encourage and reward the involvement of both children and adults in matters of mutual interest, in the identification and solution of vital community problems: isolation, poverty, physical deterioration. They encourage and reward a more empowered form of learning for students and adults, helping them to overcome the inertia that personal or individual isolation often breeds.

Although the concept of "social responsibility" is integral to the success of learning communities, it should not be turned into "school subject matter." Rather, it should be used to infuse and shape school learning in powerful ways. It can provide enriched opportunities for students to integrate disciplinary learning and, more importantly, to apply the knowledge and skills that they acquire in the study of school subjects to valuable social ends.

Students would be more committed to school learning that recognized and accepted the rich contribution of cooperative decisionmaking and problem-solving, in institutions that expected their active engagement and participation in the sort of collaborative and individual work that is found outside of school. Adults could continue their learning and broaden their opportunities for making a meaningful social contribution by participating in an educational environment that assumed responsibility for action on a variety of community matters. Adults from all walks of life would be able to contribute to the children's learning, and all adults would be able to benefit from the intellectual and emotional resources that schools could provide.

Many predict that America will become a learning society in the twenty-first century, as educational obsolescence becomes pervasive in all fields. The growing adult-education functions of schools will probably continue to increase, giving schools a good opportunity (if they seize it creatively) to become reconnected to their communities.

TEACHER EFFICACY

Teacher efficacy is central to the discourse about educational reform and restructured schools, because teacher efficacy is essential to the vision of quality schooling that is developed herein. Teacher knowledge, in turn, exerts a critical influence on the nature and extent of teacher efficacy. Further, the role definitions and professional responsibilities expected of teachers profoundly limit the nature and extent of both teacher knowledge and teacher efficacy.[42]

Efficacy refers to the power one has to bring about a desired effect. Teachers' efficacy refers to the power teachers have to bring about the desired student learning we described earlier. The concept of teacher efficacy received attention over a decade ago but then faded during the growth of the effective schools movement. Perhaps it was diminished by the various waves of management strategies and testing for minimal objectives; those efforts focused on the basic rote learning that was thought to be foundational at the time. Some suggest that the notion of efficacy has reemerged under the guise of teacher empowerment—a plausible circumstance in light of the lively discourse on empowered learning. On the other hand, the growing interest in teacher empowerment may be largely associated with recent efforts to create new standards and control boards. The slight variation in meaning that accompanies empowerment implies official authority and legal power, which would lend some credence to this possibility. However, for purposes of this discussion, the concept of efficacy will be used—the term suggested by the hosts of the Texas conference.[43]

"Teacher efficacy" is used here to mean the extent to which teachers have sufficient power to bring about the higher-order thinking and social learning that empowers students. The amount of power teachers need is directly related to the amount of powerful learning that is desired. It is indeed a matter of *powerful* learning, which carries broad conceptual understanding but is critical; which is flexible and creative; which provokes problem-finding as well as problem-solving; which is not easy to abide. Such powerful learning on the part of students demands substantial efficacy on the part of teachers—not only to teach students to think and reason and be successful in their intellectual work, and not only to contribute to the learning community of which they are a part—but efficacy to help transform the schools of America into places that can accomplish this task.

Resurrecting a Vision of Teachers as Public and Professional Leaders

This call for teacher efficacy may sound ambitious and vastly different from recent uses of the term. However, it is simply the resurrection of a noble but largely dormant vision of teachers as "public leaders" that has existed since the mid-nineteenth century. This vision creates a powerful role for teachers in the reconstruction and success of schools. It expands their professional role to include responsibility for maintaining the public's commitment to quality schooling by challenging efforts to narrow the concept and standards of school learning. Teachers would lead their communities in converting the nature of learning in school; they would serve as the advocates and guardians of empowered learning for the young. This view of public leadership for teachers may sound radical today, but the vision was actually articulated more than a century ago by a handful of civic leaders on the eve of the common school movement (not seen as particularly radical until women came into the teaching force in large numbers). Although the vision has been endorsed by a variety of educational authorities ever since, the U.S. has moved steadily away from it.

An important thesis here is that the quality of children's learning, the system's ability to attract, engage and retain effective teachers, and the ability of schools to play a variety of important social functions are affected by prevailing definitions of "teaching." Two distinctive definitions of the professional role of teachers have evolved in this nation. The dominant one is a classroom-bounded role for nurturant, pedagogical specialists; the less well-known role is that of a classroom-school-community activist who works to foster public learning. It is useful to unravel the origins and implications of these roles, for they are valuable in clarifying the current movement to reform teaching practice and the preparation and induction of teachers.

The two role definitions or visions are closely bound up with early efforts to provide formal education for prospective teachers. Just as it does now, designing a program for preparing teachers during the 1840s required a definition of teaching—an understanding of the parameters of its role and the nature of its responsibilities. University reformer Francis Wayland defined the responsibilities of teaching to include "public leadership," *as well as* "proficiency in the classroom," according to Merle Borrowman.[44] Wayland and others proposed a broad role for teachers that involved decisionmaking in matters of policy and curriculum. Correspondingly, they argued for an integration of liberal and professional studies, in the belief that a broader collegiate education would help "the teacher acquire competence for this larger calling."[45]

In contrast, many of the leaders of the American normal school movement, including Cyrus Peirce and Calvin Stowe, held a dramatically different definition of the teacher's professional competence and role. As Borrowman has observed, "they considered craftsmanship in the elementary-school classroom, not public leadership" to be the standard of professional competence. "The art of teaching must be made the great, the paramount, the only concern," Peirce wrote to common school reformer Henry Barnard.[46]

Well-meaning private citizens, like Barnard, Horace Mann, and other civic leaders, would determine policy and would have procedures and expectations standardized and enforced by representatives of the local educated elite, to whom teachers would defer in virtually all matters related to the operation of their schools. The initial cadre of normal school leaders were convinced that graduates of their programs would never assume leadership responsibilities, that educational governance and leadership would remain rightfully in the hands of "talented amateurs like Mann," noted Borrowman.

> Most [teachers] would remain in the classroom, teaching a curriculum prescribed by the board of education, through texts selected by that board or provided on a chance basis by parents, and according to methods suggested by master teachers or educational theorists, most of whom had been educated in the colleges.[47]

Although some normal school leaders, like William Phelps of New Jersey, resented these limited aims or assumptions about the teaching role and the education of teachers, the most prominent figures in the campaign, including Mann himself, favored severe restrictions on professional practice. In general, the leaders of the American normal schools, who dominated the professional training of teachers for more than half a century, endorsed the narrow, limited vision of teaching.

The two visions of teaching articulated a century and a half ago by Wayland and Peirce have contemporary expressions. Peirce's legacy has had the greatest impact on teaching and teacher education as it is now practiced in most schools and colleges. It has dominated thinking, discourse, and policy development. Over the past century, its specific terms have naturally changed, but its impact on learning and teaching has unfortunately remained substantial. For the most part, the teacher's role in America has remained limited to classroom instruction. Only by fleeing teaching altogether for administration or university work have teachers been able to exert more influence over educational matters.

This vision continues to rest on assumptions about a circumscribed sphere of influence, a constrained arena of legitimate action, a limited professional role for teachers. It perpetuates Peirce's exclusive focus on craft skills, defined as those that promote subject-matter learning in students. Even in its powerful contemporary incarnation, it is not likely to expand or broaden the professional role responsibilities of teachers; it could even make their work more specialized. Because the focus on subject matter apparently promises to strengthen teachers' skills and to improve the breadth and depth of student learning in the disciplines, it has enormous appeal.

It has additional appeal because it promises to not disturb or challenge professional relations in schools. Nor will it necessarily disturb that isolation which is so troubling to genuine educational improvement but which also makes so many lives convenient. Both teachers and administrators in many schools have adapted comfortably to this arrangement, to the detriment of genuine educational improvement.

It is Wayland's broad vision that should be resurrected: to expand the legitimate professional responsibilities of teachers beyond classroom instruction and subject-matter competence by having schools become learning communities. It is essential that teachers be effective in their classrooms, of course, and that they possess sound subject-matter and pedagogical knowledge, but such classroom competence should constitute only a portion of the requisite professional knowledge and expertise. In order to improve the educational enterprise, it is also essential that teachers understand their organizations in ways that will help them to reconstruct schools and lead other adults to improve their communities.

The concept of teacher efficacy, therefore, goes beyond classroom-bounded definitions of teaching to include public leadership. Such efficacy can only come through professional expertise and the opportunity to use that knowledge in the reconstruction of schooling. However, there are numerous barriers that diminish the benefits of the application of professional knowledge and undermine the potential contribution of working conditions in schools. Not the least of the barriers is the curious argument about which should come first: improved professional education or expanded work opportunities.

Teacher Knowledge as the Core of Teacher Efficacy

With some reluctance, we address the chicken-or-egg problem here. Should some persons with power first change schools so they become fitting work places for highly educated teachers, capable and eager to assume responsibility for new levels of student learning? Or should some persons with power first change universities and schools of education so that preservice and in-service education prepares highly educated, capable, and eager-to-be-responsible teachers, who then change schools? As with most such questions, the answers remain obscure. Both fronts must be addressed at once, and they must be addressed by those with and those without power, if the slow rate of educational change is to be quickened. Those with and those without power in the schools must begin the work of eliminating institutional constraints for teachers and learners. Those with and those without power in the universities must begin the work of eliminating the knowledge constraints with their faculty counterparts in schools. Substantial change will be needed in both types of institutions.

Still, teacher knowledge is at the core of teacher efficacy. It is central to teachers' ability to bring about sustained student learning of the sort judged critical to quality schooling. Even if some magical transformation could suddenly free America's teachers from the institutional constraints of their work with students in schools, much of the same teaching and learning that we want to change would continue. If, on the other hand, some magical transformation could suddenly free America's teachers of their knowledge constraints, there would be rapid, dramatic change in school learning and, not far behind, rather profound changes in schools. Since there is no magic, both must be addressed at once, even though knowledge may be considered to be the key.

Teacher efficacy, and therefore enhanced teacher knowledge, must be expected of *all* professional teachers, not just a subset of the school's teaching force. Some reformers recommend that a selected set of the best and brightest assume responsibility at the top of a new hierarchy, or career ladder, and become the real pros. These people seem to envision an elite corps of professionals selected to oversee the work of the many; they may be called master teachers, certified teachers, lead teachers, or department chairpersons. This chapter, however, addresses efficacy and professionalism for all teachers and career professional teachers. The argument in favor of some but not all being professionals seems to emerge from concern that there will either be too little talent among those pursuing teaching to meet the demand or too few dollars to meet the added costs of preparing, remunerating, and equipping with adequate support large enough numbers of efficacious professionals.

We reject such scarcity fears. It is better to work on ways of obtaining the human talent and financial resources needed to afford all professional school faculty the opportunity to be responsible and successful in developing quality schooling in America. All faculty must have sufficient efficacy to ensure that all students obtain the opportunity to develop higher-order learning capacities. This point is emphasized because *different* professional knowledge and values would be required if it were believed that only some, rather than all, teachers were to be efficacious. For example, in considering teacher knowledge about organizational operations, we will emphasize liberal knowledge for collegial participation rather than technical, supervisory know-how for constructing teaching as closely managed work.

A Necessarily Broad View of Professional Knowledge

Given our role conception for teachers—professionals capable of and dedicated to improving the educational enterprise—their knowledge and skills must be deeper and broader than today. Their professional preparation cannot be as limited as contemporary preservice and in-service education, nor as limited as teacher knowledge and skills are now cast in a growing number of reform initiatives.

Absolutely no one argues with the premise that teachers must know the subjects they teach, although few seem genuinely curious about why a good number of them do not. For now, imagine that teachers could all come to know their subjects well—not only just as well as college graduates pursuing some of the more prestigious professions, but for example, as well as most college professors. It is known that deep knowledge and passion for one's subject would be insufficient for ensuring higher-order learning, because of the massive weight of evidence to the contrary. Just look to higher education. If autonomy in the workplace, combined with deep understanding, high motivation, and intellectual flexibility with academic subjects constituted adequate knowledge, teaching at the universities would be exemplary.[48] So content knowledge is not sufficient, although it is necessary.

At the very least, for example, teachers must understand the higher-order cognitive skills possessed by expert readers, writers, or mathematicians. They need to be able to model these skills and strategies to students. Expertise in teaching must also include the ability to convert subject-matter content into forms accessible to children. As Lee Shulman and his colleagues have argued, effective teachers must be able to "elucidate subject matter in new ways, reorganize and partition it, clothe it in activities and emotions, and in examples and demonstrations, so that it can be grasped by students."[49] They need to construct and protect an environment that allows students to acquire and practice higher-order skills, and they must be able to judge whether or not students can use the skills without a teacher's prompting and oversight. They must be able to tolerate their own ignorance and publicly and gracefully reveal the limitations of their own knowledge. In exemplifying the cognitive processes that occur during expert problem-solving, the teacher must be able to challenge students to bring difficult problems to class, then model what one must go through in any genuine attempt to solve them. "Occasionally," Collins and his associates comment,

> the problems are hard enough that the students see him flounder in the face of real difficulties. During these sessions, he models for students not only the use of heuristics and control strategies, but the fact that one's strategies sometimes fail. . . . Seeing how experts deal with problems that are difficult for them is critical to students' developing a

belief in their own capacities. Even experts stumble, flounder, and abandon their search for a solution until another time. Witnessing these struggles helps students realize that thrashing is neither unique nor a sign of incompetence.[50]

Most of all, teachers must be able to continue in the face of a variety of intimidating uncertainties. They must act on limited knowledge about the issues confronting them and the consequences of their actions. They must make defensible, professionally responsible best choices. The enduring uncertainties of teaching are rooted in a variety of sources, including the shifting nature of knowledge in the disciplines, the inability to know exactly what impact one has on an individual student, and the obligation to manage both the social relations of the classroom and the cognitive development of students simultaneously.[51]

To have efficacy, teachers must understand that these uncertainties cannot be eliminated. They need to know that their uncertainties—and the ways they are tempted to respond to them—are related to their conception of learning. For example, if teachers have a one-dimensional conception of learning (that "covering the topic" is a legitimate professional goal), they may try to reduce uncertainty in ways that would cripple alternative avenues of strengthening students' learning—ways that might be more worthwhile. Many prospective teachers who read Vivian Paley's descriptions and analyses of her classroom teaching comment, "Why doesn't she just tell the students the answer and get on with the lesson?" They are uncomfortable with the uncertainty that they see in Paley's classroom because their conception of learning is that the teacher's job is to get through the lesson, test students to determine if they understand it, and move on. Paley's conception of learning is far richer. She views her students' groping and stumbling as evidence of their genuine intellectual struggle to get control of their own learning, and she recognizes that such behavior needs to be encouraged and protected, even though her classroom is, as a result, more explicitly uncertain.[52]

Virtually all of the scholars who have focused on the weaknesses associated with the tradition of typical school learning have recognized the essential role that empowered teacher judgement plays in reorienting students' posture toward, and engagement with, academic content and the development of cognitive skills.[53] Building on his own critique of typical school learning, Dewey himself argued that in order to empower students, teachers had to accept the intellectual responsibility to develop children's inner reflective attention. He endorsed higher learning in the disciplines for all teachers, for it was only through such study that teachers could appreciate the meaning and processes of genuine intellectual activity that could be applied to solving problems outside of school-specific contexts. He was particularly concerned about teachers who adopted the typical school learning posture toward their own professional education. "Everything should be discouraged," he wrote, "which tends to put the student in the attitude of snatching at the subject matter which he is acquiring in order to see if by some hook or crook it may be made immediately available for a lesson in this or that grade."[54] He was obviously disturbed by prospective teachers who themselves wasted powerful educational opportunities by grasping prematurely for answers to specific situations. Most contemporary teacher education, however, still errs on the side of technical preparation. Most of it still treats professional learning as most children learn to treat subject-matter learning: with little concern for its larger empowering potential, as an exercise with only immediate (and often trivial or counterproductive) results.

Problems Needing Remedy, If Professional Knowledge Is to Foster Teacher Efficacy

The nature and amount of pedagogical instruction must be dramatically different from that which prevails today. Direct pedagogical instruction traditionally includes theory, methods, and practice. The weakness of pedagogical theory has been its unrelatedness to school contexts, the weakness of pedagogical method has been its unrelatedness to school subjects, and the weakness of pedagogical practice has been its imitation of teaching models that reinforce the status quo. Recent reforms are beginning to address these traditional problems.

A move in the right direction addresses the obvious insufficiencies of isolated subject-matter knowledge and concern with knowledge about pedagogy. Here too, problems are encountered, even though some recent developments are beginning to show substantial promise.[55] Most of the pedagogy learned by prospective and practicing teachers reflects the passive, authoritarian model that teachers need to abandon in schools. The dominant models of pedagogy at all levels of education are more overpowering than they are empowering.

The movement to address the pedagogy of particular subjects more fully is a move in the right direction and must be applauded. Knowledge of predictable student misconceptions and confusions can be particularly helpful, when added to a sound grasp of subject matter. However, most of the pedagogy modeled in every grade and level of today's schools and colleges—yes, even in schools of education—does not represent the "participatory, critical, values-oriented, multicultural, student-centered, experiential, research-minded, and interdisciplinary" pedagogy that thoughtful critics call for.[56]

The exemplary models of school and university instruction that Holmes Group institutions are struggling to develop (Professional Development Schools) are important to teacher knowledge, for they promise at least glimpses of critical pedagogical alternatives to the textbookish lecturing and factual testing that now universally characterizes pedagogy. The Professional Development Schools also promise to remedy the decontextualized problems of educational theory. Long recognized for its weak explanatory power for teachers, educational theory may become more efficacious if more teachers of educational theory are more in touch with practice. However, even taken together—improved models of educational practice, educational theory that is connected to practice, and stronger subject-matter and pedagogical knowledge—these reforms remain inadequate for enabling teachers to counter existing norms.

Knowledge of the Broader Educational Enterprise Is Also Necessary

Three major areas are critical to further discourse on the teacher knowledge that is necessary for the level of teacher efficacy requisite to quality schooling. These areas involve broad knowledge of (1) the institutional and organizational enterprise of education itself, with a concomitant valuing of collegiality, (2) the substance and pedagogy of civic education as it can be appropriately integrated into the teaching of knowledge in a discipline, and (3) knowledge about the professional norms and expectations for teaching, with its emphasis on uncertainty, and other governing values for professional teachers.

Institutional and organizational knowledge. Why would professional teachers need to know about organizational theory, bureaucracies, and how educational organizations work (and don't work) in contemporary society? Isn't this far removed from classrooms, where teachers as knowledge workers become chief executives for younger knowledge workers? Isn't this too much to ask, when teachers are already asked to have more and better content knowledge and more and better pedagogical knowledge in order to manage more complicated and challenging classroom learning environments? Why a broad knowledge of organizations? Wouldn't understanding school operations be enough?

Institutional and organizational knowledge is necessary because the rhetoric about quality schooling and restructured schools will not change classroom realities much until teachers see beyond individuals and discrete acts. Large numbers of teachers must come to know that schools and classrooms are not closed systems that can be understood in their own terms. Rather, they must be understood in the context of their larger environments—in terms of their local, state, regional, and national social structures and of their links to other organizations and institutions.

Teacher efficacy will also remain dormant for most teachers until they understand the deleterious cognitive influences of prolonged mental and physical confinement in classrooms. Teacher preparation now focuses almost exclusively on preparing adults for continuous work with children in isolated settings; the preparation necessarily assumes continuous daily interaction with youngsters in a small cellular room. Opportunities for professional exchange with other adults are severely limited, and opportunities for interaction with the larger world are essentially nonexistent. Unfortunately, contemporary knowledge in teacher education and teacher testing programs continue to reinforce this narrow, basically technical view of professional practice. Professional knowledge that is confined to classroom-bounded conceptions of teaching competence limits, for all practical purposes, teachers' understanding of the broader policy arenas, and it inhibits their professional options to assume responsibility for quality student learning.

Rosabeth Kanter describes the theoretical underpinnings for the ways in which this limited perspective is deleterious in her "Contemporary Organizations" chapter in Ernest Boyer's volume, *Common Learning*.[57] Kanter argues that "informed citizens need to learn the limits imposed on their own and others' actions by the design of organizations and by institutional interdependencies," since such knowledge promotes empathy, humility, and the freedom to participate in the construction of one's own work environment.[58] Empathy is important because it promotes understanding of the circumstances confronting others: a sense that if one were in the same place, one might do likewise. Humility is valuable because it leads to the understanding that jobs themselves have high and low opportunity values. They have differing beneficial circumstances that are often more responsible for success than is individual superiority. Perhaps most important, freedom is critical, for it brings knowledge of the limits imposed by existing structures, permits people either to remove constraints or to add options that could encourage more constructive behavior.

Understanding institutional pressure and constraints diminishes the tendency to blame and punish individuals for circumstances that are not of their making. As Kanter explains, "recognition of the socially patterned nature of conduct permits the person to step aside, review his or her actions, and, by noting the effect of external forces, gain some mastery of them."[59] An example of the application of such general organizational knowledge to teaching and teacher education may be helpful. Consider the results of numerous analyses of organizational behavior:

> Certain well-known bureaucratic pathologies, such as leadership styles characterized by control, overly close supervision, rules-mindedness, and territorial defensiveness, are associated with organizational situations rather than individual characteristics. Relative power or powerlessness is the issue. When people lack the resources needed to do

their job, and when their outward influence is limited, they feel powerless and tend to turn to control over others in their own limited domain and to use whatever weapons they do possess to assert at least
minimal control.[60]

The long-standing tensions between teachers and principals (and
even many of those between teachers and students) would be more productively handled if teachers interpreted them through this sociological,
organizational perspective, in addition to the individual, psychological
knowledge they now customarily acquire. Too often, the behavior of
principals (or that of students) is rationalized in terms of implied individual failure—he or she is lazy, unimaginative, authoritarian, or not
very bright. Instead, teachers should try to understand and help remove
the environmental constraints that so predictably give rise to unproduc-
tive conflict.

Consider the importance of teachers understanding the predictable
institutional behaviors of organizations that have multiple, often conflicting, goals. For example, such organizations have great difficulty in
knowing when they have accomplished the purposes for which they
were designed. They serve many different purposes for many different
people, and assessing their own claims of success or failure is problematic. Schools have conflicting, competing goals, and if teachers are to
share responsibility and accountability for the outcomes of schooling,
then knowledge of the organizational context and relations is critical to
teacher efficacy.

Another type of organizational knowledge needed by professional
teachers who would participate in restructuring schools for quality
learning is based on delegation and role differentiation. The more extensively an organization differentiates, the more likely it is that tensions
will arise between subgroups pursuing limited ends rather than the
goals of the whole enterprise. While specialization and differentiated
staffing are clearly needed, professional teachers and their career professional colleagues must know how to avoid "trained incapacity," a term
commonly used to describe the inability of specialists to manage any
task outside of their own limited domain. As adaptable public institutions requiring people capable of thinking and acting in a variety of ways
become increasingly essential, the potentially deleterious effects of over-
specialization are being recognized and addressed.

Teachers also need knowledge about the predictable effects of the
bureaucratic tendency to prescribe calculable rules that specify the elements of performance. The extent to which people must rely on rules in
lieu of judgment causes them to be rigid in the face of change. Professional teachers must understand and be able to convince others that
change is a necessary part of teaching, since so many situations require
professional judgment and cannot be specified in advance. Similarly,

they must understand and be articulate about the unintended tendency of impersonal and easily measured performance criteria to encourage participants to gear their behavior to attain only minimal standards, a process that clearly subverts formal organizational objectives. These are but a few illustrations of the organizational knowledge teachers need to possess in order to participate effectively as public and professional leaders. Without such knowledge and the opportunity to use it, they will be unable to remedy the learning problems in the nation's schools.

Knowledge of the schools' civic mission and connections with American society. The commentary earlier in this chapter on the civic ends of quality schooling does not conform to traditional discourse on the subject. Discussions of civic learning, citizenship, and school–community relationships have had too long and rocky a history to address here. Nor can the pros and cons of diverse schools of thought regarding citizenship education be argued here. Instead, we recommend that the multiple meanings of and bases for civic learning be given important places in teachers' professional knowledge. Without such understanding, teachers cannot participate in the continuing dialogue and determination of appropriate avenues for professional teacher development and action in the affairs of civic learning. Professional teachers must understand the ways in which education, like constitutional government, provides the foundations for liberty and justice in a democratic republic.

All professional teachers must understand, therefore, how the subjects they teach are related to the pursuit of justice, dignity, compassion, and freedom. This includes not only social studies teachers, but all elementary and secondary teachers, whether they emphasize the arts, the sciences, or the humanities. Such understanding is an *extension* of teachers' more traditional knowledge of their disciplines, not a replacement of this other important dimension. Quality schooling must allow knowledge of the discipline to be acquired through the development of meaningful, higher-order thinking skills, just as application of knowledge and the moral ends of education must also be addressed. Teachers must understand how the application of knowledge to worthy civic ends provides a means of (1) increasing meaningful subject matter learning, (2) emphasizing the importance of civic learning, and (3) connecting learning in and learning out of school.

Broad knowledge of the civic ends of education for all teachers should counter the traditional narrow, technical models of professional education that have been dominant for many years. Such knowledge is intended to strengthen the public leadership role of professional teachers, enabling them to interact more effectively with other adults from the community when they encounter them in professional roles in and out of school. As Barbara Finkelstein points out, technicist models of professional education disjoin the adventure of education from intellectual, literary, and social adventuring, placing its practitioners at a distance from centers of inquiry, discourse, learning, and criticism that are available in universities, libraries, policy centers, and artistic circles. And it ill prepares them to understand and engage in the hustle and bustle of educational politics—where options and possibilities are effectively created.[61]

Teacher efficacy will be possible when the technicist models of professional teacher education are replaced, and broad civic learning permits teacher participation in the full educational life of schools and communities.

Knowledge of the uncertain nature of professional work. As new conceptions of the educational and operational norms for tomorrow's professional teachers emerge, expectations must shift from a system of preparation and practice that has been governed by rigidly prescribed rules and certainty to one that anticipates—and prepares teachers to act upon—a broad range of judgment and uncertainty. Conceptions of teachers' roles and expertise must change, as well as their relationships with students and colleagues. New values must come to govern the teacher's self-image. Permeating these new conceptions and values must be an abiding understanding of and appreciation for the need to tolerate the endemic uncertainties of teaching.

There are several kinds of uncertainty that professional teachers must face beyond those discussed above. One kind results from incomplete or imperfect mastery of available knowledge; no one can have all skill or all knowledge about teaching and learning at his or her command. A second kind of uncertainty results from the limitations of educational knowledge itself. While new discoveries of ways to facilitate learning are emerging with increased regularity, vast areas of understanding about human learning and teaching remain unknown. A third type is rooted in the difficulties of distinguishing between the first two—between personal ignorance or ineptitude and the limitations of present professional knowledge. Drawing a line between one's own limitations and those of the field is not easily done.[62]

If meaningful, higher-order learning is to emerge from the mixture of facts, concepts, principles, and experience that teachers select and provide for students, teacher preparation must include knowledge about the uncertain nature of this type of professional work. Naturally, if teaching means only carrying out someone else's professional decisions, and teachers are merely implementers, such preparation will not be necessary. However, early studies conducted by Robert Merton and his colleagues in professional schools of medicine indicate that attitudes about uncertainty are important for prospective professionals. They are important aspects of the social and psychological environments in professional medical schools, and they are addressed directly and indirectly throughout the curriculum. As the exercise of professional judgment in teaching becomes increasingly accepted, the cognitive and attitudinal dimensions of uncertainty must also become incorporated into programs of teacher preparation.

No longer, for example, would teachers (or administrators) assume that a quiet classroom where students are writing busily in district-approved workbooks is automatically a good learning environment. Teachers must judge the intellectual worth of assignments, and they must be prepared to defend their decisions, knowing full well that sometimes they will be in error. Often the learning tasks they select will be appropriate for some students but not others; it is sometimes difficult to tell until after one or more trials. At other times, when teachers create a learning environment for students that encourages high-interest, open dialogue and freedom to express thinking, constructive discourse may degenerate into disorder and disrespect. The professional teacher will have to make corrections, and reconstruct the learning situation. During their professional preparation, teachers must learn to expect challenges to their judgment, as well as occasional failure. However, the risks of occasional challenge and failure are not as costly as the further loss of the right to exercise professional judgment in teaching. The tensions of uncertainty are worth the potential gains in student learning, teaching efficacy, and quality schooling.

The case for professional decisionmaking, with its requisite call for judgment and uncertainty in teacher education and teaching, has been greatly advanced by the teachers who helped plan the Texas conference, and who spoke about "Quality Schooling for Texas Today and Tomorrow." Their voices decry the dominance of certainty and the absence of uncertainty in their work environments, and the concomitant loss of quality in school learning and teaching. They provide an eloquent conclusion to this chapter:

- "Everything today is kind of hand-me-down. The state hands me down the essential elements, and I hand them down to the students."
- "I feel no influence in the profession in general. I've been told to follow one prescribed teaching strategy. I've been told I will be evaluated in a particular manner and if I meet such, good for me. If not, I will be told what to do to meet Texas standards. I'm held accountable, but I have little or no influence."
- "Teach for the test. That's the message I get continually. Even if that's all they know, at least we'll look good to the public when test results get published."
- "No one knows my students better than I do. I want to be able to

choose what they need and teach them, not just to make a passing grade but to get them prepared for life beyond my classroom. But no one asks me what I think or recommend."[63]

NOTES

We take this opportunity to express our appreciation to John Zeuli for his contributions to this chapter.

1. Lauren B. Resnick's presidential address to the American Educational Research Association illuminated this distinction; see "Learning in School and Out," Presidential Address, Annual Conference of the American Educational Research Association, Washington, D.C., April, 1987.

2. John Dewey, "The Relation of Theory to Practice in Education," in National Society for the Scientific Study of Education, *The Relation of Theory to Practice in the Education of Teachers*, 3rd Yearbook, Part I (Bloomington, Ill.: Public School Publishing Co., 1904), pp. 9–30; reprinted in Merle Borrowman, ed., *Teacher Education in America: A Documentary History* (New York: Teachers College Press, 1965), p. 155.

3. John Dewey, "How Much Freedom in New Schools?" *New Republic 63*, July 9, 1930, pp. 204–206.

4. See, for example, Theodore Sizer, *Horace's Compromise* (Boston: Houghton Mifflin, 1984); Arthur Powell, Eleanor Farrar, and David Cohen, *The Shopping Mall High School: Winners and Losers in the Educational Marketplace* (Boston: Houghton Mifflin, 1985); Michael Sedlak, Christopher Wheeler, Diana Pullin, and Philip Cusick, *Selling Students Short: Classroom Bargains and Academic Reform in the American High School* (New York: Teachers College Press, 1986).

5. David Cohen, quoted in Richard Elmore, "Reform and Authority in the Culture of Schools," *Educational Administration Quarterly 23* (4), Fall 1987, pp. 60–78; Elmore cites Cohen's forthcoming essay "Educational Technology, Policy and Practice," *Educational Evaluation and Policy Analysis 9* (2), 1987, pp. 153–170.

6. See, for example, Sedlak, Wheeler, Pullin, and Cusick, op. cit.; Linda McNeil, *Contradictions of Control* (Boston: RKP, 1986); Powell, Farrar, and Cohen, op. cit.; Philip Cusick, *The Egalitarian Ideal and the American High School* (New York: Longman, 1983); Randall Collins, *The Credential Society* (New York: Academic Press, 1979); David Cohen and Barbara Neufeld, "The Failure of High Schools and the Progress of Education," *Daedalus 110*, 1981, pp. 62–89; Robert B. Everhart, "Classroom Management, Student Opposition, and the Labor Process," in Michael Apple and Lois Weis, eds., *Ideology and Practice in Schooling* (Philadelphia: Temple University Press, 1983).

7. Resnick, op. cit.; Frederick Erickson, "School Literacy, Reasoning, and Civility: An Anthropologist's Perspective," *Review of Educational Research 54*, 1984, pp. 525–546; Jean Anyon, "Social Class and School Knowledge," *Curriculum Inquiry 11*, 1981, pp. 3–42.

8. Deanna Kuhn, "Education for Thinking," *Teachers College Record 87*, 1986, p. 496.

9. Irene Athey and Harry Singer, "Developing the Nation's Reading Potential for a Technological Era," *Harvard Educational Review 57*, 1987, pp. 84–92.

10. R. C. Anderson, E. H. Hiebert, J. A. Scott, and I. A. G. Wilkinson, *Becoming a Nation of Readers*, Report of the Commission on Reading (Pittsburgh: National Academy of Education, 1985); Linda Anderson, "The Environment of Instruction: The Function of Seatwork in a Commercially Developed Curriculum," in G. Duffy, L. Roehler, and J. Mason, eds., *Comprehension Instruction: Perspectives and Suggestions* (New York: Longman, 1984), pp. 93–103.

11. Allan Collins, John Seely Brown, and Susan E. Newman, "Cognitive Apprenticeship: Teaching the Craft of Reading, Writing and Mathematics," in Lauren B. Resnick, ed., *Cognition and Instruction: Issues and Agendas* (Hillsdale, N.J.: Lawrence Erlbaum Associates, 1986); Kuhn, op. cit.

12. Curtis McKnight et al., *The Underachieving Curriculum: Assessing U.S. School Mathematics from an International Perspective* (Champaign, Ill.: Stipes, 1987).

13. See Collins, Brown, and Newman, op. cit.; Carl Bereiter and Marlene Scar-

damalia, "An Attainable Version of High Literacy: Approaches to Teaching Higher-Order Skills in Reading and Writing," *Curriculum Inquiry 17*, 1987, pp. 9–30; Daniel Resnick and Lauren Resnick, "The Nature of Literacy: An Historical Explanation," *Harvard Educational Review 47*, 1977, pp. 370–385; Lawrence C. Stedman and Carl F. Kaestle, "Literacy and Reading Performance in the United States, from 1880 to the Present," *Reading Research Quarterly 22*, 1987, pp. 8–46; A. Shoenfeld, *Mathematical Problem Solving* (New York: Academic Press, 1985); K. K. Wixon and M. Y. L. Lipson, "Reading (Dis)ability: An Interactional Perspective," in Taffy Raphael, ed., *Contexts of School-based Literacy* (New York: Random House, 1986).

14. Kathleen Devaney and Gary Sykes, "Making the Case for Professionalism," in Ann Lieberman, ed., *Building a Professional Culture in Schools* (New York: Teachers College Press, 1988).

15. Collins, Brown, and Newman, op. cit.

16. Ibid.

17. Ibid.

18. Thomas A. Romberg and Thomas P. Carpenter, "Research on Teaching and Learning Mathematics: Two Disciplines of Scientific Inquiry," in Merle C. Wittrock, ed., *Handbook of Research on Teaching*, 3rd ed. (New York: Macmillan, 1986).

19. Walter Doyle, "Academic Work," *Review of Educational Research 53*, 1983, pp. 159–199; see also Magdalene Lampert, "Mathematics Learning in Context: The Voyage of the Mimi," *Journal of Mathematical Behavior 4*, 1985, pp. 157–167, which provides an excellent example of a more integrated approach to teaching mathematics.

20. Romberg and Carpenter, op. cit.; C. M. Clark and R. J. Yinger, *Research on Teacher Thinking* (East Lansing, Mich.: Institute for Research on Teaching, 1978).

21. Anderson et al., op. cit., p. 73.

22. Bereiter and Scardamalia, op. cit.

23. Athey and Singer, op. cit.

24. Collins, Brown, and Newman, op. cit.

25. Devaney and Sykes, op. cit.

26. Norman Frederiksen, "Implications of Cognitive Theory for Instruction in Problem Solving," *Review of Educational Research 54*, 1984, p. 363.

27. Devaney and Sykes, op. cit.

28. Doyle, op. cit., p. 169.

29. Dewey, op. cit., p. 148.

30. Ibid.

31. Ibid., p. 149.

32. Ibid.

33. Ibid.

34. Willard Waller, *The Sociology of Teaching* (New York: Wiley, 1932); Resnick, op. cit.; Sedlak, Wheeler, Pullin, and Cusick, op. cit.; Devaney and Sykes, op. cit.

35. Annmarie S. Palincsar and Ann L. Brown, "Reciprocal Teaching of Comprehension-fostering and Monitoring Activities," *Cognition and Instruction 4*, 1984, pp. 117–175; A. L. Brown and B. B. Armbruster, "Instructing Comprehension—Fostering Activities in Interactive Learning Situations," in H. Mendl, N. Stein, and T. Trabasso, eds., *Learning and Comprehension of Text* (Hillsdale, N.J.: Lawrence Erlbaum Associates, 1984); Bereiter and Scardamalia, op. cit., Schoenfeld, op. cit., T. Raphael and P. P. Pearson, "Increasing Students' Sources of Information for Answering Questions," *American Educational Research Journal 22*, 1985, pp. 217–235.

36. Collins, Brown and Newman, op. cit.

37. Ibid. See also T. P. Carpenter and J. M. Moser, "The Acquisition of Addition and Subtraction Concepts," in R. Lesh and M. Landau, eds., *The Acquisition of Mathematical Concepts and Processes* (New York: Academic Press, 1983), pp. 7–44; L. B. Resnick, "Syntax and Semantics in Learning to Subtract," in T. P. Carpenter, J. M. Moser, and T. A. Romberg, eds., *Addition and Subtraction: A Cognitive Perspective* (Hillsdale, N.J.: Lawrence Erlbaum Associates, 1982), pp. 136–155; Lampert, op. cit.; L. M. Calkins, "When Children Want to Punctuate: Basic Skills in Context," *Language Arts 57*, 1983, pp. 567–573.

38. Mary G. Deitz, "Context Is All: Feminism and Theories of Citizenship," *Daedalus 116*, 1987, p. 14.

39. Ibid.

40. Joseph Schwab, "Education and the State: Learning Community," in Robert M. Hutchins and Mortimer J. Adler, eds., *The Great Ideas Today, 1976* (Chicago: Encyclopedia Britannica, 1976), p. 235.

41. Ibid., pp. 239–240.

42. Richard Elmore, op. cit. See also Philip C. Schlecty and Anne Walker Joslin, "Images of Schools," in Ann Lieberman, ed., *Rethinking School Improvement* (New York: Teachers College Press, 1986), pp. 147–161; David K. Cohen, "The Conditions of Teachers' Work," *Harvard Educational Review 54*, 1984, pp. 11–15; Joseph B. McDonald, "Raising the Teacher's Voice," *Harvard Educational Review 56*, 1986, pp. 355–378; Samuel B. Bacharach, Scott C. Bauer, and Joseph B. Shedd, "The Work Environment and School Reform," *Teachers College Record 88*, 1986, pp. 242–255.

43. Earlier definitions have been reviewed in Patricia T. Ashton and Rodman B. Webb, *Making a Difference: Teachers' Sense of Efficacy and Student Achievement* (New York: Longman, 1986).

44. Merle Borrowman, "Liberal Education and the Preparation of Teachers," in Merle Borrowman, ed., *Teacher Education in America: A Documentary History*, pp. 1–53.

45. Ibid., p. 30.

46. Quoted in ibid., p. 31.

47. Ibid., p. 22.

48. See, for example, the discussion in Ernest Boyer, *College: The Undergraduate Experience in America* (New York: Harper and Row, 1987).

49. Suzanne M. Wilson and Lee S. Shulman, "150 Ways of Knowing: Representation of Knowledge in Teaching," in J. Calderman, ed., *Exploring Teacher Thinking* (New York: Holt, Rinehart and Winston, 1987).

50. Collins, Brown and Newman, op. cit.

51. See, for example, Robert Floden and Christopher Clark, "Preparing Teachers for Uncertainty," unpublished paper (East Lansing, Mich.: Institute for Research on Teaching, 1987); Philip Jackson, *The Practice of Teaching* (New York: Teachers College Press, 1986); Dan Lortie, *Schoolteacher* (Chicago: University of Chicago Press, 1975).

52. For example, Vivian Paley, *White Teacher* (Chicago: University of Chicago Press, 1979); *Boys and Girls* (Chicago: University of Chicago Press, 1984).

53. See, for example, Athey and Singer, op. cit.; Anderson et al., op. cit., Kuhn, op. cit.; Bereiter and Scardamalia, op. cit.

54. Dewey, op. cit., p. 165.

55. Wilson and Shulman, op. cit.

56. Ira Shor, "Excellence is Equity," *Harvard Educational Review 56*, 1986, pp. 406–426.

57. Rosabeth Kanter, "Contemporary Organizations," in Ernest Boyer, ed., *Common Learning* (New York: Carnegie Foundation for the Advancement of Teaching, 1981), pp. 75–93.

58. Ibid., p. 83.

59. Ibid.

60. Ibid., pp. 82–83.

61. Barbara Finkelstein, "Thinking Publicly about Civic Learning: An Agenda for Education Reform in the 80s," in Alan H. Jones, ed., *Civic Learning for Teachers: Capstone for Educational Reform* (Ann Arbor, Mich.: Prakken, 1985), p. 21.

62. Renee Fox, "Training for Uncertainty," in Robert K. Merton, George G. Reader, and Patricia L. Kendall, eds., *The Student Physician: Introductory Studies in the Sociology of Medical Education* (Cambridge, Mass.: Harvard University Press, 1957), pp. 207–241; Joseph P. McDonald, "Raising the Teacher's Voice and the Ironic Role of Theory," *Harvard Educational Review 56*, November 1986, p. 377; Floden and Clark, op. cit.; Jackson, op. cit.; and Lortie, op. cit.

63. *Teachers Speak: Quality Schooling for Texas Today and Tomorrow*, a report from the Brackenridge Forum for the Enhancement of Teaching (San Antonio, Tex.: Trinity University, 1987), pp. 6–9.

CHAPTER 7

Balancing Specialized & Comprehensive Knowledge: The Growing Educational Challenge

HOWARD GARDNER

Harvard University

UNIVERSAL KNOWLEDGE: A VANISHING IDEAL

At least in the West, the ideal of the intellectually well-rounded individual has dominated educational discussions for centuries. From Plato's philosopher-king to a Renaissance man such as Leonardo, from the philosophers of the Enlightenment to the Victorian amateur, the ideal educated individual has sought to encompass the full range of human knowledge as it was then constituted. Though the pursuit of knowledge is perhaps a distinctly Western affliction, we find intimations of this ideal in other civilizations—for example, in the model of the Confucian literati, well-versed in music, painting, poetry, archery, calligraphy, and mathematics.

The fully knowledgeable individual has not been often realized, of course, but the ideal has at least appeared as a viable possibility. The greatest minds of the past, such as Plato and Aristotle, Leonardo and Immanuel Kant, have come dauntingly close to mastering the range of their era's knowledge. However, in light of the proliferation of disciplines and subdisciplines, and the discovery of diverse products and values from the many cultures of the world, a different state of affairs has begun to prevail during the past century. However reluctantly, we have all come to realize that the ideal of universal knowledge (or even of universal knowledgeability) is no longer tenable. The renowned mathematician John von Neumann put it trenchantly when he noted that a century ago it was possible to understand all of mathematics, but by 1950, even the most well-informed mathematician could have access to only 10% of the knowledge of his field.

While the possibility of comprehensive knowledge within and across fields has lessened, the need for it has most certainly not. Many of the most urgent problems of the world demand not just specialized expertise but the wider perspective and wisdom that comes with broadly based knowledge. Equally, the most basic questions facing all humans—about the meaning of life, the nature of truth, beauty, and goodness, the relation of the individual to the family, the local community, and the world community—by their very nature transcend narrow or conventional disciplinary boundaries. Moreover, even if the goal of universal knowledge cannot be attained, it seems wrong-headed for educators to deny to their charges the *opportunity* at least to sample the spectrum of disciplines.

Whether education should favor the acquisition of specialized knowledge, as opposed to adhering to an ideal of general comprehensive knowledge, is a vexed question. It is to a significant extent a question of values; no line of scientific evidence or logical argument can by itself resolve the question of *what* to teach or *how* to teach. In recent writings on this issue by Allan Bloom,[1] Ernest Boyer,[2] E. D. Hirsch,[3] and many others, the competing value systems are clear. Nonetheless, this value facet does not mean that empirical evidence is irrelevant. Given the need to acquire some specialized knowledge, without sacrificing completely the ideal of generalized knowledge, it is proper to ask *in what manner* these two educational pulls might best be balanced. This chapter draws on some lines of evidence from developmental and cognitive psychology in an effort to indicate how the balance between these contrasting educational goals might best be achieved.

THE SCIENTIFIC EVIDENCE FOR SPECIFICITY

Until fairly recently, the ideal of universal knowledge fit quite comfortably with the prevailing models of mind. That is, most psychological theories favored the notion of the mind as a single instrument, with intelligence as its most desirable property. In this "unitarian" view, the human mind carried out basic processes like perception, memory, attending, and learning, and these processes unfolded in similar ways, independent of the subject matter or material with which the mind happened to be engaged. By the same token, individuals could be compared with one another in terms of the power and efficiency of the mind, and those individuals at the proper end of the scale were deemed "most intelligent." Although the ensuing corollaries were not obligatory, it became commonplace to assume that differences in intelligence could be reliably assessed using that paper-and-pencil instrument called the IQ test and that these differences were probably present during the early years of life, if not at the moment of conception.[4]

Some scientists and educators, along with much of the lay public, still subscribe to such a unitary view of mind, featuring "across-the-board" psychological processes and a single metric labeled intelligence. So long as this perspective prevails, the tension between specialized and comprehensive knowledge need not appear acute. Yet it seems fair to say that these articles of faith have undergone searching critiques in recent years. Part of the critique has simply involved a recognition that particular mental processes, like learning and memory, are far more complicated and multifaceted than had generally been realized. A more probing critique has proposed that the mind is itself composed of different components, modules, or "intelligences," each of which operates according to its own principles. As a frequent corollary, it is held that power in one intellectual domain holds little if any predictive value for power in other intellectual domains—thus the notion of an unidimensional intelligence makes dubious scientific sense. The ideal of comprehensive knowledge becomes more elusive.

My own theory of multiple intelligences[5] was developed with particular reference to educational issues, and that fact may serve as one justification for reviewing it here, in preference to alternative modular positions.[6] To arrive at a set of candidates for "intelligences," I reviewed several bodies of evidence: the facts of development in different cognitive realms; knowledge about the breakdown of cognitive capacities under different forms of brain damage; the existence of isolated capacities or isolated lacunae in "special" populations, such as prodigies, idiot savants, and autistic children; as well as scattered evidence obtained from studies of cognition in different cultures, cognition in diverse species, psychometric correlations, and studies of training and generalization of skills.

Weaving together these disparate lines of evidence, I identified seven different families of abilities, which humans as a species have evolved over the millenia. The seven candidate "intelligences" include linguistic and logical mathematical intelligences, the two forms that are most honored in school and are also at a premium in most standardized tests of intellect. In addition, five other intelligences are posited: spatial, musical, bodily kinesthetic, and two forms of personal intelligence—interpersonal and intrapersonal intelligence.

While it is theoretically possible that an individual could excel in all intelligences, or perform at the same level in all intelligences, both of these outcomes would be empirically rare. In most cases, individuals exhibit a fairly jagged profile of intelligences, revealing relative strengths in some areas, comparative weaknesses in others. The theory also posits that these different profiles can be detected early in life and that, while they are not immutable, it is probably prudent to go with the grain, rather than wholly against it. Empirical evidence on these two assertions is still limited, but there is at least suggestive evidence that different profiles of intelligence can be detected fairly early in life and may turn out to be quite enduring.[7]

The concept of an intelligence is a psychological notion and also a biological one. Individuals possess a profile of intelligences as a reflection of their genetic heritage and their early experience. Yet intelligences cannot be manifest in a vacuum, and their development and expression presupposes a culture with certain practices and values. In work carried out after the publication of *Frames of Mind*, I have, with my colleagues David Feldman and Mihaly Csikszentmihalyi, sought to investigate the interface of individual intelligences and cultural products. In this work, distinctions are made among the *intelligences* (as defined above), the *domains* of knowledge—the epistemological structures of given areas of experience, ranging from academic disciplines to various arts and crafts, and the *fields* of knowledge—the social institutions and reward systems within which any individual must negotiate his or her way vocationally and avocationally. By taking into account this trio of perspectives, it should prove possible to offer a finer-grained analysis of what happens to an individual over the course of education.[8]

Trends counter to unitary formulations of mind in the area of psychology have been echoed in other disciplines. In cognitive science and artificial intelligence, for example, there has been a sea change: Twenty years ago, authorities searched for general heuristics of problem solving, while today the focus has shifted to specific areas of expertise[9] and to mind as a society of diverse agents.[10] Analogously, in the neurosciences, the conception of the brain as an undifferentiated mass, with equivalent potential for all kinds of competences, is no longer viable. Instead, it is recognized that brain tissue becomes committed early to specific forms of specialization, that important functions (like language or spatial perception) are highly localized, and that specific patterns of ability can be spared or destroyed in relative isolation.[11]

Even though these diverse lines of study have not been pursued with educational questions in mind, they all support the emerging notion of the mind as a set of special-purpose mechanisms. The accumulating evidence on the modularity of mind makes the prospect of gaining comprehensive knowledge even dimmer. As they reflect on the nature of human thought, researchers are nonetheless aware that individuals are capable of tying together diverse lines of thought, of creating powerful analogies that cut across domains, and, if only occasionally, of obtaining integrating syntheses or wisdom. Yet the challenge of explaining these synthesizing capacities remains daunting; some experts, like Jerry Fodor, question whether cognitive and neural science can ever go beyond the explication of specific modules of mind.[12]

EDUCATIONAL CONSIDERATIONS

While science may promote pessimism about the possibility of obtaining universal knowledge, many educators have (perhaps wisely) ignored these apparent limitations and continued to pursue the ideal of some specific and some comprehensive knowledge. Perhaps the most enduring tack in the West has been the notion of "general education" or a "core curriculum." It is held that every educated individual ought to have at least some familiarity with the great ideas of civilization (often limited to Western civilization) and with the major bodies or approaches to knowledge. Therefore, in high school and college (though not in graduate or professional schools), individuals are urged to spurn undue specialization by taking a smattering of courses across the arts, humanities, natural and social sciences and only a limited number in the so-called major field of study. At best, this method ensures at least some familiarity with the range of our culture, though more often it simply spawns superficial knowledge.

In some countries, of course, the ideal of specialization has received more prominence. In China and the Soviet Union, for example, efforts are made early on to determine which children have strong aptitudes. Thereafter, these children are guided or compelled to spend the bulk of their time pursuing their areas of particular expertise, whether it be mathematics, painting, or athletics. This approach fosters a high level of performance, but only a very few youngsters have the stamina and ingenuity to broaden the base of their knowledge.

Whatever their differences, these approaches share one distinctive feature: They begin with an attempt to inculcate the more general forms of knowledge and then move over time toward increasing specialization. In the Russian model, specialization begins early and is relatively unrelenting; in Europe the narrowing-down begins in the Gymnasium or lycée and moves into high gear in the university; in the United States, for good and bad reasons, specialization occurs in many cases only following four years of college.

However, it is possible to take other tacks. Rather than moving inexorably from general or comprehensive knowledge to specialized knowledge, one could begin with the specific and then become increasingly general, or begin with the general, move to the specific, and then back again to the general, and so on. There are even historical precedents for this. In Plato's Academy, the philosopher king at age 50 confronted the most general issues; in the American college of the nineteenth century, the senior year was devoted to the consideration of broad issues under the guidance of the college president; in Confucian China, the 70-year-old was free to explore whatever he wished.

On the basis of my reading of cognitive and developmental psychology, and in the light of my educational values, I shall propose here yet another pedagogical tack. In my own view, certain phases of development lend themselves better to the consideration of broad and comprehensive issues, while other phases of development seem suited to the focused pursuit of one or two specialized domains of knowledge. Moreover, even within a particular developmental phase, I also discern the possibility of an oscillation between periods of general exploration and periods of focused specialization. The particular plan proposed here may not bear the stamp of scientific validity, but it is at least consistent with the evidence as I read it.

The following treatment, then, is based on my value judgment that each individual should know well at least one or two domains of knowledge; have a sense of the range of those domains he or she cannot personally come to know in detail; be cognizant of significant perspectives and alternatives in the realms of truth, beauty, and goodness; and have the skills and the inclination to think about the important issues in life, ranging from his or her personal role and relation to the immediate family, to engagement with the wider community, to his or her niche in the world. As I have said, science cannot dictate exactly how to proceed, but the educational road map ought at least to be so charted that it is consistent with what can be ascertained about the development of human intellectual competence.

AN OVERVIEW OF STAGES OF EDUCATIONAL DEVELOPMENT

The field of developmental psychology has been fortunate in the talents that it has attracted in this century. From the ranks of psychoanalysts, it has been enriched by the contributions of Sigmund Freud, Erik Erikson, and John Bowlby; in the area of cognitive development, there has been the pivotal work of Jerome Bruner, Jean Piaget, and Lev Vygotsky; and much has also been learned about moral reasoning (Lawrence Kohlberg), symbolization (Bernard Kaplan and Heinz Werner), and cultural differences (Michael Cole, Robert LeVine, Margaret Mead, John Whiting).

Synthesizing the works of these individuals, and those of other researchers and theorists in the field, I find it reasonable to divide the developmental progression in the first half of life into five broad phases. (There may be additional phases in later life.) Each phase features a specific form of knowledge to be obtained and a specific realm within which it operates. In this section, I will outline the five phases, saving more detailed documentation for the succeeding sections.

1. Infancy—Period of sensory and motor knowledge. This phase involves the formation of basic Piagetian-Kantian categories of space, time, object concept, incipient concepts, and numerical sense.

Sphere: The baby's own world and his or her relation to the parents
Aspects of intelligence: Sensory and motor
Educational regimen: Play, exploration, practice

2. Early childhood: Period of exploration and the emergence of cognitive inclinations. This phase is characterized by acquaintance with the rules of different symbol systems (language, music, picturing, gesture, number) and symbolic competence acquired without direct tutelage (such as Piagetian object knowledge).

Sphere: Immediate family, close neighbors or relatives
Aspects of intelligence: Emergence of multiple intelligences
Educational regimen: Rich and varied exposure; specialized training only for the prodigiously gifted; "spectrum approach" for assessment of cognitive strengths

3. Middle childhood: Period of skill-building and school. This phase involves the acquisition of basic literacies and notational knowledge. Its task is to connect common sensory and practical experience to culturally devised symbol and notational systems.

Sphere: Peers and local community
Aspects of intelligence: Introduction to domains of knowledge (culturally structured disciplines and crafts)
Educational regimen: Acquisition of basic literacies; specialization in one art, one academic discipline, one physical activity (dance or athletics)

4. Adolescence: Period of sensitivity to issues of theory and value.
Relation of self and the world and introduction to the concerns of various social fields are characteristic of this phase.

Sphere: Wider community (heading toward global consciousness)
Aspects of intelligence: Introduction to the *fields* of knowledge and effort to connect domains of knowledge
Educational regimen: Develop thinking about broad-gauged moral and

political issues; encourage comprehensive learning while spurning precocious specialization

5. Early adulthood: Period of vocational and avocational choice. People in this phase need to make decisions about their personal style of life and to make some accommodation to the field.

> *Sphere:* Balancing of personal-familial and broad community concerns
> *Aspects of intelligence:* Heightening of specific intelligences as mobilized in particular domains and fields
> *Educational regimen:* Specialization, except for a cadre of individuals with proclivities toward general knowledge

6. Later stages. Oscillations between specialized and comprehensive concerns may occur in the period beyond early adulthood.

As should be clear, I envision a broad oscillation over these periods: Early childhood and adolescence feature more generalized concerns, while middle childhood and early adulthood call for relative specialization. Within these periods, I feel that there should also be a dynamic oscillation. That is, in each phase, there should be a period of relatively open-ended exploration at the beginning, followed by relative focus on more specific kinds of skill acquisition, then an increasingly broad and flexible deployment of these skills. The actual realization of this pendular swing will differ distinctly among individuals and fields, but the notion of a dialectical process seems to make good sense across stages and domains.

INFANCY

During the first two years of life, the infant's principal cognitive task—supported by his or her mother and father—is to discover the nature of the physical and the social worlds. The infant is well equipped in this task by virtue of natural sensory capacities and motor skills. As Piaget has amply documented in his studies of his own children, the young child constructs during this period a world that occupies space and unfolds over time, a world replete with objects that enter into causal relations and continue to exist even when they are no longer visible or tangible. Among these are those special objects called human beings, toward whom the child becomes attached and with whom he or she interacts, plays, and communicates.

The child's eagerness to look, listen, and manipulate can be thwarted, but with only a modicum of encouragement, the child occupies many hours of the day in coming to know the persons and the objects around him or her. Even at this early age, individual children may show certain biases or preferences, but in general, this is a time for maximal flexibility and absorption of information. Accordingly, from an educational perspective, the first two years of life mark a time in which the child should be encouraged to explore, with much support and encouragement but with relatively little direction or tutelage from others.

EARLY CHILDHOOD

Sometime after the first eighteen months of life, all normal children begin to interact with the world on a new and vital plane—that of symbols and symbol systems. Symbolization is appropriately considered to be the hallmark of human cognition. Many higher animals have rich knowledge gained by virtue of their sensory and motor systems, but only human beings live in a world where symbolic messages are the principal source of information and the principal vehicle of communication.

In a normally rich environment, children between the ages of two and seven gain a "first draft" familiarity with a raft of symbol systems. They learn to draw pictures and to interpret pictorial representations; they can read gestural messages and also communicate meanings and moods through movement of the whole body or parts of the body; they arrive at an understanding of numbers and can handle simple counting and arithmetical operations; they are able to sing songs, to appreciate many genres of music, and even to create little tunes on their own. Perhaps most dramatically, every normal child becomes a competent speaker of language in the first five to seven years of life. Such children can understand spoken language, express themselves fluently, listen to and appreciate stories and poems, and even create literary specimens on their own.

Just how this symbolic competence comes about is a long and complex story that is only beginning to be understood.[13] Undoubtedly, important forms of support are furnished by other individuals and by the media and institutions of the society, ranging from picture books to television and movies. Yet, just as the infant seems equipped "by nature" to master his or her physical and social world, so too the young child seems to be strongly inclined to become a "symbolic creature." Given a reasonable amount of exposure to stories and songs, to pictures and dances, to songs and numerical exercises, all normal children seem able to achieve the aforementioned "first draft mastery" by the time of their entry to school.

In light of this analysis, it would seem that the educational regimen for the preschool years ought to follow closely upon that recommended for infancy: rich exposure, ample support and encouragement, but relatively little direct tutelage. Indeed, there is informal evidence to suggest that rearing in a symbolically rich environment is the optimal way to ensure the achievement of a first-draft level of symbolic mastery.

Yet the full picture of this developmental phase is somewhat more complex. By the age of three, four, or five, children are distinguished from infants in at least two important ways. First of all, most children at this age are already demonstrating certain inclinations—some strong, others less potent but still detectable. Research at Project Spectrum has demonstrated that preschoolers may have different profiles of intelligences, exhibiting characteristic areas of strength and weakness.[14] It is thus possible at this age to undertake an instructional regimen that speaks to the child's emerging strength or, conversely, seeks to bolster weaknesses.

Some authorities would in fact recommend that education should already begin to take into account these characteristic profiles. My own view is that such an intervention would be premature in most cases. At this age, children learn so readily in different media, and their nervous systems are so "plastic," that it would be unfortunate to engage in early streaming. Only in those cases where a child exhibits an unusual gift—for example, prodigious musical talent—or a severe deficit—for example, marked problems in speaking or understanding—would I recommend an educational intervention addressed to one or two intelligences.

The second distinguishing feature at this age is that children become able to advance rapidly in a domain, provided that they receive strong structured instruction. Such a regimen breaks a desirable behavior down into small steps and features ample imitation, reward, and perhaps negative sanctions as well. A number of cultures, and some individuals within this culture, favor structured classes for preschoolers, with a strong focus on music, reading (or prereading), dance, drawing, or some other activity valued by the culture. There is no question that dramatic progress can be made in the preschool years if the resources of the society are placed at the service of such a skill area. Methods like the Suzuki Talent Education approach in Japan, organizations like the Institute for Human Potential in Philadelphia, and entire systems like that which undergirds Chinese kindergarten education have all documented remarkable "performances" by young children. In my own view, however, this early learning is purchased at too great a cost. To be sure, a given child may stand out in one or two realms, and with this additional "feeding," he or she may emerge as truly exceptional. However, losing the opportunity to sample a broad swath of materials and to engage in unstructured exploration of the gamut of symbol systems may well place the child at a later disadvantage, particularly in a culture that values innovation rather than "mere" realization of an earlier tradition.

MIDDLE CHILDHOOD

It is surely no coincidence that children throughout the world begin schooling "in earnest" at around the age of 7. In my own view, most children have by this age proceeded as far as they can in coming to know the physical and social worlds and the world of symbols through the use of their natural learning processes. For some purposes, this untutored absorption of patterns may be enough. Indeed, in certain nontechnological cultures, it already makes sense to consider these children as young adults.

In literate and technologically oriented cultures, however, children are still remote from the concerns and capacities of competent adults. They must become able to read and to master the various notational systems of the culture: mathematical ones, scientific ones, graphing techniques (like maps and charts), and perhaps other specialized notations such as those used in music, dance, or specific vocations. It is the job—and the genius—of schooling to transmit this notational knowledge in the succeeding decade or so.

Children of this age differ in other ways from their younger counterparts. Pre-schoolers enjoy free exploration, fantasy, and experimenting with boundaries; their speech favors metaphors, and they readily embrace synesthetic connections. By the age of 8 or 9, however, most children have become quite different creatures. During this middle childhood phase, they want to master the rules of their cultures and of its specific vocations and avocations. They want to use language precisely, not allusively; they want to draw pictures that are photographically realistic, not fanciful or abstract; and they expect a strict adherence to rules in dress, behavior, games, moral situations and other cultural activities, brooking little deviation.[15]

These shifts in mood and focus offer pedagogical opportunities. Certainly the first years of school are a time when it is important to master the notational systems of the culture. By and large, children cannot master these notations on their own; that is why school begins the world over at around the age of seven. It is now realized that this is a more difficult task than previously thought, because notational systems are not mastered in a knowledge vacuum. Rather, they must build upon and relate to the "common-sensical" understanding of domains that has been achieved in the preschool years.[16] Thus, written language must be related to oral language skills; musical notational skills to the child's intuitive or "figural" perception of music; scientific concepts to common-sense understanding of the physical world. Effecting this connection is a crucial challenge. Otherwise, the child may be burdened with two disembodied systems of knowledge, neither adequate on its own, rather than one integrated understanding.

Also, at this age, children are both ready and eager to master skills in specific areas. They want to be able to draw in perspective, to compose in rhyme, to perform chemical experiments, to write a computer program. It would be desirable, in the best of all possible worlds, if all children could be exposed to each of these activities. Human finitude, however, guarantees that such a goal is utopian. An attempt to train children in all art forms, all athletic forms, and all scholastic activities would be certain to achieve superficial knowledge at best and a breakdown in less happy circumstances.

It is for these reasons that I recommend some degree of specialization during middle childhood—roughly from the ages of 8 to 14. While children are mastering the crucial literacies, they should also have the opportunity to attain significant levels of skill in a small number of domains: perhaps, on the average, in one art form, one area of physical training, and one scholastic subject. Thus a 10-year-old might take music or art lessons, engage in one after-school sport, gymnastic, or dance activity, and have regular cumulative lessons in a subject like history, biology, or mathematics.

I favor this early specialization for two reasons. First of all, I think it is important that youngsters early on receive some demonstrations of what it means, on a day-to-day basis, to master a subject matter or a cluster of skills—to drill, practice, monitor one's own progress, reflect upon it, compare it to that of peers at work in the same domain. Bereft of this opportunity, children may be at a severe disadvantage later on, when it becomes essential to achieve mastery in a vocational area. The need to experience mastery first-hand is nowhere more acute than in contemporary America, where so many of the cultural signals favor the quick fix rather than the lengthy apprenticeship.

The second reason relates more directly to subsequent careers. In my own view, an individual is most likely to achieve a satisfactory life— to make a contribution to society and gain self-esteem—if he or she finds vocational and avocational niches which complement his or her own aptitudes.[17] If a child has had plenty of exposure to the range of domains and intelligences in early life, it seems reasonable that he or she should begin to narrow the focus to some extent in the years of middle childhood. At best, the child will then have already begun to gain needed expertise for later life. At the very least, he or she will at least have had the experience of gaining some competence and monitoring that process.

How should one go about choosing these areas? In a pluralistic and democratic society, the choice must be that of the child and the family, making use of whatever evidence and advice they care to secure from other sources. I believe that reasonable assessments of a child's strengths can already be made in middle childhood and that, therefore, the matching of child and discipline can be informed. It is possible, however, that even when these couplings are made at random, the results need not be unhappy. My observation in China, where such early matching is made in a relatively unsystematic manner, is that children become quite attached to those areas to which their attention has been directed and in which their skills have been assiduously cultivated.

Talking of the need to find some areas of specialization and the desirability of attaining clear skills through apprenticeships in these areas runs the risk of suggesting that this need be a serious and even painful experience. However, specialization need not resemble a diet of castor oil at all. An inspired teacher, a lively curriculum, a sympathetic mentor, a congenial group of peers can make the early stages of mastery a wonderful and enjoyable experience. In fact, I would urge that at the beginning of any specialization, there needs to be a period of relatively unstructured exploration, during which the possibilities of the medium or symbol system are widely sampled. More constrained training thereafter can build upon this initial survey and can be united with it as the incipient master begins to handle the medium in a more personal and more assured way.[18]

There is never a need to suggest a single right answer or a prescribed way to do things. Indeed, just because children at this age are likely to make these erroneous assumptions, it is important for their elders to stress a plurality of approaches and responses.

ADOLESCENCE

In contrast to the realm of the "middle-aged" child, the world of the adolescent bursts open in at least three directions. It becomes *wider*—the youth's arena is now the larger society, even the world, and not merely the family or the local community. It becomes *higher*—the youth is capable of more abstract forms of reasoning, of speculation, and of dealing with the hypothetical and the theoretical. It also becomes *deeper*—the youth probes more insistently into his or her own life, dealing with personal feelings, fears, and aspirations in a much fuller way than a few years before.

While Piaget's characterization of "formal operational" thought is no longer accepted in its original form, it is still useful to think of the adolescent as one who can deal comfortably with whole systems of thought.[19] The preadolescent is interested in facts, rules, and "sheer" skills, whereas the adolescent in our culture becomes more involved with values, with wide-reaching principles, with pregnant exceptions, and with the legitimacy of uses to which skills are put. The adolescent becomes newly concerned with the relations among different bodies of knowledge, different points of view, and different fields in which individuals can become productive. He or she tries to relate these issues to personal concerns—the emerging sense of identity and decisions about career, schooling, and personal relationships, including those with individuals of the other sex and of quite different backgrounds.

In our culture, adolescence is a time of "higher school"—high school and college. In many pockets of the world, developed as well as underdeveloped, this period is thought of as a time for increased specialization. In my view, this trend is ill-timed and unfortunate from a developmental perspective. Since people of this age are defining themselves with reference to a wider arena, I think it is particularly important that they remain (or become) exposed to a broad range of topics, themes, subject matter, value systems, and the like and that they be encouraged to engage in thinking that spans these topics.

Thus, in contrast to the years of middle childhood, and also in opposition to educational practices in many places, there should be a shift of emphasis toward more comprehensive knowledge during the ages 14 to 21. In old-fashioned terms, this would be viewed as a call for the liberal arts, but defined in such a way as to include scientific and technological subjects as well as the classics and the humanities. It is also a call for the inclusion within the curriculum of a consideration of ethical issues, current events, and communal and global problems. It recommends student involvement in rich and multifaceted projects, which encourage them to sample widely and to make diverse connections.[20]

Of course, whatever constraints applied to middle childhood do not mysteriously disappear in adolescence. If it is not possible in the years from 7 to 14 to survey the universe, it is obviously equally impossible to do so in the succeeding seven-year period. Nonetheless, I still call for a more catholic emphasis at this time, for three reasons. (1) Such a broadening of curricula and concerns is consistent with the youth's own information-processing propensity at this life stage. (2) It is imperative that every growing individual in the world have at least a modicum of exposure to the principal disciplines and concerns of our planet. (3) Youths in this phase are far more willing to transcend boundaries and to risk interdisciplinary thinking.

Nearly all educators are wrestling with the problem of just how to ensure such exposure. They search for short-cuts: core curricula, major and minor subjects, courses that convey concepts or ways of thinking rather than attempting to provide all information from the ground up. Some go so far as to recommend a definite list of facts and terms, which everyone who would be educated needs to know.[21]

Even if I had arrived at one, there would be no room here to introduce the universal curriculum for adolescence. Nor do I feel that every student needs to study every subject or the same set of subjects as a matter of course. Rather, what I want to urge is that the third seven-year period of life, like the first, be a time when relatively wide-ranging exploration is encouraged and narrow specialization is put aside or suspended, at least for most students, and that activities that synthesize, draw connections, or link school knowledge to extrascholastic concerns be encouraged and even mandated.

FOLLOWING ADOLESCENCE

In years past, it was customary to conclude educational (and developmental) treatments with the termination of adolescence (or roughly the end of college). This strategy makes little sense today. It is now understood that intellectual development, like personal and emotional development, continues through life. It is also beginning to be appreciated that education continues for many years, whether or not it is carried out full-time on a college campus.

Recommendations for education after college are even more speculative than those offered before, particularly since there has been so little research on older populations. However, I view post-college life as the next logical time for specialization, for mastering of materials that are crucial to an individual's vocation. Indeed, having passed through a period of relatively unfettered exploration, the novice adult is now in a favorable position to begin more focused study.

It is painfully clear, however, that many of the most crucial problems in the world, by their very nature, will elude the efforts of the narrow specialist. There must be people with general skills, with broad interests and knowledge, who can help to conceptualize and approach vexing problems—intellectual CEOs, if you will. Some such generalists may well emerge from the ranks of the discipline-trained, but my own view is that such individuals ought to be trained specially. I would recommend that those college students who display special gifts for synthetic thought and for absorbing large bodies of knowledge be encouraged to continue such broad-based studies for as long as possible. Perhaps, indeed, they can be "apprenticed to the generalist," just as their peers are apprenticed to specialists.

The rest of the people need not complete their learning with increasingly precious specialization. By the age of 30 or so, most educated individuals will have been well launched in professional careers, be it business, law, medicine, teaching, or some other of the professions. From then on, I would hope that many individuals would continue to follow the pendular swing that I have described—opening up their worlds to broader study and thinking for a time, then repairing for a time of more specialized study, and then back again. During periods of specialization, they might continue to harbor "margins" where they can engage in the kind of untrammeled exploration that so often precedes significant innovations.

CONCLUSION: TOWARD THE OPTIMAL BALANCE

Education has always been a struggle against human finitudes: limitations of mental ability or information-processing capacity, impoverishment of motivation and will, and, dwarfing all, the brevity of human existence. Our civilization as a whole spawns ever-expanding bodies of knowledge, but ever-smaller percentages of it can be accessed by any specific individual. Such are the bitter costs of the knowledge explosion.

Some thinkers dream that heuristics—mechanical, psychological, or medicinal—will once again condense or summarize human knowledge or, alternatively, will expand the human mind so that it can connect and master all. Short of such occurrences, however, it becomes necessary to consider the educational options that are currently available.

In this chapter, having surveyed trends in contemporary cognitive-scientific work as well as alternatives in current educational practice, I have proposed a scheme of educational development. For each of five major stages of human development, I suggest certain principal concerns and themes and recommend a particular educational regimen. It has not been possible to go into detail about each particular discipline, field, or vocation, but one can expect, on the basis of recent research, that the terrain will differ across areas and that what works well in one discipline may prove inappropriate or even counterproductive in another. Thus, greater specialization renders attempts at uniform curricula increasingly misguided.

In addition to recommending educational regimens at each stage, I have also urged a more general tack which can be implemented across stages: beginning with a general and relatively unstructured exploration of materials and media; following upon this a period of more rigorous and circumscribed drill and skill acquisition; and culminating in a concluding phase, where the developed skills are yoked to wider or to more personal concerns.

In making these recommendations, I am clearly putting froth my own value judgment. American society favors the cultivation of skills that can be used in imaginative and creative ways. A contrasting model exists in a country like China, where the ideal has been the faithful re-enactment of performances that have been perfected and valued over the long haul. In following such a model, one begins with the careful cultivation, through imitation and memory, of the procedures evolved over time within the culture. Only at the tail end of development does there even arise a possibility of significant departures from current and past practices. From the perspective of Western cultural judgments, such departures as are tolerated turn out to be quite modest.

Quite specific suggestions have been made without hesitation in this chapter, but a closing cautionary note is in order. Psychology, that most elusive of sciences, is scarcely a century old; cognitive science and neuroscience are inventions of the latter half of the twentieth century; and educational science is still but a glint in the eye of even the most optimistic speculative thinkers. Any pretense that the current scheme has been "validated by research" must be specifically disavowed. Yet one lesson gleaned from contemporary philosophy of science is that programs or principles never simply emerge from the data: It is necessary to conceptualize a program, to propose a theory, to see how it meshes with or reorganizes existing data, and then to devise experiments to test the power of the scheme. It is in this spirit—in the recognition that a simple, or indeed even a simplistic, scheme may stimulate better thinking—that the present chapter has been formulated.

NOTES

The research described in this paper was supported in part by grants from the Rockefeller Brothers Fund, the Rockefeller Foundation, and the Spencer Foundation.

1. A. Bloom, *The Closing of the American Mind* (New York: Simon and Schuster, 1987).

2. Ernest Boyer, *College: The Undergraduate Experience* (New York: Harper and Row, 1986).

3. E. D. Hirsch, *Cultural Literacy* (Boston: Houghton Mifflin, 1987).

4. N. Block and G. Dworkin, *The IQ Controversy* (New York: Pantheon Books, 1976).

5. H. Gardner, *Frames of Mind: The Theory of Multiple Intelligences* (New York: Basic Books, 1983).

6. J. A. Fodor, The Modularity of Mind (Cambridge, Mass.: MIT Press, 1983); U. Neisser, "General Academic, and Artificial Intelligence," in L. Resnick, ed., *The Nature of Intelligence* (Hillsdale, N.J.: Lawrence Erlbaum Associates, 1976); R. Sternberg, *Beyond IQ* (New York: Cambridge University Press, 1985).

7. U. Maklus, D. H. Feldman, and H. Gardner, "Dimensions of Mind in Early Childhood," in A. Pelligrini, ed., *The Psychological Basis of Early Childhood* (Chichester, U.K.: Wiley, 1987); C. Sherman, H. Gardner, and D. H. Feldman, "A Pluralistic View of Early Assessment: The Project Spectrum Approach," *Theory into Practice* 27 (1) 1988.

8. M. Csikszentmihalyi "Society, Culture, and Person: A Systems View of Creativity," in R. Sternberg, ed., *The Nature of Creativity* (New York: Cambridge University Press, 1988); D. Feldman, "Creativity: Dreams, Insights and Transformations," in R. Sternberg, ed., *The Nature of Creativity* (New York: Cambridge University Press, in press); H. Gardner, "Creative Lives, Creative Works," in R. Sternberg, ed., *The Nature of Creativity* (New York: Cambridge University Press, in press).

9. E. A. Feigenbaum, B. G. Buchanan, and J. Lederberg, "On Generality and Problem Solving: A Case Study Using the DENDRAL Program," in B. Meltzer and D. Michie, eds., *Machine Intelligence*, vol. 6 (Edinburgh, U.K.: Edinburgh University Press, 1971).

10. M. Minsky, *The Society of Mind* (New York: Simon and Schuster, 1987).

11. H. Gardner, *The Mind's New Science: A History of the Cognitive Revolution* (New York: Basic Books, 1985).

12. Fodor, op. cit.

13. H. Gardner and D. Wolf, "Waves and streams of symbolization," in D. R. Rogers and J. A. Sloboda, eds., *The Acquisition of Symbolic Skills* (London: Plenum Press, 1983);

H. Gardner and D. Wolf, "The Symbolic Products of Early Childhood," in D. Goerlitz and J. Wohlwill, eds., *Play, Curiosity and Exploration* (Hillsdale, N.J.: L. Erlbaum, 1987); D. Wolf and H. Gardner, eds., "Early Symbolization," *New Directions for Child Development 3*, 1979.

14. Sherman, Gardner, and Feldman, op. cit.

15. H. Gardner and E. Winner, "First Intimations of Artistry," in S. Strauss, ed., *U-Shaped Behavioral Development* (New York: Academic Press, 1982).

16. J. Bamberger, "Revisiting Children's Drawings of Simple Rhythms: A Function for Reflection in Action," in S. Strauss, ed., *U-Shaped Behavioral Growth* (New York: Academic Press, 1982); L. Vygostsky, *Mind in Society* (Cambridge, Mass.: Harvard University Press, 1978).

17. J. Walters and H. Gardner, "The Crystallizing Experience: Discovery of an Intellectual Gift," in R. Sternberg and J. Davidson, eds., *Conceptions of Giftedness* (New York: Cambridge University Press, 1986).

18. B. Bloom and L. Sosniak, "Talent Development vs. Schooling," *Educational Leadership*, Nov. 1981, pp. 86–94.

19. H. Gardner, *Developmental Psychology*, 2nd ed. (Boston: Little, Brown, 1982).

20. H. Gardner, "An Individual Centered Curriculum," in David Imag, ed., *The Schools We've Got, The Schools We Need* (American Association of Colleges for Teacher Education, 1987).

21. Hirsch, op. cit.

CHAPTER 8

Teaching Alone, Learning Together: Needed Agendas for the New Reforms

LEE S. SHULMAN

Stanford University

A skeptic approached the great rabbi Hillel and asked that sage to teach him the full message of the Torah in a single proposition. Hillel responded, "Do not do unto your fellow man what you would not have him do unto you. That is the essence; the rest is commentary." There is a parallel proposition I now suggest as the essential principle of educational reform. Do not do unto teachers what you would not have teachers do unto students. This is the essence; the rest (which I shall not, alas, spare you) is commentary.[1]

The theme of this volume, directing reforms to issues that count, echoes the recurrent calls for reform of the nation's schools and of the preparation of its teachers. Those reform agendas have many authors and many locations, but they are remarkably similar in many of their visions, if often mixed in their motives.

Tracing back the discussion of quality education to first principles, one is bound to examine, not issues of schooling or even teaching, but of learning. The argument of this chapter is that twenty-first century conceptions of learning now coexist with nineteenth-century conceptions of teaching. What is held to be true of learning in students must, of necessity, hold true for teaching and teachers. Most reform agendas rest on the assumption that teachers are capable of learning, both in programs of formal preservice preparation and in the course of an extended professional career, and that teachers can improve with experience. Changes are needed in classrooms to render them more powerful environments for student learning, and similar changes are needed in classrooms and schools to make them suitable settings for teacher learning. Teacher collegiality and collaboration are not important merely for the improvement of morale and teacher satisfaction (which always sounds like a lame argument in favor of satisfied teachers, regardless of whether they succeed in teaching kids); they are absolutely necessary if teaching is to be of the highest order and thus compatible with the standards of excellence demanded by the recent reforms. Collegiality and collaboration are also needed to ensure that teachers benefit from their experiences and continue to grow during their careers. However, few accomplishments are as hellishly difficult as learning from experience. Both teaching and learning to teach are remarkably challenging tasks.

THE REFORMS AND THEIR ASSUMPTIONS

In looking at the new reforms, one must examine the assumptions that undergird them and the assertions they share. The reforms that have been proposed since 1982, whether by the Excellence Commission, the Carnegie Task Force on the Teaching Profession, the Holmes Group, or the many state advisory groups, generally share certain key assumptions and characteristics. These can be organized under three headings: assumptions about teachers, about learners, and about schools and schooling.

Learners

The "first wave" of reform called for much greater emphasis on the achievement of excellence for all students, and "excellence" increasingly took on a more "classical" character. The generally improving results of the National Assessment of Educational Progress (NAEP) testing around the country and the apparent reversal of the decline in SAT scores have quieted the call to go back to basics, at least basics as defined by the fairly simple fundamentals of reading, computation, and writing. However, the NAEP results also reported that the American learner is incapable of employing higher-order thinking, that his or her problem-solving abilities are stunted and critical thinking skills untapped. Moreover, this learner is ignorant of the most basic ideas of Western civilization and is unenlightened by the culture's most central texts. These texts include works of the great philosophers, works of great writers from Homer and the Bard to Sinclair Lewis and Ralph Ellison, and fundamental tracts on the formation of U.S. government, such as the Federalist Papers and the Constitution.

In a tone reminiscent of earlier calls for reform (such as that of Joseph Mayer Rice in the 1890s), reformers urge a reduction of rote learning and uninspired teaching in the schools and a quest for the higher-order thinking and reasoning that ought to characterize American classrooms. Dumbed-down curricula are to be shunned; dumbed-down teachers are to be unemployed. Moreover, in recent critical reviews of the research on Title I programs for disadvantaged students, it was concluded that principles of excellence are not limited in their application to the most advantaged learners. The children of the poor have been frequently mistaught in programs that overemphasized remedial and basic-skills orientations, thus depriving them of the stimulation of needed schoolwork on problem solving and reasoning. Thus, emphasis on higher-order goals is the strategy of choice for the achievement of equity as well as for the promotion of excellence.

This conception of learning as higher order, constructive, and inventive is not all that new, yet for the first time it has a substantial body of psychological and anthropological research to support it. The view of the learner as someone who can discover new principles through active involvement with the materials and media of instruction is predicated on fairly recent concepts of how meanings are constructed in the learning process. Those views will be examined shortly, after first focusing on the reform assumptions associated with that other indispensable partner in the educational process, the teacher.

Teachers

Without question, teachers and the professionalization of teaching are at the heart of the recent "second wave" of reform initiatives. The first assumption is that teaching is difficult. It requires substantial content preparation, so a minimum standard of a bachelor's degree in a discipline is called for—even for elementary school teachers, who have not traditionally been viewed as content specialists. Teaching requires additional preparation in pedagogy, perhaps including a master's degree as a minimum standard. Teaching requires a serious period of supervised internship or residency. Most of all, teaching requires the definition and application of rigorous standards for entry into the occupation and progress through it. The current standards (or lack thereof) will simply not do.[2]

These reform documents link the vision of a profession peopled by more talented and better prepared practitioners to a new image of schools as organizations and of a teaching career. The schools, reformers say, should be organized to provide far greater opportunities for leadership and differentiation of role for the gifted veteran teacher. The career of a teacher should develop alternative trajectories that would permit the able pedagogue to remain in the classroom for substantial periods, yet also perform other roles as teacher educator, mentor, curriculum developer, university faculty member, and the like. A greater variety of teaching roles should be defined, as befits the variations in both degrees of preparation and advanced specialization that could become commonplace.

These reform recommendations are rooted in several fundamental assumptions. Teachers can learn to teach. Moreover, they can become better teachers as they learn from experience. They are capable of reflecting on their own practice (both in action and in reenactment), thereby discerning the proper ways to adapt their thoughts and actions to future challenges. Yet the vision of learning to teach, of improving with experience through the employment of strategies of reflection and review, is predicated on the availability of that most precious and rare commodity for a teacher—time. This includes both time for individual reflection and for collective deliberation, for thinking alone and for being thoughtful with others. Thus, there is a need to reorganize schools to become places where the opportunities for thought, the organizational characteristics that promote thinking, and an institutional reward system can work jointly to make learning from experience (and teaching by the experienced) commonplace.

Empowerment and Responsibility

The word that is bandied about most frequently in discussing the needed reforms of teaching is "empowerment." It is an unfortunate choice of terms, because it conjures up visions of a struggle for control over the schools. Empowerment in my terms is not expressed in collective bargaining victories or in wresting authority from principals and distributing it among juntas of teachers. The empowerment needed in the current reforms is a complex phenomenon that would enable teachers to exercise the talents and capacities that the new conceptions of teaching require.

Teacher empowerment in this sense is an empowerment of *mind*, of *spirit*, of *status*, and of *role*. The teacher is enabled by a knowledge base—the knowledge and skill needed to be effective in teaching; by commitment—the passion, motivation, and ethical norms necessary to persevere responsibly in the face of discouragement and difficulty; by the status of a professional—the standing associated with a trusted and respected individual whose functions are viewed by the society as absolutely essential for its survival; and by his or her formal institutional roles—ascribed functions within organizations that permit the fruits of mind, spirit, and status to be exercised productively in the education of students.

Without such elaborations, the concept of empowerment is empty and even dangerous. Societies should not grant power to those who do not have the intellectual commitments and moral capacities to wield it justly. Teacher empowerment is justified when it affords teachers the autonomy needed to perform their tasks effectively and the freedom required to engage students productively.

The Schools

With this new image of a setting and a career path for teachers, new images of schools emerge. These tend to take on two competing forms. Those that derive from the first wave of reform emphasize the model of "effective schools." They identify leadership with charismatic and powerful administrators, who help create a climate of shared high academic expectations for all students and a collective commitment to academic values and activities. However, in the more recent teacher-centered reform conceptions of groups such as Holmes and Carnegie, quite a different view emerges. Teachers are now seen as exercising substantial leadership at the building level. Schools are asked to become more like our best corporations, employing modern methods of management to decentralize authority, to make important decisions where the street-level bureaucrats reside. Leadership is not monopolized by administrators but is shared with teachers.

I began with the argument that we should guide the reform of teaching and schooling with a variation on the principle of Hillel. We should not treat teachers in a manner inconsistent with the ways in which we treat students. Teaching must be viewed as resting on a base of learning, thinking, and reasoning quite similar to the standards of student learning, thinking, and reasoning that have inspired the first wave of reform.

In the next section, I describe the current conceptions of learning and teaching that underlie efforts to reform the conditions for student learning. These efforts rest on ideas about human rationality and its enhancement that emphasize the centrality of higher-order reasoning and its fostering in the real world. The next section examines the extent to which these notions of rationality and deliberation also characterize valued conceptions of schooling in a democratic society, as reflected in the writings of John Dewey. Then follows a discussion of the ways in which the requirements for student learning are also requirements for teacher development, as the parallels between the conditions for learning and the conditions for teaching are reviewed.

VARIETIES OF RATIONALITY: CONCEPTIONS OF LEARNING AND TEACHING

Several years ago I published a paper with Neil Carey,[3] in which we explored the ways in which human learning had been represented by philosophers and psychologists. We argued that there were at least four ways in which philosophers and psychologists had attempted to explain why human beings reason and act as they do. They are all responses to Aristotle's claim that man is a rational animal. These accounts can be summarized in the following assertions:

- Humans are rational; they think and act in a manner consistent with their goals, their self-interest, and their reinforcement histories. To induce them to behave in a given way, make the desired behavior clear to them and make it worth their while to engage in it.
- Humans are irrational; they are driven by motives and needs of which they are generally unconscious and over which they exercise little control. To induce them to change, help them grasp and come to terms with their underlying motives and fears, so that they can exercise more direct control over their intentions and actions.
- Humans are limited in their rationality; they can make sense of only a small piece of the world at a time, and they strive to act reasonably with respect to their limited grasp of facts and alternatives. They must therefore construct conceptions or definitions of situations rather than passively accept what is presented to them. To induce them to change, engage them in active problem solving and judgment; don't just tell them what to do.
- Humans are rational only when acting together; since individual reason is so limited, men and women find opportunities to work jointly on important problems, achieving through joint effort what individual reason and capacity could never accomplish. To induce them to change, develop ways in which they can engage in the change process jointly with peers.

The first principle (man as rational) was consistent with claims that individuals learned to do those things for which they were rewarded, learned best through imitation, drill, and practice, and generally learned to act in ways consistent with their self-interest as they understood it. Thus, schools were defined as places where the contents of a culture were arranged and transmitted, where pupils were evaluated on the basis of their mastery of the contents of that culture, and where teachers were most likely to improve when they could receive rewards based on their merit—which was defined as their success in transmitting the cultural capital to their students.

According to the second principle (man as an irrational animal), the human being's sources of inconsistency and anxieties were of greatest moment. Why did people so often appear to act against their own self-interest? Why did they fail to feel motivated toward activities that they sincerely felt were desirable? Why did they misunderstand the "plain meaning" of a communication and distort their interpretation in such outlandish ways? Applied to schools, these principles called upon educators to engage the emotional and affective commitments of teachers and students—to influence their unconscious motives as they responded to the goals and processes of schools as sites for human interaction and passions.

The third principle (man as boundedly rational) held that human beings were always constructing meanings because they had no other way to keep track of everything that was going on around them. Individuals had no choice but to simplify the world around them in terms of some principles, the most powerful of which was that new learnings must be rendered consistent with older knowledge and belief. Thus, children sitting in classrooms always reinterpreted whatever teachers said to them, the better to coordinate what they were learning with what they had learned earlier. Teachers were also forced to simplify their perceptions and understandings of students; it was simply impossible to be accurate in thinking about all 160 or more students that an average high school teacher saw in a day. Simplifications should not be read as distortions, but as unavoidable adaptations.

Thus, young children learning new methods of calculation in primary arithmetic classes regularly adapt the method they are taught by the teacher and invent new algorithms of their own. High school students learning about natural selection in a biology course often manage to leave the course continuing to believe that evolution involves the transmission of acquired characteristics, even though teachers never teach them that. Teachers adopt modes of instruction that reduce the complexity and unpredictability of classroom life, especially when they feel relatively unfamiliar with the content being taught.[4]

The fourth principle, called *collective rationality*, argues that the solution to the limitations of individual rationality does not lie exclusively in the construction or invention of individual solutions. On the contrary, human beings regularly accomplish tasks whose complexity exceeds the limitations of individual information processing, by collaborating on the different aspects of an otherwise overwhelming task. For an individual, piloting a Boeing 747 is impossible; for a three-person crew, it is straightforward. However, the crew does not work in isolation; they are dependent on large numbers of mechanics and other service personnel, cabin attendants, air traffic controllers, pilot educators who keep crewmembers abreast of the latest developments and sharp in their responses to problem situations, and many others. From the prosaic demands of repairing a flat tire on a dark highway ("If you'll just hold that flashlight while I . . .") to the complex requirements of flying a modern passenger jet, collective rationality is the most frequent human response to the challenges of coping with otherwise impossible tasks.

The four conceptions of rationality, while posed as alternatives, are not necessarily incompatible. There are aspects of each that can be invoked appropriately to characterize different facets of human activity, or different settings in which human beings employ reason and emotion in the pursuit of their goals. Nevertheless, I write this chapter from a particular point of view. The demands being made on teachers call for them to act critically, decisively, and self-correctively under conditions that do not promote or support those processes. The solution to the dilemma is inherent in the principles of collective rationality.

It is now understood that teaching is, in many ways, an impossible job in which to succeed as an individual. The demands are too great, the range of talents required is too broad and varied, the requirements for learning from experience exceed the capacities of an individual learner. Nevertheless, the jobs of both students and of teachers are defined in ways that treat collectivization as odd or sinful. When students work together on an assignment or test, they are often accused of cheating. Teachers who seek to collaborate are provided with few facilitating structures (scheduling changes to encourage joint planning, or team teaching arrangements) and even fewer incentives.

Ironically, the lessons of recent research attest to the virtues of collective learning and teaching. They testify to the ways in which both students and teachers can come to achieve more and learn more effectively when the artificial barriers that limit collaboration are removed. It is no accident that the "real world" of work and play treats collaboration as a norm. Professionals as diverse as nurses, lawyers, newspaper reporters, and football players meet together daily in working groups to review their responsibilities, check their progress, solicit ideas for next steps, and design ways to work together on tough problems. Their workplaces are built around the recognition of the necessity for such meetings. Neither hospital nurses' stations nor newspaper staff meeting rooms are organizational accidents. However, schools are not organized like the world outside them; the individual student and the individual teacher are the units around which the structures of classrooms and schools are built. Opportunities for collective work are afterthoughts.

In her presidential address to the American Educational Research Association, Lauren Resnick summarized the ways in which school learning and learning in the real world are different.[5] Since learning in schools appears to be far less successful than its out-of-school counterpart, this contrast can be useful for understanding how to make schools more effective places. Resnick argues that there are four general characteristics that distinguish in-school from out-of-school learning.

1. Learning in the world is cooperative; learning in schools is pursued alone.
2. Learning in schools uses "pure mentation." Learning in the outside world uses tools—the efforts needed to complete a task are shared with others who have invented cognitive tools such as "ready reckoners," statistical tables, or computer simulations. Using tools devised by others is not cheating; it is acting intelligently.

3. In schools, the learners reason about and with symbols; outside of school they reason about real things. In the real world, therefore, you rarely see people make the kinds of really stupid mistakes regularly made by youngsters learning arithmetic, who will often, in manipulating symbols, make errors that are orders of magnitude off target.
4. Learning in school is directed at generalization; outside of school, learning is usually situation-specific.

Resnick concludes that school itself should perhaps become more like life. In itself this is no great innovation—Dewey argued for a compatibility between life and school nearly a century ago, as did educational thinkers both before and after him—but Resnick can bring new evidence in support of her recommendations. She reviewed dozens of programs that claim to teach youngsters to think critically or engage in better problem solving. The few such programs that could present evidence of success tended to share five characteristics. Successful critical thinking programs:

1. Involve socially shared intellectual work.
2. Are organized around mutual accomplishment of tasks, so that elements of the skills to be learned take on meaning in the context of the whole.
3. Make usually hidden processes overt and thus subject to explicit observation and commentary by participants and teacher.
4. Permit skills to be built up bit by bit, yet allow participatory roles even for the relatively unskilled. They thus enable learning by social sharing.
5. Are organized around particular bodies of knowledge and interpretation rather than general abilities.

Thus, contemporary thinking about learning borrows from two recent traditions: humans as boundedly rational and humans as collectively rational. The more complex and higher-order the learning, the more it depends on reflection—looking back—and collaboration—working with others. For example, studies of expertise in the solving of physics problems indicated that the most able problem solvers did not learn by doing; they did not learn from simply practicing the solving of physics problems. They learned from looking back on the problems they had solved (or, less frequently, had failed to solve) and learned by reflecting on what they had done to solve them. They learned, not by doing, but by thinking about what they were doing.[6]

Resnick[7] has commented on the scenario that opens a major section of the Carnegie Task Force's *A Nation Prepared*, describing a school in which students are working together in small groups on quite difficult problems, with the assistance of teachers. She observed that, in the light of her review of critical thinking programs, the Carnegie description could be characterized as that a "critical thinking school."

The real world is regularly organized to provide opportunities for such planning, reflection, and review in the company of others. The schools are not. Thus, Tamir[8] has reported that a most frequent error of laboratory teaching in biology, chemistry, and physics is to provide sufficient time for students to conduct the assigned experiment but insufficient opportunity for discussion of the meaning of the experiment and the observations it made possible. Learning in a science laboratory occurs when a group is looking back on the experiments and discussing what they mean, why not all results yielded the same values, and how the experiment related to other topics that had gone before.

If learning to learn requires the establishment of such conditions, then learning to teach will also demand them. Learning to teach is enormously complex, a clear example of learning the highest-order forms of knowledge, skill, and problem solving. If the conditions described above are needed for student learning to occur, they are certainly needed to foster learning and development among teachers. The preconditions for school reform, therefore, are to create circumstances in schools that permit and support teacher learning, and it is likely that teacher learning will require conditions quite similar to those needed for student learning.

Before proceeding to a discussion of the needed circumstances for learning from experience within the teaching profession, I wish to consider one other aspect of the current emphasis on the importance of higher-order thinking, problem solving, and critical reasoning. Resnick points out in her address that a democratic society must place particular emphasis on students learning to reason, to consider alternative views. This is a perspective on the relationship between learning in schools and living in a democratic society that was strongly emphasized by John Dewey in his writings on teaching and schooling.

THE SEARCH FOR UNDERSTANDING: A DEWEYAN PERSPECTIVE

In the preface to his masterful *Experience and Education*,[9] Dewey presents his analysis of the tyranny of dualisms, the "either/or" arguments against which he railed for so many years. I do not wish to focus on the dualisms themselves, or any particular dualism, in this chapter. Instead, I will look more closely at the underlying psychology and philosophy that led Dewey to his dialectical style of analysis.

Dewey presented an idea of education that rooted the pursuit of truth in the creation of dialogue. His argument against "either/or" thinking was also, somewhat ironically, an assertion about its inevitability.

Powerful ideas always generate refutations; theses breed antitheses; stipulations bring about their contradictions. People state their positions by uttering straightforward propositions. Politics is not unique in its dependence on the slogan; the simple claim guides us all.

Because such claims are intrinsically incomplete relative to the complexities of the world whose actors they purport to guide, they will inevitably stimulate counterclaims rooted in recognition of the missing ideas. Thus, calls for greater freedom and self-direction in learning predictably elicit pleas for teaching the young the eternal verities of our culture.

Dewey argued that the reason why human discourse is characterized by controversy is that we are intrinsically incapable of uttering the whole truth and nothing but the truth. Claimed truth is inherently incomplete. Assertions can never do justice to the full complexity of the world, any more than perceptions and cognitions can grasp the full richness of any setting. For this reason, controversies are both inevitable and desirable. Individuals or groups will sense the incompleteness of any argument and oppose it with an alternative that builds on what was left out of the original position, thus advancing the overall deliberation and deepening the analysis.

Thus, arguments for more content in teaching predictably elicit calls for more critical processes. Arguments for excellence breed counterarguments for equity. A case for basic skills is refuted with a case for higher-order reasoning. "Either/or" thinking is at the very heart of social and intellectual discourse, because all arguments are intrinsically incomplete.

What, then, is knowledge? Since what is held to be true by any individual or group is intrinsically incomplete, knowledge is a process of continuous debate, dialogue, deliberation, and reasoning. Reason is a process of constantly comparing incomplete, insufficient views. "Either/or" thinking is therefore always the starting point for deliberation. If the achievement of knowledge is a good thing, then a good society is one that permits (even fosters) the competition between different views. The more different a view, the more likely it is to contain a seed of truth absent in prevailing notions. Freedom of speech and the encouragement of open dialogue and debate are therefore not only political virtues; they are epistemological ones. If the survival and flourishing of a society is dependent, in large measure, on its capacity to seek out what is warranted, then its openness to new and different ideas is essential.

What must schools look like in such a society? They should be microcosms for the kinds of debate and deliberation needed by the society more generally. They must be organized to permit and encourage competition among ideas. They must discourage doctrine and dogma. Both the selection of content and the organization of interactions within the classroom should reflect the collaborative/competitive conception of the search for knowledge.

For Dewey, this image of an inquiring society defined the character of learning, of teaching, of classroom organization, and of schooling. As Larry Cuban,[10] among others, has repeatedly stated, the image has more often been fulfilled in dreams than in reality, and there are probably understandable reasons for that. However, the Deweyan quest must proceed if reformers are serious about these "higher-order" educational goals. Yet it is unlikely to be accomplished without creating conditions in which teachers can learn as readily as do their students.[11] Teacher learning in schools does not occur in formal classes and through a formal curriculum, as does student learning. Teacher learning depends on the possibility of learning from experience. What is needed to foster such learning? An examination of the conditions for experiential learning is a prerequisite for addressing that question adequately.

LEARNING FROM EXPERIENCE

The great challenge for teaching and teacher education is the demand that teachers learn from their teaching experiences. How does teaching become learning for the teacher? Teaching, like learning, is an act of construction, simplification, and invention, but often without an adequate opportunity to learn from the experience.

What is required for someone to learn from experience? The general paradigm for such learning is simple. An individual or group engages in a particular action for the sake of achieving a desired end. A pitcher throws a particular pitch to strike out a given batter. A woman invests in a given stock to increase her net worth. A doctor prescribes a specific treatment to alleviate a patient's pain. A teacher changes a child's seat to reduce the frequency of classroom disruption. When the desired end is achieved, people learn to use the action again under similar circumstances. When the end is not achieved, or a less desirable condition arises, people learn to avoid that action or class of actions.

The general paradigm of experiential learning is thus a fairly simple and quite rational one. Unfortunately, both the limits of human rationality and the complexities of the real world render that apparently simple model badly flawed in practice. There have been substantial programs of research demonstrating why human beings are such abysmal experiential learners.[12] I shall spare my readers yet another review of the literature and instead tell two stories that illustrate why learning from teaching experience is so difficult. They demonstrate respectively that the two most obvious requirements—knowing what you did and accurately identifying the consequences of what you did—can be hard to achieve.

Cases of Socratic Teaching

During the past summer my research group ran a two-week field test of new exercises for the assessment of teaching, designed in conjunction with the development of a National Board for Professional Teaching Standards.[13] Forty teachers, twenty elementary and twenty secondary level, came to Stanford for four days each to participate in the field test. A local elementary school was transformed into an assessment center, and each teacher participated in ten different exercises, ranging in length from forty-five minutes to three hours.

One of the exercises was "Teaching a Familiar Lesson," in which a candidate was to send ahead to the center a lesson plan from which he or she had already taught. The candidate was first interviewed for about thirty minutes over the lesson plan. The interviewer asked the teacher to provide a rationale for the selection of the lesson, to discuss how this particular lesson fit into a larger unit, and how that unit related to a larger curriculum. The teacher was asked to describe how the lesson would be taught, what assumptions were being made about the students, and how he or she would know if the lesson were going well.

After completing the interview, six youngsters were brought into the classroom to serve as pupils. They were instructed to act naturally, to avoid creating discipline problems, but otherwise to participate in the class as they normally would. Each teacher was given about fifteen minutes to become acquainted with the pupils in any way he or she desired, and then the balance of an hour to teach the lesson. The full lesson was videotaped for later analysis. At the conclusion of the lesson, the pupils were debriefed by one of the observers, while the original interviewer conducted a "reflection interview" with the candidate to discuss how things had gone, what had been learned about each of the individual pupils, and what he or she would do differently if given an opportunity to teach this lesson again under similar conditions. The videotape was not reviewed with the teacher.

I remember quite vividly one candidate whom I interviewed. He described a lesson he would be teaching on an aspect of the U.S. Constitution. When asked how he would conduct the lesson, he replied that he would teach Socratically, asking the students questions and following up their answers with more penetrating follow-up questions. Knowing how hard it is to teach Socratically, I awaited the lesson expectantly. The candidate opened the lesson with a question for the students. The students remained silent. After waiting no more than a couple of seconds, the teacher proceeded to answer his own question. He then asked another question. Student silence was again interrupted by the teacher's answer to his own question, and so it proceeded for nearly thirty minutes, with hardly a variation. The Socratic dialogue had become a Socratic monologue! The students had realized quite early that a little patience on their parts—an exhibition of student wait-time, if you will—would relieve them of any obligation to respond.

When we sat down together for the reflection interview, I asked the candidate to describe the lesson he had just taught. Without hesitation, he reported that he had conducted the lesson Socratically; he appeared to have no idea that the students had deferred to him to provide both questions and answers. He apparently had no idea that there was a discrepancy between his intention to teach in a particular manner and the reality of his performance.

I had had a similar experience nearly twenty years earlier while teaching a seminar on teaching to the members of a medical school faculty. A young pediatrician had volunteered to videotape his bedside teaching to a group of four medical students. He too had characterized his plan as Socratic teaching, but he had conducted a series of Socratic monologues at the bedsides of the youthful patients, responding energetically to the encouraging yet silent nods of his medical students. When we viewed the videotape in the faculty seminar a week later, he had truly been in a state of shock as it slowly dawned upon him that the students themselves had almost never contributed to the discussion.

I offer these brief "cases" to illustrate a basic principle of teaching performance. The act of teaching itself demands so much attention and energy that it is difficult for any teacher, especially when under some pressure, to monitor his or her own performance with great accuracy. Distortions of perception occur, especially in the direction of consistency with prior expectations. Yet if it is difficult to depend on one's own perceptions or recollections of what was actually done, then the first precondition for learning from experience becomes problematic. We may not be able to discern what we have actually done without the assistance of colleagues who can help us observe or monitor our own teaching behavior or a system of recordkeeping or reporting that transcends the limitations of our own subjective recollections. Since a teacher cannot be observed by someone else all the time, he or she must learn to use the feedback of colleagues, videotaping with supervised review, and reports from students, among other direct and vicarious strategies, to improve the calibration of his or her own observations and recollections.

The Case of the Unanticipated Vectors

If having a clear grasp of what one has actually done can be a problem, so can discerning the *consequences* of one's actions. In the next vignette, it becomes clear that establishing what students have learned from one's teaching—that is, knowing the consequences of one's actions—is not always particularly easy.

My teacher education course has designed an assignment in which students engage in reciprocal observation and interviewing. Teacher education candidates pair off and interview one another about a lesson that will be conducted in the immediate future. In each interview they are expected to describe the goal of the lesson—the concepts, facts, skills and/or attitudes they intend their high-school students to learn—and how the lesson will be conducted. The students of teaching then observe one another teaching the respective lessons that have been planned, taking detailed notes on the classroom events. After the lesson is completed, two high school students are selected for interviewing. Each is asked independently what the lesson was about and what the main ideas were. They are asked probing questions designed to tap the depth of their understanding. The observer then provides feedback to the teacher, who subsequently reciprocates when roles are reversed.

Bob was a fine physics graduate who was learning to be a physics teacher. As part of his year-long internship, he taught an honors physics class, which was the setting for the reciprocal observation exercise. His colleague Alice interviewed him regarding the lesson on conceptions of force he planned to introduce the unit on mechanics in the physics course. During the lesson he conducted an animated lecture-discussion on the various kinds of force. Alice thought it was one of the most effective lessons she had ever observed. She interviewed the students and opened each interview with the question: "What was this lesson about?" Both students answered, "This was a lesson about vectors."

She was shocked. Bob had devoted no more than ten minutes of a forty-five minute period to a blackboard demonstration of how to represent the direction and magnitude of forces using arrows with lines of varying length called vectors. How had they concluded that this brief presentation, at best a kind of subordinate clause in the main exposition, was the key point of the lesson? When Bob was informed of the student responses, he was also surprised. If there had not been an interview immediately after the class, there was no way in which he could have guessed that there was such a substantial gap between what he had taught and what the students had learned. Given that information, he was able to generate some hypotheses with his observer and other science teaching candidates to account for the anomalous finding. Their best guess was that the students were fooled by the fact that Bob had used the blackboard only one time in the period—during the ten-minute discussion of vectors—and they associated blackboard work with what was "really important." Whatever the cause, this story illustrates how very difficult it can be for a teacher working alone to know what his teaching has accomplished unless he is trained to do so and gets assistance in learning from experience.

Learning from experience requires that a teacher be able to look back on his or her own teaching and its consequences. The ordinary school setting does not lend itself to such reflection. It is characterized by speed, solitude, and amnesia. Too much is occurring too rapidly. One is alone attempting to make sense of the buzzing, blooming confusion of classroom life. The students are unlikely to help the teacher to pin down either causes or consequences unless he or she has learned how to elicit and exploit such feedback. Sadly, there is evidence from other sources that even when learning does occur in a classroom setting, it is often forgotten from year to year. All too often, a teacher laments, "I was halfway through the lesson before I remembered that I was making the same mistake I had made the year before while teaching the same unit." Even when learning has occurred, the speed and solitude often combine to produce pedagogical amnesia. Are there any possible cures for these problems of learning from experience or for the amnesia that so often attends the learning that does occur?

The difficulties of learning from experience are characteristic of the limitations of any individual trying to make critical sense of a complex world while working alone. A strategy of solution must transform individual work to collective activity. In the next section, collegiality in schools will be considered as a strategy for fostering experiential learning among teachers.

THE CONCEPT OF COLLEGIUM

One of the terms most frequently associated with the necessary reform of teaching and of schools is collegiality. A collegium is a setting in which individuals come together with a shared mission. One of the central features of that shared mission now becomes clear. Collegiality is needed to overcome the limitations of individual rationality. If any individual actor's capacity to learn is bounded, if human reasoning of all kinds—theoretical, practical or moral—remains restricted when pursued alone or without access to a competing point of view, then the collegium is indispensable as a vehicle for educational reform.

Yet it is necessary to be realistic. It is surely impossible logistically and fiscally for most teaching to be accompanied by peer observation and feedback. The reasons for the solitary classroom teaching experience relate to economic and social factors that are not readily ignored. How then can the principle of the collegium be achieved within reasonable bounds?

If collegiality is defined as that set of strategies needed to overcome the limitations of individual rationality and to make learning from experience possible, I suggest that those strategies be divided into two classes: the visible college and the invisible college. The visible college is the forum for direct, face-to-face interactions and deliberations among colleagues in the same building. The "invisible college" refers to the communication among colleagues who do not work in physical proximity but share knowledge of one another's work through the exchange of publications, correspondence, and occasional scholarly meetings. If the problems of affording teachers opportunities to communicate within the same building get in the way of the functioning of visible colleges, collegiality via invisible colleges is even less likely in a teaching community with few forums for joint deliberation and even fewer for recording and analyzing experiences in a scholarly manner. I now propose a number of strategies for promoting the development of both visible and invisible colleges among the nation's school teachers.

Visible Colleges

What might foster greater face-to-face collegiality within existing school buildings? The growing number of mentor teacher programs nationally, especially in conjunction with beginning teacher induction and support initiatives, promises to increase the role of collegiality between more and less experienced teachers (or among teaching peers whose respective experiences are simply different). If the mentoring relationship is accompanied by some expectations for systematic observation, coaching, and eventually some forms of documentation and evaluation, this should go a long way toward creating a new climate of collaboration within schools. Some of the newer conceptions of teacher evaluation for purposes of certification[14] include the design of portfolios that would document the accomplishments of candidates during the course of their teaching. These portfolios would require the attestations and commentaries of mentors or lead teachers who work with the candidate and guide his or her efforts at improvement through modeling and coaching. The visible college would thus include examples of one-to-one teaching within the professional teaching community itself.

Other structures that can foster the creation of visible colleges include the establishment of weekly or biweekly case conferences in schools. These would be conducted in the spirit of the teaching hospital's weekly grand rounds or clinical conferences, in which interesting or problematic cases from the hospital's own recent experience are presented and discussed for the educational benefit of the entire staff. Case conferences in schools, however, should not focus on case studies of youngsters who are "tough to teach." These conferences should be presentations by teachers, individually or in teams, on exciting new teaching units they have implemented (complete with videotapes of their operation and discussions of student work), new forms of classroom organization, approaches to the mentoring of new teachers (co-presented by mentor and novice), as well as experiences with particular students or groups. Case conferences would be one strategy for preserving the experiences of individual teachers and making those experiences and their analysis available to colleagues for review and discussion. Videotapes of these conferences or written versions of the case presentations (perhaps prepared as part of collaborations with local colleges or universities) would be accumulated in school archives creating the beginnings of an institutional memory.

Invisible Colleges

An invisible college is created when the boundaries of a collegium are stretched beyond the walls of a shared building or department. A serious problem for teaching as a profession has been the absence of opportunities to communicate what has been learned from experience through literature that can be shared with colleagues at remote sites. To achieve this form of communication, I would propose the fostering of the written version of school-based case conferences, the writing of cases and casebooks of teaching.

Teachers are capable of writing about their work in ways that can stimulate and enlighten other teachers. The writing of cases serves as an occasion for reflection and deliberation on teaching by the case authors themselves. The cases, when written and distributed, can elicit commentaries by other teachers as well as by education scholars and teacher educators. These case-based exchanges can well create an entirely new form of educational discourse that centers on the experiences, reflections, and lessons learned by teachers. They may constitute the long-sought antidote for pedagogical amnesia.

This new literature of case and commentary has been pioneered in the casebooks created by Judith Shulman of the Far West Laboratory.[15] Shulman first wrote a series of case studies of mentor teacher programs in California during their initial year of implementation. She then presented these cases to a group of new mentors who had come together to learn about and from each other's experiences. Highly stimulated by Shulman's case studies of mentors, the participants began to write their own short cases, brief vignettes capturing their experiences as mentors and the ways they had coped with them. Shulman and her school-based colleague, Joel Colbert, edited and organized the cases from the perspective of the recurrent problems of learning to mentor. They also solicited commentaries from the mentors on one another's cases, thereby simulating the ways in which physicians comment on one another's case presentations during a clinical case conference. The edited volume of cases and commentaries is now used in the invisible college, by other mentors and trainers in school districts and teacher education programs around the country. Others, including policymakers planning new mentor programs, can now reflect on and learn from the experiences of their invisible peers.

In the most recent casebook,[16] the teaching interns with whom the mentors are responsible for working write their own cases—perspectives on learning to teach written from the vantage point of the learners. These new cases are somewhat longer than the mentor vignettes, but the real innovation in the second casebook is in the treatment of the commentaries. Shulman has solicited and organized *layers of commentary*, in which other novices, mentors, teacher educators, and educational scholars add their interpretive comments to the original cases and to one another's comments. The invisible college that is represented in this casebook now extends the boundaries of collegium from the teaching community to include the world of higher education. For example, a set of cases describing the classroom management dilemmas confronted by interns teaching in the inner city elicits commentaries from experienced inner-city mentors, from teacher educators, and from Professor Jere Brophy, who is perhaps the leading research authority on classroom management. Brophy's comments, while remaining focused on the intern teacher-authored cases, connects them to the research literature on classroom control and discipline, thereby linking the invisible college of teachers with the invisible college of educational scholars on teaching.

If the limits of learning from experience derive from the speed with which experiences occur and the impossibility of deliberation on those fleeting events, then all strategies that help to freeze experience for subsequent analysis and review are promising. There is a need for antidotes (or at least palliatives) in response to the epidemics of pedagogical amnesia and teaching aphasia, of forgetting what has been learned and of being incapable of communicating even what has been remembered. The strategy of creating a case literature of teaching to preserve teacher experiences and to prepare them as a vehicle for teacher learning may well be one of the most important ways available to create and enhance the collegium.

FOR THE FUTURE

What is the desired image of the future? At this point in the history of contemporary educational reform, the position is paradoxical. The first wave has reached the beach and brought with it higher standards for pupils and more demanding expectations for teachers. The second wave is cresting, with its emphasis on the professionalization of teaching and its stress on the importance of teachers learning from teacher education and from their own experiences. However, the force of the second wave is being diminished by the undertow created by the first wave. One reform is caught in the other's backwash.

One of the demons of the current reform movement, a force that will bedevil most of the attempts to improve the qualities of teaching as a profession and a career, is the absence of time. Time tyrannizes teaching. The quest for excellence has been captured by the twin terrors of time on task and the tasks of covering enormous amounts of material. If one play by Shakespeare is good, five are splendid. If one Federalist Paper is desirable, five are dandy. Teachers have no time to think, either alone or with others. Students have no time to think, because they are too busy covering their assignments. Group work takes time; individual worksheets promote efficiency. Accelerated schools should improve by raising expectations for the achievement of all students and then by slowing down so that learning can become deeper, more collaborative, and more critical—not merely more extensive in its coverage.

There is reason to believe that many of today's youngsters are failing to learn what they are now covering. Advanced Placement courses move even more quickly than honors courses, which in turn zoom along faster than ordinary ones. The long lists of E. D. Hirsch[17] notwithstanding, a critical thinking curriculum will entail the study of fewer topics with greater care and collaborative deliberation than is currently the case. The problems of both student learning and teacher learning will require that we recapture control of both pace and time.

One of the most popular research programs of the past fifteen years has been Mary Budd Rowe's work on wait-time. I received a letter from a teacher educator who had been working on teaching teachers to wait longer in the interests of eliciting higher student levels of thinking. I had suggested in my paper "The Wisdom of Practice"[18] that the impediments to increased wait-time were an increase in discipline problems and the greater unpredictability of classroom life that were likely to accompany longer silences on the part of teachers. My correspondent suggested yet a third reason why teachers would not increase their wait-times, even after being convinced of the research grounds for the tactic. The teachers who would not increase their wait-times explained that the tactic slowed teaching down to the point where they could not have covered all the material they were expected to teach in their state or district curriculum standards. The state tests were linked to the pace dictated by the curriculum. The twin demons of time and pace strike again!

Yet, in the final analysis, much of the burden of the proposed reforms rests on assumptions about teachers learning from experience. What, then, is experience? It is reading and studying the teaching materials and the disciplinary sources from which they often derive. It is learning from students. It is watching videotapes, hearing audiotapes, observing peers, mentors and proteges. It is studying research, reading and writing cases, preparing for and participating in case conferences, planning and teaching in collaboration with fellow professionals. Are these fostered or rewarded in the present structures?

Learning from experience in teaching is more than honing or tuning a skill so that it becomes automatic. It is raising the skill to thinking, giving reason to action and value to goals. It is the transformation of showing and telling into pedagogy. This will require that teachers work in structures that permit such interactions, be prepared in programs and institutions that both teach and model such processes, and be themselves individuals who can engage in the effort.

All the talk of reforming schooling must never lost sight of the ultimate goal: to create institutions where students can learn through interactions with teachers who are themselves always learning. The effective school must become an educative setting for its teachers if it aspires to become an educational environment for its students.

NOTES

1. This chapter was written, in part, with support from the Spencer Foundation and the Carnegie Corporation of New York. The opinions expressed are the author's.

2. There is a curious ambivalence with regard to the emphasis on higher *preparation* standards as against higher *entitlement* standards. Thus, the Carnegie Task Force, in the same text that advocates higher standards of preparation, also recommends strongly in favor of encouraging alternative routes into teaching for those without professional preparation as long as they can pass the individual hurdles of licensure and certification standards.

3. Lee S. Shulman and Neil B. Carey, "Psychology and the Limitations of Individual Rationality: Implications for the Study of Reasoning and Civility," *Review of Educational Research 54*, Winter 1984, pp. 501–524.

4. See my discussion of the phenomenon in Lee S. Shulman, "Knowledge and Teaching: Foundations of the New Reform," *Harvard Educational Review 57*, February 1987, pp. 1–22, especially the discussion of Colleen on pp. 17–18; Pam Grossman, *A Passion for Language: From Text to Teaching* (Stanford, Calif.: Knowledge Growth in Teaching Publications Series, Stanford University School of Education, 1985); and Lee S. Shulman, "Sounding An Alarm: A Reply to Sockett," *Harvard Educational Review 57*, November 1987, pp. 473–482. See also my discussion of teaching as the management of complexity in Lee S. Shulman, "The Wisdom of Practice: Managing Complexity in Medicine and Teaching," in David C. Berliner and Barak V. Rosenshine, eds., *Talks to Teachers: A Festschrift for N. L. Gage* (New York: Random House, 1987).

5. Lauren Resnick, "Learning In School and Out," *Educational Researcher 16*, 1987, pp. 13–20.

6. J. Larkin, J. McDermott, D. Simon, and H. A. Simon, "Expert and Novice Performance in Solving Physics Problems," *Science 208*, 1980, pp. 1335–1342.

7. Resnick, Lauren, Comments during a symposium on the implications of the Carnegie Task Force report made at AERA meetings, April, 1987.

8. Pinchas Tamir, personal communication.

9. John Dewey, *Experience and Education* (New York: MacMillan, 1938).

10. Larry Cuban, *How Teachers Taught: Constancy and Change in American Classrooms: 1890–1980* (New York: Longman, 1984).

11. The writings of Joseph Schwab further reflect this Deweyan emphasis on the cen-

trality of deliberation, dialogue, and dialectic in the fostering of critical educational thinking among teachers and students. His papers on "the practical," which emphasize the role of practical deliberation and the eclectic, as well as his writings on the "learning community," eloquently discuss these principles. See Joseph J. Schwab, "The Practical: A Language for Curriculum," *School Review 78*, 1969, pp. 1–29; Joseph J. Schwab, "Learning Community," *The Center Magazine 8*, May–June 1975, pp. 30–44; Schwab's collected papers in Joseph J. Schwab, *Science, Curriculum and Liberal Education: Selected Essays* (Chicago: University of Chicago Press, 1978).

12. See Hillel J. Einhorn and Robin M. Jogarth, "Confidence in Judgment: Persistence of the Illusion of Validity," *Psychological Review 85*, 1978, pp. 395–416; Amos Tversky and Daniel Kahneman, "Judgment Under Uncertainty: Heuristics and Biases," *Science 185*, 1974, pp. 1124–1131.

13. For a full description of that research, see Lee S. Shulman, "Assessment for Teaching: An Initiative for the Profession," *Phi Delta Kappan*, September 1987, pp. 38–44.

14. Ibid.

15. Judith H. Shulman and Joel A. Colbert, eds., *The Mentor-Teacher Casebook* (San Francisco: Far West Laboratory for Educational Research and Development, and Eugene, Ore.: ERIC Clearinghouse on Educational Management, 1987).

16. Judith H. Shulman, ed., *The Intern Teacher Casebook: Cases and Commentaries* (San Francisco: Far West Laboratory, in press).

17. E. D. Hirsch, *Cultural Literacy* (Boston: Houghton-Mifflin, 1987).

18. Lee S. Shulman, "The Wisdom of Practice: Managing Complexity in Medicine and Teaching," in David C. Berliner and Barak V. Rosenshine, eds., *Talks to Teachers: A Festschrift for N. L. Gage* (New York: Random House, 1987).

CHAPTER 9

Professional Knowledge & Reflective Practice

DONALD A. SCHÖN

Massachusetts Institute of Technology

THE CRISIS OF CONFIDENCE IN PROFESSIONAL KNOWLEDGE

Although American society has become thoroughly dependent on professionals, so much so that the conduct of business, industry, government, education, and everyday life would be unthinkable without them, there are signs of a growing crisis of confidence in the professions. In many well-publicized scandals, professionals have been found willing to use their special positions for private gain. Professionally designed solutions to public problems have had unanticipated consequences, sometimes worse than the problems they were intended to solve. The public has shown an increasing readiness to call for external regulation of professional practice. Laymen have been increasingly disposed to turn to the courts for defense against professional incompetence or venality. The professional's traditional claims to privileged social position and autonomy of practice have come into question as the public has begun to have doubts about professional ethics and expertise.[1] In recent years, professionals themselves have shown signs of a loss of confidence in professional knowledge.

Not very long ago, in 1963, the editors of *Daedalus* could introduce a special volume on the professions with the sentence, "Everywhere in American life the professions are triumphant."[2] They noted the apparently limitless demand for professional services, the "shortages" of teachers and physicians, the difficulty of coordinating the proliferating

188

technical specializations, and the problem of managing the burgeoning mass of technical data. In the essays that made up the volume, doctors, lawyers, scientists, educators, military men, and politicians articulated variations on the themes of professional triumph, overload, and growth. There were only two discordant voices. The representative of the clergy complained of declining influence and the "problem of relevance,"[3] and the city planner commented ruefully on his profession's lagging understanding of the changing ills of urban areas.[4] Yet in less than a decade the discordant notes had become the dominant ones, and the theme of professional triumph had virtually disappeared.

In 1972, a colloquium on professional education was held at the Massachusetts Institute of Technology. Participants included distinguished representatives of the fields of medicine, engineering, architecture, planning, psychiatry, law, divinity, education, and management. These individuals disagreed about many things, but they held one sentiment in common—a profound uneasiness about their own professions. They questioned whether professionals would effectively police themselves. They wondered whether professionals were instruments of individual well-being and social reform or were mainly interested in the preservation of their own status and privilege, caught up in the very problems they might have been expected to solve. They allowed themselves to express doubts about the relevance and remedial power of professional expertise.

It is perhaps not very difficult to account for this dramatic shift, over a single decade, in the tone of professional self-reflection. Between 1963 and 1972 there had been a disturbing sequence of events, painful for professionals and the public alike. A professionally instrumented war had been disastrous. Social movements for peace and civil rights had begun to see the professions as elitest servants of established interests. The much-proclaimed shortages of scientists, teachers, and physicians seemed to have evaporated. Professionals seemed powerless to relieve the rapidly shifting "crises" of the cities, poverty, environmental pollution, and energy. There were the scandals of Medicare and, at the end of the decade, Watergate. Cumulatively, these events created doubts about professionally conceived strategies of diagnosis and cure. They pointed to the overwhelming complexity of the phenomena with which professionals were trying to cope. They raised questions about the adequacy of existing theories and techniques to relieve the most urgent sources of societal distress.

Sharing, in greater or lesser degree, these sentiments of doubt and uneasiness, the participants in the M.I.T. colloquium analysed their predicament in terms of four main factors.

They believed a shift in the nature of social reality had created problems of a complexity and uncertainty ill-suited to the traditional division of labor. A noted engineer observed that "education no longer fits the niche, or the niche no longer fits education." The dean of a medical school spoke of the complexity of a huge health care system that could be influenced only marginally by the actions of the medical profession. The dean of a school of management referred to the puzzle of educating managers for the task of judgement and action under conditions of uncertainty.

They were troubled by the irreducible residue of art in professional practice. Art was deemed an indispensable part of professional practice, even in the fields of science and engineering, and there were doubts that this indispensable art could be codified and taught. As one participant said, "If it's invariant and known, it can be taught; but it isn't invariant."

Professional education had tended to focus on problem solving, but several participants thought the most important issues for professional practice were those of problem *finding*. "Our interest," as one participant put it, "is not only how to pour the concrete for the highway, but what highway makes sense? When it comes to designing a ship, the question we have to ask is, which ship makes sense in terms of the problems of transportation?"

Representatives of schools of architecture, planning, social work, and psychiatry spoke of the pluralism of the schools, the conflicting views of the competences to be acquired, the problems to be solved, and the nature of the profession. A leading professor of psychiatry described his field as a "babble of voices."

Finally, there were calls for a liberation of the professions from the tyranny of the professional schools and the universities. "American universities are products of the late nineteenth and early twentieth centuries," one participant observed. "The question is, how do you break them up in some way, at least get some group of young people who are free of them? How do you make them free to do something new and different?"

The years that have passed since the 1972 colloquium have tended to reinforce its conclusions. Nowadays, no profession would celebrate itself in triumphant tones. In spite of the continuing eagerness of the young to embark on apparently secure and remunerative professional careers, professionals are still criticized (and criticize themselves) for failing to live up to their own norms and adapt to a changing social reality. There is widespread recognition of the absence or loss of a stable institutional framework of purpose and knowledge within which professionals can live out their roles and confidently exercise their skills.

Nevertheless, there is something puzzling about the ways in which participants in the 1972 colloquium accounted for the troubles of the professions. Professionals in many different fields do sometimes find ways of coping effectively, even wisely, with situations of complexity and uncertainty. If the element of art in professional practice is not invariant, known, and teachable, it does appear occasionally to be learnable. Problem setting is an activity in which some professionals engage consciously and skillfully, and some students and practitioners of the professions do seem to make thoughtful choices from among the multiple views of professional identity.

Why, then, should leading professionals and educators have been so troubled by the phenomena of complexity, uncertainty, instability, art, and pluralism? It was not, I think, because they were unaware that practitioners sometimes display artistry and cope with uncertainty. I suspect it was, rather, that they found it difficult to account for the processes by which they do so.

Complexity and uncertainty are not dissolved through the application of specialized knowledge to well-defined tasks; on the contrary, tasks become well-defined through the restructuring of complex and uncertain situations. The irreducible element of art in practice cannot be reduced to the exercise of known technique. Problem finding has no place in a body of professional knowledge concerned exclusively with problem solving. One cannot rely on professional expertise in order to choose among competing paradigms of professional practice.

The participants were disturbed to find that their underlying model of professional knowledge left them unable to account for processes they had learned to see as central to professional competence.

THE DOMINANT MODEL OF PROFESSIONAL KNOWLEDGE

The epistemology that dominates most thinking and writing about the professions, and is built into the very structure of professional schools and research institutions, has been clearly set forth in two recent essays on professional education. Both of them treat rigorous professional practice as an application of research-based knowledge to the solution of problems of instrumental choice.

Edgar Schein, in *Professional Education,* proposes a threefold division of professional knowledge:

1. An *underlying discipline* or *basic science* component upon which the practice rests or from which it is developed.
2. An *applied science* or *"engineering"* component from which many of the day-to-day diagnostic procedures and problem solutions are derived.
3. A *skills and attitudinal* component that concerns the actual performance of services to the client, using the underlying basic and applied knowledge.[5]

In Schein's view, these components constitute a hierarchy that may be read as an order of application, justification, and status. The application of basic science yields engineering, and engineering provides the models, rules, and techniques applicable to the instrumental choices of everyday practice. The actual performance of services "rests on" applied science, which rests, in turn, on the foundation of basic science. In the epistemological pecking order, basic science is highest in methodological rigor and purity, and its practitioners tend to be superior in status to those who practice applied science, problem solving, or service delivery.

Nathan Glazer, in a much-quoted article, argues that the schools of such professions as social work, education, divinity, and town planning are caught in a hopeless predicament.[6] These "minor" professions, beguiled by the success of the "major" professions of law, medicine, and business, have tried to substitute a basis in scientific knowledge for their traditional reliance on experienced practice. In this spirit, they have placed their schools within the universities. Glazer believes, however, that their aspirations are doomed to failure. The "minor" professions lack the essential conditions of the "major" ones. They lack stable institutional contexts of practice, fixed and unambiguous ends with "settled men's minds,"[7] and a basis in systematic scientific knowledge. They cannot supply scientific knowledge to the solving of instrumental problems, and they are therefore unable to produce a rigorous curriculum of professional education.

> Can these fields [education, city planning, social work, and divinity] settle on a fixed form of training, a fixed content of professional knowledge, and follow the models of medicine, law and business? I suspect not because the discipline of a fixed and unambiguous end in a fixed institutional setting is not given to them. And *thus* [my emphasis] the base of knowledge which is unambiguously indicated as relevant for professional education is also not given.[8]

Glazer and Schein share an epistemology of professional practice that I shall call "positivist" because it is rooted historically in the positivist philosophy that so powerfully shaped both the modern university and the modern conception of the proper relationship between valid theory and rigorous practice.[9] The positivist epistemology of practice still underlies what Schein describes as the normative curriculum of professional education, which follows the hierarchy of professional knowledge: first, the relevant basic science, then the relevant applied science, and finally, a practicum in which students learn to apply classroom knowledge to the problems of practice. The dominant conception of the proper relations between research and practice, the conception embedded in the institutional arrangements of research and practice, is still very much what Thorsten Veblen propounded some seventy years ago.[10]

The university and the research institute are devoted to the production of new knowledge in the protected setting of the scholar's study or in the carefully controlled environment of a scientific laboratory. They are kept separate from the relatively unprotected and uncontrollable context of practitioners whose purpose is the useful application of knowledge. Research and practice are conceived as entering into a relationship of exchange. Researchers are supposed to give practitioners theories and techniques useful in solving day-to-day problems, and practitioners are supposed, in return, to give researchers new problems to work on and practical tests of the utility of research results.

The positivist epistemology of practice depends critically on the separation of research from practice, but it also depends on the separation of ends from means and knowing from doing.

Rigorous professional practice is conceived as an essentially technical activity; it consists in the use of described, tested, replicable techniques of problem diagnosis and solution. From this it follows that professional problem solving can be objective, consensual, cumulative, and convergent. However, in order for practice to be technical, it must be oriented to ends that are clear and fixed, like Glazer's examples of profit, health, and success in litigation. Technical means, on the other hand, are variable. Their appropriateness varies with the practice situation. It is the business of applied science to provide a rigorous basis for the selection of the means best suited to established ends. Means and ends must be conceived as separately defined and determined, so that the solution of means–ends (instrumental) problems can be seen as a technical activity.

If professional practice is technical and science-based, then it must also be seen to consist of a kind of knowing—problem solving, judging, or deciding. The practitioner is supposed to use research-based theory and technique to *decide* on the strategies best suited to the solution of instrumental problems. When rigorous practice is equated with rigorous deciding, the actual "doing" comes to be seen as nothing more than the implementation of technically sound decisions.

It is not hard to understand why those committed, explicitly or implicitly, to the model of technical rationality should be troubled by the phenomena of uncertainty, complexity, instability, professional pluralism, and the irreducible element of art in practice. Each of these phenomena transcends the dichotomies of technical rationality. In the conversion of uncertain situations to technical problems, on which technical rationality depends, ends and means are *reciprocally* determined. Artistry is in the doing as well as in the knowing. Also, conflicts of professional paradigms affect research as well as practice; they cannot be resolved for practice by research.

THE DILEMMA OF RIGOR OR RELEVANCE

For professional practitioners and educators and for students of the professions, the positivist epistemology of practice contributes to an urgent and essential dilemma, which I shall call the dilemma of rigor or relevance.

Given the dominant view of professional rigor, the view that prevails in the intellectual climate of the universities and is embedded in the institutional arrangements of professional education and research, rigorous practice depends on "well-formed" problems of instrumental choice to whose solution research-based theory and technique are applicable.[11] However, real-world problems do not come well-formed. They tend to present themselves, on the contrary, as messy, indeterminate, problematic situations. A civil engineer worrying about what road to build, for example, does not have a problem that can be solved by an application of locational techniques or by decision theory. It is a complex and ill-defined situation in which geographic, financial, economic, and political factors are usually all mixed up together. To arrive at a well-formed problem, the engineer must construct it from the materials of the problematic situation, and the problem of problem setting is not a well-formed problem.[12]

A practitioner, in setting a problem, chooses what to treat as the "things" of the situation and decides what to attend to and what to ignore. He or she names the objects for attention and frames them in an appreciative context that sets a direction for action. A vague worry about hunger or malnourishment may be framed, for example, as a problem of selecting an optimal diet, but situations of malnourishment may be framed in many different ways.[13] Economists, environmental scientists, nutrition scientists, agronomists, planners, engineers, and political scientists debate over the nature of the malnourishment problem, and their discussions have given rise to a multiplicity of problem settings worthy of *Rashomon*. Indeed, the practice of malnourishment planning is largely taken up with the task of constructing the problem to be solved.

When practitioners succeed in converting a problematic situation to a well-formed problem, or in resolving a conflict over the proper framing of a practitioner's role in a situation, they engage in a kind of inquiry that cannot be subsumed under a model of technical problem solving. Rather, it is through the work of naming and framing that the exercise of technical rationality becomes possible.

Similarly, the artistic processes by which practitioners sometimes make sense of unique cases, and the art they sometimes bring to everyday practice, do not meet the prevailing criteria of rigorous practice. Competent practitioners recognize things like the families of symptoms associated with a disease, the peculiarites of a building site, or the irregularities of materials, for which they cannot give a complete (or often even a reasonably accurate) description. They make judgments of quality for which they cannot state adequate criteria and display skills for which they cannot describe procedures of rules.

The centrality of problem setting and of such artistic processes as these, together with the prevailing, institutionalized commitment to the positivist epistemology of practice, creates the dilemma of rigor or relevance. Defining rigor only in terms of technical rationality excludes as nonrigorous much of what competent practitioners actually do, including the skillful performances on which technical problem solving depends. Indeed, the most important components of competent practice are excluded.

In the varied topography of professional practice, there is a high, hard ground that overlooks a swamp. On the high ground, manageable problems lend themselves to solution through the use of research-based theory and technique. In the swampy lowland, problems are messy, confusing, and incapable of technical solution. The irony of this situation is that the problems of the high ground tend to be relatively unimportant to individuals or to society at large, however great their technical interest may be, while in the swamp lie the problems of greatest human concern. The practitioner is confronted with a choice. Remain on the high ground and solve relatively unimportant problems according to the standards of rigor, or descend to the swamp of important problems and nonrigorous inquiry?

Consider medicine, engineering, and agronomy, three of Glazer's major or near-major professions. In these fields, there are areas in which problems are clearly defined, goals are relatively fixed, and phenomena lend themselves to the categories of available theory and technique. Here, practitioners can function effectively as technical experts. When one or more of these conditions is lacking, however, competent performance is no longer a matter of exclusively technical expertise. Medical technologies like kidney dialysis or tomography have created demands that stretch the nation's willingness to invest in medical care. How should physicians behave? How should they try to influence or accommodate to health policy? Engineering solutions that seem powerful and elegant when judged from a relatively narrow perspective may have a wider range of consequences that degrade the environment, generate unacceptable risk, or put excessive demands on scarce resources. How should engineers take these factors into account in their actual designing? When agronomists recommend efficient methods of soil cultivation that favor the use of large land holdings, they may undermine the viability of the small family farms on which peasant economies depend. How should the practice of agronomy take such considerations into account? These are not problems, properly speaking, but problematic situations from which problems must be constructed. If practitioners choose not to ignore them, they must approach them through kinds of inquiry that are, according to the dominant model of technical rationality, nonrigorous.

The doctrine of technical rationality, promulgated and maintained in the universities and especially in the professional schools, infects the young professional in training with a hunger for technique. Many students of urban planning, for example, are impatient with anything other than "hard skills." In schools of management, students often chafe under the discipline of endless case analysis; they want to learn the techniques and algorithms that are, as they see it, the key to high starting salaries. Yet professionals who really tried to confine their practice to the rigorous application of research-based technique would find not only that they could not work on the most important problems, but also that they could not practice in the real world at all.

Nearly all professional practitioners experience some version of the dilemma of rigor or relevance, and they may respond to it in several ways. They may choose the swampy lowland, deliberately immersing themselves in confusing but crucially important situations. When asked to describe their methods of inquiry, they speak of experience, trial and error, intuition, and muddling through. When teachers, social workers, or planners operate in this vein, they tend to be afflicted with a nagging sense of inferiority to those who present themselves as models of technical rigor. When physicians or engineers do so, they may be troubled by the discrepancy between the technical rigor of the "hard" zones of their practice and the apparent sloppiness of the "soft" ones.

Practitioners who opt for the high ground confine themselves to a narrowly technical practice and pay a price for doing so. Operations research, systems analysis, policy analysis, and management science are examples of practices built around the use of formal, analytic models. In the early years of the development of these professions, following World War II, there was a climate of optimism about the power of formal modelling for the solution of real-world problems. In subsequent decades, however, there has been a growing recognition of the limits of these techniques, especially in situations of high complexity and uncertainty.[14] Some practitioners have responded by confining themselves to the limited class of problems—for example, to inventory control. Others have continued to develop formal models for use in problems of high complexity and uncertainty, quite undeterred by the troubles incurred whenever a serious attempt is made to put their models into practice. They may become researchers, pursuing an agenda driven by evolving questions of modeling theory and technique, increasingly divergent from the context of actual practice, or they may try to cut the situations of practice to fit their models. In its more general form, this Procrustean strategy is a further response to the dilemma of rigor or relevance.

The Procrustean response makes use of a variety of strategies. Practitioners may employ selective inattention,[15] blocking out the phenomena that do not fit their models of the world of practice. Educators may preserve their confidence in the techniques of "competency testing," for example, simply by ignoring the kinds of understanding and skill that competence testing fails to detect. Practitioners may use junk categories[16] to explain away discrepant data, as when physicians or therapists use the term, "patient resistance" to dismiss the cases in which an indicated treatment fails to lead to cure. Practitioners may try to make their technical expertise effective by exerting unilateral control over the practice situation—for example, by removing "rebellious" or "slow-learning" children from the field of education.

All such responses to the dilemma of rigor or relevance serve to protect the positivist epistemology of practice. Those who confine themselves to the limited range of technical problems, or cut the situations of practice to fit available models and techniques, seek a world in which technical rationality works. Those who choose the swamp tend to pay homage to the prevailing models of rigor; what they know how to do, they have no way of describing as rigorous.

Writers about the professions tend to follow similar paths. Both Glazer and Schein recognize, for example, that professional practice manifests uncertainty, instability, and uniqueness, but they try to square their recognition of these phenomena with their underlying epistemology of practice. Glazer localizes uncertainty and instability in the "minor" professions, of which he despairs. Schein treats applied and basic science as increasingly "convergent," while locating the "divergent" phenomena of uncertainty, complexity, and uniqueness in the concrete situations of practice. He believes that practitioners match convergent knowledge to divergent practice by the exercise of "divergent skills."[17] About these, however, he can say very little. For in his view of professional knowledge, which is the prevailing view, if divergent skills fall into the categories of theory or technique, they belong on one of the other levels of the hierarchy of knowledge. If divergent skills are neither theory nor technique, how can they be described? They function as a kind of junk category, serving to protect an underlying model of technical rationality.

Yet the epistemology of practice embedded in American universities and research institutions, and ingrained in habits of thought about professional knowledge and in the dilemma of rigor or relevance, has lost its hold on the field that nurtured it. Among philosphers of science, no one wants any longer to be called a positivist.[18] There is a rebirth of interest in the ancient topics of craft, artistry, and myth—topics whose fate positivism seemed once to have finally sealed. Positivism, and the positivist epistemology of practice, now seem to rest on a particular *view* of science that is largely discredited.

It is timely, then, to reconsider the question of professional knowledge. Perhaps there is an epistemology of practice that takes full account of the competence practitioners sometimes display in situations of complexity, uncertainty, and uniqueness. Perhaps there is a way of looking at problem setting and intuitive artistry that presents these activities as describable and susceptible to a kind of rigor that falls outside the boundaries of technical rationality. In the following section, I shall briefly describe my approach to the development of such a view.

REFLECTION-IN-ACTION

When people go about the spontaneous, intuitive performance of the actions of everyday life, they show themselves to be knowledgeable in a special way. Often, they cannot say what it is they know. When they try to describe it, they find themselves at a loss or produce descriptions that are obviously inappropriate. Knowing is ordinarily tacit, implicit in patterns of action and in a "feel" for the stuff being dealt with. It seems right to say that one's knowing is *in* one's action. Similarly, the workday life of the professional practitioner reveals, in its recognitions, judgments and skills, a pattern of tacit knowing-in-action.

Once one has put aside the model of technical rationality, which leads one to think of intelligent practice as an *application* of knowledge to instrumental decisions, there is nothing strange about the idea that a kind of knowing is inherent in intelligent action. Common sense admits the category of know-how, and it does not stretch common sense very much to say that the know-how is *in* the action—that a tightrope walker's know-how, for example, lies in, and is revealed by, the way she takes her trip across the wire, or that a big-league pitcher's know-how is in his way of pitching to a batter's weakness, changing his pace, or distributing his energies over the course of a game. There is nothing in common sense to indicate that know-how consists in rules or plans that a person entertains in the mind prior to action. Although people sometimes think before acting, it is also true that in much of the spontaneous behavior of skillful practice they reveal a kind of knowing that does not stem from a prior intellectual operation. As Gilbert Ryle has put it,

> What distinguishes sensible from silly operations is not their parentage but their procedure, and this holds no less for intellectual than for practical performances. "Intelligent" cannot be defined in terms of "intellectual" or "knowing *how*" in terms of "knowing *that*"; "thinking what I am doing" does not connote "both thinking what to do and doing it." When I do something intelligently . . . I am doing one thing and not two. My performance has a special procedure or manner, not special antecedents.[19]

Andrew Harrison has recently put the same thought in this pithy phrase: When someone acts intelligently "he acts his mind."[20]

Over the years, several writers on the epistemology of practice have been struck by the fact that skillful action often reveals a "knowing more than we can say." Chester Barnard wrote of "non-logical processes," which are not capable of being expressed in words or as reasoning, which are made known only by a judgment, decision, or action. His examples included an athlete judging distance in throwing a ball, a high school boy solving quadratic equations, and a practiced accountant who can take "a balance sheet of considerable complexity and within minutes or even seconds get a significant set of facts from it."[21] Michael Polanyi, who invented the phrase "tacit knowing," drew examples from the recognition of faces and from the use of tools, where, for example, the feeling of a probe in the hand becomes transparent to a "sense of its point touching the objects we are exploring."[22] Geoffrey Vickers pointed out that not only in artistic judgments, but in all of our ordinary judgments of quality, "we can recognize and describe deviations from a norm very much more clearly than we can describe the norm itself."[23]

In examples like these, knowing has the following properties:

- There are actions, recognitions and judgments that people know how to carry out spontaneously, without having to think about them prior to or during their performance.
- People are often unaware of having learned to do these things but simply find themselves doing them.
- In some cases, people were once aware of the understanding that has subsequently become internalized in their feeling for the stuff of action. In other cases, they may never have been aware of them. In both cases, however, people are usually unable to describe the knowing their action reveals.

It is in this sense that I speak of knowing-*in*-action, the characteristic mode of ordinary practical knowledge.

If common sense recognizes knowing-in-action, it also recognizes that people sometimes think about what they are doing. Phrases like "thinking on your feet," "keeping your wits about you," and "learning by doing" suggest not only that people can think about doing but also that they can think about doing something while doing it. Some of the most interesting examples of this process occur in the midst of a performance.

When good jazz musicians improvise together, they manifest a "feel" for their material and make on-the-spot adjustments to the sounds they hear. Listening to one another and to themselves, they feel where the music is going and adjust their playing accordingly. They can do this, first of all, because their collective effort at musical invention makes use of a schema—a metric, melodic and harmonic schema familiar to all the participants—which gives a predictable order to the piece. In addition, each of the musicians has ready a repertoire of musical figures that can be delivered at appropriate moments. Improvisation consists in varying, combining, and recombining a set of figures within the schema that bounds and gives coherence to the performance. As the musicians feel the direction of the music that is developing out of their interwoven contributions, they make new sense of it and adjust their performance to the new sense they have made. They are reflecting-in-action on the music they are collectively making and on their individual contributions to it, thinking what they are doing and, in the process, evolving their way of doing it. Of course, their reflection-in-action may not take place in the medium of words. More likely, they reflect through a "feel for the music" that is not unlike a pitcher's "feel for the ball."

Much reflection-in-action hinges on the experience of surprise. When intuitive, spontaneous performance yields nothing more than the results expected for it, people tend not to think about it. Sometimes, however, intuitive performance leads to surprises. These may be pleasing and promising, or they may be unwanted. In either case, people may respond to surprise by reflection-in-action. Like a baseball pitcher, people may reflect on their "winning habits," or like the jazz musician, on their sense of the music they have been making, or like a designer, on the misfit they have unintentionally created. In such processes, reflection tends to focus interactively on the outcomes of action, the action itself, and the intuitive knowing implicit in the action.

Professional practitioners, such as physicians, managers, and teachers, also reflect-in-action. The character of their reflection indicates how a professional practice is both different from and similar to other kinds of action.

When speaking of a lawyer's practice, one refers to the kinds of activities he or she performs, the kinds of clients he or she serves, and the kinds of cases he or she is called upon to handle. When speaking of practicing the piano, one refers to the repetitive and experimental processes by which a person tries to increase his or her proficiency on that instrument. The two senses of "practice" are distinct, but related to one another in an interesting way. Professional practice also includes a necessary element of repetition. A professional practitioner is a specialist who encounters certain types of situations again and again, building, in the process, a repertoire of expectations, examples, images, and techniques. As many variations on a relatively small number of types of cases are experienced, the professional is able to "practice" his or her practice. This knowing-in-practice tends to become increasingly tacit, spontaneous, and automatic, thereby conferring on the professional and his or her clients the benefits of specialization. On the other hand, specialization can lead into a parochial narrowness of vision, or it can induce a kind of overlearning that takes the form of a tacit pattern of error to which the practitioner becomes selectively inattentive.

Reflection can serve as a corrective to overlearning. Through reflection, a practitioner can surface and criticize the tacit understandings that have grown up around the repetitive experiences of a specialized practice. He or she can experience and make new sense of situations of uncertainty and uniqueness. This inquiry may take the form of retrospective reflection *on* past practice, undertaken either in a spirit of idle speculation or in a deliberate effort to prepare for future cases. Or, one may reflect on practice while in the midst of it—in an "action-present," an interval of time (minutes, hours, days or months, depending on the pace of activity and the situational boundaries of the practice)—in which action can still make a difference to the situation.

The possible objects of this reflection are as varied as the kinds of phenomena present and the knowing-in-practice that is brought to the situation. The professional may reflect on the feeling for a situation which has led to a particular course of action, on the way in which the problem has been framed, or on the professional role that he or she has constructed within a larger institutional context. In all of these modes, reflection-in-action is central to the art through which practitioners sometimes cope with the "divergent" situations of practice.

When the phenomenon at hand eludes the ordinary categories of knowledge-in-practice, presenting itself as unique or unstable, the practitioner may surface and criticize his or her initial understanding of the phenomena, construct a new description of it, and test the new description by an on-the-spot experiment. Sometimes, he or she arrives at a new theory of the phenomenon by articulating a feeling about it.

When stuck in a problematic situation that cannot be readily converted to a manageable problem, the professional may construct a new way of setting the problem, a new frame that might be imposed on the situation.

When confronted with demands that seem incompatible or inconsistent, the professional may respond by reflecting on the appreciations that have been brought to the situation. The dilemma may be attributed to the way a problem is set, or even to the way in which rules have been framed. The professional may then find a way of integrating, or choosing among, the values at stake in the situation.

SCHOOL KNOWLEDGE AND REFLECTION-IN-ACTION

What forms might reflection-in-action take in the educational professions? Consider this episode, drawn from the records of the Teacher Project, an experiment in in-service education for elementary school teachers conducted by Jeanne Bamberger and Eleanor Duckworth between 1978 and 1980.[24]

A group of seven teachers watched a videotape of two boys seated at a table, separated from each other by a screen. One boy had in front of him a pattern made of pattern blocks. The other was to use similar blocks to build the same pattern, following the first boy's instructions. After the first few instructions, the boys lost touch with each other, though neither of them was aware of the fact. The teachers saw the situation as a "communication problem." The second boy seemed to them to be unable to follow instructions, while the first seemed "orderly and clear," with "well-developed verbal skills." One of the observers suggested, however, that she had heard the first boy tell the second to take a green square, although there were no green squares (all the squares were orange, and only the triangles green). She thought this misleading instruction had been the starting point for the second boy's troubles. He had put a green triangle where the first boy's pattern had an orange square. From then on, all the instructions had been ambiguous, unbeknownst to the boys.

When the teachers watched the videotape again, checking on this observation, they were astonished. The whole situation now seemed upside-down. They could see exactly why the second boy made the moves that got him into difficulty. He no longer seemed dull. He had, in fact, followed instructions and had actually been remarkably inventive in his efforts to reconcile later instructions with the pattern before him. One of the teachers then said of the observer's remark, "She gave him reason"—a phrase that became the slogan for the group's later attempts to find sense in behavior they would once have judged stupid or stubborn. "Giving a child reason" became associated with a readiness to find children's behavior puzzling and to seek, in interaction with the child, to discover its source.

The teachers' shift of view suggests two ways of looking at what children know, how they learn, and how teachers may help them do so.

The first view, suggested (though by no means fully illustrated) by the teachers' initial reaction, I shall call "the school's view of knowledge." It is a powerful view of knowledge built into the schools—a view of the knowledge teachers are supposed to convey to kids. There is a view of the knowledge teachers are supposed to have in order to do their job and a view of knowledge built into prevailing ideas of educational reform. This epistemology suits the bureaucratic requirements of the school, which are geared—as in most bureaucracies—to requirements of predictability and control. It lends itself to a conception of educational reform that depends on a center-periphery model for the diffusion of improved educational methods and practices. Its main features are these:

- Knowledge is seen as a body of accepted facts, theories and skills—seen, after the fact of inquiry, as a set of *products*.
- Knowledge is determinate; questions have right answers that can be delivered by those who know.
- Knowledge is molecular. Basic skills and facts are the building blocks from which more advanced complex skills and theories are constructed. Hence, in the movement from simple to ever more complex wholes, the acquisition of knowledge is cumulative.
- Knowledge is formal and categorical. It is explicitly formulable in propositions that assign properties to objects or express, in verbal or symbolic terms, the relations of objects and properties to one another. The more general and abstract the meanings expressed by such propositions, the higher the level of knowledge involved.
- Knowledge that possesses these characteristics is *privileged*. It is the privileged knowledge of the schools, and it is communicated to each new generation through school-based training.

The view of knowledge I have described as school knowledge corresponds to a particular view of the teacher's task: to communicate school knowledge to children. On this view, teachers convey knowledge; children receive it and show that they "get it" or fail to get it by their performance on tests designed to reveal the knowledge they have absorbed. A child's failure to "get it" may be attributable to a teacher's inadequate communication or to such deficiencies in the child as "slow learning," "poor motivation," or "short attention span."

The second view of knowledge—the one I have associated with what the teachers called "giving the kid reason"—focuses attention on what kids already know, as indicated by the things they do in the pursuit of their everyday activities. This knowing-in-action may be unschooled, delivered spontaneously and without "taking thought," as in riding bicycles, fixing bicycles, playing basketball, dancing, and ordinary conversation. Often such knowledge is, in Michael Polanyi's word, *tacit:* kids cannot say, or can only partly say, what they know. In school, they reveal what they know by their "errors," by the puzzling or surprising things they do, as much or more than by their "right answers." In their knowing-in-action, they group things together, treat things as similar or different, in ways that reflect the familiar coherence of everyday life rather than the formal categories in terms of which school knowledge is ordered.

When attention turns to knowledge-in-action, teaching includes getting in touch with, enhancing, and building on what kids already know, helping them *connect* their knowing-in-action with the privileged knowledge of the school. Teaching in the mode of "giving kids reason" involves listening to the things kids say, adopting a stance based on the assumption that what they say or do makes sense; attending to the surprising, puzzling things they do or say; discovering the sense that underlies their words and actions; fashioning descriptions or demonstrations of privileged knowledge that meet their initial understandings; and creating situations that enable them to coordinate school knowledge with the knowing already built into their doing.

At its best, such teaching becomes a form of artistry—beautifully described by Leo Nicholaevitch Tolstoy in his essay on "Teaching the Rudiments" of reading:

> Every individual must, in order to acquire the art of reading in the shortest possible time, be taught quite apart from any other, and therefore there must be a separate method for each. That which forms an insuperable difficulty to one does not in the least keep back another, and vice versa. One pupil has a good memory, and it is easier for him to memorize the syllables than to comprehend a most rational sound method; another has a fine instinct, and he grasps the law of word combination by reading whole words at a time.
>
> The best teacher will be he who has at his tongue's end the explanation of what it is that is bothering the pupil. These explanations give the teacher the knowledge of the greatest possible number of methods, the ability of inventing new methods, and above all, not a blind adherence to one method but the conviction that all methods are one-sided, and that the best method would be the one which would answer best to all the possible difficulties incurred by a pupil, that is, not a method but an art and talent. . . .[25]

Reflective teaching, the kind of teaching whose source is "giving the kid reason," "the art of teaching described by Tolstoy, is a special case of the kind of inquiry I have called reflection-in-action. It is a kind of process in which, when people are presented with a surprise, they turn thought back on itself, thinking what they are doing as they do it, setting anew the problem of the situation in which they find themselves, conducting on-the-spot an action experiment by which they seek to solve the new problem they have set—an experiment in which they try both to test their new way of seeing the situation and change the situation for the better.

Like knowing-in-action, the reflection-in-action of a skillful bicycle rider, jazz musician, or teacher may be spontaneous and tacit; people can engage in spontaneous improvisatory inquiry without having to stop and think. However, there are times—when people get stuck and want to get unstuck, or want to help someone else learn to do something, or want to build on their own spontaneous artistry—when people also reflect *on* their reflection-in-action. Then people become observers of their own on-the-spot experiments, reflect on what they observe, and try to describe their knowing, their inquiry, and their change in view.

They give themselves reason and try to make explicit the reason*ing* they have produced without having had to take thought. So the teachers' slogan, "give the kid reason," is a reflection on the reflection-in-action they have just experienced, and Tolstoy's paragraph is a reflection on the reflection-in-action that seems to have characterized the artistry he displayed as a teacher in the peasant school he founded at Yasnaya Polanya.

The difference between the two views of knowledge and teaching I have described affects teachers' capacity to bridge certain dichotomies that (just to the extent that they remain in being) undermine and deaden the experience of school.

- To heal the split between school and life, so that kids' spontaneous knowing-in-action becomes admissible, indeed central, to their school experience
- To reduce the gap between teaching and doing, so that what teachers teach is less estranged from the ways in which *they* actually know, think, and learn; to help teachers become less dependent on externally given right answers, to help them connect kids' knowing-in-action and kid's confusions with their own
- To make a bridge between educational research and educational practice (working against the increasing divergence of these activities); to see teachers engaged in exploring the puzzles of kids' utterances, discovering their ways of understanding things, testing their understandings of kids' understandings by actions that are both explorations and interventions—to help teachers become researchers *in* practice

NOTES

1. Everett Hughes, "The Study of Occupations," in Merton and Broom, eds., *Sociology Today* (New York: Basic Books, 1959).
2. Kenneth Lynn, introduction to "The Professionals," *Daedalus*, Fall 1963, p. 649.
3. James Gustafson, "The Clergy in the United States," *Daedalus*, Fall 1963, p. 743.
4. William Alonso, "Cities and City Planners," *Daedalus*, Fall 1963, p. 838.
5. Edgar Schein, *Professional Education* (New York: McGraw-Hill, 1973), p. 43.
6. Nathan Glazer, "The Schools of the Minor Professions," *Minerva 12* (3), July 1974.
7. *Ibid.*, p. 363.
8. *Ibid.*, p. 363.
9. For a discussion of positivism and its influence on prevailing epistemological views, see Jergen Habermas, *Knowledge and Human Interests* (Boston: Beacon Press, 1968). For a discussion of the influence of positivist doctrines on the shaping of the modern university, see Edward Shils, "The Order of Learning in the United States from 1865 to 1920: the Ascendancy of the Universities," *Minerva 16* (2), Summer 1978.
10. Thorsten Veblen, *The Higher Learning in America* (New York: Kelley, 1954).
11. I have taken this term from Herbert Simon, who gives a particularly useful example of a well-formed problem in *The Sciences of the Artificial* (Cambridge, Mass.: M.I.T. Press, 1972).
12. Martin Rein and I have written about problem setting in "Problem-Setting in Policy Research," in Carol Weiss, ed., *Using Social Research in Public Policy Making* (Lexington, Mass.: D. C. Heath, 1977).
13. For an example of multiple views of the malnourishment problem, see Berg,

Scrimshaw, and Call, eds., *Nutrition, National Development, and Planning* (Cambridge, Mass.: M.I.T. Press, 1973).

14. See Russell Ackoff, "The Future of Operational Research is Past," *Journal of Operational Research Soc. 30* (2), 1979, pp. 93–104.

15. I have taken this phrase from the work of the psychiatrist Harry Stack Sullivan.

16. The term is Clifford Geertz's. See his *The Interpretation of Cultures* (New York: Basic Books, 1973).

17. Schein, op. cit., p. 44.

18. As Richard Bernstein has written in *The Restructuring of Social and Political Theory* (New York: Harcourt, Brace, Jovanovich, 1976), "There is not a single major thesis advanced by either nineteenth century Postivists or the Vienna Circle that has not been devastatingly criticized when measured by the Positivists' own standards for philosophical argument. The original formulations of the analytic-synthetic dichotomy and the verifiability criterion on meaning have been abandoned. It has been effectively shown that the Positivists' understanding of the natural sciences and the formal disciplines is grossly oversimplified. Whatever one's final judgment about the current disputes in the post-empiricist philosophy and history of science . . . there is rational agreement about the inadequacy of the original Positivist understanding of science, knowledge and meaning."

19. Gilbert Ryle, "On Knowing How and Knowing That," in *The Concept of Mind* (London: Hutcheson, 1949), p. 32.

20. Andrew Harrison, *Making and Thinking* (Indianapolis, Ind.: Hackett, 1978).

21. Chester Barnard, *The Functions of the Executive* (Cambridge, Mass.: Harvard University Press, 1968), p. 306; first published in 1938.

22. Michael Polanyi, *The Tacit Dimension* (New York: Doubleday, 1967), p. 12.

23. Geoffrey Vickers, unpublished memorandum, M.I.T., 1978.

24. The staff of the Teacher Project consisted of Jeanne Bamberger, Eleanor Duckworth, and Margaret Lampert. My description of the incident of "giving the child reason" is adapted from a project memorandum by Lambert, 1981.

25. Leo Tolstoy, "On Teaching the Rudiments," in Leo Wiener, ed., *Tolstoy on Education* (Chicago: The University of Chicago Press, 1967), pp. 58–59.

PART III

RESTRUCTURING
SCHOOL MANAGEMENT

When one searches for critical leverage points in bringing about school reform, the question of school management quickly surfaces. Superintendents, principals, and other school leaders have access to the important levers that can help or hinder progress toward improvement. It is naive to assume that distant reform measures reach teachers and students without any interpretation and shaping by administrators. The reality is that school administrators shape policy daily as they implement it.

The American system of schools is loosely connected, in a managerial sense. Local schools, as a result, enjoy wide discretion despite spirited efforts to the contrary from distant reformers. The same is true within the individual school. Teachers have considerable de facto autonomy behind the closed classroom door. School improvement strategies must take this managerial looseness into account, and innovative leadership models must be created to build the needed cooperation, coordination, and order for the system to work effectively. On behalf of the Education Commission of the States, E. Patrick McQuaid wrote recently (in *Education Week*, June 17, 1987, p. 19), "Leadership is quickly replacing literacy as the new catchphrase in social commentary. But like literacy, and its many prefixes, our concept of leadership—and our efforts to fill a leadership void—are rooted in yesterday's assumptions and yesterday's national need. Just as it is time to identify the literacy needs of a coming generation, so too must we recognize the need for a new understanding and a new appreciation of leadership." It is clear that little progress will be made with respect to meaningful school reform unless there are serious attempts to examine critically the traditional management posture and to develop better alternatives. The chapters of Part III examine issues of leadership and management, seeking to provide an account that is both practical and efficacious with respect to school improvement.

In Chapter 10, Thomas J. Sergiovanni suggests that present school improvement efforts are limited in effectiveness because they are based on inadequate management premises and a theory of leadership that has reached its limits. This transactional view of management and leadership, when articulated in practice, is able to ensure a minimum level of commitment from followers, to bring standards up to par, and to elicit "a fair day's work for a fair day's pay." He concludes that transactional leadership has run its course and thus cannot do anything more to tap the potential of followers, to increase individual performance, or to bring about improved school productivity.

Sergiovanni proposes *transformative* leadership as an alternative to *transactional*. Transformative leadership has the potential to tap higher levels of human potential, to build commitment, and to motivate followers, with improved consequences in both satisfaction and performance. Relying on motivational theory, the research associated with increased work performance, and recent studies of leadership effectiveness, he points out that transformational leadership can sustain performance beyond external conditions and beyond normal expectations in both quantity and quality.

Sergiovanni points out that one of the reasons why transformative leadership is more efficacious than transactional is that it can bring about a sense of order and coordination in the loosely connected world of schooling. In such a world, leadership and the roles of school administrators remain important, but leadership practice is different. He then reviews a number of key values that characterize transformative leadership in action. Among them are leadership by purpose, leadership by empowerment, leadership density, and leadership by outrage. Sergiovanni concludes his discussion of the leadership needed for quality schooling by noting that leadership and management are linked in such a way that one supports the other. He recommends, therefore, that the concept of management not be omitted from discussions of leadership. Instead, it must be recognized that the leader-manager is to be preferred to the routine-manager as the template for school administrators.

In Chapter 11, Roland S. Barth asserts that teaching is in trouble and that little can happen to improve schools in the long run unless repairs are made in the basic structure of work for teachers and in the quality of work life they experience. He believes it is essential to make teaching less a job and more a profession. He notes that efforts to improve teaching to date, such as career ladders, pay incentive schemes, raised certification requirements, and improved evaluation procedures, have only limited value because they are "outside-of-school remedies to inside-of-school problems."

Barth argues that principals can and should play key roles in enhancing the profession of teaching. He reasons that what matters most is what teachers experience in their daily work lives and that principals are in a unique role to improve this setting. The building of collegiality within the school is all-important. Collegiality, he points out, is not the same as congeniality. Congeniality has to do with how well people get along together, while collegiality involves how well people work together. Barth then reviews research on characteristics of school faculties where the value of collegiality is strong and principals' behaviors seem related to building collegiality.

A second dimension of teacher professionalism over which principals have strong influence is allowing and encouraging teachers to participate in the decisionmaking structure of the school. Barth notes that teachers make literally thousands of decisions in each day about supplies, discipline, and matters of teaching, but other important decisions that affect their work are typically made by someone else. This results, he maintains, in a feeling of inefficacy that erodes professionalism and thus endangers continuous, long-term school improvement. He then provides a number of illustrations of decisions that teachers can either make by themselves or can help the principal make. In his words, "Principals can recognize teachers not as competitors but as capable practitioners and help them develop skills that will improve their professional practice. Principals need to find ways to share with teachers as much responsibility as both are able to handle."

Barth feels that principals can also contribute to the professionalism of teachers by encouraging them to be more visionary and by creating a learning community within the school that encourages not only students but also principals and teachers to become learners. To this end, he advocates school-based staff development as a more effective alternative than districtwide attempts or university-based programs. Barth also addresses the need for teachers to accept greater responsibility for helping one another; within this context, he discusses the concept of mentoring. Throughout this discussion, the norm of collegiality looms large. Collegiality, Barth believes, can help focus the energies of the faculty on the work of the school and can bond teachers together as colleagues in pursuit of that work. This bonding then produces norms that govern the standard teachers are to uphold, thus serving as a built-in quality control mechanism.

Barth points out that as principals work to increase the professionalism of the staff, their own power and status is enhanced. He believes that principals are not only important but critical in bringing about school improvement. Barth then shifts his attention to increasing the effectiveness of principals. He acknowledges that behind every successful school is a successful principal; for better or for worse, principals have a disproportionate influence on what teachers teach and what students learn. For this reason, improving the effectiveness of principals must be a top priority in efforts to improve the schools.

Writing as a superintendent turned professor, Larry Cuban, in Chapter 12, provides a realistic appraisal of the district superintendent's role in restructuring schools. He points out that the environment for school administration is turbulent and that conflict is the DNA of the superintendency. Given this context and the order and stability required by individuals and organizations alike, superintendents are more apt to manage than lead.

In response to the question of why conflict is so basic a part of the superintendency, Cuban provides a historical analysis of the evolution of the role. He notes that conflict is embedded in each of the three core roles of "superintending": instructional, managerial, and political. In answer to the question of why superintendents manage more than they lead, Cuban cites once again the origins of the position and the multiple roles and expectations that are inherent in this position as main contributors. To these he adds such factors as socialization and training, uncertainty in determining effectiveness, and convenience.

Despite these overwhelming odds, Cuban points out that planned changes by superintendents do occur with some regularity. "How can superintendents driven by an impulse toward the managerial still initiate, adopt, and implement changes in a district? One way to answer this question is to ask about the varied meanings of the word 'change.'" Cuban then provides an analysis of two types of change. *First-order* changes are those that assume that existing goals and structures are basically adequate and that what needs to be done is to improve policies and practices. In the language of engineering, first-order changes are solutions to quality control problems. Within the context of school, they include recruiting better teachers, raising salaries, distributing resources more equitably, selecting better texts, changing the curriculum, and introducing a longer school day. These changes do little to alter the basic structure of schooling with respect to how time and space are used and how teachers and students are organized and assigned. They are designed to make what exists more effective and efficient.

Second-order changes, by contrast, are directed at altering the fundamental way of achieving goals or at introducing new goals and interventions that transform traditional ways of doing things into novel solutions to persistent problems. "The point is to reframe the original problem and restructure organizational conditions to conform with the redefined problems. Engineers would call such changes solutions to design problems." Such solutions would include the use of vouchers, the elimination of attendance boundaries, the introduction of conceptually different models of teaching such as open classrooms, and other changes in teaching and learning that significantly modify the relationships of teachers and teaching. These solutions represent changes in basic governance and authority and in fundamental philosophical premises. Putting second-order changes into practice alters roles, routines, and relationships within the school.

It should surprise no one, Cuban observes, that for the most part superintendents engage in the process of school reform largely by introducing first-order changes. Yet there is a small number of school superintendents who have been successful at introducing second-order changes. Cuban provides a brief historical overview of some of these successful school leaders. He then turns his attention to sketching out "the necessary conditions that have to be in place for second-order changes to occur."

In Chapter 13, David L. Clark and Judith M. Meloy provide a provocative and critical appraisal of the dysfunctions of bureaucracy as a model for schooling. In a country governed constitutionally and committed to democratic values, those who seek to improve schools should look to management principles and organizational designs that reflect these values rather than those of bureaucracy. "The concern is that contemporary organizations have sacrificed the freedom of their employees in favor of control over those employees, to the detriment of both the employee and the organization."

Clark and Meloy ask, what if, instead of bureaucracy, the metaphor of the Declaration of Independence were the basis for organizing schools, school districts, and state school systems? However, they are not content to leave the issue at the level of values. Instead, they provide a review of management thought as developed by such distinguished thinkers as Chester Barnard, Douglas McGregor, Chris Argyris, and Harry Stack Sullivan to support their contention that bureaucracy, in the long run, has negative effects on human performance. They propose a view of management and organization that taps more fully the dimensions of human potential and results in increased performance at work. The evidence they provide in support of this view is too compelling to be ignored by those interested in improving schools.

Clark and Meloy's analysis of democratic values and their place in developing organizational structure and management designs, as well as the social psychological research in support of increased performance at work, lead them to propose a number of propositions that they believe should be the basis for leadership in schools. They conclude their analysis by noting that "the bureaucratic structure is failing in a manner so critical that adaptations will not forestall its collapse. It is impractical, and it does not fit the psychological and personal needs of the workforce." The authors believe that there is overwhelming evidence in support of a shift from bureaucratic to democratic school structures, whether one wishes to rely on the practical grounds of organizational research and its relationship to human performance or on more philosophical grounds.

CHAPTER 10

The Leadership Needed for Quality Schooling

THOMAS J. SERGIOVANNI

Trinity University

The concept of leadership gets a fair amount of attention in the current school reform debate.[1] How can the principal be a more effective leader? What kind of leadership works in getting schools to improve? How can the principal be more effective in getting teachers to teach better? What is the proper leadership role of the state? How can the governors provide the leadership that is needed, and what form should this leadership take? What role should teachers play in the leadership process? How can leadership make schools better places for teaching and learning?

Leadership is the process of persuasion by which a leader or leadership group (such as the state) induces followers to act in a manner that enhances the leader's purposes or shared purposes. How leadership is conceived and practiced makes a difference. To some policymakers and administrators, the power of leadership is in ideas and symbols that touch followers in ways that inspire and create meaning. To others, by contrast, the power of leadership is in the cleverness of the leader in sizing up situations and people, in managing the psychology of followers, and in engineering the workplace to make the difference.

A common mistake of many well-intentioned policymakers and administrators who seek to improve schools is to equate leadership with authority. Authority is the means by which one obtains compliance, even if it is given grudgingly. As John Gardner points out, those who comply grudgingly become subordinates rather than followers.[2] The performance of subordinates is typically marginal, sometimes satisfactory, but rarely extraordinary. Quality schooling will not be achieved by teachers and principals who view themselves as subordinates. Instead, it is necessary to encourage and develop followers, in the truest sense of the word, for followers have the capacity for continued performance beyond expectations. Followers are moved by compelling ideas, meanings, opportunities for higher levels of need fulfillment, and moral purposes. Subordinates are pushed from the outside, but followers are pulled by forces within themselves.

Traditionally, the study of leadership has dwelled on issues of leadership style, levels of decisionmaking (and the consequences of variations of these on teacher satisfaction, compliance, and performance), and school effectiveness. Which style is better: autocratic or democratic, task or relationship, directive or participatory? Contingency theories of leadership ask similar questions. When is it best for the leader to tell, sell, participate, and delegate? Do the job circumstances favor the related or dedicated leadership style? Management theory of this genre relies heavily on change strategies that seek to influence what teachers do by programming how they work. How best to control what people do? What incentives can be offered in order to obtain compliance? "Best" is defined as getting teacher and schools to do whatever it is that the leader wants to accomplish and to be happy with that prospect. Ideally, both the teacher and the leader gain. If enough teachers respond in the way desired by the leader, school effectiveness presumably follows.

AN EMERGING VIEW

James MacGregor Burns provides a language system and set of concepts for sorting and understanding traditional leadership and an emerging view of leadership that provides a more realistic basis for school improvement.[3] Traditional and emergent leadership are not considered to be mutually exclusive. Though one represents a higher and more potent view than the other, both types may be present at the same time and practiced by the same leader. It does make a difference, however, which view of leadership is emphasized and becomes the basis for school improvement efforts. For Burns, leadership is exercised when persons with certain motives and purposes mobilize resources to arouse and satisfy the motives of followers. To this end, he identifies *transactional* leadership and *transformative* leadership; the former focuses on basic, largely extrinsic motives and needs, while the latter focuses on higher-order, more intrinsic needs.

In transactional leadership, administrators and teachers exchange needs and services in order to accomplish independent objectives. The objectives may be related (for example, both apply to a specific school context) but still separate. This exchange process can be viewed metaphorically as a form of *leadership as bartering*. Positive reinforcement is given for good work, merit pay for increased performance, promotion for increased persistence, a feeling of belonging for cooperation, and so on.

Many experts believe that transactional leadership has run its course and thus can do no more to deliver insights and understandings of leadership and management, tap the potential of followers, or increase individual performance and organizational productivity.[4] They maintain that it is based on a limited view of human potential, an inadequate view of how the world works, and an outdated conception of the field of management theory and practice. Other experts point out that transactional leadership provides a "phonetic" view of behavior and needs that overlooks the more "semantic" side of leadership in action.[5] They reason, for example, that it is less important how a principal behaves than what this behavior means to teachers. Focusing on behavior itself and not the meaning of this behavior misses the point. Further, in transactional leadership, the nature of the bargain that is struck as administrator and teachers exchange behaviors and needs emphasizes too much self-interest, overlooking the more moral aspects of school life.

In transformative leadership, by contrast, administrators and teachers are united in pursuit of higher-level goals that are common to both, regardless of their special interests and goals. Both, for example, want to become the best. Both want to shape the school in a new direction. In Burns's language, "such leadership occurs when one or more persons *engage* with others in such a way that leaders and followers raise one another to higher levels of motivation and morality."[6] Their purposes, which might have started out as separate but related, become fused. Initially, transformative leadership takes the form of *leadership as building*. The focus is on arousing human potential, satisfying higher needs, and raising expectations of both leader and follower to motivate them both to higher levels of commitment and performance.

Leadership as bartering responds to the physical, security, social, and ego needs of followers. Leadership as building responds to esteem, competence, autonomy, and self-actualization needs. Examples of concepts associated with transactional leadership are the development of management skills designed to engineer work behaviors, using appropriate leadership styles, and applying the principles of contingency, exchange, and path-goal theory. Examples of concepts associated with transformational leadership as building are empowerment and symbolic leadership.

Transformative leadership ultimately becomes *moral*, in that it raises the level of human conduct and ethical aspiration of both the leader and the follower, thus transforming both.[7] When this occurs, transformative leadership takes the form of *leadership as bonding*. The focus is on arousing an awareness that elevates goals and purposes to the level of a shared covenant. This covenant, in turn, bonds together leader and followers in a moral commitment. Leadership as bonding responds to such human needs as the desire for purpose, meaning, and significance in what one does. Selfishness is replaced by selflessness, and self-interests are transcended in favor of moral purposes. Principals and teachers are engaged in service to teaching and learning, not to protecting turf. State and schools forsake their struggle over power and resources on behalf of quality schooling and society's future.

Each of the forms of leadership have their consequences. Leadership as bartering—the trading of this for that, the striking of bargains—results in calculated commitment and involvement in one's work.[8] Teachers and administrators (school and state) engage in transactions as long as each feels that the other is holding up his or her end of the bargain. When this is the case, all is well for schooling. Administrators, for example, get what they want, and teachers' objectives are also met. However, since continued performance is contingent upon all parties keeping the bargain, it is withdrawn when the bargain is not upheld.

In leadership as building, the involvement of followers is intrinsic. Instead of reacting to forces and conditions outside of themselves, administrators and teachers are driven by inner forces. Instead of being pushed into a bargain by the exchange of wants and needs, they are pulled or attracted to work by its inherent characteristics and the sense of worth and achievement it provides. In leadership as bonding, the stakes are even higher, as involvement becomes moral. In both cases, *performance is sustained beyond external conditions* and (as Bass points out) *is beyond normal expectations in quantity and quality.*[9]

BEYOND EXPECTED PERFORMANCE TO EXCELLENCE IN SCHOOLING

Accumulated research on motivation and performance reveals that transactional leadership, competently practiced, leads only to expected performance.[10] Transformative leadership, by contrast, yields levels of work performance that are beyond normal expectations.[11] Motivation theory can help explain this difference. A basic principle in motivation theory is that people invest themselves in work in order to obtain desired returns or rewards. Rewards can take a variety of tangible and intangible forms, including money, respect, comfort, a sense of accomplishment, acceptance, and security. It is useful to categorize expressions of investment in work as being of two types: *participation* and *performance.*[12] For teachers, the participation investment includes doing all that is necessary to obtain and maintain satisfactory membership in the school. Meeting classes, preparing lesson plans, obtaining satisfactory evaluations from supervisors, following school rules and regulations, attending required meetings, being cooperative, bearing one's fair share of committee responsibility, projecting an appropriate image to the public, meeting deadlines—in short, giving a fair day's work for a fair day's pay—are considered to be examples of the participatory investment. One cannot require teachers to give more of themselves, to go beyond this level of investment.

The performance investment, by contrast, occurs when teachers decide to exceed the limits of the traditional work relationship. They then give more than can be reasonably expected and, in return, are provided with rewards and benefits that are of a different kind. In a sense, they are drawn to higher levels of performance and commitment. In Burns' terms, the leadership that evokes the performance investment transforms one's state of needs from lower to higher by arousing different dimensions of human potential. Ultimately, this leadership becomes moral in its tone and direction, enhancing the significance and meaning of work and life for both leader and followers.

Two questions remain to be considered. Why does transformative leadership work? What are the principles and values that characterize this leadership in action? Transformative leadership works because of its ability to tap higher levels of human potential and because it fits better the way in which the world of organizations work.

CULTURALLY TIGHT AND STRUCTURALLY LOOSE COUPLING IN SCHOOLS

One current controversy in educational administration is the extent to which schools are tightly or loosely connected and what the implications of these configurations are for effective schooling.[13] *Schools are indeed tightly connected, but around cultural, not management, themes.* Teachers and students are driven less by bureaucratic rules, management protocols, contingency tradeoffs, and images of rational reality than by norms, group mores, patterns of beliefs, values, the socialization process, and socially constructed reality. Thus, in a structural sense, schools are loosely connected, but in a cultural sense, they are tightly connected. On the one hand, there is little *sustained* connection between what teachers do and the management systems of which they are a part. On the other hand, most schools have strong informal traditions and norms to which teachers respond. How teachers decide to teach is an example. Though most will "showboat" an official approach to teaching when required, their daily teaching reflects more their patterns of socialization and the norms of the work group.

Transactional leadership works best in an organizational world that is tightly connected managerially but loose culturally. When such is the case, management can rely on bureaucratic linkages and psychological tradeoffs to get teachers to do what they are supposed to. Cultural connections, being weak, are presumed to be of little consequence. School improvement measures that seek to program what teachers do and how they are to teach are based on those premises.

When schools are characterized by loose managerial and tight cultural connectedness, it is transformative leadership that is needed. Transformative leadership is able to bring about order and direction, as well as coordinated efforts, by "domesticating" the "wild" cultural system to which teachers are tightly aligned. In the process, the self-interests of leader and follower are transcended as both respond to a set of shared values of a higher order.

School leaders who rely heavily on transactional leadership believe that goals can be achieved by closely linking various parts of the system and by providing the necessary management controls to ensure that this linkage works properly. Thus, the process of ensuring quality schooling becomes a matter of providing the necessary paths and goals to objectives, linking objectives to the curriculum, and aligning the curriculum to teaching and teaching to testing. A management-oriented supervisory and evaluation system is usually added to allow for proper monitoring of this tightly aligned system. Inducements and exchanges become the psychological energy that drives the system. The system itself represents the "clockwork's" main gears and pins, which must be properly established and monitored to ensure that all the other gears and pins operate reliably and predictably.

By contrast, school leaders who rely primarily on transformative leadership are likely to have a very different view of the workings of the enterprises they lead. When they "open the clock," they see a mechanism gone awry. The wheels and pins are not connected but instead turn and swing independently of each other. They accept the reality that most schools and classrooms are characterized by a great deal of de facto autonomy.

THE NEED FOR COORDINATION AND ORDER

Although transactional and transformative leaders do not share the same view of how schools function or how teaching works, they do share a common commitment to achieving identifiable goals. Further, both types of leaders believe that the work of various school professionals must be coordinated if these goals are to be served well. In other words, the issue of tight or loose connectedness does not bear on the fact that coordinated work is needed and that goals should be pursued in some systematic fashion. The issue is how each of the two groups of leaders work to bring about this coordination.

In both transactional and transformative leadership, the leader is considered to be central to the success of the enterprise. In schools, for example, the issue is not whether leadership is needed or whether principals count, but rather the type of leadership that is provided. With respect to states, the issue is not whether policymakers and state departments should lead or not, but rather the way leadership is exercised. As Weick points out, "Organizational theory is about ways in which indeterminacy can be organized, but what the concept of loose coupling has highlighted is that indeterminacy can be organized not just by rules, job descriptions, and prior specifications, but also by such things as shared premises, culture, persistence, clan control, improvisation, memory, and imitation."[14] He continues:

> In a loosely coupled system, you don't influence less, you influence differently. The administrator . . . has the difficult task of affecting perceptions and monitoring and reinforcing the language people use to create and coordinate what they are doing. A loosely coupled system requires strong leadership of the kind where administrators model the kind of behavior they desire. Charisma becomes more important . . . because it helps to define what the system stands for. Administrators must identify key issues so they can centralize control over a few (not all) issues and help people see them similarly. Leaders in loosely coupled systems have to move around, meet people face-to-face, and do their influencing by interaction rather than by rules and regulations.[15]

His comments are also appropriate when the word "state" is substituted for "administrators." In a loosely connected world, it is culture, not management, that is the key to bringing about the coordination and sense of order needed for effectiveness, and the leadership best suited to this task is transformative.

What are the values underlying transformative leadership? How do these values bring about the order and predictability schools need, in a world characterized by loose connectedness structurally and tight connectedness culturally? A number of values that are central to transformative leadership are described below.

LEADERSHIP BY PURPOSE

Transformative leaders practice leadership by purpose. Vaill defines *purposing* as "that continuous stream of actions by an organization's formal leadership which has the effect of inducing clarity, consensus and commitment regarding the organization's basic purposes."[16] Purposing is a powerful force that responds to human needs, sensing what is important and of value. Alone, one teacher can make sense of his or her work life and derive satisfaction from it, but experts agree that meaning, significance, and satisfaction are considerably enhanced when this process is shared. The key to the concept of purposing is the building of a *shared* covenant. When shared meaning and significance are present, people respond to work with increased motivation and commitment. In practicing purposing, the leader's behavioral style is not as important as what the leader stands for and communicates to others. The objects of purposing are to stir human consciousness, to enhance meaning, and to spell out key cultural strands. These activities give both excitement and significance to one's work.

Bennis considers vision to be a key concept, aligned with purpose. To him, transformative leadership requires "the capacity to create and communicate a compelling vision of a desired state of affairs, a vision . . . that clarifies the current situation and induces commitment to the future."[17] Leaders who are remiss in expressing and articulating a vision in terms of values and dreams miss the very point of leadership. The vision of a school must also reflect the hopes and dreams, the needs and interests, the values and beliefs of the group. When a school vision embodies the sharing of ideals, a covenant is created that bonds together leader and followers in a common cause. This larger concern is the point of leadership by purpose.

LEADERSHIP BY EMPOWERMENT

Transformative leaders practice the principle of power investment. They distribute power among others in an effort to get more power in return. They know it is not power over people and events that counts, but power over accomplishments and the achievement of organizational purposes. To gain control over the latter, they recognize that they need to delegate or surrender control over the former. Transformative school leaders understand that principals and teachers need to be empowered to act—to be given the necessary responsibility that releases their potential and makes their actions and decisions count. In a structurally loose world, they are resigned to the reality that delegation and empowerment are unavoidable. Empowerment without purposing is not appropriate; the two go hand in hand. When directed and enriched by purposing and fueled by empowerment, principals and teachers respond with increased motivation and commitment to work.

Transformative leaders are more concerned with the concept of power to than with power *over* people. They are concerned with how the power of leadership can help people become more successful, to accomplish the things that they think are important, to experience a greater sense of efficacy. They are less concerned with what people are doing than with what they are accomplishing. Empowerment and efficacy are closely connected ideas. When teachers and principals are empowered, their sense of control increases, as does the belief that they can make a difference. Teacher efficacy has been convincingly linked to more effective teaching and to gains in student learning, as measured by achievement test scores and other indicators of school effectiveness.[18]

LEADERSHIP DENSITY

In *Every Employee a Manager*, Scott Meyers observes that the more management-like jobs are, the more readily workers accept responsibility and respond with increased motivation.[19] "Every employee a manager" is a common goal among highly successful leaders, because they recognize the importance of leadership density and its relationship to organizational effectiveness. "Leadership density" means the extent to which leadership roles are shared and leadership broadly exercised.

Principals and other school administrators get uncomfortable when one starts to talk about shared leadership, leadership density, and similar ideas. Are such murmurs subtle attempts to undermine the leadership roles of administrators? Does anyone really believe that a school or school district can be run by a committee of equals? Such a suggestion flies in the face of well-established management principles, they point out. Does the concept of leadership density imply undermining the legal structure of schooling? Schools, they argue, are *public* organizations, and teachers are more like civil service professionals than independent operators. That being the case, administrators are needed to protect the public trust. Though teachers can be expected (and should be empowered) to respond to professional norms and accepted standards of best practice, accountability in education must be institutionalized at the level of school and district. For these reasons, it is impossible to forsake hierarchical structures and administrative systems of accountability in favor of peer-administered schools. This argument is persuasive. Despite occasional experiments with peer-run schools,[20] principals are here to stay. However, the arguments for maintaining principalship are not sufficiently compelling to preclude the acceptance and use of the principle of leadership density.

When leadership density is practiced, the leader is still in charge, but in a different way. Principals are not solo performers but lead members of collegial teams. Among physicians, the leader is "head surgeon"—a head, certainly, but first of all a surgeon. In law, the leader is a "senior partner"—first of all a partner. Similarly, in schools, the leader should be a "principal teacher"—first of all a teacher. Head surgeons, senior partners, and principal teachers are leaders among colleagues. A close reading of the case study research on highly successful schools reveals that the line between principal and teacher is not drawn very tightly; successful principals typically view themselves as principal-teachers. Teachers, in turn, assume a great deal of responsibility; they exercise leadership freely.

In institutions that are culturally tight but managerially loose in their organization and functioning, leaders have no choice but to rely on leadership density concepts. As John Gardner points out, American society is characterized by dispersed leadership. In his words, "we tend to forget that the nation is made up of innumerable subsystems loosely related in ever-changing configurations, subsystems that sometimes mesh but often clash. The difficult task of making fluid, interacting systems function effectively cannot be ordained from a central point. We cannot expect top leaders, working alone, to make the system work without the help of many others throughout the society. A great many individuals throughout the system must be in a state of psychological readiness to take the initiative, to take leaderlike action to improve the functioning at their level."[21]

If the practicality of leadership density is not sufficiently shown by the internal loose connectedness of school institutions and the reality of leadership dispersion, then consider the "ability–authority gap."[22] In enterprises of even modest technical complexity, a gap exists between those who have the ability to do and those who have the authority to decide. Clearly this is the case in schools. The wise leader acknowledges this gap and lends his or her authority to others as the means to borrow their ability.

LEADERSHIP BY OUTRAGE

When one observes transformative leaders at work, it becomes apparent that they know the difference between sensible toughness and merely looking and acting tough. Real toughness doesn't come from flexing one's muscles simply because one happens to have more power than another. Real toughness is always principled and value-based. Transformative leaders, for example, view empowerment, delegating, sharing, and other leadership values within a target frame of reference. The center of the target represents the core values and beliefs of the school; the distance between the center and the outer boundary of the target represents how these values might be articulated and implemented in the practices and work of the school.

Transformative leaders expect adherence to common values but provide wide discretion in implementation. They are outraged when they see these common values violated. The values of the common core are "non-negotiables," making up the covenant that defines the way of life in the school. On the other hand, teachers enjoy wide discretion in organizing their classrooms and deciding what, when, and how to teach, providing that the decisions they make embody the shared values that make up the school's covenant.

In this sense, transformative leaders seek to develop schools that are both tightly and loosely structured—tight on values and loose on how values are embodied in the practice of teaching, supervision, and administration. Schools and state are tied together similarly when transformative leadership is provided at that level.

School cultures are concerned with the values, beliefs and expectations that administrators, teachers, students, and others share. Transformative leaders help to shape this culture, work to design ways and means to transmit this culture to others, and, most important, behave as guardians of the values that define the culture. When the leader acts as guardian of school values, the values enjoy a special verification in importance and meaning; they become real-life cultural imperatives rather than abstractions. This kind of leadership transforms followers by arousing higher levels of need and tapping higher dimensions of human potential, as well as bonding followers and leaders together as part of a shared covenant.

In many school improvement efforts, there is a glaring lack of understanding of what accountability is and how it works. Accountability and responsibility go hand in hand. One cannot hold teachers accountable without first giving them responsibility, nor can one hold principals accountable in the absence of responsibility. Authentic accountability can be achieved only when teachers and principals are provided with authority to match their responsibility. The leadership values described above can provide policymakers, administrators, and teachers with the ideas needed to build real accountability into America's schools.

ROUTINE-MANAGER AND LEADER-MANAGER

Eventually, discussions of leadership address the question of leadership versus management. Should the principal, for example, be a leader or a manager? "Managers are interested in doing things right, and leaders are interested in doing right things." Cast in that light, it is clear that schools need both management and leadership. If both qualities are not present in the same administrator, they should be built into the administrative team.

Nonetheless, American schools are too often overmanaged and underled. Present reform efforts have a tendency to encourage that trend. As legislated learning leads to bureaucratic teaching, so does legislated schooling lead to bureaucratic management. The choice should not be between management and leadership but between conceiving of school administrators as routine-managers or as leader-managers.

As Gardner points out, leader-managers can be distinguished from routine-managers in several respects. Translated to the school context, leader-managers

1. Think about the longer term—beyond the day's crisis, beyond the next testing period, beyond the end of the school year
2. Look beyond the school or school district they are heading and grasp its relationship to larger realities—the broader community context, conditions external to the school or school district, and societal trends
3. Reach and influence constituents beyond their jurisdictions and boundaries, overcoming bureaucratic constraints and rising above jurisdictions to bring together fragmented constituencies that must work together to solve a problem
4. Put heavy emphasis on intangible visions, values, and motivations and have an intuitive understanding of the nonrational and tacit elements in leader-follower interactions
5. Have the political skill to cope with conflicting requirements, multiple goals, and multiple constituencies
6. Think in terms of renewal, not accepting existing structure and processes as the routine manager does, but seeking the revision of structure and processes required by ever-changing reality.[23]

One important characteristic of the leader-manager is an understanding of what each of these dimensions can and cannot do. As H. Ross Perot, an accomplished leader-manager, points out: "People cannot be managed. Inventories can be managed, but people must be led."[24] Applying this principle to schools, it is clear that quality schooling is a goal that cannot be managed bureaucratically but must result from leadership.

Transformative leadership deals with values, covenants, and shared purposes, and moral action is thus unavoidable when it is practiced. Ultimately, transformative and moral leadership become one and the same. The emphasis shifts from such "means" values as honesty, fairness, loyalty, patience, and openness to what Burns calls "end" values.[25] These values are concerned with the larger purposes to be served by the actions and decisions of leaders, followers, and the institutions they represent. Examples of such values are justice, community, excellence, democracy, and equality.

The culture of management in general, and educational administration in particular, sometimes makes it awkward to speak of transformative leadership in moral terms. People are not accustomed to talking about leadership and organization in such dramatic language. However, if there is to develop a theory and practice of leadership that fits the real world of schooling, little choice is available.

The more comfortable technical language of transactional leadership does not produce efficacious leadership theory and practice that is able to move teachers, students, and school much beyond expected performance. However, by building on transactional leadership, transformative leadership offers a great deal. It can tap higher levels of human potential and produce inspired levels of performance that will lead to excellence in schooling. It also seems better fitted to a world of schooling that is characterized by structural looseness and cultural tightness. Finally, as Thomas Green asserts, "The moral character of the profession does not derive from its body of technical expertise. It derives rather from the fact that a profession is a social practice that is already moral."[26] On this basis, transformative leadership comes closer to the point of leadership. These are, I believe, compelling reasons for using the new leadership values as a basis for future school improvement efforts.

NOTES

1. See, for example, E. Patrick McQuaid, "Go to the Head of the Class: Leadership Critical for Restructuring Schools," *Education Week,* June 17, 1987, p. 19.

2. John W. Gardner, "The Nature of Leadership: Introductory Considerations," Leadership Paper No. 1, Leadership Studies Program, Independent Sector, 1986.

3. James MacGregor Burns, *Leadership* (New York: Harper and Row, 1978).

4. See, for example, Bernard Bass, *Leadership and Performance Beyond Expectations* (New York: The Free Press, 1985).

5. See, for example, Louis Pondy, "Leadership is a Language Game," in Morgan McCall, Jr. and Michael M. Lombardo, eds., *Leadership: Where Else Can We Go?* (Durham, N.C.: Duke University Press, 1978), pp. 87–100.

6. Burns, op. cit., p. 17.

7. Ibid.

8. Amitai Etzioni, *A Comparative Analysis of Complex Organizations* (New York: The Free Press, 1961).

9. Bass, op. cit.

10. See, for example, Bass, op. cit.; Thomas J. Sergiovanni, "Leadership and Excellence in Schooling," *Educational Leadership* 45 (5), 1984, pp. 4–13.

11. See, for example, Bass, op. cit.; Burns, op. cit.; Warren Bennis and Burt Nanus, *Leaders: the Strategies for Taking Charge* (New York: Harper and Row, 1985); Terence Deal and Alan Kennedy, *Corporate Cultures* (Reading, Mass.: Addison-Wesley, 1982); Sara Lightfoot, *The Good High School* (New York: Basic Books, 1983); and Joan Lipsitz, *Successful Schools for Young Adolescents* (New Brunswick, N.J.: Transaction, 1984).

12. Thomas J. Sergiovanni, "New Evidence on Teacher Morale: A Proposal for Staff Differentiation," *North Central Association Quarterly* 63 (3), 1968, pp. 259–266; Thomas J. Sergiovanni, "Factors Which Affect Satisfaction and Dissatisfaction of Teachers," *Journal of Educational Administration* 5 (1), 1967, pp. 66–82.

13. See, for example, Karl E. Weick, "Educational Organizations as Loosely Coupled Systems," *Administrative Science Quarterly* 21 (1), 1976, pp. 1–19; and Weick, "The Concept of Loose Coupling: An Assessment." *Organizational Theory Dialogue,* December 1986, pp. 8–11.

14. Weick, op. cit. (1986), p. 8.

15. Ibid., p. 10.

16. Peter Vaill, "The Purposing of High-Performing Systems" in Thomas J. Sergiovanni and John E. Corbally, eds., *Leadership and Organizational Culture* (Urbana, Ill.: University of Illinois Press, 1984), p. 91.

17. Warren Bennis, "Transformative Power and Leadership," in Sergiovanni and Corbally, op. cit., p. 66.

18. Patricia T. Ashton and Rodman B. Webb, *Making a Difference: Teachers' Sense of Efficacy and Student Achievement* (New York: Longman, 1986). See also Peter Mortimore and

Pam Sammons, "New Evidence on Effective Elementary Schools," *Educational Leadership 45* (1), 1987, pp. 4–8.

19. M. Scott Meyers, *Every Employee a Manager* (New York: McGraw-Hill, 1971).

20. See, for example, "In Minnesota Experiment, Committee of Teachers Replaces Principal," *Education Week*, June 17, 1987.

21. Gardner, op. cit., p. 17.

22. Amitai Etzioni, *A Comparative Analysis of Complex Organizations* (New York: The Free Press, 1961).

23. Gardner, op. cit., p. 8.

24. James M. Kouzes and Barry Z. Posner, *The Leadership Challenge* (San Francisco: Jossey-Bass, 1987), p. xv.

25. Burns, op. cit.

26. Thomas E. Green, "The Conscience of Leadership," in Linda T. Sheive and Marian B. Schoenheit, eds., *Leadership: Examining the Elusive*, 1987 Yearbook, Association for Supervision and Curriculum Development (Alexandria, Va.), p. 108.

CHAPTER 11

The Principal & the Profession of Teaching

ROLAND S. BARTH

Harvard University

Teaching has become an extraordinarily difficult occupation, one made no easier by the public, who have little confidence in what teachers do and who pare away the resources with which they are expected to do it. Teachers are dejected. Many would not enter the profession if again given a choice. They commonly report a sense of discontent and malaise; they feel unappreciated, overworked, and demeaned as professionals. They feel little trust for or from either school and district administrators or the public. They are even alienated from one another. They feel trapped in their jobs, powerless to effect change, and frustrated at the never-ending nonteaching demands.

Increasingly, schools are staffed with veteran, tenured teachers who are afforded little horizontal or vertical professional mobility. For most there is little to do next September except what they did last September: same books, same room, same associates, same curriculum, same subjects, and same grade level—a formula for personal and professional atrophy. Many would agree with what one fourth-grade teacher told me recently: "Excellence is no longer a goal toward which to aspire. Now I'm satisfied if I can do it at all, let alone well." Teachers are encountering times more difficult than any other period in American education. The social value of their work, which has fueled them through past difficulties, no longer provides sufficient compensation and professional invigoration. A bumper sticker appearing in parking lots of many public schools sums it up: I Feel Better Now That I've Given Up Hope.

Theodore Sizer observes that prior to 1960 a position in public education was a "calling."[1] During the 1960s and 1970s, education became more of a profession. In the 1980s, says Sizer, it has become a job. As a calling or a profession, education offers much to teachers and their students; as a job it offers little. Fortunately, the crisis in teaching—attracting capable persons into the classroom, retaining them, and supporting them in their important work—has become an issue of national importance. However, now we must determine under what conditions teaching can become less of a job and more of a profession. Several remedies are proposed: improve all teachers' salaries; compensate the best teachers through merit pay; construct career ladders that will pay those who assume more responsibility; support the training of the best and the brightest so that they will choose to enter teaching; make teacher evaluation more rigorous; and raise teacher-certification requirements.

Although these proposals promise much, all are outside-of-school remedies to inside-of-school problems. Therefore, they offer little hope of influencing the basic culture of the schools. And in the ethos of the workplace is where the problems reside—and where, I believe, the most promising solutions reside as well. The moment of truth for the teaching profession comes when the alarm rings at 6:30 A.M. How does the teacher respond? Higher salaries, career ladders, and certification requirements will little influence the reaction of the waking teacher. Yet it is the satisfaction that teachers experience in their daily work that, more than anything else, defines their professionalism.

Four years of public-school teaching in Massachusetts and California and ten years as a principal in urban New Haven and suburban Newton and Brookline convince me that the nature of the relationships among the adults who inhabit a school has more to do with a school's quality and character, the accomplishments of its pupils, and the professionalism of its teachers than does any other factor.[2] The success of a school depends on interactions between teacher and teacher, teacher and administrator, and all school staff and parents. I am convinced that the school principal is in the best position to influence these relationships and thereby the profession of teaching. In this chapter I attempt to support these beliefs and to determine how changes in the relationship between teachers and principal and among teachers can contribute to the professionalization of teaching.

COLLEGIALITY

The relationship between teacher and principal has become increasingly strained by the growing emphasis on teacher accountability, pupil minimum competence, parent involvement, and collective bargaining and by declines in the student population and in the teaching force. All of this is accompanied by increased litigation against schools and teachers.

The pathology of the principal–teacher relationship in schools is symbolized by "the parking lot syndrome." As principal, I prepared carefully for my first faculty meeting. I arranged chairs in circles and encouraged several teachers to contribute. Yet during the meeting I found that I did most of the talking while the teachers sat quietly by. A few minutes after the meeting I looked out my office window at the school parking lot and there the *real* faculty meeting was taking place. Little clusters of teachers were abuzz, expressing their ideas about all the subjects on the agenda. In faculty rooms principals talk; in parking lots teachers talk. But seldom do teachers and principals talk openly together.

Similarly, the pathology of the relationship among teachers in schools is symbolized by my experience during a recent visit to a public junior high school. On the way to the teachers' lounge I noticed a sign on the door: No Students Are Allowed. When I commented on the message, a teacher said: "There are two rules for this room. That's the written one. The unwritten one is, 'No talking about teaching in the teachers' room.'" Probably no statement so well captures the absence of professionalism among teachers.

The relationships among adults in most schools are primitive, affording administrator and teacher little satisfaction or assistance. Sociologist Dan Lortie found that in the eyes of most teachers, learning, success, and satisfaction come largely from interaction with students in the classrooms and that ". . . all other persons [parents, the principal, other teachers] without exception were connected with undesirable occurrences. Other adults have potential for hindrance but not help.[3] This condition of adult alienation must be redressed if teaching is to become a satisfying profession.

Strangely, collegiality is seldom mentioned in the effective-schools literature of the past decade. It is not listed with such factors as strong leadership, emphasis on basic skills, a clear sense of purpose, monitoring of academic progress, and an orderly school environment. Nor is collegiality part of the vocabulary of recent national studies of American education. It is recognized neither as part of the problem nor as part of the solution.

Relationships among adults in schools—*all* schools, from preschools to graduate schools—take several forms. One of them is described by a wonderful term from nursery-school teachers' parlance, "parallel play." Two 3-year-olds are busily engaged in opposite corners of a sandbox. One has a shovel and bucket; one has a rake and hoe. At no time do they borrow each other's toys. Although in proximity and having much to offer one another, each works and plays pretty much in isolation. This description serves remarkably well as a characterization of adult relationships in schools.

But, of course, not all adult relationships in schools are independent. I observe three different forms of interaction:

Adversarial relationships. Recently, a Boston-area principal made a sage observation: "You know, we educators have drawn our wagons into a circle and trained our guns—on each other." When we adults in school interact, all too often we attack one another. Somehow we manage to create opponents under our own roofs. It may be that adversarial relationships among adults in school make "parallel play" a welcome alternative.

Competitive relationships. Typically, competition takes the form of withholding. My experience suggests that most school staff have extraordinary insights about their important work—about discipline, parental involvement, budgeting, child development, leadership, and curriculum. These hard-won insights have as much value as elegant research studies and national reports. But our work at the Harvard Principals' Center indicates that adults in schools have a strong reluctance to make their craft knowledge available to others who are competitors for scarce resources and recognition—that is, to almost everyone else. No profession can survive, let alone flourish, when its members are cut off from others and from the rich knowledge base on which success and excellence depend.

Collegial relationships. The least common form of relationship among adults in schools is one that is collegial, cooperative, and interdependent. Collegiality is not the same as congeniality. According to Little, collegiality is the presence of four specific behaviors.[4] First, adults in schools talk about the practice of teaching and learning frequently, continuously, and in concrete and precise terms. Second, they observe each other teaching and administrating. Third, they work on the curriculum together by planning, designing, researching, and evaluating. Finally, they teach each other what they know about teaching, learning, and leading. As obvious, logical, and compelling as these ideas are, they find all too small a following in schools. Enormous risks and costs are associated with observing, communicating, sharing knowledge, and talking openly about the work that we do. Yet somehow most good schools that I have been in are ones where parallel behavior and adversarial and competitive relationships among adults have been transformed into cooperative, collegial ones.

There is growing evidence that principals who hold collegiality as a goal can help schools move toward it. Principals may not have tremendous resources at their disposal, but most have more than they use. For instance, Little found that a norm of collegiality in a school was related to four specific behaviors of the principal: (a) explicitly stating expectations for cooperation among teachers ("I expect all of us to work together, help one another, and make our knowledge available"); (b) providing a model for collegiality, that is, enacting it by joining with teachers and other principals in improving conditions in the school; (c) rewarding collegiality by granting release time, recognition, space, materials, or funds to support it; and (d) protecting teachers who engage in collegial behavior and who risk the retribution of their fellows.[5]

In my own experience as a principal, I found other ways to counter the taboo against teacher collegiality that exists in schools.[6] We decided to hold each faculty meeting in the classroom of a different teacher. During the first 20 minutes, host teachers told us what they did in their rooms and something about the curriculum, grouping practices, and special characteristics of the class. Although initially these parts of the meetings were tense, the faculty grew more comfortable—both as "presenters" and "receivers"—at these sessions. This rather contrived activity "primed the pump" and legitimized talk about instruction.

Students were placed with teachers each spring on the basis of two considerations. Under what instructional conditions does each child in a class seem to work best? Which of next year's teachers comes closest to providing those conditions? In order to answer these questions, teachers had to observe carefully each student in the class. They also had to learn something beyond faculty-room gossip about how their colleagues taught. Each "sending" teacher spent a half day during the winter observing the classroom of each "receiving" teacher, for the purpose of finding the optimal placement for students. After each visit the two teachers had lunch together. This process, of course, violated the taboo against one teacher invading the sanctuary of another's classroom. But it led to better pupil-teacher matches (and therefore to better school experiences for students), updated the stereotypes teachers held of one another, and frequently stimulated conversations about how a teacher might handle a student's unique problem.

It has long been my belief that the optimal number of adults working together for children is two. One teacher in a self-contained classroom gets pretty lonely and depleted. Large teams, on the other hand, spend too much time and energy in meetings, trying to achieve consensus. Consequently, I encouraged teachers to pair with one another, and almost half of them did so. The exchange might simply be "You take my kids for math, and I'll take yours for language" or a more elaborate set up in which the two teachers trade all the time in different subjects. Or it might be that they treat the two classrooms as one large class and divide their responsibilities. Teachers working in teams are provided with a built-in support system, an adult with whom each can talk about teaching, learning, and students. In short, teachers who work together enjoy a professional, collegial relationship.

MAKING IMPORTANT DECISIONS

A second building block of teacher professionalism over which principals have particular influence is allowing and encouraging teachers to make decisions about important elements of their work. Teachers, of course, make thousands of decisions each day in their classrooms—decisions about supplies, discipline, the beginning and ending of activities, and so forth. But other important decisions that directly affect teachers' work are made by someone else. Exclusion from critical choices leads to a pervasive feeling of inefficacy that erodes the profession. As one teacher put it: "I would not advise any of my children to become a teacher. There is no room to do things that I believe in as an educator." Teaching cannot become a profession until teachers influence important decisions. Let me give a few illustrations of decisions to which teachers can be a party and can often make by themselves.

1. Sabbaticals and leaves of absence

In a good school each adult chooses to be there. All too many teachers feel that school is as compulsory for them as it is for their students. Teachers need periodic opportunities to commit and recommit to their work; otherwise the profession becomes a job. I know one principal who each week declares "my 1-hour sabbatical," leaves her building, and walks along a riverbank to contemplate. When she returns she chooses to go back into the school.

A request by any teacher for a leave of absence for any purpose should be granted. The teacher is requesting an opportunity to stop, reflect, replenish, and consider other options. If the teacher returns to the school, everyone wins—the teacher, students, and school; if the teacher decides to leave, everyone also wins. Sabbaticals would be preferable, but automatic availability of leaves of absence without pay can also help relieve the trapped feeling that is so prevalent in teaching. A school full of indentured servants is not a good school for anyone. Teachers become professional to the extent that they make a genuine commitment to be there. Principals facilitate these important efforts.

2. Changes in work

As a principal, I met annually with each teacher who had recommitted to such employment and asked him or her: "If you could decide under ideal conditions what you would like to do next year and with whom, what would it be?" I provided one boundary condition: teachers had to work in the school in some way with children. In short, I invited teachers to disregard all practical constraints for a few moments and reflect on their work as educators; consider current interests, ideas, skills, and relationships; and engage in some "if only" brainstorming. My objective was that all of us might come to school each September with at least one significant new element in our professional and personal lives—something to dream about, think about, worry about, get excited about, be afraid about, become and remain alive about.

Many teachers expressed the wish to do "the same thing" next year. But more teachers came ready to dream. A teacher aide wanted to become a librarian; a teacher wanted to become a principal; two teachers wanted to work together. It came as a surprise to us how closely we were able to comply with most of these "fantasies." The results suggest that following the best interests of teachers is often in the best interests of their students and the school. Teachers do not have to spend another year doing the same thing in the same place in the same way. Fundamental changes replenish the professional and the profession.

3. Spending money

Money is a symbol. It is also an antidote to a feeling of inefficacy. A little money is a large antidote. Each year our school was allocated about $30.00 per child for all instructional purposes. As principal I chose to divide the funds into 25 pieces by allocating a "fair share"—$400.00 per year—to each teacher. How this money was spent was left to the discretion of each teacher; it could go for texts, games, food, teacher courses, field trips, or testing materials.

Many things happened. Book salespeople had to convince teachers that a product was helpful to teachers and valuable for children. Teachers were very resourceful with their limited funds. A box of geoblocks costs about $40.00, a sizable portion of a year's budget. Each of three fourth-grade teachers contributed $13.00, and all of their students used the blocks as often as they might have had the blocks belonged to one class. Thus, important decisions about teaching materials rested in the hands of those most qualified to make them. Teachers talked with each other about what the children were doing, even came into each other's rooms to observe, and occasionally grouped their classes for activities using the blocks.

Four hundred dollars is not much, but it is $400.00 more than many teachers have to spend. It is meaningless to give people responsibility without giving them the resources with which to exercise that responsibility. In that sense, the money is almost as important as a symbol as it is as a means for teachers to buy materials and supplies. It is a vote of confidence. What teachers do with limited funds is what most people do with their budgets: they become responsible and resourceful; they feel empowered.

4. Curriculum

The profession of teaching does not face the same crisis in colleges and universities and in independent schools that it does in public elementary and secondary schools. One reason for this is that professors and teachers in private schools have a major influence over what they teach, how, and with which materials. Public elementary and secondary teachers have less control over curriculum, but they can have more. Again, the school principal can be part of either the problem or solution for teachers.

Each June, I asked teachers to prepare for the following year curriculum outlines that revealed what they expected to teach. The outlines might reflect a little or a lot of the system's guidelines, but above all they were to be "honest." This practice shifted the teacher's role. Teachers were expected to be creative rather than compliant. Although exposing themselves in this way caused both labor and risks, most teachers gladly accepted the accountability because with the costs came a large measure of control over classroom instruction.

Unlike the system's guidelines, the teachers' never corresponded neatly to one another. Their curriculum outlines did not form anything resembling a coherent blueprint for the elementary years, suitable for solemn presentation at a PTA meeting. So each year we selected a different subject—science, for instance—and collated each teacher's plans for the year. A huge poster in the faculty room revealed what each teacher was doing in science—and showed some startling omissions and redundancies. Why was everyone growing bean seeds? Questions emerged. Teachers had to talk with one another, establish priorities, and make decisions. The curriculum began to be articulated because the teachers became expressive.

The biggest problem besetting schools is the primitive quality of human relationships among children, parents, teachers, and administrators. Many schools perpetuate infantilism. School boards infantilize superintendents; superintendents, principals; principals, teachers; and teachers, children. This results in children and adults who frequently behave like infants, complying with authority because of fear or dependence, waiting until someone's back is turned to do something "naughty." To the extent that teachers become responsible for their own teaching, they not only help children become responsible for their own learning, they also become professional.

SCHOOLWIDE RESPONSIBILITIES

The model of an individual who unilaterally "runs" a school no longer works very well. Problems are frequently too big and too numerous for any person to address alone. Schools need to recognize this and develop many kinds of leadership among many people to replace the venerable, patriarchal model.

School leadership can come from principals who transform adversaries into colleagues, from teachers who individually or collectively take responsibility for the well-being of the school, and from parents who translate a basic concern for their children into constructive actions. School leadership, then, can be considered not only in terms of roles but also in terms of functions. Teachers, principals, and parents need skills, insight, and vision that will equip them to assume responsibility for their schools.

In a law firm, the partners are vitally involved in and influence the organization as well as their particular practices. In schools, however, the principal looks after the organization and teachers look after their individual classrooms. I believe strongly that everyone should look after the organization. The principal can enlist the best efforts of every teacher toward this end.

Principals can recognize teachers not as competitors but as capable practitioners and help them develop skills that will improve their professional practice. Principals need to find ways to share with teachers as much responsibility as both are able to handle. Principals often find it difficult to delegate responsibility. This leaves teachers uninvolved in an important part of school life, unprepared when a principalship opens up in the next town, and feeling not very professional.

As principal, I enlisted committees of teachers to be fully responsible for decisions over matters such as schedules, budgets, staff development, and, yes, fire drills. Teacher "coordinators" were appointed in each subject to mediate between the central office and the faculty while coordinating curriculum within the school.

Involving teachers as committee members and coordinators encourages teachers to relate directly and frequently with one another over conflict-laden issues. Teachers learned that assuming responsibility for school problems frequently means assuming responsibility for one another's problems. The title of coordinator made cooperation not only legitimate and appropriate but expected. Also, both committees and coordinators frequently determined acceptable behavior for teachers. When teachers have legitimate authority that is sanctioned by the principal and faculty, they find the courage to make demands on their colleagues in one instance and to comply with their colleagues' demands on them in another.

Nonteaching responsibilities, then, can enable members of the school community to contribute their strengths and to share the power, the satisfaction, and the price of influence. This exchange contributes to the professionalism of teachers.

TEACHER AS VISIONARY

I can think of nothing so sorely missing in the teaching profession as the engagement of teachers in contemplating what schools should be, what children should learn, and what teaching might become. Schools badly need inhabitants who ask *why*—that is, philosophers. This important function—questioning the way things are—is now performed by 6- and 7-year-olds. Why are there 25 students in a class? Why are the upper grades upstairs and the lower grades downstairs? Why do teachers talk 95% of the time while 95% of the persons in a classroom talk only 5% of the time? Why indeed? We need to devise mechanisms in schools that will allow adults constantly to question embedded ways of doing things. Above all, we need to juxtapose the way things are with school people's visions of how they might become.

Conceptions of quality in schools currently abound—"excellent" schools, "effective" schools, "good" schools, "successful" schools. Yet teachers and principals have developed extraordinary defenses to ward off these and other new ideas imposed from outside.[7] Then where will schools obtain an organizing principle or a sense of moral order? Is there a vision of good education that those who work in the schools will take seriously?

I think that there are many such visions—visions that those who work in schools have. I know of no teacher, principal, counselor, or department head who does not have a sense of the kind of classroom or school he or she would like to see. Many have well-developed visions of the kinds of places in which they would like to have their own children study or in which they themselves would like to work.

All of us who entered teaching brought with us a conception of a desirable school. Each of us had a valued personal vision and was prepared to work, even fight, for it. Over time our personal visions became blurred by the visions, demands, and requirements of others. Many teachers' personal visions are now all but obliterated by external prescriptions. Recently I talked with a group of principals about vision, and one observed, "It's gotten so that what's me is hard to figure out." We have become so habituated to reflecting the visions of others that what we believe is hard to discern. I remember that as a principal I succumbed to what I called "PTA rhetoric," using words like "discipline," "rigor," "work," "basics," "respect." These are good words, but none is part of the vocabulary of my personal vision. In short, I found myself, as most other teachers and principals do, becoming obsessively political while becoming less of a professional.

Why honor the visions of school people? I believe there are several reasons. First, massive research studies stand little chance of having a major and direct influence on schools. In the loosely coupled world of schools, adults usually act on their own conceptions of quality and rarely on the ideals of someone else. One reason to honor the visions of school people, then, is that these are the only prescriptions for school reform that will be taken seriously and sustained.

There is a second reason. Research frequently provides a broad view that is badly needed in schools. Yet, most large-scale research studies are, by nature, a mile wide but only an inch deep. Researchers pay brief visits to many schools, frequently with all the effect of a tea bag swished through a bathtub. The visions of school people, by contrast, stem from many years' experience in only a few school settings. These experiences may be limited in scope, but they are deep. These rich insights, gained from years of practice, give credibility to the visions that school people hold about good education. Strong tea, indeed.

A third reason why I believe that it is essential to elicit the conceptions that school practitioners have about reforming their schools is that, as I vividly recall, the excitement of working in schools, the satisfactions, and the rewards come from studying a difficult situation and then generating one's own plan for improving things. Why should educators be placed—or place themselves—in the position of implementing the grand ideas of others, ideas with which they may not agree? The greatest tragedy I know is to be caught every day in the position of doing something that one does not want to do or does not believe in. Too many educators are playing out this tragedy—functioning as assembly-line robots whose main business is production, not learning. This condition, more than everything else, diminishes professionalism in the public schools.

It is astonishing that the voices of teachers and principals are not more audible in the current discussions and debates about school improvement. It is unthinkable that any other profession undergoing the same close scrutiny would allow all the descriptions of practice, analyses of practice, and prescriptions for improving practice to come only from outsiders looking in. Where are the voices of the insiders?

Those who work in schools can no longer have it both ways, dismissing the many conceptions of quality education that currently bombard them from outside but still refusing to push forward their own visions or goals and approaches for achieving them. If teachers and principals want to participate in attempts to improve the schools, they will have to offer suggestions for improvement.

How to encourage teachers continuously to consider, reflect on, and articulate their visions about what their classrooms and schools might become is a formidable job and right at the heart of what it means to be a professional. Principals have been successful in creating schools of visionaries by becoming more conscious of their own visions, articulating them, and thereby modeling vision making.

Questions that principals ask communicate the importance of vision and the importance of everyone having a vision: Do I have a vision about what this school could be? What are its really important elements? How might I sharpen and clarify it? What would happen if I flew my vision from the flagpole in front of the school? How can I encourage the development of vision in others? How do I reconcile my vision with the hopes and aspirations of so many others? Finally, how can we celebrate personal and collective visions in the daily life of the school?

Nothing so professionalizes teaching as teachers who create within the schoolhouse visions of good education. Each of us who works in a school is not only entitled to his personal vision of what the school might become but has an obligation to uncover, discover, and rediscover what that vision is and to contribute it toward the betterment of the school community. A middle-school teacher said it all: "I need to be part of the forest—creating. I like seeing the whole picture and helping guide toward it."

Ultimately, there are probably two workable strategies for improving schools: (a) somehow getting teachers and principals to work on closing the gap between the way their schools are and the way people outside these schools would have them be or (b) working toward closing the gap between the way schools are and the way those within the schools would like them to be. The latter defines a professional; the former does not. Only when teachers and principals take responsibility for creating an environment conducive to both their students' and their own learning will they be able to carry out some of the visions of the school community.

TEACHER AS LEARNER

A good school ought to be a community of learners, a place where students, principals, and teachers learn and teach. It can be a place where children discover and adults rediscover the joy, the difficulty, the excitement of learning. Learning is lifelong. It is not, as one teacher observed, "something like chicken pox—a childhood disease that makes you itch for a while, then leaves you immune for the rest of your life." School is not a place for little people who are learners and big people who are learned but a place where all people are learners.

Those who value public education should be worried about the stunted growth of teachers because teacher growth is closely related to pupil growth. Probably nothing within a school has more effect on students' skills development, self-confidence, or classroom behavior than the personal and professional growth of their teachers. When teachers examine, question, and reflect on their ideas and develop new practices that lead toward their ideals, students benefit. When teachers stop growing, so do their students.

Yet the professional development of individual teachers is more than a means toward the end of delivering services to students. It should also be an end in itself. Learning ennobles the learner. But because schools and teachers are held accountable for pupil achievement and because any amount of pupil growth is never enough, pupil growth preempts adult growth. Schools are viewed as places where children learn and adults teach. Until teachers are seen as being worthy of receiving services, especially the service of adult education, they will see themselves neither as learners nor as professionals.

Most school districts operate from a "deficiency" model of adult growth. Certain skills—writing behavioral objectives, employing a new language arts program—are deemed by the central administration to be essential for teachers to master. Most teachers do not have the requisite skills, so after-school or release-day workshops are mandated to remedy the weakness. Staff development has thus taken the form of workshops done to someone by someone else, as in the phrase, "to in-service teachers." When a school or school system deliberately sets out to foster new skills by committing everyone to required workshops, little usually happens, except that everyone feels virtuous about having gone through the motions.

School-based staff development tends to be more effective than district-wide attempts and university-based programs. I am convinced that the greatest opportunities for the professional development of teachers reside under the schoolhouse roof and that the principal can be a powerful force in assisting teacher growth. Although it is clear that a principal may have little effect, no effect, or even a negative effect on teacher growth, it is far less clear that a principal can have a positive effect. Although there seems to be widespread agreement about the potential for principals to contribute to teachers' growth, a major reason for the recent proliferation of a new educational cadre called "staff developers" is that school principals have failed to realize their enormous potential as staff developers.

There are good reasons, of course. Is it reasonable to expect the principal, the person with the capacity to terminate the professional life of teachers, to promote that professional life? The culture of schools does cruel things to teachers and to principals and to their relationships. Most people I know who are beginning principals enter their new roles as advocates, friends, helpers, supporters, and often former colleagues of teachers. By December of their first year they have become adversaries, requirers, forcers, judges, and setters of limits.

As an administrator in three elementary schools, I vigorously attempted to promote the personal and professional development of teachers.[8] I encountered many obstacles, only some of which I was able to overcome. When I began as a principal I thought that successful staff development had occurred if teachers did what I expected them to do— followed the curriculum outlines, arrived on time, and wrote careful pupil evaluations. But soon I became dissatisfied with this definition and broadened my conception of effective staff development to having teachers do what I expected them to do and do it *well.* I expected teachers not only to teach about the Navajos but to build hogans with children, to learn Navajo dances, and to write poems about the Indians.

Still, many teachers did not seem passionately committed. So my conception of staff development subsequently extended to something like "Do what is expected of you, do it well, and love it!" I was finding, of course, that although teachers were following the guidelines, they did so with all the eagerness of a child confronting a plate of spinach. I then became intent on finding conditions over which I had control that would make it likely that teachers would conform to my expanded definition. More frustration. Only recently have I begun to realize that I was promoting not staff development but institutional compliance, not the personal and professional growth of teachers but, at best, in-service training.

To be sure, if an organization as complex as a school is to survive, it is important that members conform to certain expectations and norms, such as teaching literacy skills and coming to school on time. But to make these norms the sole content of professional growth is inadequate.

I have since come to a quite different conception of staff development. It consists of listening in a hundred different ways for statements from teachers, usually in the form of "here's what I want to try." Staff development means responding—supplying assistance or encouragement. I have become conscious of a hierarchy in the quality of responses to teachers: (1) not listening; (2) listening; (3) listening and hearing; (4) listening, hearing, encouraging, and valuing the teachers' initiative; (5) listening, hearing, encouraging, valuing the request, and agreeing to share the risks and consequences.

Any initiative emanating from a teacher, whether a request to buy 1,000 tongue depressors or to deviate from the prescribed curriculum in order to build a new one based on last summer's trip to Alaska, carries with it considerable potential for professional growth. The way to ensure that a teacher becomes a deeply engrossed student is to allow and encourage the teacher to identify a problem to be addressed. For adults, as for students, the source of the problem determines the energy and motivation that will be expended to resolve the problem. Some call it "ownership."

I have found professional development most likely to occur as a consequence of teacher and principal pursuing regular school issues and functions thoughtfully and imaginatively. The distinction between principal as "manager" and principal as "instructional leader" is rather misleading and simplistic. *Everything* a principal does has potential for staff development. Through a huge number of small, daily decisions and interactions, the principal, teachers, and pupils live and work. The so-called management functions of principals—student discipline, budgets, scheduling—are occasions, opportunities for the principal to exercise creative instructional leadership.

TEACHER AS MENTOR

I find the common conception that the knowledge base for improving schools resides in universities but that practice resides in schools to be inaccurate, simplistic, and disturbing. I know of no schoolteacher or principal who works without some organizing principle or framework—or, in university language, a theory. Theories about teaching, parent involvement, curriculum improvement, and motivation abound in schools. Some of these school-based theories are good, some fragmentary, and a few elegant. Be that as it may, educational practitioners are theory makers as well as theory consumers.

The knowledge base for school improvement comprises research from the academic community and craft knowledge from teachers and principals. One reason for teachers to be providers as well as consumers of information is that their craft knowledge can contribute to the betterment of schools.

A second reason for teachers to convey to other adults what they know is that by so doing they derive enormous professional satisfaction and recognition. Despite the good rhetoric about the importance of schoolteachers that has been offered in recent state and national reform proposals, few teachers feel valued or recognized for their work. This is hardly what PTAs, superintendents, school boards, and principals convey to teachers each day. Yet, of all the pressing needs of public-school professionals, none is more vital than the need for personal and professional recognition from a society that values an education far more than it values those who provide it.

For teaching to become a profession, teachers must feel professionally recognized. Recognition for teachers can come from inviting them to share their craft knowledge with colleagues and others, from allowing them to make major decisions, and from enabling them to become mentors to others who would like to become capable of the craft of teaching.

In schools there is a taboo against a teacher professing to know something, let alone daring to share it with others. A teacher seldom stands up in a faculty meeting and says, "I want to tell you about this terrific idea I have for grouping students—or evaluating them, or disciplining them." Many teachers believe that one's knowledge, skills, and success in schools are private matters.

How can a teacher working full-time in the classroom assume responsibility as colleague and mentor to other practicing teachers as well as to prospective teachers? Once again, I find that the principal occupies a central position.

I find that principals who are successful in unlocking the talents of their teachers seem to hold several assumptions: that every teacher possesses strengths and insights of value to others; that we should rely as much on the strengths of public educators as on universities and other resources outside the school; and that teachers have a great capacity to stimulate professional growth and effective practice in their colleagues. A major challenge for a principal is to devise ways to reveal this abundance of thinking and practice so that it can be made more widely available to improve the school and teaching.

At one school where I was principal we devised a contract with Brandeis University to cooperate in their undergraduate teacher-certification program. About a dozen students were placed with as many of our teachers. In addition, the teachers ran what we called "Brandeis seminars," which helped the student teachers learn instructional methodology. Each year a committee of teachers paid by Brandeis led these seminars. These teachers in turn engaged many of their fellow teachers as faculty for the seminars. Topics included "discipline," "observing children," "record keeping," "curriculum," and "getting a teaching job." Teachers also assisted others through the Greater Boston Teacher Center, which offered faculty-led workshops and courses.

In both of these activities, teachers were paid to share their knowledge with prospective or practicing teachers. This opportunity and the remuneration for it conveyed several important messages: we are aware of the many good things you are doing; we value these things; we believe others would benefit from knowing what you are thinking and doing; we believe strongly enough about this and value your expertise enough that we will convene the other teachers and pay you. These messages, so seldom communicated, affirm importance, dignity, and professionalism. When teachers receive this kind of recognition, they go to extraordinary lengths to justify it. They reflect on their practice translating intuitive and unconscious behavior into more conscious, deliberate, visible information that can be useful to others. Of course this process results in extraordinary learning and classroom improvement for the teachers themselves. There is no more sophisticated form of staff development for teachers.

The issue then is not whether school people know much of value to others but rather under what conditions they will reveal their rich craft knowledge so that it may become part of the discussion to improve schools. Recognition is the commodity in least supply to teachers these days, and the process of being helpful to others is a means of conveying recognition to others as well as to oneself.

TEACHERS AND QUALITY CONTROL

Nothing destroys the morale and sense of professionalism of good teachers more than bad teachers. Nothing infuriates good teachers more than no one doing anything about bad teachers. Responsibility for monitoring, evaluating, and dismissing incompetent teachers rests chiefly with the school principal, who can establish high expectations for performance and ensure that all teachers move toward them.

As principal, I told teachers that there was room under the roof for everyone. I explained that in questions concerning goals, neither parents nor teachers could make unilateral decisions. Teachers could not decide to omit teaching reading simply because they believed that children would somehow learn to read. However, in questions of means—for example, how to teach reading, how to teach math—the responsibility was with the teachers, not with the parents, principal, students, or central office. I set two conditions. First, teachers could teach subject matter in any way that they thought best, provided that they accepted and respected the way in which the teacher across the hall was doing it. Second, at least twice a year I expected the teachers to convey to me, to one another, and to the parents that, as a result of teaching the subject in their particular way, children were learning and enjoying that subject area.

Like most principals I also formally evaluated teachers each year, as the school committee required. There were several familiar components. First, I observed in a teacher's classroom two or three times during the fall. Before each visit, the teacher and I shared ideas and, after the observation, more ideas. Then we each filled out the official form, commenting on work in the different subject areas and on relationships with parents, other teachers, and children. After that, we brought the two sets of forms, reflecting our perceptions, to another conference. I was always particularly interested in differences in our perceptions. When I identified difficulties I almost always found that teachers were well aware of them. The last step was to incorporate both sets of observations into a final report, which went to the personnel office with a recommendation for reappointment. In a small number of cases—when teachers were not meeting their own, mine, or the system's expectations and, despite my efforts, showed no improvement—I recommended dismissal.

Part of my own vision of teacher professionalism is that teachers accept responsibility for the performance of their colleagues. I would like to see the day when teachers in effect police themselves, by maintaining standards of performance for their own work and that of their peers. Teaming teachers and having them visit one another's classrooms are examples of moves in the right direction. We are a long way from the day when teachers will maintain standards for their profession. Yet nothing better marks the coming of professionalism to teaching than the willingness and ability of teachers to monitor the performance of their colleagues.

THE PROFESSIONAL DEVELOPMENT
OF PRINCIPALS

I have argued that the principal of a school occupies a position of central influence over the professionalization of teaching. I have found that transforming relationships among teachers and between teachers and principal by developing collegiality, engaging teachers in important decisions affecting their classrooms and schools, developing personal visions, becoming active adult learners, serving as mentors to other teachers and prospective teachers, and maintaining quality in their own and others' performances are all ways in which principals can make good use of their extraordinary influence. Each of these characteristics contributes to the profession of teaching; collectively they define a school culture of professionalism.

The role of the principal in professionalizing teaching suggested here is, of course, not a common one—and for good reason. Powerful and persistent forces that work within the culture of school systems make it extremely difficult for a school principal to support the profession of teaching. Principals who would engage in the kinds of activities outlined here encounter resistance from state departments of education, central offices, other principals, parents, and, indeed, from many teachers themselves. Other educators are more concerned with attaining uniformity by trying to control what teachers do in classrooms than with bringing dignity to the teaching profession.[9] Consequently, many principals attempt to exercise an authoritarian, hierarchical kind of leadership: they arrange schedules that mandate who is supposed to be where and doing what; they maintain tight control over money, supplies, and behavior; and they dictate curriculum, goals, and means. An inevitable consequence of this patriarchal model of leadership—aside from a certain amount of order, productivity, and consonance—is the creation of a relationship of dependence between principal and teacher. Teachers learn not to move without orders from principals; principals cannot leave "their" buildings without fear that things will disintegrate in their absence. This dependency immobilizes teachers and principals—when maximum flexibility and imagination are what they both need.

Like college presidents, principals are effective less as charismatic authority figures than as successful coalition builders. Increasing specialization of teachers, for instance, signals that principals can no longer pretend to be master teachers well versed in instructing handicapped children, students who are gifted and talented, beginning reading, and advanced math.

In order not only to survive but to flourish, principals must learn to share problems without worrying about appearing inadequate; believe that adult learning is legitimate; and become more secure about their visions, values, ideas, and practices so that they can act consistently and confidently. All this learning requires support systems within the school, from other principals, from the central office, and from outside the system.

The school principal has been rediscovered. A growing body of literature suggests that behind every successful school is a successful principal.[10] For better or worse, principals have a disproportionate influence on what teachers teach and students learn. There seem to be three major policy implications suggested by this literature: strengthen the preservice training of aspiring principals by improving certification requirements and formal academic coursework, improve the process of selecting principals, and improve and increase the professional development opportunities for practicing principals. All three of these areas require rigorous attention in the process of improving the effectiveness of practicing principals.

It is the last of these areas in which I have been actively engaged for the past several years and that I would therefore like to consider here. The professional development of the nation's principals deserves our attention because these individuals have a profound influence on their schools and on the teaching profession. On average, each will retain the position for nearly two decades. Moreover, surrounding principals are conditions that are promising for promoting their learning: difficulties, a context for resolving them, and a person who wants them resolved. How, then, might school principals learn to work with teachers in order to create a profession of teaching? For all the agreement about the importance of school principals, surprisingly little is known about their professional development.

It is much easier to mention such elements as leadership and school climate than it is to define them for purposes of either research or practice. It is also easier to define them than it is to produce them through training—or to transfer them from one person or organization to another. Professional development for principals has been described by an official of one of the national principals' associations as a "wasteland." Principals take assorted courses at universities. They attend episodic in-service activities within their school systems, and they struggle to elevate professional literature to the top of the sedimentary pile of papers on their desks. Staff-development programs for principals are often more coherent when designed by state departments of education, large school systems, and universities. Many of these activities stem from a common set of assumptions and draw on a common logic: (a) find schools where pupils are achieving more than what might be predicted by their backgrounds; (b) observe principals in those schools and find out what they are doing; (c) identify these behaviors as "desirable traits"; (d) devise training programs to develop these traits in all principals; (e) enlist principals in these programs; (f) then, to the extent that this group of principals successfully acquires these traits, students in their schools will also come to achieve at a level beyond what might be predicted given their social class, race, and family background.[11]

I find this model to be simple, straightforward, compelling, and logical. Its only major flaw is that it does not work very well. I suspect that there may be several reasons. The assumption that strong leadership results in high student test scores suggests a very limited—and, I think, demeaning—view of both students and principals. Good education is more than good scores, and good leadership is more than generating good scores. Also, conditions in one school are seldom similar to those in another. To treat schools as a generic class is easier said than done. A third reason is that people who run things, as principals run schools, do not want to be run themselves—especially badly. Principals resent attempts by others to fix them.[12] Finally, even if principals are successfully trained by means of these staff-development activities, without sustained feedback and skillful coaching, little comes of it. The linkages from principal behavior in a workshop setting to principal behavior in a school, to teacher behavior, to student learning are convoluted and tenuous indeed.

These may be among the reasons why the logical model of staff development for principals encounters difficulty—and are the reasons for my belief that there is a pressing need both for different conceptions of staff-development programs for principals and for a wider variety of inventive models for promoting principals' professional growth.

In our work at the Harvard Principals' Center it is becoming clearer just why it is so difficult for school leaders to become learners. One difficulty is, of course, a lack of time. "If I participate in that teachers' math workshop, the phone messages from parents will go unattended." For principals, as for all of us, this is another way of saying that other things are more important and perhaps more comfortable. So the leader's learning takes a back seat.

A second impediment is principals' experience as learners. Few come to professional development activities without baggage from the past. District in-service and university course work, for instance, have left principals turned off. Principals resist new learning opportunities because they have been there before and found what is there to be wanting. Few of them retain much confidence that staff development will be engaging, let alone helpful to them in running their schools.

Third, the culture of schools promotes the belief that it is immoral for principals to be learners. The purpose of schools is to promote student learning. Taking $100 from the school budget to join the Harvard Principals' Center is tantamount to snatching bread from the mouths of babes. Think of what the school could do with $100—teacher aides, books, magic markers. And think of what could be done at school during those two hours of workshop. Principals are public servants whose place is to serve, not to be served. Principals who would become professionals would do well to remember the words of Elizabeth Cady Stanton, a nineteenth-century feminist: "Self-development is a higher duty than self-sacrifice."

Another obstacle to principals becoming learners is that by publicly engaging in learning, principals reveal themselves as being flawed. The world out there expects principals to know how to perform their duties. Principals often pretend to know how. A few even believe that they know how. Thus, principals find themselves forbidden not to know. To become a learner is to admit that the screening committee and superintendent made a mistake.

It is also inappropriate for principals to be learners. Learning always begins one rung on the ladder below the teacher. Teachers want children to learn but see their own learning as less necessary. Principals want teachers to learn but do not believe that a math workshop is appropriate for principals. Superintendents want principals to shape up, but few engage seriously in their own professional development. And so it goes. The moral order of the school places the principal in authority as knower; the principal as learner is out of place.

Finally, if principals engage in a learning experience and learn something—a new way of thinking about curriculum, a new interpersonal skill, a new idea about improving school climate—they are then faced with having to do something with it. Principals are rewarded for learning by being provided with additional work. It seems to be one of the paradoxes of professional development that it can be both energy and time depleting and energy and time replenishing.

These impediments suggest just how difficult it is for principals to become learners. Yet I am convinced that being a learner, a lifelong adult learner, is the most important characteristic of a school leader and of a professional.[13] Learning is not just another on the long list of critical characteristics of the leader: rather, the leader as learner belongs at the top of the list. Many of the characteristics—that is, the skills most of us recognize as being important to the effectiveness of principals—are learned skills. A principal can learn how to monitor performance of pupils, convey high expectations to teachers and pupils, and make teaching more professional.

Learning is replenishing. We deplore teachers who will do more of the same next September that they did this September and last September. I think this condition is equally unfortunate for principals. After several years principals tend to switch on to "automatic pilot" in PTA meetings, teacher-evaluation sessions, and parent conferences, a sign of clinical death. Not only do teachers and students suffer; the principal suffers. Learning is an antidote to routinization.

And the leader as learner is critical because there is a striking connection between learning and collegiality. The most powerful form of learning comes not from listening to the good words of others but from sharing what we know with others. Learning comes more from giving than from receiving. Every principal I know is good at something. By reflecting on what we do, by giving it coherence, and by sharing and articulating our craft knowledge, we make meaning; we learn. The best way, perhaps the only way, that schools are going to improve is by school people learning from and helping other school people.

I find that the most powerful reason for principals to be learners as well as leaders come from the extraordinary influence of modeling behavior. In many schools, the more important you are, the further you are removed from learning. But when the leader is learner, when the principal's learning is continuous, visible, and exciting, a crucial and very different message is telegraphed: this school is a community of learners; learning is its most important characteristic; the principal is a first-class citizen of the community of learners, the head learner.

CONCLUSION

I began by describing the personal and professional malaise that shrouds the teaching profession. I believe that school principals have an extraordinary opportunity to influence the renewal of teaching. A most pressing item on the agenda of school reform is how to help principals make more effective use of their central place in the professionalizing of teaching.

No longer can principals dominate. The top-down model is too unwieldy, subject to too much distortion, too infantilizing, and too unprofessional. Neither can the structures and constraints of the school system dictate what happens within the schoolhouse. Leaders need to set general directions and to create environments and structures that enable teachers to discover their own skills and talents and thereby be free to help students discover theirs. The role must be one of enabling rather than controlling. How will principals learn this? Principals must engage in their own professional development. Principals too need replenishment and invigoration and an expanded repertoire of ideas and practices with which to respond to overwhelming demands. And, even more, principals need a sense of their own professionalism.

Despite severe declines in both budgets and public confidence in education, teachers and principals will persist. Principals alone cannot make a profession of teaching. And teachers alone cannot professionalize their work. But principals and teachers working together can create an ecology of reflection, growth, and professionalism. My experiences as teacher, principal, and now at the Harvard Principals' Center suggest that the best—and perhaps only—way to influence principals to join with teachers in creating a profession of teaching is first to arrange conditions in which principals can join with principals in creating a profession among school leaders. The relationships among teachers and principals that I have discussed—collegiality, shared decisionmaking in classrooms and within schools, personal vision, the teacher as learner and mentor, and control of the quality of teaching—are what being a professional is all about. These are the conditions that will cause teachers and principals alike to blossom rather than wilt when that alarm rings at 6:30 in the morning.

This conception of professionalism has some of the elements of higher education, particularly the professional recognition and the balance of power between dean and faculty; it has some aspects of British schools, particularly the collegial relationship between teacher and the head teacher; and some of the characteristics of a teaching hospital, especially the emphasis on a climate of continuous experimentation. But what I have discussed here cannot easily be reduced to a model or a theory. Rather, it is above all a way of thinking about teaching, about leadership, about good schools, and about the relationships among the adults who inhabit them.

NOTES

The original version of this paper was prepared for the California Commission on the Teaching Profession in April 1985. it also appeared in *Elementary School Journal 86* (4), March 1986. It is included here with permission of the author and The University of Chicago Press.

1. T. R. Sizer, *Horace's Compromise* (Boston: Houghton Mifflin, 1984).
2. R. S. Barth, "Sandboxes and Honeybees," *Education Week 3* (33), 1984, p. 24.
3. D. C. Lortie, *Schoolteacher* (Chicago: University of Chicago Press, 1975), p. 169.

4. J. W. Little, *School Success and Staff Development in Urban Desegregated Schools: A Summary of Recently Completed Research* (Boulder, Colo.: Center for Action Research, 1981).

5. Ibid.

6. R. S. Barth, *Run School Run* (Cambridge, Mass.: Harvard University Press, 1980).

7. R. S. Barth, "Outside Looking In—Inside Looking In," *Phi Delta Kappan 66*, 1985, pp. 356–358.

8. R. S. Barth, "The Principal as Staff Developer," *Boston University Journal of Education 163* (2) 1981, pp. 144–162.

9. R. S. Barth, 1980.

10. R. Edmonds, "Effective Schools for the Urban Poor," *Educational Leadership 37*, 1979, pp. 15–24.

11. R. S. Barth, "Principal-Centered Professional Development" (paper presented at the annual meeting of the American Educational Research Association, Chicago, 1985).

12. R. S. Barth, "The Leader as Learner," *Educational Leadership 42* (6), 1985, pp. 92–94.

13. R. S. Barth, "The Professional Development of Principals," *Educational Leadership 42* (2), 1984, pp. 93–94.

CHAPTER 12

The District Superintendent & the Restructuring of Schools: A Realistic Appraisal

LARRY CUBAN

Stanford University

To argue that district superintendents are in a position to restructure schooling (and presumably to improve what occurs in classrooms), attention must be paid to the origins of the post, the varied roles that superintendents must perform, and the nature of leadership and change in schools. I have paid attention to each of these factors over the last fifteen years as a practitioner and researcher. Based upon that combined experience, I make the following assertions:

1. Conflict is the DNA of the superintendency. The genetic inevitability of conflict grows out of the origins of the position, the roles required to discharge obligations inherent in the post, and the setting of tax-supported public schools.
2. Because conflict is embedded in the genetic material of the post, creating fundamental dilemmas[1] for the superintendent, those who hold these positions are commonly driven by a managerial imperative to keep the organization stable. That is, they try to reduce tensions and avoid major changes and instability by striking a balance favoring constancy over change.
3. When superintendents do overcome the managerial imperative and initiate changes, they frequently favor ones that improve efficiency and effectiveness; such changes seldom rearrange or alter the fundamental organizational structures of schooling.

4. Those superintendents who have made deep changes in schooling, fundamentally altering how these institutions were governed, ordered, and operated, did so when their visions and substantial skills converged with conditions within the setting favorable to undertaking such structural changes.[2]

In making these claims, I want to be very clear that these statements are not intended as criticisms of school chiefs. Having served as a superintendent for seven years, I know well the potential and the limits to change inherent to the position as the superintendent interacts with the setting. After leaving the superintendency, I have had time to reflect and understand better what I experienced. If anything, I have to check my natural compassion for the men and women who serve in these dilemma-ridden posts.

Nor are these statements meant to imply that some changes are better than others. Improvement and change are not synonymous. Notions of improvement are in the heads of the beholders; a change that appears as progress to one person may appear to another as a disaster. The changes I describe are ones that readers will need to judge as worthwhile, worthless, or some mix of the two.

The rest of this chapter takes these four assertions and makes the case for understanding the nature of the district superintendency and change in the closing decades of the twentieth century. To elaborate each of these claims, I begin with questions: Why is conflict the DNA of the superintendency? Why do most superintendents manage rather than lead? What does fundamental change in schools mean (the current slogan is "restructuring"), and under what conditions does it occur?

WHY IS CONFLICT THE DNA OF THE SUPERINTENDENCY?

Conflict was present from the beginning. When part-time, elected school boards of the midnineteenth century found the tasks of supervising teachers, examining students, and buying supplies too burdensome, they began appointing superintendents to do the work. In addition to purchasing pencils and coal and hiring teachers and janitors, the first two generations of superintendents kept records, taught teachers, prepared examinations, administered these exams to students, and chose the textbooks that their school systems would use. Turn-of-the-century superintendents also faced the problem of one-year contracts that were tied to annual school board elections. Meanwhile, sporadic attacks from reformers bent on altering schooling forced these early school chiefs to wrestle periodically with the unexpected.

Turnover among superintendents—the most readily observable measure of conflict—was highest in the 1870s and during the decade that bridged World War I. By the 1920s, progressive school reformers, determined to make the public schools hum like successful corporations, stumped for small school boards, to be appointed from the ranks of business and the professions. The reformers conferred on superintendents the status of experts—engineers who would design educational blueprints.[3]

The advent of appointed school boards and of professional training for superintendents insulated superintendents from partisan politics. This insulation guaranteed the rise of less noisy (and thus less visible) organizational politics, however. If political parties no longer sought favors from friendly school boards, now superintendents began to engage in pitched battles and guerrilla skirmishes with their school boards, principals, and teachers.

Civil rights, community participation, accountability, enrollment declines, and economic recessions buffeted superintendents during the 1960s and 1970s, producing the highest turnover rates in the twenty-five largest urban school districts since World War I. In the 1980s, casualties of political and organizational warfare in urban school systems persist, but the number is considerably lower than during the peak periods of the 1870s, 1910–1924, and 1965–1979.[4]

Why the persistent waxing and waning of political and organizational conflict since the establishment of the superintendency a century and a half ago? I have already suggested one explanation: Schooling is public business. To survive, school boards and their chief executives must have public funds and public confidence.

The constant quest for adequate funds to underwrite the many complex goals that schools have been expected to achieve forces school boards and superintendents to seek friends and to neutralize enemies among groups both within and outside of the school community. Social movements such as civil rights and demographic changes such as declining birthrates also create political and organizational conflict within school districts. For school superintendents, the outcomes are often premature resignations, early retirements, or 3–2 votes that terminate their contracts.

Conflict, then, springs from the simple fact that schooling in this democracy is public business where factions compete for their versions of how tax dollars should be spent for the children of the community. Moreover, when shifts in the economy, political culture, and social norms occur, they reverberate in the schools. When the country has a cold, the schools sneeze. As I have suggested, conflict is also embedded in the varied roles that superintendents must perform.

CORE ROLES OF SUPERINTENDING: INSTRUCTIONAL, MANAGERIAL, AND POLITICAL

Instructional

From the birth of the position in mid-nineteenth-century America, superintendents taught both teachers and children. In small districts, superintendents taught one or more classes; in larger districts, superintendents would teach demonstration lessons for teachers. School boards expected their appointed executive to be a pedagogical expert who could alter the existing beliefs and behaviors of teachers and principals to create an improved instructional program.

By the mid-twentieth century, although few superintendents (except in tiny districts) taught students regularly, the career path to the top post included teaching. By the 1980s, becoming a superintendent *without* having taught would spur newspaper articles and references to the uniqueness (or notoriety) of the fact. While occasional superintendents would substitute for an absent teacher or teach a special lesson to illustrate particular approaches, they remained a rare breed. For those superintendents who still viewed themselves primarily as teachers, instructing teachers and principals emerged as their central instructional duty.

The concept of an instructional role for superintendents shifts meaning from direct teaching of students and teachers to a concept of superintendent as the teacher of the *school community*. At one level, the superintendent as teacher means the familiar instructional supervision historically sought by earlier generations of school executives: helping teachers improve their pedagogy, helping principals understand the curriculum, and teaching principals how to supervise and evaluate teachers.

At another level, the superintendent's instructional role is broader. Through shaping the mission of the district, establishing a district climate that signals seriousness in purpose, designing rituals that infuse life in the district's mission and through communication skill and personal example, the superintendent, in effect, teaches. In effect, the school board, the district organization, and the community become a classroom. Intentions and strategies become lesson plans and units of a curriculum invented to achieve desired ends. At this level, a superintendent who teaches is one who not only persuades children and adults, professionals and lay people, parents and nonparents to see schooling in a slightly different way than before but also bends their efforts toward new activities and new goals.

Most superintendents perform *neither* level of the instructional role directly. Many delegate the instructional role to a subordinate director or assistant superintendent. Some pursue only instructional supervision to principals with great passion; others embrace both levels.

An illustration may help capture concretely the two dimensions of the instructional role I have described. The two levels of teaching embodied in the instructional role can be seen occasionally in a superintendent.

Chicago superintendent Ella Flagg Young performed this dual instructional role between 1909 and 1915. She broadened the formal academic curriculum to include manual arts for all elementary schools and vocational courses at secondary schools. She introduced elements new to the curriculum (field trips, handicrafts, drama), which she and John Dewey had developed at the University of Chicago's Laboratory School, thereby expanding the curriculum beyond the usual books, paper, and pencils.

She persuaded the board of education to authorize teachers' councils for letting teachers give professional advice to the superintendent about curriculum, instruction, school organization, textbooks, and other topics, at a time when the prevailing image of a teacher was that of a bureaucrat, a public servant that had better pay attention to his or her superiors. Young's credibility as a teacher, principal, district superintendent, and top administrator of the second largest district in the nation was anchored in her prowess as a teacher in and out of schools.[5]

While Ella Flagg Young was unusual, there have been since and are currently superintendents who have played a dominant instructional role. In the 1980s, for example, the instructional role of the superintendent has again reemerged as central to what superintendents *should* do. In the growing literature on "effective schools," what began as an effort to improve the local school by focusing upon teachers and principal has now expanded to the district superintendent and, in some instances, the state superintendent, elevating the instructional role to a central position. Setting goals, establishing standards, selecting and supervising staff, and ensuring consistency in curricula and teaching approaches have become benchmarks of instructionally active superintendents.

Managerial

The familiar administrative tasks associated with carrying out school board policies, such as planning, collecting and disbursing information, constructing budgets, hiring and firing, supervising subordinates, and managing conflict across a broad array of activities constitute this role. Managerial actions range from supervising the busing of students and evaluating principals to allocating parking spaces at the district office and monitoring standardized test scores.

If the instructional role aims to alter existing beliefs and behaviors of members of the school community, the fundamental purpose of the managerial role is to maintain organizational stability. For those superintendents who envision a direction for the district, who aim to achieve certain purposes with students, teachers, and principals beyond preserving existing arrangements, the managerial and instructional roles merge. For those superintendents whose orientation is to accomplish no more than what the school board directs, the managerial and instructional roles are largely separate.

The managerial role was embedded in the very origins of the post over a century and a half ago. Aaron Gove, Denver's nineteenth-century superintendent who served the longest tenure in the district's history down to the present day, lived the managerial role. After a decade in Denver, Gove told the National Council of Education in 1884 what a superintendent must do to be considered an expert advisor to the school board.

First, "he must be familiar . . . with the financial affairs of the district. He must know about the assessment roll and about the tax collector's returns; he must be acquainted with the sources of income, and with the ratio of school expenses to other municipal expenses." Why? "Money," he explained, "is the greatest power in upbuilding school interests."

Next, because school boards tend to overspend, the superintendent should advise the school board swiftly and in detail about the worth of their expenditures. He should also advise the school board on prudent investments of district funds.

Finally, proper maintaining of school buildings is essential. "A broken pane, pencil, or chalk marks or whittlings in outhouses or on fences not only indicate weakness in supervision but are also a postive barrier to making desirable character among pupils." It is the superintendent who will "make visits to inspection and spur janitors and principals to eternal vigilance."

While Gove devoted a section of his speech to instructional supervision and the importance of teaching teachers, the opening line of his talk captures the emphasis in both his speech and his Denver superintendency: "The technical duties of a city superintendent are administrative."[6]

The Political Role

Since the first superintendents sat behind their desks, they have spent time meeting with parents, businessmen, local officials, and others to nourish public support for schools or to offset criticism. Most superintendents simply recognized the central fact of their workaday lives: Any public institution supported by taxes in a democracy will seldom be left to experts to run alone.

I use the term "political" to embrace activities beyond those that later generations of administrators came to call "community leadership" and "public relations." The word "political" includes the process superintendents used to determine and transform personal and public goals into policies and actions; it also refers to the authority, rules, and influence that superintendents exert in working with a school board and governing a school district.

Superintendents stand between what state and local school boards direct, what parents expect, what teachers and principals need (and these differ), and what students want. Their position is like that of a police officer at a traffic circle where cars from four different directions enter and exit. There to slow and speed up traffic, the officer also must sense when it will bunch up and even out and determine when to call a halt to one line while urging another to move ahead with dispatch. Figuring out when the traffic of competing interests and expectations will ebb and flow while simultaneously handling the inevitable crashes of conflicting interests in order to avoid gridlock becomes a superintendent's major task. By their decisions and actions, by their exercise of formal and informal power, their display of interpersonal skills, their core values, and their perspectives on what is and is not possible, superintendents determine to what extent a policy is implemented as intended, converted to fit the particular contours of the district, or shelved.

School chiefs, then, act politically when they persuade, argue, sell, and bargain with school board members, principals, teachers, students, taxpayer coalitions, parent activitists, state department of education officials, and fired-up reverends of the local ministerial association. Because political action means working towards achieving particular goals, such work is just as intensely moral as that of those ministers working the other side of the street.

Some superintendents have savored the political role. Frank Cody, veteran Detroit superintendent (1919–1942), relished the work. He was a joiner par excellence—from the Odd Fellows to the Chamber of Commerce, from churches to professional groups. He moved easily from the bar of the Saint Claire Hotel, where he met frequently with school board members, to the presidency of the NEA (1927).

To Cody, a superintendent has three major functions: administration, supervision, and "community relations." To him, "community relations are the contacts which are designed to discover the educational needs of the community and to interpret the schools to the community." In a large school district, the superintendent cannot do everything, so functions must be delegated to staff. "He may delegate almost every other type of work," Cody wrote, "but not this one completely." The superintendent's "chief assignment is community relations."

> He must know his public in order to be able to sense its desires and its needs. Further, he must be able to "sell" the program of the schools to his local community.[7]

Cody engaged in a political process because he saw linkages in daily tasks to larger goals that they sought. He used his formidable skills and influence to sell, lure, shove, and pull staff and citizens toward larger goals that contained values he prized. Both the process and the outcomes were political, in that policies negotiated in the crucible of the school board and community were initially sensed and formulated by the superintendent and then transformed into managerial and instructional decisions.

All three roles form the core of superintending. No superintendent can ignore any one and survive. Superintendents experience conflict continually in serving a school board, staff, parents, students, taxpayers, and other constituencies—each of which has competing expectations for what should occur. What roles the superintendent wishes to perform frequently clash with the desires of others to whom the school chief must respond. As mundane an example as the superintendent who chooses to give a plaque at a high school assembly honoring a retiring teacher, rather than chair the Kiwanis meeting where the mayor will be speaking, suggests the conflict that inevitably arises from discharging these core roles.

Conflict, then, is embedded in the origins of the post within a tax-supported public school system and the multiple roles called for in exercising the authority delegated by the school board. Conflict is also connected to how much superintendents manage and how much they lead. By this I mean that most superintendents view their varied roles as tools to reduce tension, maintain stability, and manage conflict. Some superintendents, with a picture of what should be, view the same roles as opportunities to push the organization to change itself even to the point of making conflict and generating tensions among the varied constituencies. The concept of managing conflict and consciously generating it as a tactic in leading an organization is derived from different superintendents' perspectives on the three roles and the desired ends they seek.

Let me distinguish further what I mean by "managing" and "leading." In the present period, managing is increasingly viewed as insufficient, as technical work that is marginally important but not equivalent to "leading." This has not always been the case. Recall the educators' passionate embrace of scientific management in the early twentieth century and its dominance in occupations such as engineering and in graduate schools of business. In the 1980s, "leadership" is the buzz word. The two concepts are not polar opposites; they are related but separable.

Managing requires the technical skills of allocating efficiently and effectively toward organizational goals and resources (including people), monitoring, evaluating, and navigating. When these technical skills are harnessed to goals that go beyond maintaining organizational stability (which in some instances may be all that can be expected), it becomes a matter of leadership. This implies taking initiatives and risks, creating new conflicts, transforming existing goals, and even adding new ones. Not all managers lead, but organizational leaders must be able to manage.

TABLE 12-1   Distribution of superintendents' time devoted
to various functions (as reported by city and rural chiefs, 1950)

	City (%)	Rural (%)
Administration	58	55
Instructional supervision	31	35
Teaching	0	0
Community/public relations	11	10

Source: American Association of School Administrators, *The American School Superintendent* (Washington, D.C.: AASA, 1952), pp. 452, 460.

I value both managerial and leadership concepts; I do not believe that "merely" to manage is to engage in some low-level activity unrelated to important outcomes. In effect, educators need to be both leaders and managers. I do argue, however, that most superintendents manage (that is, seek occasional changes to improve organizational effectiveness and efficiency) but essentially maintain the institution as it is. One way of further clarifying the distinction between managing and leading is to find out what superintendents actually do when they come to work.

For the years since 1920, there is little systematically collected evidence about what superintendents have done in and out of their offices. What is available comes from a few studies drawn from self-reports, interviews, surveys, and occasional direct observation. Table 12-1 summarizes superintendents' self-reports of their work. It shows that more time is spent on administration than instructional supervision; public relations and teaching share a third level of priority.

In 1928, one national survey of 663 principals and superintendents in different-sized districts reported on which tasks were done and how often. Unfortunately, the data on managerial, instructional, and community work are not reported in relation to one another as is done in Table 12-1. Four of five superintendents reported the following activities:

- Go to the post office
- Deliver messages to teachers
- Draft special reports to state and U.S. Bureau of Education; prepare annual reports for school board
- Prepare letters of sympathy
- Conduct visitors through schools
- Examine school work sent to office
- Prevent salesmen from canvassing schools
- Answer questionnaires
- Gather school publicity data
- Adjust complaints of parents
- Consider applications, examine credentials, consult with principals in selecting teachers for district
- Secure substitute teachers
- Suggest professional books and articles for teachers
- Investigate criticism of teachers

- Assist teachers to find lodgings
- Attend summer school
- Visit schools elsewhere
- Talk before community groups
- Attend church social functions[8]

Between 1950 and the mid-1970s, there were no comprehensive or systematic descriptions of what superintendents did on a daily or weekly basis. Apart from occasional individual accounts written by former or sitting superintendents and articles in professional journals that described what individual school chiefs did, few descriptions existed.

When I had completed my research in 1973 on *Urban School Chiefs Under Fire* (a study of Chicago's Benjamin Willis, San Francisco's Harold Spears, and Washington, D.C.'s Carl Hansen), I said, "While we know to the penny what salaries suburban administrators received, what degrees they earned, and where they were born, we know very little about what they, as executives, actually do each day." I cited Henry Mintzberg's study of five managers (including a suburban school chief) as a hopeful end to that ignorance.[9]

Since 1973, Mintzberg's structured observation approach, (which used to be called "shadowing" or, in a slightly critical vein, "neo-Taylorism") has produced time-and-motion studies recording in minutes and hours how much time superintendents spent on various tasks each day for a week or more of direct observation.[10] There are a number of strengths to this stop-watch, time-and-motion approach, particularly in offering a detailed, up-close view by an outside observer of how superintendents spend their time, but there are also decided limitations.

The data up to 1950, which consists largely of self-reports, and the surge of shadow studies since the early 1970s cannot be directly compared, since the categories used by the researchers differ as well as the methodologies. However, the two snapshots of the superintendent's work at least provide a fuller, if mildly contradictory, portrait of the post.

The self-reports show superintendents spending most of their time in administration and less in instructional supervision, with brief moments squeezed into "community leadership," implying an orderly and prosaic routine. The superintendent-watching of the 1970s shows wide variation in behavior, with some common patterns. (1) Superintending is a constant stream of brief encounters, mostly with school board members and subordinates in the central office. (2) There are constant interruptions; seldom can extended periods be spent at the desk or in the schools. There seems to be a decided concentration upon verbal exchanges with people—both planned and spontaneous. In short, superintending is a world of action. A picture of superintendent behavior as planned and organized receives little support from these studies. The

TABLE 12-2   A comparison of school superintendents' activities and contacts

	STUDIES				
	Bussom	*Pitner*	*Kurke*	*Mintzberg*	*Feilders*
Activity					
Desk work					
(% of time)	31	20	20	16	4
Telephone calls					
(% of time)	11	8	3	6	2
Scheduled meetings					
(% of time)	13	51	69	75	50
Unscheduled meetings					
(% of time)	30	10	5	3	30
Tours (% of time)	5	2	0	1	3
Contacts					
With School Board	4	19	28	17	26
With subordinates	59	54	40	61	58
With others	37	27	32	22	16

evidence portrays the superintendent as no Superman or leader, but rather as a frazzled Clark Kent struggling to get out of a phone booth.

Where the two sets of studies appear to converge is in the bulk of available time being spent with superiors and subordinates in meetings and desk work, and so little time seemingly devoted to instructional supervision. The image of a superintendent as a leader trying to improve classroom teaching and the curriculum in either small or large systems appears to have little credibility in these studies, given the few hours that superintendents spend in schools—much less classrooms.

WHY DO MOST SUPERINTENDENTS APPEAR TO MANAGE RATHER THAN LEAD?

I have already suggested how the origins of the position and the multiple roles and expectations inherent in the post generate conflict and influence what superintendents do. Together with other factors, such as socialization and training, uncertainty in determining effectiveness, and convenience, this drives school chiefs toward the managerial end of the continuum of leadership. Let me take up each to illustrate how these factors accumulate to produce a managerial imperative.

Origins of the position

The initial rationale for establishing superintendencies was to have subordinates of the school board perform clerical and administrative tasks. Such obligations had to be met. As decades passed, such tasks persisted and multiplied as the mission of schooling incorporated broader services to both children and the community, such as day care, preschool programs, bilingual education, special services to handicapped children, and free and reduced price lunches. Hiring clerical and administrative aides reduced the workload somewhat, but the need for managerial oversight persisted.

For superintendents, the mission of maintaining order in schools remained central to the community's definition of a satisfactory education. Time had to be invested in assuring that the adults controlled the young. Concerns over attendance, truancy, proper behavior, and suspensions produced policies and procedures that required monitoring. From the beginnings of the superintendency, then, managing assumed a large chunk of time and attention from administrators.

Socialization and training

Except for the priesthood, no other occupation places people in classrooms and administrative offices after almost two decades of informal apprenticeships. From kindergarten through high school, from teacher education to student teaching, from the first classroom job to becoming a principal, from one administrative post to another before appointment to a superintendency, decades pass within different classrooms, different buildings, different offices—but the same institution. Superintendents have spent all but the first few years of their lives in schools watching people practice their skills expertly and ineptly.

The subtle and obvious absorption of norms, expectations, habits, and beliefs tends toward conserving what is, rather than seeking what can be. There is a very minimal tendency to take moderate or high risks, to begin new ventures, or to invest high energy into prized initiatives. Among those who view the system as filled with inviolable rules and policies, the inclination is to comply. Compliance and loyalty produce an orientation toward keeping things as they are; this results in a tilt toward the managerial.

For administrators, advanced training (especially since the 1920s) incorporated a strong managerial orientation, under the influence of Cubberley, Thorndike, and other administrative progressives. State certification policies tightened further the concentration on efficiently administering schools and districts by requiring courses on finance, facility maintenance, and personnel management. The cumulative effects of socialization as a teacher, graduate training, and daily experiences nudge superintendents toward the managerial.

Multiple roles and expectation

The structure of the workplace and the history of the superintendency subject school chiefs to conflicting demands from individuals and groups, to whom they must pay varying degrees of attention. These contradictory roles and expectations generate an inescapable element of conflict that requires constant attention.

The need to be on top of things, to have what Jacob Kounin calls "with-it-ness," to prevent a slow-burning brush fire from erupting into a blaze that might disrupt relationships, causes superintendents to prize routines and activities that maintain organizational stability. The glue that holds the school and district together amidst the centripetal force of competing demands is the routine of administrative tasks. Thus, the managerial role is salient in the minds of many administrators as a conflict-reducing strategy.

Uncertainty in determining effectiveness

Faced with multiple and conflicting obligations, superintendents have a tough time figuring out not only whether they are successful, but also why. For a superintendent, do improved SAT scores mean superior performance? Column inches in the local newspapers? A contract renewal? How many school board agenda items are approved unanimously? Is working 60 hours a week a sign of a job well done?

The criteria, measures, and standards in judging superintendent effectiveness are varied, incomplete, and contested. Moreover, proving that what a superintendent did caused desired or detested outcomes exceeds the science of measurement, further complicating any judgment of effectiveness.

There is, however, one set of tasks upon which there is general agreement over what needs to be done and how to determine whether or not the tasks have been done: managing. To evaluate the management of a superintendent, one checks whether the budget is balanced, principals and teachers follow procedures, personnel are hired and fired without fuss, and decisions are made tidily and expeditiously. Thus, focusing on managerial work provides a common yardstick for administrators (as well as for all those who peek over their shoulders) to use in assessing effectiveness.

Convenience

Within the current structures of schooling, it is simply easier for administrators to concentrate on routine managerial tasks and maintain stability than to risk increasing the level of conflict and the further uncertainty that usually arise from introducing changes. By "easier" I do not mean that a person works less intensely, puts in less hours, or malingers; I mean dealing with less conflict, spending less energy, and creating a sense of control over an uncertain, very complex enterprise.

A superintendent who works toward reducing class sizes to twenty students per primary grade teacher finds strong support among elementary teachers but not secondary school teachers and among some parents but not others, and the school board is likely to be split over the worth of the policy and its funding. Conflict erupts. It is far easier for school executives to focus on the managerial, on keeping things humming as they are rather than altering existing arrangements.

These reasons are plausible. They are rooted in history and the potent influence that workplace structures have upon behavior. In no way, however, do they exhaust the universe of explanations for why most superintendents spend the bulk of their time on managerial activities. I offer these reasons for the managerial imperative to stir the reader to speculate about their persuasiveness and especially to consider possible consequences.

There are organizational consequences of the managerial imperative. The press toward maintaining existing structures, norms, and relationships assumes that what is present is better than what can be. In some settings, this assumption is both appealing and preferable (for example, fiscal retrenchment during a recession). In other settings, such as swift demographic changes in student population, it can hinder action. The drive toward the managerial offers little incentive to look ahead, respond to environmental changes, and see emerging problems in their entirety.

Furthermore, the workplace structures within which administrators find themselves not only shape managerial behavior but also produce a fragmented view of problems. Frequently, superintendents see the "problems" of schooling and their solutions in narrow terms of individuals. "If I could only get rid of those three union troublemakers from my district. . . . If I had a more supportive school board chairman. . . . If parents in the community did a better job with their children. . . ." In short, hierarchical, fragmented and complex work settings cultivate splintered, narrow, and incomplete framing of problems and their solutions.

The result is ad hoc, constricted defining of problems. Problems are broken into tiny parts that can be easily managed by individuals isolated from one another: teacher problems, principal problems, etc. Thus, the managerial imperative is enhanced further by viewing solutions in narrow, individual terms rather than broader, organizational ones. These consequences, I believe, are both subtle and real.

Yet, even in the face of these arguments for a dominant managerial imperative, changes planned by superintendents (and approved by school boards) do occur. How can superintendents, driven by an impulse toward the managerial, still initiate, adopt, and implement changes in a district? One way to answer this question is to ask about the varied meanings of the word "change."

WHAT DOES CHANGE IN SCHOOL MEAN AND UNDER WHAT CONDITIONS DOES IT OCCUR?

Historically, major efforts to improve schooling have come from outside the schools. Amateur and professional reformers affiliated with universities, school districts, or lay coalitions have sought changes in schools, ranging from the elimination of one-room rural schools to the use of desktop microcomputers and from federal subsidies for vocational education to the banning of science texts that treat evolution as a fact. On occasion, such reformers have called for state intervention. For example, at the turn of the century, states mandated that public schools teach the physical harm done to the body and morals of youth when they smoke, drink alcohol, and use drugs. In a later decade, reformers lobbied successfully for the Smith-Hughes Act (1917), which subsidized training of high school boys and girls in specific occupations. For the most part, however, school change concentrated on districts. Coalitions of reformers organized into state, regional, and national networks pressed local boards of education to institute particular improvements.

Of course, teachers and administrators *have* initiated improvements and bottom-up changes. However, as schooling has become larger, more complex, and bureaucratized, such internal moves to make substantial alterations in existing arrangements become increasingly difficult when unaided by external forces.

Distinctions in types of change

Distinguishing among different types of change in school will help in understanding what changes superintendents commonly undertake. To distinguish among planned changes introduced into schools, consider the experience of the National Air and Space Administration (NASA).

In the mid-1980s, NASA endured a number of grave setbacks within three months. By all accounts, an agency that had soared with the successes of lunar landings and shuttle flights that included space walks and satellite repairs now staggered to a halt with the deaths of seven astronauts and the failure of two rockets.

Faced with the public perception of a complete performance collapse, the new leadership of NASA had to define the problem clearly. Was the Challenger accident a design problem, a lapse in quality control, or some mix of the two? Defining the problem became crucial, since the definition would chart the direction for changes in NASA's formal structure, relationships with government contractors, and a multitude of ripple effects. Similarly, for school reforms over the last century, it must be determined whether school problems were defined as design or quality control issues or some mix of the two.

First-order changes are reforms that assume that the existing organizational goals and structures are basically adequate and that what needs to be done is to correct deficiencies in policies and practices. Engineers would label such changes as solutions to quality control problems.[11]

For schools, such planned changes would include recruiting better teachers and administrators, raising salaries, distributing resources equitably, instituting a longer school day, selecting better texts, materials, and supplies, and adding or deleting courses in the curriculum. When such changes occur, the language used to describe the changes uses the vocabulary of fundamental reordering, but little is actually done to alter basic school structures of how time and space are used or how students and teachers are organized and assigned. First-order changes, then, try to make what exists more efficient and effective without disrupting basic organizational relationships or the ways people perform their roles. Compensatory education programs since the 1960s, including Title I of the Elementary and Secondary Education Act and Chapter I, are instances of first-order reforms. The school effectiveness movement, with its emphasis on high expectations, strong instructional leadership, academic performance in basic skills, aligning goals with curriculum, texts, and tests, is a recent instance of a cluster of first-order, planned changes.

Second-order changes, on the other hand, aim to alter the fundamental ways of achieving organizational goals or to introduce new goals and interventions that transform familiar ways of doing things into novel solutions to persistent problems. The point is to reframe the original problems and restructure organizational conditions to conform with the redefined problems. Engineers would call such changes solutions to design problems.

For late nineteenth-century schools, a second-order change was going from the one-room schoolhouse, with one unsupervised teacher and children ranging in ages from 6 to 16, to an eight-room building divided into grades and a formal curriculum where a teacher is supervised by a principal.

Teacher-run schools or ones operated by parents are instances of second-order changes in governance and authority. The use of vouchers or the elimination of attendance boundaries within a district are second-order changes in the existing structure of choice available to parents. Open classrooms (or informal education) were second-order changes, because they required teachers to adopt different roles in the classroom and develop different relationships to students regarding what is knowledge, what is teaching, and what is learning.

Second-order changes, then, involve visions of what ought to be that are different from those embedded in the existing organization. Putting those visions into practice alters fundamental roles, routines, and relationships within an organization.

The history of school reform has largely been a matter of superintendents and school boards introducing first-order changes to the basic structures of schooling established in the late nineteenth century. Incremental changes to schooling that maintained fundamental structures (the graded school, self-contained classrooms with one teacher and thirty students, varied curricula, fifty-minute periods in secondary schools) have been the dominant pattern. Most superintendents introduced first-order changes (better scheduling, smarter books, modern furniture, efficient purchasing procedures, new tests, and the like) to improve what already existed.

None of this, of course, is surprising. Why would anyone expect a superintendent hired by a school board to do more than manage a system effectively and efficiently? That is an achievement in itself. However, some superintendents have been hired by school boards to alter the existing structures of schooling and introduce certain second-order reforms.

SUPERINTENDENTS WHO RESTRUCTURED SCHOOLS

To establish that there have been (and will continue to be) superintendents who introduced deep changes in how schools and classrooms were governed, organized, and operated, one begins with the first two generations of school chiefs who built *systems* of schooling in the cities of the middle to late century. Such superintendents took collections of one-room schools, uncoordinated in staffing, curriculum, instruction, facilities, and equipment, and systematically introduced hierarchies of authority, graded schools, and standards for staff and students. Such system-builders as John Philbrick in Boston, William Torrey Harris in St. Louis, William Maxwell in New York City, and Aaron Gove in Denver created the landscape of schooling that still seems familiar a century later.[12] Such superintendents labored one or more decades in the service of school boards. When they left their districts, schooling in each city had become fundamentally different in its governance, organization, and operation.

There are other school chiefs who altered substantially the districts they headed. Francis Parker, who was hired to lead the Quincy (Massachusetts) schools in the 1870s and whom John Dewey called the father of progressivism, introduced novel curriculum and instructional procedures that required teachers to alter what they commonly did. Carleton Washburne came to Winnetka (Illinois) in 1919 and stayed a quarter of a century to reorganize the schools, introducing individualized instruction to that Chicago suburb's classrooms.[13]

However, one does not need to look to the past for examples of superintendents restructuring parts or the whole of schooling in their districts. It continues today. In East Harlem, one community school district abolished attendance areas; individual schools compete to attract parents to their special programs. A variety of classroom options has developed for students to choose from. In a small Minnesota district, teachers elected five of their number to take the place of the principal in operating the school. Another superintendent has introduced an outcome-based curriculum that requires teachers and principals to alter what they ordinarily do.

Such superintendents do exist now, but they are rare, for many of the reasons that I have already offered. Beyond those historical, structural, and occupational reasons, however, there are necessary conditions that have to be in place for second-order changes to occur.

NECESSARY CONDITIONS

1. A sense of crisis.   Informed members of the community, especially the board of education, believe that the performance of schools is mediocre or has deteriorated gravely. The sense of unsatisfactory performance may stem from demographic changes in the community, such as urbanites moving into a rural town thirty miles from the city or an influx of non-English-speaking immigrants. The perception may also arise from forces in the economy, culture, or political arena that influence public views about what is acceptable and unacceptable in schooling. For example, the civil rights movement in the mid-1960s emphasized equal schooling; the launching of Sputnik meshed with the academic attack on life adjustment curricula in the 1950s; and the erosion of America's international economic primacy coincided with the report of the Commission on Excellence in Education in the 1980s.

The problem of unsatisfactory performance is then framed in terms of inadequate leadership on the part of those on the board, or the superintendent, or both. The solution is to seek and install better policymakers and an executive that can turn the situation around.

2. An enlightened school board.   It is necessary that there be a school board that seeks a person who mirrors its views of the problem, places its trust in the new appointee, is willing to grant sufficient latitude to achieve changes, and stands behind its choice until those improvements are visible to the community. No superintendent can lead well or long without substantial authority delegated by the board of education.

3. A vision. The superintendent must be one who shares the school board's vision or has enough of another vision to induce the board to reshape its original picture of what should be. He or she possesses the stamina, ambition, and daring, plus the technical, social, and mental skills, to direct that vision into practice over at least a five-year period.

These are the necessary conditions that need to be in place for second-order changes to occur. As for the sufficient conditions that need to be present, they are usually unique to the individual district and can seldom be generalized, much less listed. In one district, it might be a question of more money, but in another district the support of the mayor might be a sufficient condition. The art of leadership probably resides in figuring out what the other conditions within the setting must be in place for fundamental changes to occur. Such specification remains beyond the grasp of researchers and practitioners who lamely try to quantify, explain, and list what should be done.

Because the necessary conditions are seldom in place, and because many boards and superintendents have difficulty figuring out what the sufficient conditions for improvement are, first-order continue to be more common than second-order changes.

CLOSING THOUGHTS

I offer this extended commentary on the types of change in schools and the distinctions between leading and managing because of three major fallacies that, I believe, characterize much of the writing on what should be done in schools.

- *All problems are solvable.* Conflict is a natural condition of the superintendency, a dilemma that is insoluble. Compromises can be struck, but conflict will occur again and again in the superintendency.
- *All planned changes (solutions to problems) are generally the same in intent, direction, and implementation.* In fact, first-order and second-order changes are quite different in all three respects.
- *Superintendent leadership cures all problems.* Besides the critical importance of the school board in authorizing their executive to act, it is well to remember that most superintendents manage rather than lead. In some settings, that is all that can be expected; in others settings, aggressive leadership can disturb a precarious calm that has been laboriously constructed after years of instability. In other settings, managing is simply inappropriate to the conditions within the district. The art of judging whether a particular superintendent's approach will fit the district is the primary task of the school board.

These assumptions need to be made explicit and debated openly, since they often underlie the discussion about conflict, change, and leadership in improving schools. Much of the debate about the restructuring of schools and the superintendent's role mirrors these unexamined assumptions. It sounds to me more like cheerleading than informed analysis of the structure of schools, the long history of school reform, and the practice of superintending. It is now close to the twenty-first century, and those who would improve American schools in the coming decades should have a clearer perspective on the role of superintendents.

NOTES

1. Dilemmas are insoluble problems offering choices between unattractive alternatives. Dilemmas frequently arise from the hidden structural arrangements within an organization. If problems have solutions, dilemmas have compromises.

2. By structures of schooling, I mean those fundamental arrangements that form the scaffolding of a school or district organization. For schools, the following illustrate what I mean by structures:

• Compulsory attendance laws
• The graded school with its self-contained classroom
• The state vested formal authority given to a district school board
• The hierarchical authority that projects formal goals, policies, and routines

The arguments and some passages in this chapter are drawn from my book, *The Managerial Imperative: The Practice of Leadership in Schools* (Albany, N.Y.: State University of New York, 1988).

3. See Larry Cuban, *Urban School Chiefs Under Fire* (Chicago: University of Chicago Press, 1976), Chapter Five, "The Vulnerable Superintendent," pp. 111–139. See also Arthur Blumberg, *The School Superintendent: Living With Conflict* (New York: Teachers College Press, 1985).

4. I have updated turnover statistics for superintendents since the turn of the century in twenty-five cities. See Cuban, *Urban School Chiefs Under Fire*, Appendix 2, pp. 175–180.

5. See Rosemary Donatelli, "The Contributions of Ella Flagg Young to the Educational Enterprise" (unpublished dissertation, University of Chicago, 1971), pp. 279–429; Joan Smith, *Ella Flagg Young, Portrait of a Leader* (Ames, Iowa: Educational Studies Press, 1976), pp. 183–184.

6. Aaron Gove, "Duties of the City Superintendent," National Education Association, *Journal of Proceedings and Addresses*, 1884, pp. 26–33.

7. Frank Cody, "The Superintendent: His Administrative and Supervisory Staff," *School Executive Magazine 49*, February 1930, pp. 259–262. See also David Tyack and Elisabeth Hansot, *Managers of Virtue* (New York: Basic Books, 1983), pp. 144–152, for a delightful vignette of Cody.

8. Fred Ayer, "The Duties of Public School Administrators," *American School Board Journal*, March 1929, pp. 39–41; April 1929, pp. 39–41; June 1929, pp. 58–60.

9. Cuban, *Urban School Chiefs Under Fire*, p. xii.

10. Henry Mintzberg, *The Nature of Managerial Work* (New York: Harper and Row, 1973).

11. Paul Watzlawick, John Weakland, and Richard Fisch, *Change: Principles of Problem Formation and Problem Resolution* (New York: Norton, 1974). I need to make two further points about the distinction between orders of change. First, the terms "first-order" and "second-order" may confuse some researchers who recall Type I and Type II errors from statistics. For practitioners, the phrases may occasionally be awkward because "first-order" may seem more important than "second-order," while the opposite is true for those who see structural changes as being more significant. I am not particularly concerned with labels. Whatever the names are, I want to distinguish between two levels of change.

Simply calling attention to the difference in magnitude of changes is my purpose in distinguishing between the two kinds of reform. My purpose is *not* to value one type of change more than another. In some settings, first-order changes might be more appropriate; in other settings, less so.

12. For fuller descriptions of what these superintendents did in restructuring their districts, see David Tyack, *One Best System* (Cambridge, Mass.: Harvard University Press, 1974); Tyack and Hansot, op. cit.; Selwyn Troen, *The Public and the Schools: Shaping the St. Louis System* (Columbia, Mo.: University of Missouri Press, 1975).

13. For descriptions of Francis Parker, see Jack Campbell, *The Children's Crusader: Colonel Francis W. Parker* (New York: Teachers College Press, 1967); for Carleton Washburne, see Carleton Washburne and Sidney Marland, *Winnetka* (Englewood Cliffs, N.J.: Prentice-Hall, 1963).

CHAPTER 13

Renouncing Bureaucracy:
A Democratic Structure for
Leadership in Schools

DAVID L. CLARK
University of Virginia

JUDITH M. MELOY
Connecticut State Department of Education

This chapter has a concern and a viewpoint that go beyond the question of restructuring the roles of teachers and principals. The concern is that contemporary organizations have sacrificed the freedom of their employees in favor of control over those employees, to the detriment of both the employee and the organization. The viewpoint is that the decision to do so is based upon assumptions about people and organizational structure that are unreasonable, unwise, and unnecessary.

REFLECTIONS ON LEADERSHIP AND STRUCTURE

The images of and metaphors for structure and leadership in the literature on organizations are scant in number and similar in content. Before turning to a systematic examination of our concern and viewpoint, we offer two metaphors that affected our approach to the topic.

A Metaphor for Leadership

Consider, for a moment, an alternative metaphor for leadership suggested by Walker Percy in *The Thanatos Syndrome*. His narrator reports the following "secret belief," transmitted by Dr. Harry Stack Sullivan to his residents:

"Here's the secret. . . . You take that last patient we saw. Offhand, what would you say about him? A loser, right? A loser by all counts. You know what you're all thinking to yourself? You're thinking, No wonder that guy is depressed. He's entitled to be depressed. If I were he, I'd be depressed too. Right? Wrong. You're thinking the most we can do for him is make him feel a little better, give him a pill or two, a little pat or two. Right? Wrong. Here's the peculiar thing and I'll never understand why this is so: *Each patient this side of psychosis, and even some psychotics, has the means of obtaining what he needs, she needs, with a little help from you.* Incidentally, Doctors, how do we know you don't look like losers to me, or I to you."[1]

The narrator continues:

> But there it was, to me the pearl of great price, the treasure buried in a field, that is to say, the patient's truest unique self which lies within his, the patient's, power to reach and which we, as little as we do, can help him reach.
>
> Do you know that this is true? I don't know why or how, but it is true. People can get better, can come to themselves, . . . with a little help from you.[2]

Suspend more traditional metaphors for leadership and imagine that Dr. Sullivan had been thinking about a school and had been querying a group of administrative interns. How easily do we fall into the habit of classifying the teachers in "our" school? How many do we classify as losers, recalcitrants, drones? How many teachers do we give up on? How hard do we try to manipulate them to do what we think needs to be done or to force them to leave if they do not respond?

Suppose the object were to figure out what the teachers need rather than what the school needs? "Need" to do what? Need to tap into each one's truest, unique self; to reach so that he or she has a chance to succeed; to become what every person desires to become—an effective, recognized, rewarded individual in the work setting.

Our skills and tools of administration have not been designed to fit the psychiatric metaphor. We assume that someone, other than the classroom teacher, has the knowledge and the wisdom to assert organizational goals, which are monitored with such devices as management by objectives, teacher evaluation systems, and curricular syllabuses. The output of these control mechanisms can then be brought to bear on the analysis of the teaching staff. Consequently, they can be classified and provided with technical staff development interventions to help them become better than they are.

However, this is no technical business in which we are engaged. Success in staff training programs is like success in stopping or reducing smoking, drinking, gambling, or drugs. The individual has to want to take the action. Staff training has to follow the discovery of one's unique self. The intrinsic compulsion to succeed, in any role, follows from the discovery of one's unique self. When administrators foster that compulsion in others, then the strength of the school as an adaptive, excellent unit increases permanently. When they fail to do so, the pills and the pats are useless tools for improvement.

A Metaphor for Organizational Structure

Turn to an alternative metaphor for organizational structure, suggested by the Declaration of Independence of the United States. The assumptions posited by the framers laid the foundation for the political structures that followed. The self-evident truths were five in number, the guarantee to all persons of (1) equality, (2) life, (3) liberty, and (4) the pursuit of happiness, based on (5) the consent of the governed.

Contrast this set of conditions with the assumptions underlying classical bureaucracy. Weber noted:

> Bureaucratization offers above all the optimum possibility for carrying through the principle of specializing administrative functions according to purely objective considerations. Individual performances are allocated to functionaries who have specialized training and who by constant practice learn more and more. The "objective" discharge of business primarily means a discharge of business according to *calculable rules* and "without regard for persons."[3]

Weber continued:

> [Bureaucracy by] its specific nature . . . develops the more perfectly the more the bureaucracy is "dehumanized," the more completely it succeeds in eliminating from official business love, hatred, and all purely personal, irrational, and emotional elements which escape calculation. This is the specific nature of bureaucracy and it is appraised as its special virtue.[4]

What an interesting contrast. The Declaration of Independence is built solely on assumptions about persons. Bureaucracy assumes that organizational structure can be considered "without regard for persons." Once the structure is considered apart from people, the consent of the governed in the designation of leaders is inappropriate, because election reduces "the strictness of hierarchical subordination."[5] Domination and power assume precedence over liberty and the pursuit of happiness, as Weber noted:

> The professional bureaucrat is chained to his activity by his entire material and ideal existence. In the great majority of cases, he is only a

single cog in an ever-moving mechanism which prescibes to him an essentially fixed route of march. . . .

As an instrument for "societalizing" relations of power, bureaucracy has been and is a power instrument of the first order—for the one who controls the bureaucratic apparatus.[6]

Suppose, then, that one could imagine an organizational structure with the individual as its building block, exhibiting a total regard for persons. Reasonably, this personal model would trade off control for empowerment, domination for freedom, and authority for consent. An organization built on these principles would choose its members and leaders, concern itself with the self-actualization of all its members, share the power tools of the organization, deemphasize hierarchical relationships, and create opportunities for self-fulfilling jobs.

In fact, the Declaration of Independence as a metaphor for structure would require a leadership style and leader behavior similar to that described by the metaphor of the administrator as psychoanalyst. In both instances, the design would be built around the needs of the professional staff of the school.

These two metaphors do not fit the modal conditions in American schools. They are not the metaphors on which leader behavior and structure in schools have been based. American schools are bureaucracies. The root structural metaphor for Max Weber was clear: "the fully developed bureaucratic mechanism compares with other organizations exactly as does the machine with the non-mechanical modes of production."[7] Our metaphors for leadership suggest an individual in control, holding onto rather than passing the buck, mobilizing the troops, running a lean and mean organization, making hard decisions, not running a popularity contest. This chapter will argue that two sets of interacting assumptions about (1) people and (2) organizational structure are paralyzing all efforts to modify the roles of principals and teachers in schools. During any attempt to modify one set of assumptions, the other jumps to the fore, leading to the conclusion that the demands of practicality make basic change impossible.

However, one person's practicality is another person's will-o'-the-wisp. The definition of practicality is derived from the assumptions one makes about the factors that affect practicalness in specific circumstances or situations. Our view of today's schools is that they are impractical organizations because they are based on incorrect assumptions about both persons and structure. They are inappropriate as well as impractical because they impose on the learning situation a system of control that inhibits the successful conduct of the teaching-learning act. However, these conclusions should be held in abeyance pending a more systematic examination of assumptions that are commonly held about people in organizations and organizational structure.

ASSUMPTIONS ABOUT THE PERSON IN WORK ORGANIZATIONS

Fifty years ago, Chester Barnard was grappling with the place of the individual in organizational theory. He reminded his readers of the tendency for the "person" to become "people" as the observer thinks about him or her as "them."

> Sometimes in everyday work an individual is something absolutely unique, with a special history in every respect. This is usually the sense in which we regard ourselves, and so also our nearest relations, then our friends and associates. . . . The farther we push away from ourselves the less the word "individual" means what it means when applied to you and me. . . .[8]

The complication of talking about the individual without categorizing her or him into clusters of "them" confuses the theoretician just as it does the practitioner. How can you make assumptions about people that fit persons? Well, of course, you cannot. So the theoretician falls back to the position of modal assumptions about people. How do you think most people feel about themselves, their work, their relations with others? Are there some assumptions about people that are more valid or more heuristic in dealing with individuals than other assumptions? Are there some more likely to be true of more people in more work situations? Have some assumptions or sets of assumptions about people had more or less influence on the theories of structuring work organizations?

Organizational theorists have argued for thirty years that the answer to these questions is "yes," from the complicated explication by Robert Presthus of Harry Stack Sullivan's interpersonal theory[9] to the simpler formulations of Douglas McGregor[10] and Chris Argyris[11] based on behavioral and personality theory.

Theory X and Theory Y

Douglas McGregor asserts that there are a few pervasive assumptions about human nature and human behavior that are implicit in both the theory and practice of management:

1. The average human being has an inherent dislike of work and will avoid it if he can.
2. Because of this human characteristic of dislike of work, most people must be coerced, controlled, directed, threatened with punishment

to get them to put forth adequate effort toward the achievement of organizational objectives.

3. The average human being prefers to be directed, wishes to avoid responsibility, has relatively little ambition, wants security above all.[12]

He contended that these assumptions, which he labeled Theory X, influenced managerial strategy although they did not describe human behavior accurately. He argued that these assumptions were not straw men but were, in fact, the dominant assumptions in the heads of managers.

This assumption of the "mediocrity of the masses" is rarely expressed so bluntly. In fact, a good deal of lip service is given to the ideal of the worth of the average human being. Our political and social values demand such public expressions. Nevertheless, a great many managers will give private support to this assumption, and it is easy to see it reflected in policy and practice.[13]

In contrast, McGregor asserted a set of generalizations about human behavior that, he contended, represented a view of behavior better supported by the findings of social science:

1. The expenditure of physical and mental effort in work is as natural as play or rest. The average human being does not inherently dislike work. . . .
2. Man will exercise self-direction and self-control in the service of objectives to which he is committed.
3. Commitment to objectives is a function of the rewards associated with their achievement. . . .
4. The average human being learns, under proper conditions, not only to accept but to seek responsibility. . . .
5. The capacity to exercise a relatively high degree of imagination, ingenuity, and creativity in the solution of organizational problems is widely, not narrowly, distributed in the population. . . .[14]

McGregor concluded his argument by noting that, "if employees are lazy, indifferent, unwilling to take responsibility, intransigent, uncreative, uncooperative, Theory Y implies that the causes lie in management's methods of organization and control,"[15] not in "the nature of the human resources with which we must work."[16]

Self-Actualization: Developmental Trends of Human Personality

Three years before the publication of McGregor's work, Chris Argyris attempted to present an integrated picture of the behavioral sciences and organization in a volume subtitled "The Conflict Between System and the Individual." Argyris found the conflict to be rooted in seven assumptions about developmental personality trends of individuals in our culture. He argued that these dimensions are descriptive of a basic multidimensional process toward self-actualization that is "characteristic of a relatively large majority of the population":[17]

1. From a state of *passivity* to *activity*; increasingly self-initiatory and self-determinative
2. From a state of *dependence* to independence
3. From *behaving in only a few ways* to *being capable of behaving in many different ways*
4. From having erratic, casual, *shallow interests* to *deeper interests*
5. From having a *short time perspective* to a *longer time perspective*
6. From being in a *subordinate position* to aspiring to occupy an *equal and/or superordinate position* relative to their peers
7. From a *lack of awareness of self* to an *awareness of and control over self* [18]

Argyris contended that these developmental trends were basic properties of the human personality. Theoretically, this means that mature adults "will want to express needs or predispositions related to the adult end of each specific developmental continuum."[19] He went on to present empirical evidence "to support the proposition that the basic impact of the formal organizational structure is to make the employees feel dependent, submissive, and passive, and to require them to utilize only a few of their less important abilities."[20]

Fifty years ago, thirty years ago, twenty-five years ago, and today, these same propositions sound true and troublesome:

1. The uniqueness of the individual, a truism in the way in which people view themselves, is lost as they view others in the organization.
2. Most people, most of the time, typify their subordinates, colleagues, and often superordinates as exhibiting Theory X characteristics. They ordinarily believe that superordinates view them as Theory X performers. Each person, of course, is certain of his or her own status as a Theory Y performer.
3. Everyone concurs that Argyris' developmental continuum describes his or her own personality growth pattern but is (a) uncertain that it describes that of colleagues and subordinates and (b) certain that limits have to be placed on fostering this development in the workplace.

ASSUMPTIONS ABOUT THE STRUCTURE OF WORK ORGANIZATIONS

Why is there such stumbling progress toward modifying practice in work organizations to fit theoretical propositions about human behavior and personality that have been generally accepted for decades? In the field of education, for example, the restricted role of the classroom teacher looks little different than it did thirty years ago.

One explanation is self-contained under the heading "assumptions about the person." A reasonable argument can be mounted that a natural characteristic of people is to distrust and undervalue others. Another possibility is that people's assumptions about organizational structure reinforce that "natural" tendency by allowing them to rationalize their negative view of people in more acceptable terms. "I really believe in the creativity, energy, ambition, and independence of people, but you just can't tolerate anarchy in school or business or. . . ." In fact, these are complementary explanations. Not only can each position serve to rationalize the other, but each tends to force acceptance of the other. Presthus, quoting Harry Stack Sullivan, described what we believe to be the case in explaining the prevailing tolerance, even encouragement, of unacceptable work situations for employees in and outside education:

> "The human organism is so extraordinarily adaptive that not only could the most fantastic social rules and regulations be lived up to, if they were properly inculcated in the young, but they would seem very natural and proper ways of life." [21]

Presthus noted the blindness to alternatives in organization induced by people's organizational assumptions:

> We tend moreover to restrict our thinking about individual freedom to government, concluding that freedom is assured when public power is controlled. But somehow the logic of freedom which is so compelling in this public context is often neglected where private power is concerned. There, despite the intimate relationship between conditions of work and self-realization, the implications of the concentrated power now characteristic of our society have usually been ignored. [22]

Traditional Assumptions about Structure in Schools

The basic assumptions of bureaucracy are the foundation for structural planning and implementation in school organizations. They can be imagined, in effect, as a kind of Theory X[1]—the traditional assumptions held about organizational structure by most people who work in organizational settings.

There is an overarching assumption that bureaucracy is an inevitable structural form for work organizations that are large or complex enough that daily contact among all employees is impossible. Almost all school systems and the majority of schools meet this criterion. This leads to *Assumption 1: The basic bureaucratic form is the only way in which school systems and schools can be organized.*

Bureaucracy, as an organizational form, carries with it a set of minimal unavoidable elements. Bureaucracy makes no sense without a hierarchy. The hierarchy serves two functions of the bureaucracy—official authority and specialization. The principal of a school assumes a set of specialized functions of an administrative nature in the building while simultaneously representing the point in the scalar hierarchy where the "buck stops" within the building unit. This is *Assumption 2: All schools need principals* to carry out administrative functions and to represent the authority of a system in the building unit.

How one becomes an administrator in a bureaucracy was made clear by Weber and has never been seriously challenged: "The pure type of bureaucratic official is *appointed* by a superior authority. An official elected by the governed is not a purely bureaucratic figure,"[23] because "The designation of officials by means of an election among the governed modifies the strictness of hierarchical subordination."[24] *Assumption 3: School principals are appointed* by the elected school board on the recommendation of the chief school administrator.

The appointment of administrative officials in a bureaucratic system emphasizes the scalar characteristic of the hierarchy and ultimately its oligarchic nature. Power within the bureaucracy is centralized in the hands of a few. The mass of employees, if they are to negotiate with the oligarchy, must organize outside the hierarchy to create an external power force to deal with "their own organization." Oligarchy and hierarchy, by centralizing authority and decisionmaking, seek to create a rational organization in pursuit of a set of generally agreed-upon goals and objectives. *Assumption 4: The school system sets goals and directions at the system level.* It takes into account advice and counsel from subordinate levels. This centralization is needed to support rational decisionmaking and accountability in the organization.

Two other features of bureaucracy, specialization and specification, have had particularly important effects on the organization of schools. The former characteristic is designed to provide for technical expertise in the system where such expertise is required. The latter clarifies the assignment and scope of responsibility of individual employees. The technical expertise of the teacher has been defined narrowly—as a subject and/or grade specialization *in the classroom.* Broader instructional expertise—curriculum development and planning—has typically been vested in staff and line administrators from curriculum specialists to the principal. The consequences for teachers have been several. Teachers have become isolated from one another and from the principal during the school day. The autonomy of the teacher in the classroom has resulted in the restriction of the teacher's role and responsibility to the teaching-learning act. *Assumption 5: The teacher's role in the school occurs behind the classroom door.* The professional responsibility of the teacher does not include determining educational goals, curricular content, or making basic decisions about the operation of the school.

Finally, a unique characteristic of bureaucracy, often overlooked in descriptions of necessary elements, is its reliance on education and training. Weber foresaw the need for this development:

> The modern development of full bureaucratization brings the system of rational, specialized, and expert examinations irresistibly to the fore. . . . The development is greatly furthered by the social prestige of the educational certificates acquired through such specialized examinations.[25]

This element is not introduced here to stimulate a debate about whether teachers or administrators should be trained in their areas of specialization, but rather to highlight the field's commitment to certification and examination as a route to organizational effectiveness. The most popular reform tool introduced as a consequence of the criticism of education over the last five years has been standards manipulation through forms of external examination for teachers and students. *Assumption 6: Officeholders in schools should possess educational certificates.* Increasingly, proof of certificate eligibility will be established through external examinations.

Alternative Views of Structure: The Dilemma

Following the logic of the earlier section on assumptions about persons in work organizations, the reader might now expect that the characteristics of traditional organizational structure (Theory X^1) would be followed by a set of structural counterassumptions (Theory Y^1), constituting a system having the following characteristics. Bureaucracy is eschewed; school-level leadership might or might not be provided by a single designated leader; leaders are identified and chosen by means other than appointment; goals and directions grow out of the successful activity of professionals working with clients; job definition evolves from the work of the professional; and certification is a matter of concern among professionals, based on norms of performance. Such a hypothetical configuration would be a Y^1 approach to organizational structure, a true alternative to bureaucracy.

Suppose one did exist. How far would it stretch our credulity? Is it more difficult to believe that "schools do not need principals" than that "man will exercise self-direction and self-control in the service of objectives to which he is committed?" Is it easier to say, "principals should be elected," or "the capacity to exercise a relatively high degree of imagination, ingenuity, and creativity in the solution of organizational problems is widely, not narrowly, distributed in the population?" We submit that the latter set of assumptions is much easier to accept than the former. Our impression is that the assumptions about organizational structure are more deeply embedded in our consciousness than those about people. That, we think, is why those who assert alternative views of people are honored even though it is considered impossible to apply their ideas in practice.

This is not to say that those who asserted alternative views of persons did not attempt to apply those views to the organizational structure. The difficulty arose when they asked themselves to become "practical" in applying their theoretical schema to organizations.

McGregor, for example, had no illusions about the fit between bureaucracy and Theory Y. He noted that "the central principle of organization which derives from Theory X is that of direction and control through the exercise of authority—what has been called 'the scalar principle.'"[26] In comparing management's ineffective use of control in contrast to engineering, he argued:

> In the human field . . . we often dig channels to make water flow uphill. Many of our attempts to control behavior, far from representing selective adaptations, are in direct violation of human nature. They consist in trying to make people behave as we wish without concern for natural law.[27]

Now listen to the relatively conservative tone of the recommendations by the same author in regard to organizational structure:

> What is the practical relevance for management of these findings of social science research in the field of leadership? . . . [1] *One of management's major tasks, therefore, is to provide a heterogeneous supply of human resources from which individuals can be selected to fill a variety of specific but unpredictable needs.* . . . [2] A management development program should involve many people within the organization rather than a select few. . . . [3] Management should have as a goal the development of the unique capacities and potentialities of each individual rather than common objectives for all participants. . . . [4] The promotion policies of the company should be so administered that these heterogeneous resources are actually considered when openings occur. . . . and [5] If leadership is a function—a complex relation between leader and situation—we ought to be clear that every promising recruit is *not* a potential member of top management.[28]

None of these recommendations require the suspension of belief in any of the requisite structural characteristics of bureaucracy. They are reasonable adjustments that can be made within an existing structure that is, in fact, antithetical to the theoretical propositions about people to which the author subscribes.

That was a quarter century ago. What about today? The dilemma of practicability stultifies even the most innovative of theorists. For example, Rosabeth Kanter, in discussing the empowerment of individuals in organizations, runs directly up against the limitations of thinking about people within the traditional structural model:

> Unlimited circulation of power in an organization without focus would mean that no one would ever get anything done beyond a small range of actions that people can carry out by themselves. Besides, the very idea of infinite power circulation sounds to some of us like a system out of control, unguided, in which anybody can start nearly anything. (And probably finish almost nothing.) Thus the last key to successful middle-management innovation is to see how power gets pulled out of circulation and focused long enough to permit project completion. But here we find an organizational dilemma. Some of the focusing conditions are contrary to the circulating conditions, almost by definition.[29]

Even analysts who begin with the consideration of structural alternatives often find themselves trapped, in the final analysis, in modest adjustments still based upon the traditional assumptions. Patterson, Purkey, and Parker have published a monograph with the provocative title, *Productive School Systems for a Nonrational World*. In practice, however, the nonrational model sounds very rational indeed:

> Like the rational model, the nonrational model endorses the concept of organizational goals, but assigns a different meaning and importance to the construction of these goals. Both views of reality would argue that school districts do have a central mission: to improve learning and the quality of life in schools. When it comes to translating this mission statement into organizational goals, the nonrational and rational schools of thought part company.
>
> For instance, the board of education may have a long list of district goals as part of board policy. Individual schools could have their own list, and certain parent organizations may produce still another list they want the school or district to address. The key, within the nonrational model, is to use organizational energy optimally in serving a variety of legitimate goals across different lines—*as long as the district adheres to the overall mission of the organization*. [Italics added.][30]

In the example, Patterson and colleagues assumed that the hierarchical responsibility for establishing goals was reasonable and necessary. They noted that idiosyncratic goals might also be stated at the school level, so long as they did not conflict with board policy. They suggested that, in the nonrational model, conflicting goals can be met by delaying or sequencing their implementation—for example, postponing the implementation of a program for the gifted until a program for computer literacy is in place. That is a sensible deviation from the rigidity of the traditional model but hardly seems to justify the nomenclature "nonrational."

This is not intended to be a criticism of Patterson and colleagues, but rather to illustrate how very difficult it is to imagine what might be defined as a Y^1 organization—even one that might be termed arational rather than nonrational.

Alternative Views of Structure: Proposed Solutions

A familiar example of an organizational structure that does not conform to the necessary elements of bureaucracy is the organized anarchy described by Cohen and March.[31] They described a class of organizations with three pervasive characteristics: problematic goals, unclear technology, and fluid participation by the participants in organizational activities and interests. The authors argued that such organizations were "not limited to educational institutions; but they are particularly conspicuous there. The American college or university is a prototypic organized anarchy."[32] This description is not judgmental. "These factors do not make a university a bad organization or a disorganized one; but they do make it a problem to describe, understand, and lead."[33]

This organizational form is not a theoretical construction. Cohen and March presented it as an empirical description of an organization that evolved within a conventional bureaucratic structure. The evolution occurred in a setting in which individual interests are apparently strong enough to modify, in a few essential ways, the basic elements of the bureaucracy.

The actual form, different in degree from university to university, is an unjustified variation[34] in the bureaucratic model in response to the pressure of individual freedom. The consent of the governed, for example, may not be stretched to a vote of the faculty on a new dean, or president, or department chair (although it often is), but the faculty is almost always in the position to advise and consent. One is hard pressed to find universities without presidents, but it is common to discover departments where the role of chair is passed around from year to year. There are career administrators, but there are more career professionals who move among teaching, research, and administration. The power tools of the organization—salary level, recruitment, promotion, and tenure—are often held by the professorial staff. Curriculum is routinely in professorial hands. The university, as a consequence of this variation, is not a perfect organization, but on the other hand, it is neither anarchical nor ineffective.

Another current commentator on organizational theory and leadership in schools addressed the specific issue being discussed in this section—the paucity of alternatives to the bureaucratic model. Foster argued:

> Administration must at its heart be informed by critical models oriented toward social justice and individual freedom. This is not just

"nice"; it determines our entire way of life and the purpose of our most important social institution, education.[35]

To illustrate alternatives to the bureaucratic model, he suggested the bargaining model and the community democracy model, analogous to worker ownership in industry.

Gareth Morgan attempted to loosen the hold of X^1 assumptions by describing a variety of metaphors of organizational structure from the most conservative (organizations as machines), to less conservative but well-known (organizations as organisms, organizations as cultures, and organizations as political systems), to more unconventional images (organizations as brains, psychic prisons, instruments of domination). Morgan argued that:

Images and metaphors are not only interpretive constructs or ways of seeing; they also provide frameworks for action. Their use creates insights that often allow us to act in ways that we may not have thought possible before.[36]

He also stated:

I believe that people can change organizations and society. . . . Prescriptively, I would thus like us all to recognize that reality is made, not given; to recognize that our seeing and understanding of the world is always *seeing as*, rather than a *seeing as is*; and to take an ethical and moral responsibility for the personal and collective consequences of the way we see and act in everyday life, difficult though this may be. . . . Consistent with my overall orientation, I firmly believe that we need to break the hold of bureaucratic thinking and to move toward newer, less exploitative, more equal modes of interaction in organizations.[37]

We suggest that the clues to a Y^1 organizational structure are already present, ready to be noticed. One starting point to provoke noticing is to play a game of "antithesis." What would be the opposite of the basic requisites of bureaucracy? Rather than a hierarchy, imagine a heterarchy; rather than appointed leaders, elected leaders; rather than centralized power, diffused responsibility; rather than system goals, individual goals; generality rather than specialization; variable job definition rather than specification; permeable boundaries of responsibility rather than circumscription of responsibility; ex post facto rather than a priori expectations of satisfactory performance.

The game can be extended if one turns from antithesis to invention. What needs to be done structurally to fit the characteristics of Argyris' mature individual and McGregor's Theory Y? It is necessary to create conditions that allow for self-direction and self-control. For example, as a prior condition, the organization's goals must be derived from the goals of the individual or, better yet, be discovered in the successes of the individual. The reward system must be rooted in the intrinsic rewards of the individual's job. Empire builders must be encouraged to seek added responsibility in the organization, because responsibility is not a finite element in the organization. The conditions of discovery are such that new ideas, images, creative solutions, and (of course) problems emerge from the people of the organization. Ideas from any are treated as ideas from the influential. Individual employees can run trials of new ideas or techniques in the same manner that organizations now arrange trials. Workers develop intricate human, technical, and conceptual linkages to the organization—the kind of linkages that suggest to managers in current organizations that "this place will probably collapse without me." The contract between the individual and the organization feels like the intimate lifetime employment described by William Ouchi as characteristic of Japanese organizations.[38] While referring to Theory Z, one could also consider nonspecialized career paths, slow evaluation, decoupling of formal titles and actual responsibility, and membership in multiple work groups.

Nonbureaucratic (Y^1) structural alternatives are neither recondite nor beyond contemporary experience. Clues to Y^1 are everywhere in the practice and theory of today:

- Operating subunits within current organizations that function successfully with a nonbureaucratic structural form—for example, R&D centers or teams, some university departments, self-managing work teams in industrial settings.
- Organizations in other cultural settings that exhibit nonbureaucratic features, and the adaptation of some of these features in American organizations.
- Nonwork organizations that function effectively employing counterbureaucratic structures, such as voluntary service groups.
- Clan-like organizations that arise, at least occasionally, in the midst of or parallel to a bureaucratic structure, such as alternative schools and private schools.
- Professional organizations that are better depicted as organic or coalitional than bureaucratic.[39]
- Administrative techniques and strategies that struggle to survive in bureaucratic settings (and for which people struggle to offer bureaucratic rationalizations) although the strategies are clearly antibureaucratic in intent—self- and peer evaluation, election of leaders, empowerment, job enlargement, team building.
- Metaphors that suggest richer interpretations of everyday life in organizations than the classical machine and military metaphors.
- Theoretical formulations that, though antibureaucratic, seem to conform better to the practitioner's understanding of logic-in-use than does traditional reconstructed logic about organizations.
- Theoretical and empirical anomalies that suggest that the existing structural orientation is flawed—evidence that modal behavior in organizations is represented better by a theory in which action pre-

cedes intent; rationality is retrospective rather than prospective; individual and organizational choices do not conform to consistent preferences.

These glimpses of alternatives to the bureaucratic structure are overwhelmed not by the practicalness of the bureaucratic model but by its omnipresence. Tradition and availability are often confused with practicability. How can one imagine operable alternatives to a structure so firmly in place? That is the dilemma, the challenge, and the hope.

CONJOINING ASSUMPTIONS ABOUT PEOPLE AND STRUCTURE IN ORGANIZATIONS

Figure 13-1 displays the territory covered to this point in the chapter. Cell (1) represents modal practice in organizations today. Operationally, most organizational participants cling to a Theory X view of people. That view dominates the day-to-day life in organizations, and it is not restricted to administrators. Teachers ordinarily express similar views of other teachers, administrators, and their students. Organizational storytelling by teachers and administrators abounds with tales of incompetence, laziness, inconsiderate behavior, and intolerable domination.

However deeply alternative views of people have penetrated the literature of organizational theory, they have barely made a dent in the interactions of people in organizations—including schools. Why should they? The structure that pervades work organizations demonstrates the basic wisdom of Theory X. Administrators feel compelled to supervise, control, and motivate teachers. That is consistent with a fear that without these organizational practices teachers will be unmotivated, indolent, uncertain of their job requirements, and unclear about organizational goals. Is similar concern addressed to the lack of motivation of superintendents of schools or to the likelihood that they will be unclear about the district's goals or their own job requirements? Are slothfulness and confusion human characteristics determined by the scalar principle? Of course they are not. However, the bureaucratic structure has always assumed that the natural tendency of all people to behave in ways antithetical to the best interests of the organization can only be controlled through domination. When under pressure to demonstrate school reform, educators attempt to mandate higher standards and levels of performance; control and accountability mechanisms—tests, merit pay, standards, competitive comparisons—are the first tools to which they turn.

A Theory X view of people is in harmony with a traditional view of organizational structure. On most days of the year, that harmony is expressed in the nation's schools. However, something pulls away at people's commitment to the traditional structure. The popularity of spe-

FIGURE 13-1
A classificatory schema of the interaction between
assumptions about people and about structure in
organizations.

Assumptions about Structure

	Theory X [1]	Theory Y [1]
Theory X	**X-X [1]** Conventional assumptions about people and structure Modal view in contemporary organizational practice (1)	**X-Y [1]** Adoption of structural modifications to relieve pressures on the bureaucratic structure Symbolic response; in some ways an empty set (2)
Theory Y	**Y-X [1]** Neo-orthodox response to "humanizing" the organization Modal view in current organizational theory; emergent view in organizational practice (3)	**Y-Y [1]** Nonorthodox response to "humanizing" the organization Emergent view in organizational theory (4)

(left axis label: **Assumptions about People**)

cific devices (quality circles, peer evaluation, career ladders, matrix organization, conflict resolution techniques) and of more general strategies
(empowerment, job enlargement, strategic planning, school site management, Theory Z, shared decisionmaking) demonstrates an uneasiness and disaffection with X-X[1] organizations on the basis of human
concerns, or organizational productivity, or both. In some cases, modification is simply a response to pressure brought to bear on the hierarchy by individuals chafing under the restrictiveness of a bureaucratic
structure, or by clients dissatisfied with the product or services of the
organization. Often the adjustment is only the attempt of opportunistic

managers to modify structure while clinging to traditional views of persons in the organization—an X-Y[1] position in Figure 13-1, cell (2). It is even reasonable to argue that cell (2), by its nature, is an empty set because the adoption of structural variations, tactical or strategic, to enhance the effectiveness of ultimate control over individuals in the organization is unlikely to represent any modification in the adopter's assumptions about the necessary elements of structural control.

In contrast, cell (3) is where most people end up after deciding to do their best to think about or work toward "humanizing" an organization. The decision to operate on the basis of Theory Y within the constraints of a traditional organizational structure produces results that are well meant but essentially inconsonant. Seven years after publishing his seminal theoretical book on the individual and the organization, Chris Argyris undertook the task of theoretically integrating the individual and the organization. In a prophetic first chapter, Argyris asked the question whether it is likely that the relationships between the individual and the organization can be maximized. He answered by suggesting that the best that can be hoped for is to reduce the conflict in the relationships between the two, a kind of "satisficing" rather than maximizing the relationship.

Argyris' position in Figure 13-1 was clearly in cell (3). He noted:

> We believe that organizations and personalities are discrete units with their own laws, which make them amenable to study as separate units. However, we also believe that important parts of each unit's existence depend on their connectedness with the other. . . . Our primary interest is at the boundaries of both—at the points where they overlap and are interrelated.[40]

Further, Argyris' definition of what he called the "underlying nature" of formal organizations was traditional:

> Formal organizations are based on certain principles such as "task specialization," "chain of command," "unity of direction," "rationality," and others. These are the basic "genes" that are supported by, and at times modified in, varying degrees by the technology, the kinds of managerial controls, and the patterns of leadership used in the organization.[41]

Confronting this oxymoronic situation, how did Argyris imagine "the organization of the future"? Firstly, he did not imagine revolutionary structural alterations. "One conclusion, however, should be evident by now. The pyramidal structure has *not* been overthrown. It has simply been relegated to a more realistic position in terms of its potential."[42] Yet he did predict changes that have continued to be discussed and implemented over the past twenty years:

- Management in the organization of the future will give much more thought to its basic values and planning as to how they may be implemented. . . .
- The values about effective organizational relationships will be expanded and deepened. . . .
- The concept of directive authority or power will be expanded to include the influence of individuals through rewards and penalties that minimize dependence, through internal commitment, and the process of confirmation. The "old" values regarding influence will still be maintained to be used for the appropriate conditions. The "new" values regarding influence will be added to, not substituted for, the old. . . .
- The organization of the future will strive to enlarge the jobs. . . .
- Individuals [will be required] to become concerned for the health of the organization. . . . Thus employees (at all levels) may meet in small groups to constantly diagnose organizational strengths and weaknesses. . . .
- The pyramidal structure will now exist side by side with several other structures. . . .
- Participants [other than designated leaders] will . . . be required to accept increasing amounts of responsibility and therefore authority. . . .
- As trust increases the climate should tend to be ripe for some major changes in the controls, reward and penalty, and incentive systems. . . . Controls will change to instruments of opportunity for increased self-responsibility and psychological success. . . . The information collected "on" an individual will be collected "by" him and evaluated by him, and he will take the appropriate action. . . .
- Rewards and penalties, therefore, will also tend to be modified. There will still be the more traditional rewards and penalties, especially to the degree that (1) the foregoing changes are not possible, (2) the people's physiological and security needs are not fulfilled, (3) the individuals are psychologically threatened by growth and self-responsibility.[43]

Cell (3) is simultaneously comfortable and stressful. The position takes the individual in the organization into account at more than a superficial level. The traditional structure is adjusted to fit individual needs. Argyris was picturing job enlargement, quality circles, diffused leadership, self-evaluation, matrix organization, strategic planning, and opportunities for intrinsic job rewards. That was more than alright for 1964, but what stopped him cold was the question, "By whose leave?" The answer is by the authority vested in appointed officials in a bureaucratic system. The adaptations are dependent on the goodwill or the intelligence, or both, of designated leaders. Argyris' position, then and now, is neither cynical nor manipulative, but it is strained. The fact is, cell (3) accepts an impractical theoretical position, one that argues simultaneously for freedom with responsibility in a democratic system and control with benevolence in an oligarchic structure. Returning to Presthus' conjecture, why is it that "the logic of freedom which is so compelling in this public context is often neglected where private power is concerned"?[44]

Cell (4) is the alternative. Educators must create and experiment with structures that fit the accumulated theory and research about the human personality. They must not be constrained by the traditional structural assumptions that were derived from an incomplete and inaccurate understanding of human potential. In the following section, we will try to imagine a new school organization based on Y-Y[1] assumptions.

REFLECTIONS ON A DEMOCRATIC STRUCTURE FOR LEADERSHIP IN NEW SCHOOLS

How to start the process of imagining such a new school is no mystery, because what people need in a work organization is known: to be free, to be valued, to be challenged, to grow, to assume responsibility, to be secure, to be rewarded, to be in touch with their true selves. Such an organization is possible; it is within people's own power to create and implement if they choose to do so. We are convinced that it is necessary to move in the direction of organizations for people if excellence in performance and freedom for human beings are to be achieved.

Initially, we want to assert a small number of propositions that we feel are imperative in imagining a new school.

1. A new school must be built on the assumption of the consent of the governed. This concept is troublesome chiefly because it is strange. Yet if any organization should reflect democratic ideals, it is the school. Designated leaders, such as the principal, should be chosen by teachers. The professional staff of the school unit should choose their new colleagues. The professional staff is a work team of mature adults. They cannot manifest professional responsibility in an oligarchy.

2. A new school must be built on shared authority and responsibility, not delegation of authority and responsibility. The responsibility for a new school lies with the professional staff of the school, not solely or even predominantly with a designated leader. If the new school is a team enterprise, then the key actors on the team change from day to day and activity to activity. If there is to be delegation to authority, it must come from the team to the individual. If specialists in subject areas, or curriculum, or administration are to take on special spheres of responsibility, that assignment must be made by the staff of the school.

3. The staff of a new school must trade assignments and work in multiple groups to remain in touch with the school as a whole. The role of principal, head teacher, or chair should ordinarily be assumed for relatively short periods. The staff should include many individuals whose experience includes terms of work in administration and instructional development as well as classroom teaching. The work groups formed within the staff should provide opportunities to interact with a variety of colleagues on a variety of problems.

4. Formal rewards to the staff—salary, tenure, forms of promotion—should be under the control of the staff of the new school as a whole. There is no perfectly satisfactory way to distribute differential rewards, but no one is in a better position to deal with this difficult issue than a group of colleagues. Peer evaluation and decisionmaking may end in the decision to reduce individual distinctions and emphasize group distinctions, or it may not. In either event, the power tools of formal rewards and recognition must not be controlled by an individual outside the group. The problem is a professional issue of self-determination.

5. The goals of the new school must be formulated and agreed to through group consensus. The professional staff is responsible for negotiating the acceptability of the goals to the school community. Although formal goals probably have little to do with organizational efficacy, the school needs to represent itself to its political constituency and clarify, for itself, its raison d'être. The school *is* the professional staff, acting both individually and collectively. The staff is responsible for negotiating the relationship of individual goals to the goals of the school as an organization, translating those into programs, and subsequently expressing the goals and programs to other responsible agents and agencies in an intelligible and acceptable form.

We are going to stop with this short list of "musts." They represent sufficiently the basic change in orientation that we feel is necessary to the "new school." If they were implemented, schools would be operating on the basis of:

- Democracy
- Group authority and accountability
- Variability, generality, and interactivity in work assignment
- Self-discipline and control exercised individually and collectively
- Group commitment to and consensus about organizational goals and means

We are certain of one thing. Within the bureaucratic structure, there will never be movement to new schools, to free schools. That structure was invented to assure domination and control, and it will never produce freedom and self-actualization. You can't get there from here.

The risk of movement from here to there is not great. The bureaucratic structure is failing in a manner so critical that adaptations will not forestall its collapse. It is impractical, and it does not fit the psychological and personal needs of the work force.

It can be argued that an alternative structure is practical, on grounds of organizational productivity. Research evidence on creativity and innovation supports organizational structures that promote freedom, self-control, and personal development. Organizational studies indicate that such nonbureaucratic characteristics as activity, variability, self-efficacy, empowerment, and disaggregation are more likely to be found in effective organizations than are their bureaucratic counterparts—stability, regularity, accountability, control, and centralization. In the replacement of the bureaucratic structure, necessity may turn out to be the progenitor of practicality.

From our viewpoint, only one argument is needed to sustain the change. An oligarchic work organization is discordant in a free society. Persons need and deserve the same degree of protection of their human rights in the workplace that is assured in their broader role as adult citizens.

Finally, we counsel patience in the development of and experimentation with new organizational forms. People have been patient and forgiving of our extant form. Remember that new forms will also represent ideals; do not press them immediately to their point of absurdity. Bureaucracy as an ideal form became tempered by adjectival distinctions—bounded, contingent, situational. New forms need to be granted the same exceptions as they are proposed and tested. No one seriously imagines a utopian alternative to bureaucracy, but there can be realistic alternatives that consistently trade off control for freedom, the organization for the individual. Such alternatives can be built upon the principle of the consent of the governed.

NOTES

1. Walker Percy, *The Thanatos Syndrome* (New York: Farrar, Straus & Giroux, 1987), p. 16.

2. Ibid., pp. 16–17.

3. H. H. Gerth and C. Wright Mills, *From Max Weber: Essays in Sociology* (New York: Oxford University Press, 1958), p. 215.

4. Ibid., pp. 215–216.

5. Ibid., pp. 200–201.

6. Ibid., p. 228.

7. Ibid., p. 214.

8. Chester I. Barnard, *The Functions of the Executive* (Cambridge, Mass.: Harvard University Press, 1968), p. 12.

9. Robert Presthus, *The Organizational Society* (New York: Alfred A. Knopf, 1962), pp. 93–134.

10. Douglas McGregor, *The Human Side of Enterprise* (New York: McGraw-Hill, 1985), pp. 33–58.

11. Chris Argyris, *Personality and Organization* (New York: Harper & Brothers, 1957), pp. 20–53.

12. McGregor, op. cit., pp. 33–34.

13. Ibid., p. 34.

14. Ibid., pp. 47–48.

15. Ibid., p. 48.

16. Ibid.

17. Argyris, op. cit., p. 49.

18. Ibid., pp. 49–50.

19. Ibid., p. 53.

20. Ibid., p. 75.

21. Presthus, op. cit., pp. 119–120.

22. Ibid., p. 19.

23. Gerth and Mills, op. cit., p. 200.

24. Ibid.

25. Ibid., p. 241.

26. McGregor, op. cit., p. 49.

27. Ibid., p. 9.

28. Ibid., pp. 185–188.

29. Rosabeth M. Kanter, *The Change Masters* (New York: Simon and Schuster, 1983), pp. 171–172.

30. Jerry L. Patterson, Stewart C. Purkey, and Jackson V. Parker, *Productive School Systems for a Nonrational World* (Alexandria, Va.: Association for Supervision and Curriculum Development, 1986), p. 27.

31. Michael D. Cohen and James G. March, *Leadership and Ambiguity* (Boston: Harvard Business School Press, 1986), p. 3.

32. Ibid.

33. Ibid.

34. "Unjustified variation, as opposed to rational variation, is emphasized in evolutionary theory. . . . An unjustified variation is one for which truth has not been established, but one for which truth is not precluded." Karl E. Weick, *The Social Psychology of Organizing* (New York: Random House, 1979), p. 123.

35. William Foster, *Paradigms and Promises: New Approaches to Educational Administration* (Buffalo, N.Y.: Prometheus Books, 1986), p. 189.

36. Gareth Morgan, *Images of Organization* (Beverly Hills, Calif.: Sage Publications, 1986), p. 343.

37. Ibid., pp. 382–383.

38. William G. Ouchi, *Theory Z* (New York: Avon Books, 1982), pp. 15–22.

39. James D. Thompson, *Organizations in Action* (New York: McGraw Hill, 1967), pp. 142–143.

40. Chris Argyris, *Integrating the Individual and the Organization* (New York: John Wiley & Sons, 1964), p. 13.

41. Ibid., p. 14.

42. Ibid., p. 272.

43. Ibid., pp. 273–276.

44. Presthus, op. cit., p. 19.

PART IV

ISSUES OF PROFESSIONALISM

At the heart of the debate over school improvement is the possibility of increasing the professional status of teaching. To some, talk of professionalism elicits nervous reactions. To others, professionalism is championed as the key leverage point in bringing about significant and sustained improvements in the quality of the educational system.

Those who fear professionalism often view the movement as a conspiracy to increase the power and prestige of teachers at the expense of the public. Another source of fear is the belief that professionalism will drive away administrators and result in peer-run schools. "Peer-run" is often considered to be a synonym for anarchy.

One's view of professionalism depends on the meanings that are attributed to the term. Does it mean turning the educational system upside down, thus challenging the basic structure of school governance? Does it also mean challenging the fundamental premises of the present system of public accountability? Or does professionalism mean making the needed adjustments in schooling that will increase the efficacy of the present system of governance and accountability? The contributors to Part Four of this book are clearly aligned with the second view. They see professionalism as the means by which the present system might be loosened in part and tightened in part and, as a result, strengthened. The crux of loosening is to increase the discretion of teachers and principals, thus allowing them to make more informed and effective decisions about their practice. Tightening could take the form of raising the standards for professional entry and holding schools more accountable for their accomplishments. The arguments for more looseness and tightness are made as a matter of practicality. Considering the nature of teaching, what is known about professional work, the ways teachers and other professionals think and act, and the power of professional norms, those who want quality in the long run find themselves looking increasingly to professionalism as an important part of the answer.

In Chapter 14, Arthur E. Wise proposes professional teaching as a new model for managing schooling. He begins by summarizing his own research on how efforts to improve schooling within our present framework increase the extent to which both schooling and teaching are bureaucratized. This is followed by an analysis of the effects of bureaucracy on how teachers teach, how they see their identity and commitment to work, and how and what students learn. He provides a portrait of a school system steeped in mediocrity. Further steps in this direction, he warns, will only make things worse.

Recognizing that the public has a right to demand accountability in schools, Wise concludes that today's problems stem from using the wrong model of accountability. "Happily, there is another model of accountability: professional accountability." Professional accountability, Wise maintains, recognizes that "appropriate instructional decisions must be made at the point of service delivery. Therefore, the quality of services delivered inevitably depends upon the capacity of the teacher to make appropriate decisions." In all of the more established professions, quality control problems are solved by "substituting quality control over personnel for quality control over service delivery." Wise then discusses the standards that need to be developed to improve the quality of teachers. He gives attention to such issues as licensing and induction, testing, and reforming teacher education programs. Wise is convinced that as these standards are raised, the public trust in teaching will increase, allowing the profession to be freed from many of the constraints that may impair quality.

Wise points out, however, that professionalization of teaching does not mean the development of totally different school structures. Schools will continue to have principals, and school districts will continue to have superintendents. It is clear, however, that as the caliber of teachers improves and teaching itself takes on more complex and effective forms, principals and superintendents will need to manage and lead differently.

Wise concludes by discussing what is likely to happen if professionalism does not prevail. By the mid-1990s, schools will be hiring over one million teachers and replacing nearly all of the present school administrators. He does not believe that teaching or school administration will be able to attract the best and the brightest, given present circumstances. Moreover, few talented people from minority groups will elect to become teachers if today's low standards continue. He raises the possibility of the evolution of a school system that will be unacceptable to the middle class. If this occurs, he maintains, large numbers of parents will abandon the public schools. Professionalization is not only good for teachers and students but also essential to the "preservation of our common public school tradition."

Samuel B. Bacharach and Sharon C. Conley follow a slightly different tack in Chapter 15 as they develop their argument on behalf of professionalism. They point out that traditional bureaucratic views of management and control, which offer "patterned" solutions to school problems, do not fit the world of teaching very well. Teaching takes place in an environment of uncertainty; therefore, the level of decision-making required for effective teaching cannot be programmed. The traditional view is often followed nonetheless, resulting in the development of management structures that do not fit the realities of teaching practice. This produces, in turn, tension between the values of bureaucracy and those of professionalism.

To Bacharach and Conley, the solution is to develop a system of management and control more consistent with the nature of teaching, and that system must be a professional one. They point out that different assumptions about key underlying issues determine whether management will employ a bureaucratic or professional strategy as it seeks to direct and control. Three issues that they consider to be critical are how related knowledge is viewed, how knowledge can be controlled, and how the work flow of teachers can be regulated. Central to their analysis is the extent to which the environment of teaching is characterized by uncertainty. This uncertainty is defined in terms of variations in the problems that teachers encounter and variations in the number of possible solutions to these problems. Different mixes of these two dimensions lead to four metaphors for the role of teachers: bureaucrats, technicians, craftspersons, and professionals. The adequacy of each metaphor is then examined in light of its fit with situations of practice.

Recognizing the growing consensus that teaching is fundamentally a process of making decisions in highly uncertain settings, and providing examples from their own research, the authors identify nine basic decisionmaking responsibilities of teachers. They conclude that the work of teaching is mainly a professional activity. Management systems that support this reality enhance professionalism. A supportive management system can allow teachers to be sufficiently integrated into the formal decisionmaking process of schools.

Bacharach and Conley then examine some of the structural and political obstacles to expanding the role of teacher from classroom decisionmaker to a more complete organizational participant.

If one accepts the premise that professionalism is a good idea for teachers and that professionals work in unique kinds of organizations, what would the implications be for how schools are organized and managed? In Chapter 16, Karl E. Weick and Reuben R. McDaniel, Jr. attempt to answer that question. Relying on an organizational theory perspective, they begin with the basic purposes of organizing. Organizations are created when people need to work together. They assume roles and play out various relationships in order to achieve certain desired outputs. A particular organizational form, therefore, needs to be evaluated on the basis of its ability to help people achieve goals and objectives in an effective and efficient manner. It is therefore reasonable to assume that the nature of the organization and the ways workers engage in activities should determine the form and structure of the organization. It follows that there should be differences in how one runs a shipyard, a factory, or a school.

Weick and McDaniel then address more specifically how professions are organized. Discussing the nature of professionalization, the characteristics of professional values, and the ways information inputs are used in professional organizations, they chart the appropriate dimensions of organization and structure, management, and control. They note that most professional organizations have both routine and nonroutine tasks to accomplish and must process both routine and non-routine information. Although nonroutine information is common in professional organizations such as schools, it often poses difficulties for information processing and is therefore misperceived and handled as routine. As more emphasis is given to routine, professionals are excluded from participating in the control system, and professional values are deemphasized.

Weick and McDaniel then examine the functions of professional organizations. "Professional organizations embody the transformation process of people rather than in machines. This is a strategy for dealing with uncertainty in a marketplace." Though all organizations are responsible for interpreting events and making decisions, professional organizations give professionals a primary role in executing both. Where nonroutine information, incomplete knowledge, and uncertainty loom large, professional values become important means for providing direction and bringing about order. Matters of purpose and belief and the refinement of professional values are all-important in the development and operation of a professional organization.

Weick and McDaniel maintain that control strategies in professional organizations differ from those in other organizations. This assertion leads them to examine such issues as how one maintains control, how leadership should be exercised, how enterprises should be organized, and how power should be distributed. They then address the issue of what form professional organizations should take. They begin their analysis by examining "mechanistic" and "organic" models, defining their characteristics and analyzing their strengths and weaknesses. Weick and McDaniel then provide a careful analysis of the conditions of work that exist in schools and of the nature of the decisionmaking that occurs in classrooms and corridors. This leads them to conclude that schools are hybrid professional organizations that process both routine and non-routine information and thus require dimensions of tightness and looseness in structure and form.

The authors' conclusion that schools need to display both a bureaucratic and professional face is consistent with the view that the restructuring of schooling is not a matter of turning things upside down but of making appropriate adjustments in the ways in which schools now operate. The need for making adjustments, however, should not be taken lightly. Should the bureaucratic face be emphasized to the point where professional decisionmaking is not possible, the consequence will be the routinization of schooling, with negative effects for both teachers and students.

Phillip C. Schlechty has considerable experience with the "nitty-gritty" of implementing career ladder programs. Long before the recent uproar of reform, Schlechty and his colleagues designed and implemented the Charlotte-Mecklenburg teacher career development program. In Chapter 17, he raises the question as to whether the concept of career ladder is a good idea going awry. He points out that linking career options with salary opportunities creates serious difficulties in implementation. Prime among them is the displacement of the original goals of career ladder plans (increasing opportunities for growth and development and status and recognition) by the goal of pay for performance.

Schlechty then traces the consequences of viewing career ladders as "pay for performance" plans. Merit pay leads to the development of evaluation systems that must be technically and legally defensible, as opposed to being helpful in improving the performance of teachers. Legally defensible systems are inherently bureaucratic, because they must be measurement-oriented and standardized. It is necessary to create developmental evaluation systems that are directed less to grading and sorting and more to helping.

Relying on his own personal experience and on the literature on work motivation and performance, Schlechty then discusses eight principles that should provide the basis for developing career ladders. Essential to his analysis is the necessity of developing and implementing career ladder plans within a broad framework designed to improve the quality of work life for teachers. Such plans, he believes, should lead to a more professional work setting. Unfortunately, plans construed as "pay for performance" often increase bureaucratic characteristics. Schlechty's commitment to the concept of career ladder is strong, but he believes that unless the emphasis shifts from performance-based to skill-based career ladder systems, the unanticipated consequences of increased bureaucracy and low morale will result in less teacher commitment and have negative performance effects.

Schlechty's chapter is followed by a postscript on career ladders; a position paper prepared by the Trinity Educational Forum. The forum, composed of administrators representing several school districts in Bexar County, Texas, joined together to construct a set of alternative guidelines for developing sensible policies and practices as the state-mandated career ladder was being implemented in Texas in 1985.

CHAPTER 14

Professional Teaching: A New Paradigm for the Management of Education

ARTHUR E. WISE

The RAND Corporation

Teacher professionalism or the professionalization of teaching is an alternate paradigm for the management of education. Schools must be managed. They are now managed according to the bureaucratic paradigm, the utility of which is being questioned. I will argue that some bureaucratic management practices have been causing unacceptable distortions in the educational process. In other words, some of the very tools of management misdirect the educational process and alter the educational outcomes that schools seek to attain.

There now exists the possibility of a revolution in education: the professionalization of teaching. I would like to raise and address a series of questions. Why now? Why is it important? What is professional teaching, anyway? What would enable it to occur? What will teaching be like if it does occur? What may prevent it from occurring? What will happen if it does not occur? Finally, if you believe in it, what should you do?

THE SITUATION TODAY

In 1979, I wrote a book called *Legislated Learning: The Bureaucratization of the American Classroom*.[1] It began to trace some of the effects of the volumes of new policy that had emerged from national and state legislation and through the judiciary. This new material contained a vision of the teacher and of the educational process that would change what went on in schools. The idea seemed to be that if policymakers could regulate teacher behavior more closely, they would improve the quality of services provided. The guiding premise was that policymakers could not trust educators to do the job right. Therefore, they would "micromanage" behavior within the classroom. This, they thought, would improve the quality of education. The movement was associated with accountability legislation, "teacher-proof" curricula, and assorted other ventures.

Legislated Learning was largely a theoretical analysis, which revealed the vision of schooling, teaching, and learning implicit in the new policies. Subsequently, Linda Darling-Hammond and I began to talk to teachers about the effect of these policies on their classroom practices. In those interviews, we learned that teachers were beginning to perceive the reality of the standardized curriculum they were expected to follow, that the number of bureaucratic reporting requirements with which teachers were obliged to comply was increasing, that teachers saw a growing use of hierarchical evaluation systems to make sure that they did what they were supposed to do, and that teachers experienced a growing emphasis upon standardized tests as the measure of what they did in school.[2]

School management had been reduced to standardized curriculum, bureaucratic reporting requirements, hierarchical evaluation systems, and standardized tests. It was as if policymakers were trying to tell teachers what to do, telling them how to do it, making them fill out forms to report that they knew what they were supposed to be doing, inspecting their performance to make sure that they were doing what they were supposed to be doing, and, as a final check on the process, instituting external examinations to find out that teachers had done what they were supposed to do.

This style of management had certain effects on teachers. They selected different content and skills to teach; they devoted increasing amounts of their time to teaching students how to take tests; and they devoted substantial amounts of instructional time to preparing students for specific tests. They felt that they had less time to engage in real teaching. Increasingly, they felt under pressure. Last but not least, they experienced a discomfort that can best be characterized as ethical conflict. If they followed their own professional instincts about what to do in their classrooms, they were violating the policies they were supposed to be following. On the other hand, if they followed the policies, they had a sense that they were shortchanging their students. As a result of this ethical conflict, many teachers became increasingly disengaged from their work. Some left the field, and others adopted coping strategies designed to meet the letter of the law.

The limits of the bureaucratic regulatory management model had been reached. The harder teachers tried, the worse it got. The continuous refinement of the model aimed to make schools accountable to the public and to the legislature. It is, of course, a legitimate expectation that schools and teachers be accountable to the public. After all, schools are a public enterprise, publicly financed and serving public purposes. The public has a right to demand accountability in schools, but the wrong model of accountability was being pursued.

PROFESSIONAL ACCOUNTABILITY

Happily, there is another model of accountability: professional accountability. This concept rests a little uneasily in the necessarily bureaucratic structure of the schools. Nonetheless, substantial experience suggests that professionals can operate within bureaucratic settings. Lawyers, doctors, architects, engineers, and accountants—members of the recognized professions—have long worked for government agencies and, albeit occasionally with difficulty, managed to operate professionally. Schools must be bureaucratic in their control structures, but they need to accommodate professional control structures as well. Professional accountability can substitute, in part, for bureaucratic accountability. Teacher professionalism can be thought of as a new paradigm for school management.

The argument for professionalism in teaching is similar to the arguments that have led to the transformation of other occupations into professions. The primary rationale is a need for quality control over a process in which the service provider, in a largely private transaction, provides important services to a client who knows less than the service provider.

How, then, can the state and the client be assured that the appropriate services—those that best serve the client's needs—are being delivered? The appropriateness of instruction, like that of other professional services, must be determined by context. Because students are not standardized in their needs, stages of development, preconceptions, or learning styles, a given stimulus does not produce a predictable response. A teacher must make decisions based on knowledge of the student, the subject matter, and pedagogy in order to produce the right conditions for learning. Furthermore, what is learned (and what must be learned) is so varied as to defy any easy standardized measurement.

Teachers must constantly address complicated questions. Are particular learning objectives appropriate for particular students at a given point in time? What are appropriate materials and methods for achieving these objectives? How will their attainment be judged while maintaining other conditions for students' success, such as self-esteem and motivation? Necessarily, appropriate instructional decisions must be made at the point of service delivery. Therefore, the quality of services delivered depends upon the capacity of the teacher to make appropriate decisions.

The problem of teaching is not unique. It is like the professions in that high-quality service cannot be prescribed in advance of the professional–client interaction. High-quality service results only when the professional is prepared to apply general knowledge to the specific needs of the client. The occupations now known as professions attempt to solve the quality control problem by substituting quality control over personnel for quality control over service delivery. The professions establish standards to assure the competence of neophytes before allowing them to become full-fledged members of the profession.

The professions have created an arrangement with the state, in which they have sought and been granted the right and the obligation to control the quality of members of their professions. They have intensified their educational requirements and instituted testing procedures designed to assure the public and themselves that new members are qualified to practice and may be licensed. In this way, the professions seek to assure a high quality of service by individual members. The arrangement is not perfect; it is merely better than the alternatives. The bargain has been struck by medicine and law and increasingly by architecture, accounting, and engineering—all occupations that require discretion and judgment in meeting the unique needs of clients.

Some may wonder about the relevance of the experiences of other professions to teaching. After all, public school teaching takes place exclusively in a nonprofit, bureaucratic, publicly accountable setting. Most members of other professions operate in a market setting, where client choice and profit play a role. These major differences, however, do not negate the common core: Knowledgeable professionals must make decisions on behalf of less knowledgeable clients in settings where no "higher authority" (except professional ethics) is present.

Why is it important to think about a change in teaching at this time? There are many reasons for it, but perhaps the most important one is that America needs talented, well-educated young people who are willing to be teachers. Schools can no longer be staffed the good old-fashioned way, by denying other opportunities to talented women and talented members of minority groups. The job itself must be made more attractive so that it will attract talent to it. The problem is especially grave because the demand for teachers is rising just as the supply is beginning to run low.

WHAT IS PROFESSIONAL TEACHING?

Professional teachers have a firm grasp of the subjects they teach and are true to the intellectual demands of their disciplines. They are able to analyze the needs of the students for whom they are responsible. They know the standards of practice of their profession. They know that they are accountable for meeting the needs of their students. Under professionalism, teachers are free from the demand to teach a prescribed curriculum, using stylized methods, to prepare students for standardized tests. Instead, they are compelled to teach with intellectual honesty and practical foresight. They teach students to read for knowledge and enjoyment, not simply to acquire testable reading skills. They teach students to think mathematically rather than simply to work problems. They teach students to analyze, not simply to seek the right answer. They foster creative thinking and creative writing. Quite simply, professional teachers teach professionally, the way good teachers have always taught when allowed to do so.

WHAT NEEDS TO BE CHANGED?

What would enable the professionalization of teaching to occur? Increased public trust is necessary to allow professionalism to develop. The key is to improve the reality and the perception of teacher quality by altering the teacher education and licensing processes. Reforming teacher education and teacher licensing will unlock the door to professionalization.

First, teachers must be liberally educated, with a solid academic major. There is only one currency for that determination in our society: academic degrees. In American culture, the formal recognition that a person is educated is that he or she has the appropriate degree. The degree that signals that a person is liberally educated is a liberal arts degree. Anything short of that degree requires explanation, and once you have to start explaining, you are already in trouble.

Secondly, as Judith Lanier has made clear, there is much professional and pedagogical knowledge that teachers need to acquire. I doubt that it can all be fit into a four-year undergraduate program.[3] I believe the reform of teacher education will continue for the next decade or so. In the end, it may be realized that the four-year undergraduate teacher education program is insufficient.

Third is the realization that much practice is involved in learning to be a teacher. One can well acquire theory and concepts in a professional school setting, but learning how to put that theory into practice requires help from seasoned professionals. This underscores the importance of an internship.

Another need is to reform testing, certification, and licensing procedures. The Carnegie Forum has already spoken eloquently on that topic. In the end, there are likely to be a series of "tests" for a person to become a teacher. For the foreseeable future, tests of academic knowledge will be required to assure that teachers have acquired the appropriate knowledge. The internship will come to be seen as essential, not only as the culmination of the educational process but also as a component of the licensing process. Other professions, notably medicine and architecture, do not offer the final examination until after the completion of a structured induction. No examination for entry to any profession really tests all of the skills necessary to become a competent member of that profession. Certain skills can be tested in a formal, standardized way, and others cannot. The insistence that novices first experience a structured induction provides some assurance that they have mastered the practical skills necessary to assure the profession and the public that they are competent to practice.

The licensing process quite clearly needs to be under the control of teachers. That lesson is learned by looking at every other field that is now considered a profession. There are two reasons for this shift in power. The first is to ensure that the testing and licensing process is relevant. Practitioners in all fields, as they sit on the boards that design and select the examinations, push toward tests that really reveal whether the candidate can do the job. When the test is in the hands of the testmakers, psychometric considerations tend to predominate. The emphasis on test reliability and certain kinds of test validity seems to lead inevitably to multiple-choice examinations, because those have good psychometric properties. When the professionals are on the other side of the table, they push in the direction of job-related or performance testing. Performance testing is a lot harder to design, but it has a degree of fidelity that ensures that people who can pass the test have some of the skills necessary for performing on the job. The second reason why teachers should control the licensing process is that members of a profession have the incentives to maintain standards even in the face of shortages.

The call for teacher professionalism is not radical. It is simply part of a progression that has occurred in those fields that are now called professions. The question now is simply whether teaching will undergo that same process.

WHAT WILL TEACHING BE LIKE IF PROFESSIONALIZATION OCCURS?

Professionalism would mean changes both external and internal to the classroom, including control over the licensing process, the licensing procedures themselves, teacher preparation, teacher selection, instructional practices, control over instructional practices, teacher evaluation, and professional development. All of these things would need to change, and would change, as a teaching force that the public and policymakers trust is created.

A careful look around will reveal precursors of teacher professional-ism in many places. Studies have found schools where professional ap-proaches to teacher selection and teacher evaluation are used. I am sure that the examples identified so far are a mere fraction of the interesting developments that are now getting underway.[4]

Professional teachers—like other professionals who work in bu-reaucratic settings—should participate in the selection of their peers. The success of individual teachers depends upon the quality of their peers. How well a teacher is able to teach depends upon how well the teacher in the preceding year or in the adjacent courses is teaching. The identification of teaching quality is best pursued within a framework that involves a number of teachers and other educational personnel in the assessment of additions to a school's staff. Furthermore, the success of a school depends upon the coordination of members of the staff. One means for that coordination is the articulation of a school's instructional goals and the search for and selection of staff who share those goals. Those who oppose the professionalization of teaching conjure an image of isolated professionals, each of whom is moving on his or her own path. This view equates teacher autonomy with anarchy. The way coor-dination occurs, however, is through teacher education, where teachers come to know what needs to be accomplished with students at each stage of development and in each area of subject matter. Within a school, coor-dination occurs not through a standardized curriculum handed down from the state department, but rather as the result of communication among a school's staff.

One example of this approach is in East Williston, a small school district in New York. RAND has documented the teacher and admin-istrator selection process in that community.[5] Teachers take part in the selection of their colleagues through a committee process. Decisions re-main with management, but teachers participate in committees to de-sign job specifications and search for and select their peers. They also participate in the selection of administrators in East Williston.

Professionalization will mean changes in instructional practice, as already suggested. Professional instructional practice requires that teachers know their subjects, their students, their schools' goals, and pedagogical practices. With knowledge of these, they plan, deliver, and evaluate instruction, making appropriate instructional decisions on be-half of their students.

However, control over instructional practice in a school is the collec-tive responsibility of all the professional staff in the school. As teachers participate in setting the conditions under which they work, they coor-dinate the curriculum of a school or a school system.

Evaluation and staff development practices would change with the professionalization of teaching. In a profession of teaching, the role of evaluation would change. Extensive teacher preparation and intensive licensing procedures mean that most teachers will not require the continuous oversight involved in current and conventional approaches to teacher evaluation. Nothing, of course, is really gained by the principal's annual visit to complete the evaluation checklist.

Instead, seasoned professionals can help each other improve through classroom visits, consultations, and seminars. Occasionally, of course, instances of instructional malpractice will be found, and every school system must have a procedure for dealing with these. For these instances, exceptional evaluation procedures must exist and must be brought to bear to remove teachers who cannot or do not teach in a professionally responsible manner. RAND has identified a number of school systems that have exemplary practices. In Toledo, Salt Lake City, and Greenwich, versions of such practices now operate.

It is wrong to think that restructuring schools means a totally different school structure. Schools will continue to have principals, and school districts will continue to have superintendents. However, committees of teachers will join in the process of making the critical decisions that shape the learning environment of the schools. That means, of course, that teachers will have to have the time, preparation, and inclination to take part in those processes.

When teachers teach professionally, students benefit, for their educational needs become the predominant concern. No longer will teachers experience today's ethical conflict, which results from bureaucratic requirements and standardized tests driving the curriculum and forcing teachers to teach in ways that contradict their professional judgment.

The professionalization of teaching implies some restructuring of schooling, a redefinition of the roles and responsibilities of teachers and administrators. Administrators must be prepared to share planning and decisionmaking responsibilities, and teachers must be prepared to assume these responsibilities. To some extent, the professionalization of teaching may decrease the need for middle-level administrators in the central offices and schools. The jobs of some middle-level administrators exist because school districts now believe that they must closely direct and supervise curriculum and instruction. A professional teaching force will not require that degree of supervision. Moreover, senior teachers can perform some instructional leadership functions currently performed by middle-level administrators. Through the cost savings of a somewhat reduced administrative hierarchy, school districts will be able to pay teachers salaries commensurate with their responsibilities. The professionalization of teaching may not cost any more than schools now cost. What it does demand, however, is a redeployment of resources.

WHAT IF PROFESSIONALISM IS NOT INSTITUTED?

Of course, the professionalization of teaching may not occur. Why not? For one thing, if it does not happen soon, it will be too late. In other words, the opportunity of this generation will be lost. If reform of teacher education and licensing procedures does not begin soon, schools will be staffed with teachers in whom the public will not have confidence. Then there will be a new round of the "reforms" of the last two decades, when policymakers did not trust teachers.

Professionalism does challenge the existing administrative structure. It requires a rethinking of how school systems are managed. Schools will be hiring a million to a million and a half teachers by the mid-1990s, and they will be replacing close to 100 percent of the school administrators. There is a choice to be made. Schools can recapitulate the administrative structure that is in place, or they can begin to think strategically about how to redesign the administrative superstructure to effect certain cost savings at the same time as they create the conditions for teaching professionals.

What happens if there is no reform? What happens if teaching is not professionalized? It is pretty clear; one can even see it beginning to develop now. There will be few talented minority teachers; they are beginning to go to greener pastures. For the same reason, there will be fewer talented women teachers. Standards for becoming a teacher will be extremely low, as is now the case in Los Angeles and elsewhere. Because schools will hire people who are not prepared for the task, they will have a high turnover and chronic shortages. In the end, there will be created a school system that will be unacceptable to the middle class. When that occurs, the middle class will abandon the public schools. That, of course, has already happened in several of our largest cities, where middle-class parents (white and minority) have taken their children out of the public schools and placed them in private schools. That is what happens when the public school system does not meet the needs of affluent parents in late twentieth-century America. The professionalization of teaching is as much about the preservation of the public school tradition as anything else.

WHAT SHOULD BE DONE?

As noted, one of the keys is control over entry to the ranks of teaching. Teachers need to be in control of entry to their ranks, just as members of every other profession are. At the present time, developments are moving in two directions. States are moving in the direction of upgrading teacher education and licensing standards on the one hand, and they are eliminating all requirements for becoming a teacher on the other hand. They cannot have it both ways; the second strategy will undercut the first.

It turns out that the only people who can really be trusted to watch over the quality of members of a profession are the members themselves. The self-regulation of a profession achieves results for society that cannot be achieved in any other way. It is true that giving a profession control over entry to its ranks can result in a "premium wage" being paid, especially in times of shortage. However, that premium wage has social utility: It induces a supply of sufficient quality to maintain standards.

In short, for policymakers and the public to be able to trust individual teachers, they must trust teachers collectively to control access to teaching. Individual states should follow their own well-established practices for other professions. Each state should create a State Board of Professional Teaching Standards to work in concert with a National Board for Professional Teaching Standards. These boards should have the power to establish and enforce the standards for entry, as with the established professions.

Paradoxically, if the state retains control because it is afraid to trust teachers, the standards will fall; if the state trusts teachers and delegates control, the standards will rise. At least that is the lesson of those occupations the state has allowed to become professions.

By creating a teaching force they trust, policymakers will alter the conditions for teaching. In so doing, they will foster a new paradigm for educational management. This will create a system driven by the educational needs of students and of society rather than by the imperatives of management accountability systems. That is the promise of professional accountability for teachers.

NOTES

1. Arthur E. Wise, *Legislated Learning: The Bureaucratization of the American Classroom* (Berkeley, Calif.: University of California Press, 1979).

2. Linda Darling-Hammond and Arthur E. Wise, "Teaching Standards, or Standardized Teaching?" *Educational Leadership 41* (2), October 1983; Linda Darling-Hammond and Arthur E. Wise, "Beyond Standardization: State Standards and School Improvement," *Elementary School Journal*, January 1985.

3. See Chapter 6.

4. Arthur E. Wise et al., *Teacher Evaluation: A Study of Effective Practices* (R-3139-NIE, RAND Corp., 1984), reprinted in *Elementary School Journal 86* (1), September 1985.

5. Ibid.

CHAPTER 15

Uncertainty & Decisionmaking in Teaching: Implications for Managing Line Professionals

SAMUEL B. BACHARACH
Cornell University

SHARON C. CONLEY
University of Arizona

To a large degree, the current education reform movement began like a personnel textbook written backwards. Policymakers began by tackling the issues of teacher compensation, career hierarchies, and staffing. Only recently has there begun a serious examination of the nature of the work that teachers perform. It is somewhat peculiar (and contrary to the logic presented in any basic personnel text) to begin with explicit issues of how to manage workers before coming to an understanding of the basic nature of their work.

The first wave of reform was implicitly guided by two premises: (1) achieving quality education depends on reducing *uncertainty* in the classroom and (2) obtaining efficient schools depends on tightening bureaucratic controls, thus making teacher behavior more predictable (and less *uncertain*) to administrators.

However, any experienced teacher knows that this paradigm is incompatible with the basic nature of teaching, which is characterized by the need for teachers to respond frequently and spontaneously to situations within the classroom. Furthermore, this means that the administrator cannot know with certainty every detail that is actually happening in the classroom, just as the "fog of war" prevents a general at headquarters from knowing precisely how the battle is going. Administrators, like generals, may be able to formulate broad strategies, but it is naive to assume that they can dictate the variety of tactics that teachers must use in an uncertain classroom environment.

While most teachers would welcome the reduction of the specific uncertainty caused by their administrators' unclear expectations about their performance, the overbureaucratization of their work environment becomes a straitjacket, resulting in negative consequences like teacher burnout and dissatisfaction.[1]

The second wave of reform has tried to break away from this paradigm, which equated educational excellence with control over teachers. It has begun to take into account the uncertain nature of teachers' work. In focusing on teacher preparation and other professional issues (as in the Holmes and Carnegie reports), the second wave has begun to inch beyond bureaucratic and Tayloristic notions of how school organizations should be managed. These bureaucratic notions provided the first wave of reform with a paradigm for generating easy solutions to managerial problems, but the second wave of reform does not have such a convenient framework on which to base "quick fixes."

In this chapter, we offer a paradigm for the second wave of the reform movement. We believe that this paradigm leads to some possible solutions to common school management problems. The paradigm that we propose is based on the fact that teachers are *line professionals*—professionals who have direct contact with the organizational clients (the students). As such, they will invariably have to deal with situations that are not susceptible to bureaucratic, "patterned" solutions. On the basis of this paradigm, we argue that school managers must integrate a realistic picture of the teachers' work situation into their own managerial strategies. Effective integration of the teachers' work situation with managerial strategies is contingent upon enhancing the degree of teacher participation in both strategic and operational decisionmaking.

This chapter will make three basic arguments:

- Management should treat teachers as line professionals who cope with a critical level of uncertainty.
- Management should realize that teachers already make informal line decisions in carrying out their work activities.
- Management should establish a participatory structure that will allow teachers, as line professionals, to contribute to decisionmaking outside their classrooms.

ARE TEACHERS PROFESSIONALS?

Any discussion of the management of professionals must deal with the question of who is a professional.[2] There have been numerous debates as to whether teaching is indeed a profession. One of the primary problems faced by teachers seeking professional recognition is the old adage that familiarity breeds contempt. We have all been students and therefore assume that we know how to be teachers. The complexity of the teaching task, however, is often hidden beneath the simplicity of its execution.

Furthermore, teaching, unlike medicine or law, is not cloaked in unfamiliar terms or a language that approaches the incantations of a cult. When a good teacher speaks, any layperson understands him or her. The same may not be said for members of such professions as law or medicine, who often hide behind their respective jargons. All too often, other professionals use the mystique of their jargon to distance themselves from their clients. By definition, teachers do not have this luxury. Obviously, the use of uncommunicative jargon ensures failure in the teaching mission.

To ask whether or not teachers are professionals is slightly misleading. Most scholars writing on professionals have dismissed the notion that determination of professional status is a simple dichotomy—X is a professional, Y is not.[3] They propose the use of the concept "professionalization," which is defined as "the dynamic process whereby many occupations can be observed to change certain crucial characteristics in the direction of a profession."[4] Richard Hall, adopting this notion from Vollmer and Mills and building on the work of Caplow and Wilensky, suggests three groups of characteristics by which a given occupation's degree of professionalism can be measured.[5] These are:

1. *Structural criteria:* The degree to which there is a formalized code of ethics and a prescribed and lengthy training process in certified training institutes or the like.
2. *Attitudinal attributes of members:* The degree to which the members believe in service to the public, self-regulation, autonomy, and similar professional values.
3. *Societal recognition:* The degree to which society in general views the occupation as a profession.

Using these three criteria, it is clear that teaching is at least an occupation that aspires to professionalism. Regarding the first criterion, there is now a growing concern with the process by which teachers are trained and become certified.[6] Regarding the attitudinal perspectives of teachers, research from numerous surveys suggests that teachers possess a sense of calling and public mission.[7] When asked why they entered teaching, most teachers respond with this sense of purpose.[8] Furthermore, similar research suggests that teachers' beliefs in autonomy and self-regulation are part and parcel of their work.[9]

Finally, greater societal recognition is being accorded teaching, allowing it to be more clearly labeled as a profession. One of the latent consequences of the current reform movement has been an increased public recognition of the importance of teaching. What began as an exercise in blaming teachers has now resulted in better salaries for teachers and discussions about how to get higher-quality people into the field. All of this has apparently enhanced the public image of teaching as a profession.

The above three criteria have been discussed in the literature as an explicit operationalization of professionalism. However, there is an argument to be made that professionalism, in the truest sense, is a function of how individuals are *treated* within the organizations in which they work. We would argue that professionalism is not simply a case of credentials or public status, but a state of mind that is sustained and enhanced by how people are managed in the organization. In turn, the professionalization of workers greatly depends on the attitudes that managers have toward the line employees. More specifically, the professionalization of workers depends on the assumptions that managers make about the knowledge and skills that the line employees need to carry out their jobs.

Just as managerial attitudes can help professionalize employees, they can also deprofessionalize them. The deprofessionalization of teachers is largely caused by certain managerial assumptions concerning teachers' activities and knowledge. These assumptions are compatible with bureaucratic control mechanisms but are inconsistent with professional norms. As W. I. Thomas maintained, "If man defines the social situation as real, it is real in its consequences." This would suggest that the deprofessionalization (and professionalization) of teaching is a reality socially constructed through the interaction between managers and their subordinates.

TENSIONS BETWEEN BUREAUCRACIES AND PROFESSIONAL EMPLOYEES

Although teachers are receiving more recognition through increased salaries, and although the process by which teachers gain credentials has been upgraded, managerial attitudes still do not give teachers the discretion afforded many other service professionals. In search of predictability, control, and coordination, administrators often place primary emphasis on the bureaucratic necessities for sustaining the organizational order. Regulation, specification, and accountability become their major guidelines. Teachers, on the other hand, owe their primary allegiance to professional norms and often claim that their daily activities require discretion and on-the-spot decisions. Therefore, they tend to find the proper performance of their jobs to be inconsistent with the bureaucratic demands of administrators.

The literature on the tensions between bureaucracies and professional employees may be regarded from the perspective of how it views the outcome of this inherent conflict. Some observers suggest that this conflict is resolved by the predominance of bureaucratic managerial strategies.[10] Many of these researchers have used the accounting profession to illustrate the dominance of bureaucratic management in such firms. The studies by Sorenson and Sorenson and Lachman and Aranya suggest that, over time, new accountants entering accounting firms tend to shift from a professional orientation to a bureaucratic orientation.

Another body of research maintains that the outcome of the conflict is a set of managerial strategies that reflect the demands of the professionals rather than those of bureaucratic imperatives.[11] Frequently, these scholars use medical doctors working in hospitals to illustrate this perspective. This research suggests that hospitals as organizations are shaped by the professional norms of the doctors working in them rather than by the administrators' need for bureaucratic control.

The above literature raises the question of why the managerial strategies for the medical profession tend to be congruent with professional demands, while the managerial strategies for accounting tend to be consistent with the needs of the bureaucracy. It may be that, as we argued earlier, the managerial strategies for a given profession depend, in part, on how administrators view the knowledge and work activities of that profession. For example, the public tends to view the professional knowledge of doctors differently from that of accountants. Accountants' knowledge tends to be characterized as technocratic in nature, whereas the knowledge of doctors is more readily seen as scientific—or even mystical. Doctors may be viewed as the "priests" of everyday life and accountants as the "engineers." When dealing with the "priests" of medicine, hospital administrators become subordinate to doctors' professional norms. Conversely, when dealing with the "engineers" of accounting, management feels secure enough to impose bureaucratic control mechanisms, in spite of the fact that society recognizes accountants as professionals. One of the problems in examining the teaching profession is that professional knowledge in teaching is not viewed as either totally mystical, as in medicine or totally technocratic, as in accounting.

Differing assumptions about three key underlying issues determine whether management will employ a bureaucratic or a professional strategy towards its subordinates. These three issues and their related assumptions are presented in Figure 15-1. The first is the *nature of job-related knowledge*. When maintaining a bureaucratic attitude with respect to job-related knowledge, management assumes that the knowledge of its subordinates can be specified and delineated. Management implicitly believes that the knowledge and work activities of its subordinates may be totally objectified.[12] Alternatively, when maintaining a professional

FIGURE 15-1

Three assumptions about the knowledge and work of
teachers underlying the bureaucratic and the professional
managerial strategies.

Issue	*Bureaucratic managerial assumptions*	*Professional managerial assumptions*
Nature of job-related knowledge	Can be specified	Can be specified only within broad parameters
Control of knowledge	Upper echelons control administrative and substantive knowledge	Line personnel control substantive knowledge
Work of line professionals	Capable of total standardization	Capable of minimum standardization

managerial attitude, management assumes that line personnel bring
with them a unique body of knowledge, derived from experience as
much as from textbooks. While some of the basic knowledge may be
specified and objectified, its creative interpretation is viewed as a function of the unique skills that line professionals develop over time.

The second issue deals with the *control of knowledge.* The bureaucratic orientation to this issue contains the belief that management can
control not only administrative knowledge but also substantive knowledge to a large degree. For example, in teaching, management considers
that it can control pedagogical knowledge. The professional orientation
to this issue suggests to management that it may understand the broad
parameters of substantive knowledge, but the primary control of that
knowledge should be left to line professionals.

The third assumption deals with the *work of line professionals.* When
management feels that activities are repetitious and routine, a bureaucratic attitude is more likely than when they believe the activities demand great variation on the part of professionals.

The constant tension between these two patterns of assumption is
helpful in understanding the current debate over reform strategies. For
example, the assumption that professional knowledge can be specified,
objectified, and totally understood by the administrative bureaucracy results in strategies focusing on strict merit pay, rigid career ladders, and
"objective" evaluations of teaching performance. In this instance, teachers are viewed as simply the conduits of material to be taught.

On the other hand, the assumption that professional knowledge
cannot be totally understood or completely delineated by administrators
results in strategies that emphasize the unique pedagogical skills gained
from experience and attempt to further these skills by offering oppor-

tunities for professional growth. In this case, teachers themselves are viewed as the *sine qua non* of good teaching. This approach is understandably stressed by teachers and their associations.

Clearly, when management feels capable of specifying, standardizing, and controlling professional knowledge, management will adhere to a bureaucratic strategy for managing teachers. Alternatively, when management feels that the nature of professional knowledge is not standardized and cannot be totally controlled by administrators, then management will adhere to a less bureaucratic and more professional managerial strategy.

We have argued that the managerial strategies that emerge in schools depend in part on how the work of the teacher is viewed. Two critical questions emerge. What are the managerial assumptions about the work of teachers? What are the implications of these assumptions for the management of teachers? With regard to the first question, two managerial assumptions appear critical: whether school managers treat teachers as if they deal with uncertainty, and whether managers treat teachers as if they make decisions on a daily basis. With regard to the second question, administrations must go through a sense-making process, in which they must evaluate the outcomes of engaging in managerial strategies that are aligned more with bureaucratic or with professional norms. The following sections address these dual questions of school management concerning the work of teachers and their implications for managerial sense-making.

VIEWING THE WORK OF TEACHERS

Teacher Uncertainty: Four Management Metaphors of Teaching

As stated above, the nature of the work influences the degree to which management can place constraints on teachers' professional prerogatives. The level of uncertainty that teachers encounter must be taken into consideration. The greater the uncertainty and unpredictability teachers face every day, the less appropriate bureaucratic managerial strategies are. Alternatively, the greater the uncertainty and unpredictability, the more appropriate professional managerial strategies are.

In an interview we conducted in Boise, Idaho, in 1986, a fourth grade teacher maintained:

> One of the problems I have is the assumptions that administrators seem to be making about my job as a teacher. I don't know from one day to the next what is going to happen in this job—what students are going to do, what unexpected problem is going to come up, what a student is going to need, which students are going to finish work ear-

lier than others. Yet when the principal comes in to evaluate, nothing unexpected is supposed to happen. Sometimes I don't think administrators have a sense of the type of work that's involved in teaching.

This teacher's testimony suggests that there is a great deal of uncertainty in teaching. From one day to the next, teachers can be relatively certain of the *general* types of problems that they will need to deal with—such as attending to the needs of individual students, managing groups of students, or carrying out instructional plans—but there is a great deal of uncertainty concerning the *specific* decisions that will confront teachers.

Perrow has developed a broad framework that can be used to assess the level of uncertainty in work.[13] Perrow's work indicates that uncertainty operates on two levels: the degree of variation in specific problems faced by the line employee and the number of possible solutions to problems. Figure 15-2, loosely based on the work of Perrow, makes this apparent. The diagram suggests that to understand the primary activities carried out by members of an occupation there must be a recognition of the problems the line employee is asked to solve and the steps that he or she must follow in the solution. Problems may be characterized as having high or low variation, depending on the nature of the raw material one is asked to work with. For example, if one is weaving wool carpets, there may be some variation in the type of wool one encounters, but within limited parameters. On the other hand, if one is processing people, there will be much wider variation in the problems encountered. Furthermore, there are many more alternative solutions when one is processing people than when one is processing inanimate objects such as wool.

Using these dimensions, Figure 15-2 allows four metaphors for characterizing teachers: teachers as bureaucrats, teachers as craftpersons, teachers as technicians, and teachers as professionals. We would suggest that administrators use these metaphors explicitly or implicitly in their sense-making concerning the strategies they use to manage teachers.

Metaphor 1: Teachers as bureaucrats.   In recent years, there has been an effort to deskill teachers.[14] Rather than viewing the process of teaching as an organic whole, the job is broken down into its most basic elements.[15] Administrators assume that they can bureaucratically specify the daily problems that teachers will face and thus delineate the specific solutions teachers should pursue.

The metaphor of teachers as bureaucrats treats teachers as appendages of a bureaucracy that is primarily concerned with predictability and regulation. Unfortunately, such a metaphor does not take into account either the wide variety of problems that teachers face or the complex array of alternative solutions available. When administrators view teachers

FIGURE 15-2

Two dimensions of uncertainty as a basis for classifying the work of teachers.

| | | Variations in problems encountered | |
		Low	*High*
	Few	Teachers as bureaucrats	Teachers as technicians
Number of possible solutions			
	Many	Teachers as craftpersons	Teachers as professionals

as subordinate bureaucrats, they tend to manage them by specifying and delineating expectations and modes of operation. They force all their teachers to identify problems in a uniform way and expect them to find similar solutions. Although this mode of management allows managers to achieve tight coordination and control, it will invariably restrict the innovation and flexibility often required for good teaching. Ironically, this deprofessionalization of teachers may encourage the public and school boards to hold management more directly accountable for the results of teachers' efforts.

Metaphor 2: Teachers as technicians. Some administrators, recognizing the danger of treating teachers as bureaucrats, make a partial shift and treat teachers as technicians. The assumption underlying this metaphor is that the primary focus should be on the limited range of solutions available to teachers, rather than on the tremendous variability of the problems they face. Administrators thinking in these terms may recognize the variation of problems teachers face, such as the widely differing needs and abilities of students, but such administrators maintain that the number of solutions to any teaching problem is limited. When administrators assume that teachers have only a limited number of alternative solutions, they tend to develop managerial strategies that specify those solutions. "Teacher-free" or "teacher-proof" curricula are indicative of such an orientation.

Metaphor 3: Teachers as craftspersons. The next shift is more subtle in nature. In viewing teachers as craftspersons, administrators recognize that solutions to the problems are many, but assume that there is little variation in the problems teachers confront (for example, in the needs and abilities of students). The danger of using this metaphor is that administrators may implicitly assume that the total responsibility for student achievement rests with teachers. For example, if there is little variation in the needs and abilities of students, accountability can only rest with the teacher's ability to find solutions.

In this case, managerial strategies are characterized by "benign neglect." When administrators treat teachers as craftpersons, they attempt to disengage themselves from the problems that teachers face. They implicitly assume that any failure can be attributed to teachers' lack of skill in adapting solutions to relatively routine problems.

Metaphor 4: Teachers as professionals. Using this metaphor, management recognizes both dimensions of the uncertainty of the work of teachers—the wide array of problems encountered by teachers and the numerous solutions that may be brought to bear on the problems. In recognizing both dimensions, management casts the work of teachers in its true complexity. When managers recognize teachers as professionals, they implicitly maintain that the nature of teaching work may result in teachers being unable to achieve the best results. It is only in this instance that administrators recognize the possibility of failure, which is part of the reality of any profession.

In recognizing the true complexity of teachers' work, management recognizes teachers as professionals who identify problems and make selections among possible alternative solutions, in the hope of increasing the probability of a particular outcome. In this instance, managerial strategies are concerned not with delineating specific tasks for teachers but with helping teachers develop a repertoire of skills that they can bring to bear on multiple problems.

Furthermore, when managers recognize teachers as professionals, they assume that teachers must be accorded a high level of discretion in order to perform their work. There has been much discussion of the professionalization of teaching by creating management strategies that afford teachers more discretion. However, it is not enough to argue, as we have in this section, that teachers should be provided discretion because they deal with uncertainty. It must also be made clear that, because of the uncertainty in their job, teachers already make numerous daily decisions in their work; they are already exercising discretion, whether management recognizes it or not. In the next section, we will provide empirical support for the argument that in carrying out their activities, teachers already make numerous decisions.

Teachers as Line Decisionmakers

There is a growing consensus that teaching is fundamentally a process of making decisions in interactive, uncertain settings. Except among those who view teachers as bureaucrats or technicians, there is a growing consensus that teaching should be conceptualized as a decisionmaking process requiring the exercise of discretion and judgement in situations that rarely allow the application of routine solutions to clearly identified problems.[16] Doyle, for example, has maintained that

> teaching practice is not merely technical and rule driven, and teachers are not simply passive recipients who carry research-based practice to the classrooms. Rather, professional teachers are reflective, that is, they connect knowledge to situations through processes of observation, understanding, analysis, interpretation and decision making.[17]

This observation suggests that teachers, in their daily contact with students, constantly have to make decisions concerning students.

A recent study of the responsibilities of teachers (conducted by the authors) provides empirical support for the notion of teachers as professionals who engage in multiple decisions on a daily basis. A total of thirty-seven sets of responsibilities were identified among 1187 teachers in the city of Tucson.[18] Survey and interview data confirmed that sixteen of the responsibilities were performed daily or more often, and another nine at least weekly. The responsibilities that a vast majority of teachers (at least 80%) reported performing on a daily basis were:

- Observing and directing student behavior to keep students "on task" and to identify and avoid potential discipline problems
- Recording and reporting classroom attendance
- Observing class, group, and individual behavior and progress in order to identify when plans might need to be changed
- Communicating expectations to students concerning instructional goals and objectives, quality and amount of work, and behavior and discipline
- Actually adjusting class, group, or individual plans while class is still in session (making "midstream" changes)
- Leading class discussions and demonstrations
- Administering in-class discipline and/or referring students to others for discipline
- Assigning in-class work and homework to individuals, groups, and whole classes
- Lecturing to a class as a whole for purposes of instruction
- Instructing or reviewing work with individual students for purposes of instruction, while other students work independently or in groups
- Instructing groups of students, using a variety of techniques, while other students work independently or in groups.

Upon examining all of the responsibilities that teachers reported performing, we concluded that teachers make decisions in three critical areas: instruction (dealing with the academic skills and achievement of students), counseling (dealing with the social and emotional needs of individual students), and management (dealing with the physical and group environment). For each of these decision areas, we further identi-

FIGURE 15-3
Nine basic decisionmaking responsibilities of teachers.[20]

	Planning	*Implementation*	*Evaluation*
Instruction	Instructional planning	Instructional implementation	Instructional evaluation
Counseling	Counseling planning	Counseling implementation	Counseling evaluation
Management	Management planning	Management implementation	Management evaluation

fied three different activities: planning, implementation, and evaluation.[19] As shown in the matrix in Figure 15-3, taking the three decision areas with the three sets of activities allows the identification of nine basic decisions that teachers make on a daily basis.

The complexity of the matrix is an affirmation that, among their daily activities, teachers must make numerous decisions. Specifically, they must first decide which decision area should receive what percentage of their time. Second, they must determine the sequence in which they will carry out their activities. Third, and perhaps most important, they must integrate each of these areas of decisionmaking. Teachers do not often have the luxury of engaging in planning, then implementation, then evaluation. Many of their decisions are made "midstream"—for example, when they change plans based on their ongoing evaluation of classroom events. Indeed, teachers in the study confirmed that they rarely engage in a process of segmented decisionmaking, but rather address their various decisions simultaneously.

The ability to make simultaneous decisions in different areas of responsibility is a paramount definition of a mature decisionmaker. Simultaneous decisionmaking requires the professional to integrate action alternatives in a gestalt fashion rather than piecemeal. To take an example from another profession, the successful physician is one who is able to move back and forth flexibly among problem diagnosis, implementation of treatment, and patient monitoring.

We have argued that coping with uncertainty and making daily decisions on the line are part and parcel of the teacher's work activity. These may, in fact, be the primary characteristics of the role of a teacher. However, the managerial structure of many schools does not take into account what occurs on the line. Implicit in the above discussion is that, because of their work, teachers are the primary reservoir of organizational knowledge. Furthermore, the success of the school organization will depend on teachers' ability to cope with uncertainty and make appropriate decisions. This would suggest that one of the primary problems in schools to date is a failure to integrate line professionals sufficiently into the formal decisionmaking process of schools.

It is ironic that, compared to many contemporary private-sector organizations, so little progress has been made to involve teachers formally in making organizational decisions. Even if teachers are treated as professionals with regard to their classroom activity by granting them the discretion to make classroom decisions, little progress will be made unless there is a participatory structure that will allow teachers to express their acquired expertise beyond their classrooms.

In the next section, we will examine some of the structural and political obstacles to expanding the role of the teacher from a classroom decisionmaker to an organizational participant.

FROM CLASSROOM DECISIONMAKER TO ORGANIZATIONAL PARTICIPANT

It is now widely accepted that enhancing participation among line professionals in an organization has certain positive consequences. Research over the last few years has given convincing evidence of the benefits of participation. Participation enhances employee motivation, involvement in the organization, and commitment to change.[21] In addition, there is evidence that participation improves the quality of an organization's management decisions and enhances cooperation throughout the organization.[22]

Participation brings these effects about by giving employees more opportunities to satisfy their personal needs of control, accomplishment, meaningfulness, and collegiality. Furthermore, participation increases the effectiveness of the organization by providing management with the critical information held by those employees closest to the organization's clients and/or technology.

In research specifically concerned with teacher participation in education, a recent review by Joseph Shedd[23] indicates that participation is positively associated with four major outcomes: job satisfaction and morale,[24] trust in school leaders, reduced stress and burnout, and reduced conflict in the job. Further, several studies suggest that *lack* of opportunities to participate in decisionmaking is a factor in many teachers' decisions to leave the profession.[25]

We recently visited a Pennsylvania school district that was in the process of establishing a career ladder system. When asked whether teachers participated in decisions regarding the career ladder, the superintendent replied, with some indignation, "Of course they were. I believe in the participation of all teachers in this district."

The following day, in a separate discussion with some of the teachers, we discovered that this superintendent's effort to gather input from teachers consisted of distributing a ten-item Likert-type scale questionnaire to teachers. This superintendent may have been trained in research methods but seemed to understand very little about why participation was important. In this district (as elsewhere), participation was viewed as a method by which high-level administrators could affirm decisions already made rather than incorporate the primary line decisionmakers into the process.

The field of education is notorious for forming a teacher committee for almost every issue. In most schools, however, such teacher committees are little more than mechanisms used to elicit support for ongoing district and school policies. It is not surprising, then, that participation is often viewed by teachers as an exercise in tokenism. Administrators often recognize the need to reaffirm their policies with their professional staff, but all too often they do this within a bureaucratic mode of management. Whenever the issue of teacher participation in decisionmaking is raised, one of two reactions typically surfaces. The first, a "caring" reaction, is epitomized by the administrator who decides that teachers already have too much to do and therefore should not be bogged down with new decisionmaking responsibilities. Alternatively, a "paranoid" reaction is an assessment by administrators that teacher involvement usurps the decisionmaking authority that they need to conduct their jobs.

In truth, both reactions have a strong basis in fact, but they share the same confusion about what is meant by participation. The argument that teachers are already overwhelmed appears justified when one examines the research literature. Numerous studies have shown that teachers have only a minimal amount of time to conduct their assigned work activities. In another study, we found that lack of time to complete work activities is the highest resource concern among teachers. The time needed to engage in meaningful participation, then, becomes just another obstacle standing between the teacher and the completion of his or her work. Likewise, the supervisor who is concerned that teacher participation will enhance the power of teachers and their association has a justified point. In the context of the political reality of schools, administrators constantly deal with numerous formal and informal coalitions that can veto or seriously hamper policy efforts. To principals and superintendents, dealing with a formal coalition of teachers means that they must go through another set of political machinations, similar to those they currently carry out in relation to the school board and teacher associations.

Like administrators, teachers and their associations do not automatically embrace participation as a panacea in education. Typically, teachers' associations feel that participation is little more than a tactical cooptation mechanism, which fundamentally endangers what may be a fragile local coalition. Furthermore, it is often the case that teachers feel that participatory structures are used by management to have teachers carry out activities that are not felt to be their responsibility. Stated in a slightly different way, teachers often feel that participation is a façade, under which management is capable of mobilizing additional free labor from teachers.

However, given these hesitations on the part of administrators and teachers, the necessity for teacher input remains. As stated earlier, teachers are the only members of school systems who are literally on the line, who have direct and ongoing contact with the system's clients, the students. We have already shown in previous sections that teachers deal with a great deal of uncertainty and make numerous line decisions. They are therefore the primary holders of critical organizational knowledge, and their participation is essential for effective schools, despite the difficulties associated with sharing participation among administrators and teachers.

Unfortunately, there is little research to offer specific guidelines to school administrators for formulating managerial strategies that would enhance participation. Clearly, participation, as described here, implies a professional mode of management. However, professional managerial strategies often come into conflict with the school organization's need to have bureaucratic coordination. The most critical question that emerges in terms of strategy is how to increase participation without sacrificing the ability of management to coordinate.

There are two factors that must be considered in this context. One is the determination of the scope of participation, and the other is the delineation of the type of power that will be afforded those who will be participating. In deciding the scope of teachers' participation in decisionmaking, the following five decision areas may be considered:

1. *Organizational policies,* including staff hiring, standardized testing policies, budget development, expenditure priorities, and facilities planning
2. *Work allocation,* including school assignments, grade/subject level assignments, and student–teacher interface
3. *Student–school interface,* which includes student rights, student discipline codes, and grading policies
4. *Teacher development and evaluation,* which includes staff development opportunities and formal teacher performance evaluations
5. *Teaching process,* including what to teach, how to teach, texts available for use, texts used in teachers' own classes, counseling, and classroom management

A distinction may be made between the first four sets of decisions and the last one. The first four may be referred to as *strategic* decisions, while the last one involves *operational* decisions. Strategic decisions are broad organizational ones, dealing with overarching organizational policies. Strategic decisions affect the organizational context in which work occurs. Operational decisions, on the other hand, are made in carrying out immediate work activities. For example, decisions regarding budget allocations may be clearly seen as overarching strategic ones, whereas decisions regarding how to teach a particular student may be viewed as operational in nature. Indeed, operational decisions may be cast in terms of the nine basic decisionmaking responsibilities presented in Figure 15-3. These decisions include planning, implementation, and evaluation of instructional counseling and management activities in the classroom. The strategic and operational decision areas are not mutually exclusive; one may impact the other. However, for the sake of managerial policy, a distinction may be drawn between the two.

As discussed earlier, teachers, as line decisionmakers, already make daily work decisions and, due to uncertainty in their jobs, could not function effectively were this not the case. The problem is that teachers often make these decisions informally, without the sanction of administrators. This informal decisionmaking can give teachers the sense that they are usurping the formal decisionmaking authority of their superiors. Since the nature of professional knowledge makes it impossible for administrators to make these decisions, administrators should consider *formally* allocating operational decisionmaking authority to the classroom level.

With regard to strategic decisions, these overarching policy decisions should be made by school and district administrators. Decisions involving budget allocation and work assignments, for example, clearly have to be made in the realm of administrative prerogative. To allocate such decisions to lower levels of the organization would be to dismiss primary administrative responsibilities. However, in a participatory system, teachers should be afforded the opportunity to influence such decisions. Without having final authority for these decisions, teachers should be provided the opportunity to persuade administrators and thus attempt to influence the outcome. Currently, teachers do exercise informal influence through their ability to persuade school boards, parents, and administrators. They exert important but informal influence on strategic decisions through their local associations. Unfortunately, since the channels for informal influence are usually unspecified, this can often create conflict and suspicion. Once, some teachers went to a school board meeting to speak out against a budget reallocation; they were reprimanded by their principal for going "over her head." If management formalized teachers' influence on strategic decisions, they would go a long way toward improving this adversarial atmosphere.

It should be noted that this discussion of participation has drawn a distinction between *authority* and *influence*. During the last few years, there has been much debate over the issue of teacher empowerment.

This has given some administrators the sense that all decisionmaking authority would be allocated to teachers. In considering a system of participation for managing the professional teacher, one need not approach this extreme if one is sensitive to the distinction between authority and influence.[26]

The final authority to make most decisions is the ability to say "yes" or "no" to a particular policy. This authority should still rest with those who are accountable for the outcome of the decision. In the case of strategic decisions, this must be the administrators. The final authority for operational decisions should also rest with those who are accountable for them—teachers. Accordingly, teachers should have the ability to influence strategic decisions, and administrators should have the ability to influence work decisions. Currently, in school management, there is conflict when teachers and administrators disagree over who has the authority for decisions and who can influence those decisions. Clarifying which decisions teachers and administrators should have authority over and which decisions they should be able to influence would be an important step in lessening the conflict between the domain of the professional and the domain of the bureaucracy.

CONCLUSION

This chapter has argued that the way managers view the work of teachers (or members of any profession) will determine how they resolve the conflict between the professional ethos (and its demands for autonomy and participation) and the bureaucratic ethos (with its need for coordination and predictability). A critical component of this perception is the way managers view the level of uncertainty teachers have to deal with. It has been shown that a high level of uncertainty results in teachers making daily line decisions. Finally, we have illustrated how the needs of the bureaucracy can be strategically balanced with the needs of the professionals by creating a participatory system that draws distinctions between strategic and operational decisions and between influence and authority. Because of the nature of teachers' work, they should be accorded authority in the realm of operational decisions and influence in strategic decisions.

In the context of the present reform movement, only recently has the organizational importance of the work of teachers been considered. As the activities of teachers are examined more closely, there comes a realization that they are professionals, if for no other reason than the fact that they cope with uncertainty and make decisions on a daily basis. This reality has complex implications for the bureaucratic reform efforts that have been made in many states.

Implicit in our arguments in this chapter is the belief that both uncertainty and subjectivity are critical components of teaching. However, this runs directly against the assumptions of many reform efforts, where administrators believe that they can control teachers by minimizing the uncertainty teachers encounter. Indeed, if teachers are line decision-makers who constantly have to reshuffle their plans, how can they ever be judged on the basis of some of the rigid compensation plans attempted by such states as Tennessee? On the other hand, perhaps the issue is not one of judging them, but one of developing them to be better classroom decisionmakers and allowing them to participate in organizational decisions.

Perhaps the problem of American education is not to evaluate teachers bureaucratically, but to create an open professional environment that extends beyond the classroom door. If this chapter makes no other point, it strongly suggests that the time has come for more deliberation in recommendations about how to reform school management. Between the clichés of teacher empowerment and a teacher-proof curriculum, there is the reality of the teacher as a practicing professional.

NOTES

The authors are especially grateful to Lorie VanAtta for editorial comments and administrative assistance. We would also like to thank Peter Bamberger, Bruce Cooper, Naftaly Glasman, and Bryan Mundell for comments on and assistance with this work, and the students in Sharon Conley's Education Reform seminar at the University of Arizona. We would also like to thank our colleagues at the Arizona Education Association and the Tucson Education Association, who provided the research opportunities that made these ideas possible.

1. S. B. Bacharach, S. Bauer, and S. Conley, "Organizational Analysis of Stress: The Case of Elementary and Secondary Schools," *Sociology of Work and Occupations 13* (1), 1986, 7–32; S. Conley, S. B. Bacharach, and S. Bauer, "The School Work Environment and Teacher Career Dissatisfaction" (paper delivered at AERA, Washington, D.C., April, 1987).

2. S. B. Bacharach, P. Bamberger, and S. Conley, "A Seesaw Approach to the Management of Professionals: The Case of Hi Tech" (working paper, Department of Organizational Behavior, NYSS-ILR, Cornell University, Ithaca, New York, 1987).

3. H. Vollmer and D. Mills, *Professionalization: Reading in Occupational Change* (Englewood Cliffs, N.J.: Prentice-Hall, 1966).

4. Ibid.

5. R. Hall, *Occupations and the Social Structure* (Englewood Cliffs, N.J.: Prentice-Hall, 1969); T. Caplow, *The Sociology of Work* (Minneapolis, Minn.: University of Minnesota Press, 1954); H. Wilensky, "The Professionalization of Everyone?" *American Journal of Sociology 70*, September 1964, pp. 142–146.

6. S. C. Conley and S. B. Bacharach, "The Holmes Report: Standards Hierarchies and Management," *Teachers College Record*, Spring 1987.

7. S. B. Bacharach, S. Bauer, and J. Shedd, "Teacher Work Environment and Education Reform," *Teachers College Record*, Winter 1987.

8. S. Rosenholtz, "Effective Schools: Interpreting the Evidence," *American Journal of Education*, May 1985, pp. 352–388.

9. Bacharach, Bamberger, and Conley, op. cit.

10. J. Sorenson and T. Sorenson, "The Conflict of Professionals in Bureaucratic Organizations," *Administrative Science Quarterly 19*, 1974, pp. 98–106; R. Lachman and N. Aranya, "Job Attitudes and Turnover Intentions Among Professionals in Different Work Settings," *Organization Studies 7* (3), 1986, pp. 279–293.

11. E. Friedson, "Dominant Professions, Bureaucracy and Client Services," in Y. Hasenfeld and R. English, eds., *Human Service Organizations* (Ann Arbor, Mich.: University of Michigan Press, 1974, pp. 428–447; M. Guy, *Professionals in Organization: Debunking a Myth* (New York: Praeger, 1985); F. Katz, "Nurses," in A. Etzioni, ed., *The Semi-Professions and Their Organization* (New York: Free Press, 1969), pp. 54–81.

12. H. Braverman, *Labor and Monopoly Capital* (New York: Monthly Review, 1974).

13. C. Perrow, "A Framework for the Comparative Analysis of Organizations," *American Sociological Review 32*, April 1967, pp. 194–208.

14. M. W. Apple, "The Deskilling of Teaching," in Frances S. Bolin and Judith McConnell Falk, eds., *Teacher Renewal: Professional Issues, Personal Choices* (New York: Teachers College Press, 1987), pp. 59–75.

15. Ibid.

16. M. Mosston, *Teaching: From Command to Discovery* (Belmont, Calif.: Wadsworth, 1972); W. Doyle, *Teaching as a Profession: What We Know and What We Need to Know About Teaching* (University of Texas at Austin, Research and Development Center for Teacher Education, 1985); M. Hunter, "What is Wrong with Madeline Hunter?" *Education Leadership*, February 1985, pp. 57–60; G. Fenstermacher, "A Philosophical Consideration of Recent Research on Teacher Effectiveness," *Review of Research in Education 6* (Itasca, Ill.: F. E. Peacock, 1978); K. M. Zeichner, "Alternative Paradigms of Teacher Education," *Journal of Teacher Education 34*, 1983, pp. 3–9; K. Zumwalt, "Research on Teaching: Policy Implications for Teacher Education," in A. Lieverman and M. McLaughlin, eds., *Policy Making in Education*, 81st Yearbook of the National Society for the Study of Education, Part 1 (Chicago: University of Chicago Press, 1982); P. Jackson, *Life in Classrooms* (New York: Holt, Rinehart and Winston, 1968); D. Lortie, *School Teacher: A Sociological Study* (Chicago: University of Chicago Press, 1975).

17. Ibid.

18. J. Shedd, R. Malanowski, and S. Conley, *From The Front of the Classroom: A Study of the Work of Teachers* (Ithaca, New York: Organizational Analysis and Practice, 1985).

19. S. B. Bacharach, S. Conley, and J. Shedd, "A Developmental Framework for Evaluating Teachers as Decision Makers," *Journal of Personnel Evaluation in Education 1*, Summer 1987.

20. This matrix is elaborated in ibid.

21. D. A. Nadler, "The Effective Management of Organizational Change," in Jay W. Lorsch, ed., *Handbook of Organizational Behavior* (Englewood Cliffs, N.J.: Prentice-Hall, 1986); J. R. Hackman and E. E. Lawler, III, "Employee Reactions to Job Characteristics," *Journal of Applied Psychology 55*, 1971, pp. 259–286.

22. R. M. Kanter, *The Change Masters: Innovation for Productivity in the American Corporation* (New York: Simon and Schuster, 1983); T. J. Peters and R. H. Waterman, Jr., *In Search of Excellence* (New York: Warner Books, 1982); W. G. Ouchi, *Theory Z* (Reading, Mass.: Addison-Wesley, 1981).

23. J. B. Shedd, *Involving Teachers in School and District Decision-Making* (Ithaca, N.Y.: Organizational Analysis and Practice, 1987).

24. J. A. Conway, "The Myth, Mystery, and Mastery of Participative Decision Making in Education," *Educational Administration Quarterly 20* (3), Summer 1984, pp. 11–40; W. M. Warner, *Decision Involvement and Job Satisfaction in Wisconsin Elementary Schools* (Ph.D. dissertation, University of Wisconsin-Madison, 1981), cited in Conway (1984); D. M. Flannery, *Teacher Decision Involvement and Job Satisfaction in Wisconsin High Schools* (Ph.D. dissertation, University of Wisconsin-Madison, 1980), cited in Conway (1984); G. L. Thierbach, *Decision Involvement and Job Satisfaction in Middle and Junior High Schools* (Ph.D. dissertation, University of Wisconsin-Madison, 1980), cited in Conway (1984); S. Conley, S. B. Bacharach, and S. Bauer, "The School Work Environment and Teacher Career Dissatisfaction" (paper delivered at AERA, Washington, D.C., April, 1987).

25. D. W. Chapman, and S. M. Hutcheson, "Attrition from Teaching Careers: A Distriminant Analysis," *American Educational Research Journal 19* (1), 1982, pp. 93–105.

26. S. B. Bacharach, and E. E. Lawler, *Power and Politics in Organizations* (San Francisco: Jossey-Bass, 1981).

CHAPTER 16

How Professional Organizations Work: Implications for School Organization & Management

KARL E. WEICK

University of Michigan

REUBEN R. MCDANIEL, JR.

University of Texas, Austin

"Effective schools are schools in which teachers have the latitude and the authority to determine curricular content, craft discipline codes, define schoolwide objectives and goals, and help design standards of teacher certification that insure the integrity of our profession."[1]

Most schools are not organized and managed to meet the challenge presented above, because educational leaders often impose an industrial organization model on the schools, limiting their ability to think creatively about the organization of schools. Their perspectives would be broadened and schools would be more effectively designed if educators thought about schools as professional organizations. The purpose of this chapter is to identify the salient and enduring characteristics of professional organizations and draw implications for restructuring the organization and management of schools.

Rather than examine the role of the professional in organizations, our objective is to analyze the professional organization as a unique organizational form. We acknowledge that the professionalization of teachers is an important topic, but we also believe that the organization within which teachers operate must be appropriate for the task teachers face.

The chapter is organized as follows. First, we identify interpretation and decisionmaking as the basic purposes of organizing and then explore how these two purposes unfold in professional organizations. We discuss five components of professional organizations: their members, the special abilities of these members, nonroutine information inputs, professional constraints on interpretation and decisionmaking, and control strategies used by professionals. These five components are then combined into a generic form of professional organization, which we argue resembles more closely the organic than the mechanistic form. With these descriptions as background, we then interpret school organizations as settings that are hybrid professional organizations. We conclude with a series of implications, derived from our analysis, that need to be taken seriously if schools are to deliver on their claim that they are an effective and efficient group of professionals to whom society can entrust impressionable young people.

THE PURPOSES OF ORGANIZING

Organizations are created when people must cooperatively assume roles and play out role relationships in order to transform inputs into outputs. Since cooperation is limited by people's limited capacity to process information, people seek ways of arranging themselves and the tools of production so that they can overcome, at least to some extent, their bounded rationality. A particular organizational form can be evaluated by its ability to help people achieve, despite bounded rationality, goals and objectives in an effective and efficient manner.

There are two critical tasks for all organizations. Organizations help people interpret their worlds and, given that interpretation, to decide what to do.

Because people have limited information processing capacities, they engage in sense-making, which organizations guide by directing attention toward some information and away from other information. Through the delineation of roles and role relationships, the organization defines acceptable interpretations of the world and seeks commitment from its members by providing them with these definitions. Interpretation is strengthened by learning, because people tend to learn those things that are congruent with interpretations rather than those that challenge interpretations. People also plan in such a way as to strengthen existing interpretations. They see what they expect to see and, to a large measure, what the organization lets them see.

Given some interpretation of the world, organizations often engage in decisionmaking, "a process of choosing between courses of action that are expected to produce different outcomes."[2]

Although decisionmaking has traditionally dominated the organizational literature, more attention has recently been directed toward meaning,[3] culture,[4] problem sensing,[5] and other interpretation events[6] that precede and pave the way for decisionmaking. The thrust of this newer emphasis is that most determinants of decisionmaking involve the process of framing the decision: what needs to be decided, how it is labeled, and what alternatives are uncovered. Decisionmaking occurs within the constraints of a labeled problem, and the control of these labels is a crucial source of organizational influence. Decisionmaking relies heavily on rationality and therefore works best when directed at problems with a few stable variables. Since stability is dear in organizational life, the process of interpretation is often responsible for stabilizing situations sufficiently that they can be dealt with rationally, through decisionmaking.

As will become clear throughout our analysis, professional values, acting through the interpretation process, can impose a structure on information, allowing professional expertise to be applied through the decision process of choice-making.

Interpretation and decisionmaking are both critical tasks. However, interpretation rules out more decisions than it allows, because it occurs earlier and defines what should be decided. Therefore, it is an important constraint on decisionmaking.

HOW PEOPLE ORGANIZE PROFESSIONALS

Certain difficulties arise when the people to be organized are professionals. In order to understand these difficulties, it is necessary to understand the nature of professionals, how their expertise and values act as driving forces, what informational inputs they work on, how they interpret and make decisions, and what controls they respond to.

The Nature of Professionals

Woodring compares professions and occupations:

What distinguishes a profession from an occupation? High income is not the hallmark—some professionals take vows of poverty. A license does not identify a professional—physicians and lawyers are licensed, but priests and college professors are not. Indeed, a license is more characteristic of the skilled trades—barbers, plumbers, electricians, and bartenders.

Although the following criteria have not always been lived up to, they can be useful in identifying the professions.

- A profession requires a deep commitment on the part of all of its members, going far beyond a desire for pecuniary gain.
- A profession rests on an organized body of scholarly or scientific knowledge.
- Members of a profession engage in work that improves the human condition.
- Members of a profession meet rigorous standards of education and selection.[7]

Professionals are not all alike; there are differences among professions and among individuals within professions. However, professionally oriented people differ even more from the less professionally oriented on many dimensions, including commitment to the organization, problem-solving approach, feelings about authority, and value of organizational rewards.[8]

Compared to nonprofessional workers, professional workers tend to be less loyal to the organization, more critical of the organization and the community, more willing to relocate, happier to socialize with those with similar specializations, and less concerned with attaining influence in the organization.[9] The professional is less willing than the technical specialist to forgo practice to perform other organizational activities.[10] Professionals are also more interested in the work itself than in the social conditions surrounding it, and they draw support from colleagues rather than from supervisors.[11]

Myths and mystery surround professionals because of the special knowledge that they are supposed to have. When the possession of special knowledge becomes questionable, the power of the professional is damaged. As people in general have more experiences and are better educated, the knowledge power of the professional may be diminished. Haug states, "The logical and empirical consequence of the weakening of knowledge monopoly and decline of public belief in professional good will is that professional autonomy in work is undermined."[12]

Professionals, then, are those who through special training and socialization have gained a unique set of understandings that set them apart from nonprofessionals. Their attitudes about themselves and their work is different, and they have a different commitment to their calling than most workers. The power of the professionals is, in part, a function of their special knowledge and skills. If these are eroded and the mystery surrounding the professionals' work disappears, then the power of the professional is reduced and, in fact, the calling may be deprofessionalized.

Professional Expertise and Values as Driving Forces

The several defining properties of professionals reviewed above can be consolidated into the assertion that professionals are distinguished by their expertise and values. Professional organizations can be viewed as a strategy for reducing uncertainty about what *can* be done (using professional expertise) and what *should* be done (using the value grounding of the professional).

Both values and expertise are driving forces in professional organizations. In the vast majority of nongovernment organizations, people can do anything not expressly prohibited by law, while in most government organizations people can only do whatever the law says they can do. Thus, society needs some way, other than the law, to regain control over important activities. Therefore, society creates professional organizations, where larger societal values are protected by the value systems embedded in the profession rather than in the law.

The professional is expected to have special knowledge gained through years of specialized training and to have an internalized value system that represents these larger societal values. Selznick refers to professionals as "elites . . . any group that is responsible for the protection of a social value."[13]

A formal definition of values is that they are a "rationalized normative system of preferences for certain courses of action or certain outcomes,"[14] while our working definition of values is that they consist of beliefs about things people don't understand.

Professional values are not the same thing as personal values. Personal values come from family contacts and contacts with pre-teenage peers, whereas professional values are inculcated during professional socialization. Professional values are not ones that people grow up with; they are "owned" by and supportive of the larger society and are expressed through professionals who apply them.

In the case of teachers, professional values might include beliefs that children should be helped to grow, should be treated with respect, should learn how society works, and should apply the scientific method to validate what they are told. Values such as these are taught through student teaching, field trips, exposure to educational philosophy and history, discussions with other apprentice educators, and similar experiences that reveal what society deems important and how teachers are the vehicle by which these important matters are brought to bear on children.

Two qualities of professional values are crucial for subsequent arguments. First, they vary by profession. The values we discuss are not the same as those generic professional values discussed by Hall[15] and often referred to in literature on professionals. Examples of Hall's values include belief in service to the public, preference for self-regulation and peer control, and the belief that the profession is a significant reference group. These are general values, presumably held by all professionals; our interest is in values that are specific to professions.

The second quality of professional values that is crucial to our discussion is that they are particularistic rather than universalistic. This unexpected assertion derives from Hage's[16] argument that as people develop more complex views of the world, the idea of "one best way" breaks down and is replaced by the idea that varied responses are needed for varying environments. With a more complex view of the world goes a more particularistic value framework.[17] The importance of particularistic values is that they require more interaction among people who hold these values if they are to be refined and applied with sensitivity. More interaction, in turn, is more readily accomplished in some organizational forms than in others.

To apply universalistic values is a lot like applying a standard operating procedure; no matter what happens, the same value fits—so it is applied. Thus, universalistic values can be applied without much interpretation or discussion, which means they make minimal demands for communication, information processing, or feedback. Particularistic values, however, because they are often tailored to unique configurations of people and demands, impose much greater demands for communication.

The gradual buildup of professional values takes place during professional socialization at the same time that there is a more explicit effort to build expertise and knowledge. While apprentice teachers learn tacitly what John Dewey stands for and that they are the means by which his values will be perpetuated, they also learn explicitly what books seven-year-old children read, how multiplication is taught, and when bulletin boards can reinforce reading.

Professional expertise and values have important implications for professional organizations. A brief review of these implications sets the stage for a fuller exploration of organizational issues. Values let people create meaning in turbulent environments where there are high levels of nonroutine information. Organizations use values for the interpretation function, to give meaning to the things that are observed. Once some stability has been brought to the situation through the application of values, the organization uses expertise to make choices among the limited set of interpreted alternatives.

Professional organizations incorporate societal values by giving control over the end decisions to professionals and by allowing professionals to participate in the dominant coalition. People usually join dominant coalitions as a function of their expert and position power, but in professional organizations these elites also form around value issues. This is one of the factors that sets a professional organization apart—it takes expertise, position, and values to get into the dominant coalition.

Houston's description of a project to restructure forty-five secondary schools in the United States and Canada illustrates the importance of value issues in schools:

> The teachers and administrators in these Essential Schools-in-the-making are dedicated to the slow and laborious process of devising school structures that better serve the educational interests of adolescents and children. The impetus for this work derives from a set of nine principles that gives these educators a significant degree of philosophic unity as they design autonomous school and district programs.
>
> What do we value in teaching? What do we theoretically expect of

teachers, of schools, and of students? And what do our practices (perhaps unwittingly) reveal about our priorities? Whether we like it or not, education is a normative enterprise. Values lie at the heart of all decisions about curriculum, school organization, and teaching style. If values influence our judgements, how do we ensure that these judgements are uniformly fair without being narrowly prescriptive? On what basis does one judge idiosyncracy?

These practices and structures that are emerging in the Coalition are attempts to organize school life with particular values in mind.[18]

Information Inputs to Professional Organizations

Information is the principal input processed by professional organizations. Its crucial property is signified by the word "form" embedded in the term, since "information is the amount of formal patterning or complexity in any system."[19] As the amount of this patterning and complexity varies, so too do the appropriate organizational forms to deal with it.

For the purposes of this analysis, we will distinguish between information with clear formal patterns (routine) and information with unclear patterns (nonroutine). These two forms of input differ in several ways, suggested by Knight and McDaniel:[20]

Routine	*Nonroutine*
1. Easy to develop SOP to handle it	1. Hard to develop SOP to handle it
2. Changes slowly	2. Changes continuously or in spurts
3. Clearly recognizable pattern	3. No recognizable pattern
4. Easy to understand	4. Difficult to understand
5. Low uncertainty	5. High uncertainty
6. High familiarity	6. Low familiarity
7. Easy to classify	7. Hard to classify
8. Information treated for what it is	8. Temptation to treat it as routine or as noninformation
9. Simple search indicates how to process it	9. Complex search needed to find suitable way to process it
10. Can be processed by one system	10. Requires information exchange among multiple systems for processing
11. Easy to quantify	11. Hard to quantify

The processing of nonroutine information requires values, interpretation, and discussion, because the primary problems imposed by such information are complexity and difficulty of analysis. Nonroutine information is complex in the sense that it contains a large number of related elements that have some degree of independence from one another. This combination of relatedness and independence creates a high degree of unpredictability. Nonroutine information is also unanalyzable. Not only does it have a large number of partially independent elements; it also has unnoticed elements and relations that contribute to orderliness in unknown ways. If nonroutine information is analyzed using only those elements that are noticed, this decomposition is necessarily arbitrary because much of the problem has been ignored. When a "solution" is built to address only these noticed elements, it will be incomplete and may well make the problem worse. The only way to avoid this trap is to work with whole tasks, using values to guide the action.

As an example of this difficulty of analysis, consider the difference between a cardiologist and a family practitioner. Both deal with physical bodies that are a set of modestly understood, interrelated, compensatory systems. This complexity makes it difficult to diagnose the meaning of nonroutine information such as an irregular heartbeat. However, cardiologists and family practitioners deal with this nonroutine irregular heartbeat in quite different ways.

A cardiologist often analyzes the irregularity into heart-circulation versus everything else. The portion that is excluded from consideration as "everything else" is actually relevant, because it is part of the system that is operating to affect cardiac functioning. The error the cardiologist makes is to cut through the system that is operating rather than around it by arbitrarily treating the heart as a separate system, only incidentally related to everything else. He or she treats as analyzable and routine that which is not.

The same medical problem of an irregular heartbeat presented to a person with a more holistic view, such as a family practitioner, is seen differently. More contributions to the problem are assessed and a wider array of symptoms examined, such as tracing heart rate to the decline in the oil business.

The point is that medical symptoms are often nonroutine information, but even among medical professionals, symptoms may be handled differently, depending on professional values as well as understanding of the possible causes of disease. Furthermore, since nonroutine information takes time to process and is best processed through collegial interaction,[21] professionals who are overworked and are part of bureaucracies will be tempted to treat nonroutine information as if it were routine.

Nonroutine informational inputs are common in professional organizations, including schools. Because they pose difficulties for information processing, they are often misperceived as the more easily handled routine inputs. This misperception is likely when organizations are ill-equipped to deal with nonroutine information. Organizations become ill-equipped when they have no tools such as values to guide their processing of nonroutine information, when there is little precedent for collegial discussion to construct an understanding of nonroutine information, when bureaucratic structures and standard programs encourage everything to be seen as routine, when professionals are excluded from the dominant coalition, when professional values that exist in the middle of the organization have no way to filter upward and be implemented, and when interpretation is short-circuited in favor of making some kind of decision quickly.

A teacher with little experience may feel that most children are non-routine. If that teacher also has only a few weakly held professional values, then it will be hard to deal with nonroutine information. Three solutions are possible if people feel poorly equipped to handle nonroutine information. First, they can believe that all inputs are routine—which is a form of input people *can* handle. Teachers ignore the unusual child and treat him or her as no different from anyone else. Second, people can agonize over each nonroutine person who comes along and become overloaded and indecisive. The problem in this second scenario is not that nonroutine information is wrongly categorized; the problem is that people have no tools—such as values, colleagues, or discussion—to deal with it. Third, people can apply personal rather than professional values to handle nonroutine information. The problem here is that outsiders will evaluate the handling of cases against professional standards, not personal standards. Actions will therefore seem arbitrary and capricious and will be hard to defend.

Underdeveloped professional values, which can occur because professionals are housed in a mechanistic system or have no access to the dominant coalition or colleagues, make it hard for professionals to deal with nonroutine information. They either treat it as routine information, overdeliberate about it, or gain guidance in handling it from personal rather than professional values. Any one of these three "solutions" creates problems, although all three may occur when administrators ignore value cultivation as a criterion for the design of professional organizations.

Functions of Professional Organizations

Professional organizations embody the transformation process in people rather than in machines and represent a strategy to deal with uncertainty in the workplace. The decision to adopt a professional strategy is of fundamental importance, because it means work will be left intact and delegated to a professional workforce rather than subdivided and hierarchically controlled for a nonprofessional workforce. As Scott emphasizes, this is a watershed decision in organizational design, because it constrains most other choices.[22] The decision to delegate work rather than subdivide it "is particularly appropriate when (1) the work is also uncertain, a condition that mitigates against preplanning and subdivision; and (2) the work does not involve high levels of interdependence among workers."[23]

Professional organizations have as their major functions the same activities as other organizations—interpretation and decisionmaking. The strategy they use to accomplish these functions is to give professionals a primary role in executing both of them.

The interpretation function is often carried out through the activity of goal setting. Professional organizations can be differentiated by the congruence between organizational goals and professional goals or between the professional's interpretation of the world and the organization's interpretation of the world. In well-managed professional organizations, the people who set goals and allocate resources are professionals; therefore, their goals and aspirations are reflected throughout the organization. Because in professional organizations there are two systems operating (the professional and the organizational), the goals of the organization may be a compromise unless professionals are clearly in control of the goal-setting processes.

Early research on the nature of professional organizations suggested that there was an inherent conflict between a professional's commitment to the organization and to the profession. This early research led to a characterization of professionals as either locals, committed to the organization, or cosmopolitans, committed to the profession.[24] More recent research suggests that there is no inherent conflict between the professional's commitment to the organization and to the profession.[25] Current research supports the conclusion that the congruence of professional and organizational goals provides the best indicator of the degree to which the organization and the professional are compatible—that is, the degree to which the organization is a professional organization rather than simply an organization with professionals working in it.

Charisma is an important determinant of the professional's ability to control interpretations. Etzioni defines charisma as "the ability of an actor to exercise diffuse and intense influence over the normative orientations of other actors."[26] When the top professionals in an organization have charisma, they are able to get others to adopt their interpretations of the world. People will often accept the word of charismatic leaders as dogma, trust them completely, and follow their directions even if they do not have the legitimacy of an official rank.[27] In professional organizations, the charisma of the professional often determines whether the goals of the organization and those of the profession remain compatible.

With these issues of goal setting and charisma as background, it is possible to look more explicitly at the relation between interpretation and decisionmaking. To understand the nature of interpretation and decisionmaking in professional organizations, it is important to recall that values and expertise are the hallmarks of professionals and that interpretation precedes and constrains decisionmaking. The way in which these two realities interact in professional organizations can be illus-

FIGURE 16-1
Four types of decision issues generated by interpretation.

		Preferences regarding possible outcomes	
		Certain	*Uncertain*
Beliefs about cause/effect relations	*Certain*	Computation strategy	Compromise strategy
	Uncertain	Judgment strategy	Inspiration strategy

trated using Thompson's description of the two dimensions of decision issues.[28]

Thompson argued that decision issues involve beliefs about cause–effect relations and preferences for possible outcomes. When these two variables are dichotomized in terms of certainty/uncertainty about causation and certainty/uncertainty about outcome preferences, four types of decision issues result. (See Figure 16-1.) Each type stimulates a different strategy to resolve it. If there is complete certainty, a computational strategy such as an electronic computer can be used to make the decision. Certain outcome preferences but uncertain causation call for a judgment strategy, whereas, uncertain outcome preferences but certain causation call for a compromise strategy. When there is uncertainty on both dimensions, an inspirational strategy is called for.

The nature of interpretation and decisionmaking in professional organizations can be illustrated using just these concepts. The goal of interpretation is to create some level of certainty for both beliefs about causation and outcome preferences. These beliefs are inputs that lead to decision issues. The levels of uncertainty that are created determine the decision strategy used to decide the issue. Said differently, interpretation constructs the decision premises that will constrain decisionmaking. The amount of uncertainty in these premises affects the strategy professionals adopt to resolve the issue.

The mechanism by which these processes unfold is hypothesized to be the following. The question addressed during interpretations is, "What is going on here?" Professionals attempt to answer that question by constructing a cause–effect structure for puzzling inputs and by constructing standards of desirability against which possible causal effects in this structure could be evaluated. Professional expertise informs questions of causation, and professional values inform questions of relevant standards for assessing desirability.[29]

Attempts to construct a clear picture of causation and standards of desirability sometimes succeed, resulting in crystallized decision issues, and sometimes fail, resulting in ambiguous decision issues. These outcomes are determined by many of the variables reviewed in this chapter. For example, if there is a conflict between professional and organizational values, there will be disagreement about outcome preferences. This disagreement will create uncertainty about outcome preferences, and this will mean that the resulting decision issue will have to be decided by either compromise or inspiration, depending on the level of uncertainty that exists for causation. If existing professional expertise is incomplete, if information is nonroutine, or if inputs are dynamic rather than stable, then there will be uncertainty about causation, which means that either judgment or inspiration is the strategy that will probably be adopted for decisionmaking. If collegial support for articulating and refining values is missing, then professional values will be underdeveloped, personal values are likely to be substituted, and collective outcome preferences will be ambiguous as a result.

Notice that in each case characteristics of the professional organization affect the success professionals have when they apply their values and expertise to informational inputs in an effort to interpret the causal structure and desirability of these inputs. The output of these interpretation efforts is a decision issue that has some degree of clarity regarding both causation and preferences. This output is then fed to the decision system, where the question becomes, "If that is what is going on, what do I need to do about it?" One of four strategies will be used to answer that question, and the strategy is determined by the form in which the issue arrives at the decision process. If it arrives with neither causation nor preferences clarified, then inspiration and charisma will supply the answer. If both causation and preferences are clarified, then computation, standard operating procedures, and organizational routines can be used. If causation is clear but preferences are not, compromise will decide the issue. Finally, if causation is ambiguous but preferences are clear, then judgment will resolve the issue.

Many of the characteristics of professional organizations become clearer when we apply this framework. Nonroutine information is common in professional organizations. This information, by definition, starts out with an unclear causal structure, which also means that a relevant hierarchy of preferred outcomes is probably unclear. Nonroutine input is the only antecedant condition where all four decision strategies are possible. With routine input, causation is clear; then the only question that has to be settled during interpretation is whether the standards of desirability for this routine issue are also clear. If they are, computation is called for; if they are not, compromise is called for. The one strategy that will not be used for routine inputs, and thus the one strategy that is likely to be unique to the professional organization, is judgment. For judgment to occur, there must be uncertainty about causation, which is the defining property of nonroutine information. Because professionals are noted for their expertise, they are often delegated the tougher problems whose causal structure is problematic—situations where professional knowledge is incomplete.

The frequency with which nonroutine information, incomplete knowledge, and uncertainty about cause–effect beliefs occurs in professional organizations makes it imperative that professionals agree on values, standards of desirability, and outcome preferences to guide their interpretations. If outcome preferences and values are not clear, then all their decisions are made by inspiration—which, over time, can raise self-doubts about competence and doubts from others about legitimacy. Guidance from a consistent set of professional values is important in a world where causation is muddied. This is why, throughout this chapter, we argue in favor of organizational designs that encourage interactions leading to the development and refinement of professional values.

To summarize, it seems to us that decisionmaking represents a relatively minor portion of information processing in professional organizations. Important determinants such as expertise, values, interpretation, and discussion all shape the issue before it becomes a choice. Each of these determinants narrows the scope of that choice. While all of these professional determinants come into play during interpretation, that does not mean that they produce certainty and, therefore, computational decision strategies. Professionals are no more omniscient than anyone else, which is simply another way of saying that complete views of cause–effect relations and clear agreement on multidimensional outcome preferences are rare. However, some organizational conditions can encourage higher levels of completeness and agreement, and those conditions are the ones we want to identify to improve the professional quality of schools.

Control Strategies in Professional Organizations

A major problem that emerges in professional organizations is the problem of control: how to get unity of effort and subordination of individual, idiosyncratic behavior when the interpretation and decisionmaking functions are in the hands of those responsible for doing the work.

Professional organizations often utilize an apprentice system to provide for direct organizational control over the socialization function. Control exercised over training institutions is also control over the socialization processes. "The major means of control in professional organizations are based on prolonged and careful selection, and socialization in universities and professional schools or on the job precedes recruitment to autonomous performance positions. As a consequence, norms are as a rule highly internalized, so that informal controls and symbolic sanctions are highly effective. Social powers, formalized in the professional code of ethics and the professional association and supported by the social bonds of the professional community and professional elites, carry great weight. The use of economic sanctions such as fines, expulsion from the profession, or cancellation of license is extremely rare."[30]

Especially important sources of control in professional organizations are substitutes for leadership.[31] These substitutes affect an organizational form such that the more substitutes that are present, the closer the organization approximates a professional organization. Substitutes for leadership are individual, task, and organizational characteristics that neutralize the leader's ability either to improve or to impair a subordinate's satisfaction or performance. Substitutes in the form of individual characteristics include ability, experience, training, knowledge, need for independence, professional orientation, and indifference toward organizational rewards. Substitutes in the form of task characteristics include tasks that are unambiguous and routine, methodologically invariant, providing their own feedback, and intrinsically satisfying. Substitutes in the form of organizational characteristics include formalization, inflexibility, highly specified and active advisory and staff functions, cohesive workgroups, rewards not under the leader's control, and spatial distance between superiors and subordinates. In each of these cases, the listed characteristic performs the same functions as does an in-person leader and therefore substitutes for that leader. Leadership acts undertaken when substitutes are in place tend to be ineffective because they are imposed on a situation in which there is already sufficient structure and consideration.[32]

The close relationship between substitutes and professionalism needs to be understood fully, since substitutes may account for much of the form that exists in professional organizations. Kerr illustrates the nature of this close relationship:

> There are several reasons why the working environment of professionals employed in organizations presents special opportunities for leadership substitutes to flourish and hierarchical leadership to be consequently less important. The professional's expertise, normally acquired as a result of specialized training in a body of abstract knowledge, often serves to reduce the need for structuring information; furthermore, a belief in peer review and collegial maintenance of standards often causes the professional to look to fellow professionals rather than to the hierarchical leader for what informational needs remain. Even concerning performance feedback, which was described earlier as typically transmitted from formal superior to subordinates, substitutes for leadership may exist: First, professionals may deny that

their hierarchical superiors have the skills to determine whether performance standards are being met. From the professional's viewpoint, only fellow professionals know enough about their work to evaluate it competently. Second, professionals may deny that their superior's performance standards are even relevant. Such attributes as knowledge of the specialty, originality of approach, and impact upon the professional community may seem reasonable criteria for performance evaluation to the professional, but may not even be a part of the organization's formal evaluation procedure.[33]

Substitutes for leadership may be a point of leverage through which professional organizational forms can be created. It has been well documented that there is a reciprocal influence relationship between leaders and subordinates. Leaders affect subordinate performance, and subordinates can affect leader performance.[34] Substitutes for leadership often neutralize the influence of leaders on subordinates, but they do not neutralize subordinate influences on leaders. Substitutes unbalance reciprocal relationships and tend to increase upward influence while decreasing top-down influence. This relatively neglected pathway of influence may enable people to influence their superiors to treat them more like professionals.

Substitutes may also increase participation among hierarchical unequals because they reduce the inequalities. This occurs because a substitute, by definition, reduces the dominant position of the leader, making egalitarianism more plausible and obtainable. To illustrate how substitutes equalize power, Kerr suggests that, in an MBO negotiation, people meet as a group with the dominant leader rather than individually. The group support balances the leader's high rank, and both participate on a more equal footing. The group takes more responsibility for setting standards and monitoring adherence to these standards, which is a step toward acting in a more professional manner. The small win that moved this system toward higher professionalism was the insertion of a substitute for leadership that, when amplified, shifted responsibility closer to where the expertise was exercised and the values applied.

It is the large number of substitutes documented by Kerr and Jermier[35] and Kerr and Slocum[36] that makes substitutes potentially important vehicles for control in professional organizations. Substitutes work in two ways. First, they decrease hierarchical influence so that changes can be made at lower levels, where decisions are actually made. Second, they require subordinates to act in a more professional, self-determining manner. Substitutes are forcing functions to compel reluctant professionals to act more like they claim they want to act. When substitutes are in places, a person who says, "I would blossom if only the heavy hand of my boss were lifted," has that hand lifted when the substitutes are activated. The responsibility is then more explicitly on the individual and the group to deliver what they say they can.

THE FORM OF PROFESSIONAL ORGANIZATIONS

When professional people interpret and make decisions about non-routine inputs, the resulting distinctive system forms a template against which school organizations can be assessed. In this section, we look first at the generic form of the professional organization and then at specific ways in which this form is altered when it is adapted to schools.

The Generic Organizational Form for Professionals

The generic professional organization derives from the decision to leave work intact rather than subdivide it. However, since design decisions about delegation and subdividing are seldom all or nothing, professionals

> perform the core tasks of the organization under two general types of arrangements. The first, which we have labeled the *autonomous* professional organization, exists to the extent that organizational officials delegate to the group of professional employees considerable responsibility for defining and implementing the goals, for setting performance standards, and for seeing to it that standards are maintained. We have labeled the second type the *heteronomous* professional organization because in this arrangement professional employees are clearly subordinate to an administrative framework, and the amount of autonomy granted them is relatively small. Employees in these settings are subject to administrative controls, and their discretion is clearly circumscribed.[37]

A close reading of Scott's descriptions suggests that a more basic distinction lies behind them. The description of the heteronomous organization includes descriptive phrases such as "employees clearly subordinate," "administrative framework," "autonomy *granted* is small," "subject to administrative controls," and "discretion clearly limited." These phrases are associated with a more generic form of organization designated "mechanistic." Scott's description of the autonomous organization includes descriptive phases such as "delegate to professionals," "employees define and implement goals," "employees set performance standards," and "employees maintain standards." These phrases are associated with a more generic organizational form designated "organic." Since Scott incorporates these more general forms into his descriptions of the more specific category of professional organizations, it seems important to review the general forms themselves to see how they might be implemented in novel ways to handle the unique issues schools face.

The distinction between the mechanistic and organic forms turns on four organizational variables: complexity (specialization of tasks through a division of labor), formalization (specfied rules and procedures for dealing with work situations), centralization (degree to which authority for making decisions is concentrated at the top of a hierarchy), and configuration (number of hierarchical levels and span of control at each level). When the extreme values of these four variables are specified, a clear difference in forms occurs.

> Mechanistic structural forms, effective where changeability was low, were characterized by (a) low complexity, or differentiation of tasks into specific operations versus reliance upon specialized professional skills; (b) high formalization, or the precise definition of rights and obligations attached to each functional role; (c) high centralization, since all relevant knowledge is at the top level of the firm; and (d) the existence of a well-defined formal organizational hierarchy. In organic forms, appropriate where changeability was high, there was (a) high complexity, or use of specialized professional skills rather than differentiation into specific operations; (b) low formalization, or adjustment and continual redefinition of individual tasks; (c) low centralization, since ad hoc centers of authority developed where knowledge about problems was located; and (d) the existence of a structural configuration akin to a network.[38]

To these four basic variables, Tichy adds four more: mission and strategy, people management styles, organizational processes, and emergent networks.[39] The mission and strategies of mechanistic organizations are simple, implicit, fragmented, rigid and reactive, while those of the organic form are complex, explicit, integrated, flexible, and manipulative. Mechanistic people-management styles tend to be conservative, emphasize formal authority and power dominance, and use little participation. Organic people-management styles tend more toward risk-taking, use flexible situational authority, and are nonauthoritarian, with considerable use of participation. The organizational processes found in mechanistic organizations involve minimal communication and extensive conflict avoidance, while those processes found in organic forms involve more open communication, with less time lag and distortion and with conflict confronted and managed more openly. Emergent networks in mechanistic organizations are not task-related, whereas they are in organic organizations.

To appreciate the appropriateness of the organic form for professional organizations, it is important to understand the way that it facilitates information processing.

> The more organic a configuration is (a) the more interaction should occur, (b) the more equal should be the interpretation levels of individual participants, (c) the rarer should be interaction isolates, (d) the more interconnected should be interaction clusters, and (e) the more bridge roles should occur in the interaction network. All of these propositions derive from the reasoning that the high uncertainty in an organic con-

figuration calls forth high information-processing requirements that cause people to interact frequently. However, the reasoning can be inverted: frequent interaction produces a high capacity for information processing that looks for information-processing opportunities and so perceives contingencies and possibilities; perceiving contingencies and possibilities engenders uncertainty.[40]

The subtlety is often lost in portraits of the organic form, but it must be seen to appreciate how these forms function. A close reading of the Tichy quotation will show that the organic form itself creates uncertainty. People in an organic system have to interact a lot to reduce the uncertainty that the form itself generates. Burns and Stalker put this point well in their original description.

> The organic form, by departing from the familiar clarity and fixity of the hierarchic structure, is often experienced by the individual manager as an uneasy, embarrassed, or chronically anxious quest for knowledge about what he should be doing, or what is expected of him, and similar apprehensiveness about what others are doing. Indeed, as we shall see later, this kind of response is necessary if the organic form of organization is to work effectively.[41]

Thus, organic systems can be restless organizations where there is a continuous search for definition, information, and meaning. If everyone is slightly uncertain most of the time, then attentiveness and discussion increase, which means that more is known. However, satisfaction with organic systems may not be especially high, precisely because these systems can be unpredictable. It is because of this "anxious" quality that these systems gather more information and update their members more often. An organic system is a complex form better able to sense the complexities in the environment of nonroutine information it faces. This improvement in ability to sense complexity is often gained at the cost of composure. Glib treatments of the contrast between mechanistic and organic forms often gloss over the contentious, emotional quality of life in organic systems.

The high potential of the organic form for information processing is crucial for our analysis, because it allows people to deal with nonroutine information and encourages them to articulate, refine, and update values that make sense of nonroutine information. An organic system is important for professionals because it is the most appropriate structure for bringing expertise to bear on complexity, but it is also the most appropriate form to bring values to bear on information that is complex and unanalyzable.

The Generic Professional Form Adapted for Schools

Schools and teachers are difficult to categorize—schools because they contain a mixture of mechanistic and organic forms, teachers because they possess some characteristics of professionals but lack others. Take the simple observation that teaching involves both custodial and educational activities. The better design for routine custodial work is mechanistic, while the better design for nonroutine education is organic. The mixed or hybrid character of schools suggests a variety of issues.

For example, an organic form may be less familiar to school board members and others who evaluate schools than a mechanistic organization that deals with routine information through a hierarchy, a division of labor, and specified duties and procedures.[42] Since the curriculum looks like a standard operating procedure, the board member may tend to give it more attention than the child. Using the metaphor of figure and ground, the person familiar with a mechanistic organization will treat the curriculum as figure and the child as ground, whereas the professional, more accustomed to nonroutine information and whole tasks, will treat the child as figure and the curriculum as ground. An evaluator sensitive to professional needs will treat the curriculum as guide and look for the quality of interaction between the child and the professional rather than for the compliance of the professional with the curriculum guidelines. Evaluators familiar with the more common mechanistic form will look for curriculum compliance and pay less attention to the quality of the interaction between the teacher and the student.

People who evaluate and set policy for teachers often live in organizations unlike those in which teachers live. As a result, they evaluate teachers by an inappropriate set of criteria and impose inappropriate organizational forms on their activities. The mechanistic forms they impose magnify the unique problems of establishing a professional identity that are already troublesome for educators.

Whether an organic or mechanistic system is more appropriate for schools depends on the kind of information they process. Since the informational inputs to schools are not homogeneous, they require both mechanistic and organic systems—a difficult but not impossible combination. Gerwin suggests that an organization can enjoy the advantages of both mechanistic and organic forms by intraorganizational specialization (different groups have different forms), temporal specialization (the same group adopts a different form at different times), and interorganizational specialization (for example, elementary schools are organic, secondary schools are mechanistic).[43]

Since schools are professional organizations, they have additional ways to combine organic and mechanistic properties in the service of dealing with both routine and nonroutine information. If part of the school is made into a mechanistic form and part into an organic form, then the key design question is how well the two parts are integrated. By integration we mean, how well each understands, respects, and defers to the strengths of the other. Furthermore, there is the question of allocation. Are nonroutine issues sharply differentiated from routine issues? If so, are they then assigned to the system best suited to handle them? Schools that deal with a mixture of routine and nonroutine information by a division of labor among systems vary in their effectiveness, depending on how well they manage the allocation of issues between these two systems.

Schools can handle the coexistence of routine and nonroutine information in at least two other ways than the division of labor. First, all systems can be made organic in the interest of processing nonroutine information, with the additional provision that they can form themselves (self-designing system) into temporary mechanistic forms when the input is routine. They are intermittently mechanistic, but normally organic. They are like an all-channel network that can become a wheel when inputs become predictable and routine. It would seem easier to be organic with the option of becoming mechanistic than to be mechanistic with the option of becoming organic. This is so because the skills necessary to run an organic form are complex and are not normally developed or called for in a mechanistic form. If such skills as face-to-face communication and negotiation are underdeveloped, then the temporary organic systems that are built out of mechanistic raw materials will be badly flawed, ineffective, and not much better as a means to handle nonroutine information than the mechanistic system from which they emerged.

The second way to handle coexistent routine and nonroutine information is to rely more heavily on the collegial qualities of professionals. Complex professionals could form themselves into projects, teams, task forces, or hierarchies as the need arises. Organization design under these conditions would be nothing more than an ad hoc collection of interest groups built to solve specific problems. The interest groups would dissolve as problems were solved or wander away to different issues. This design is not that far from the organized anarchy where people, problems, choices, and solutions show different rhythms and pacing and converge in idiosyncratic configurations whenever people feel a decision has to be produced.[44]

It seems to us that professionalism is affected more substantially by organizational design than is nonprofessionalism, and that an organic form is more difficult to maintain than is a mechanistic form. From these two assumptions, we infer that prescriptions for design in schools should favor the organic-professional form in order to maintain a balance between the organic and mechanistic forms. We say this for several reasons. First, teachers have less control over entry into the profession and over the period of socialization than is true in other professions. This means that they start their lives in schools less fully developed as professionals; thus, they may be more willing to accept centralization, restrictions on autonomy, and externally imposed standards for performance. These concessions retard further professional development. Second, it is easier to direct than listen, easier to tell than persuade, easier to appeal to position power than to competence—all of which means that any administrator is more likely to think mechanistically than organically. Third, organic organizations occur less often in society than do mechanistic organizations, so people have less understanding and appreciation of the organic form and are therefore more apt to see it as a maverick in need of reform ("They need to run a tighter ship"). The very novelty of the organic form ensures that people will try to assimilate it to forms they are more familiar with. Fourth, we believe that control over value issues drifts from the bottom of the hierarchy toward the top in mechanistic systems. This drift is counterproductive, because values need to be articulated and applied close to the nonroutine situations where they become salient.

IMPLICATIONS

Our conclusion that schools are hybrid professional organizations, because they process both routine and nonroutine information, resembles Bidwell's conclusion that schools have a mixed organizational character: "both the looseness of system structures and the nature of the teaching task seem to press for a professional mode of school-system organization, while demands for uniformity of product and the long time span over which cohorts of students are trained press for rationalization of activities and thus for a bureaucratic basis of organization."[45] This interplay of bureaucracy and professionalism, based on our review, seems most economically viewed as the efforts of professionals to process nonroutine information.

Our analysis suggests that people who create organizational designs for schools should construct forms that aid the articulation and development of professional values, since these values are sources of guidance when people process nonroutine information. Our review also suggests that organic organizational forms are better designs both for developing values and for clarifying vague causal structures than are mechanistic forms. Since organic forms also encourage the development of substitutes for leadership, they encourage professional development as well as utilize current skills and attitudes.

Our assumption that nonroutine information is common in school organizations should be tested. Toward this end, the eleven-item list of characteristics that separate routine from nonroutine information is a start. The question uppermost in the mind of the assessor should be, "Where, on a scale ranging between routine and nonroutine, are the key issues that the school deals with?" Once the issues have been classified, then the question becomes "Do the more routine issues go to the mechanistic systems and the more nonroutine to the organic system?" If the answer is "no," then the question becomes "Can the issues be reassigned to the appropriate system?" If the answer is again "no," then "Can the form of the system itself be changed so that it fits more closely the demands of the information fed to it?"

We have placed the process of interpretation in a more central role than is common in the organizational literature, where the usual tendency is to spotlight decisionmaking. Interpretation assumes a key role for us because we are dealing with professionals, with information that is susceptible to multiple interpretations, and with novel issues that reflect diverse constituencies. We argue that interpretation is influential because it occurs earlier than decisionmaking and defines what should be decided and how it should be decided. The decisions people face are determined by the interpretations they make and their ability to clarify issues of causation and preference for outcomes.

When we spotlighted the interpretation process, we were able to understand several properties of professional life in schools. For example, it is often noted that the technology of teaching is poorly understood.[46] Translated into the language of this chapter, efforts to interpret issues involving teaching often produce an uncertain cause–effect structure. Thus, decisions involving teaching will usually be made either by judgment or by inspiration. The prescription implied by this analysis is that professionals should become very good at working with these two strategies because they have to use them so often. An additional prescription is that professional training should be designed to clarify the cause–effect structure of teaching. If that is done, the intervention should have far-reaching effects. As the causal structure of teaching becomes clearer, professionals will be increasingly able to use computation and compromise to make decisions, options that were formerly closed to them because of their incomplete understanding of this technology.

The scenario we have suggested for teaching technologies illustrates a larger goal for professional organizations. If professionals are encouraged to develop agreement about outcome preferences and a better understanding of the causal structure for a set of target issues, then these issues can be handled by the strategy of computation. That frees time and personnel for closer attention to issues where questions of causation and preference are more stubborn. Efforts to improve agreement and understanding are more likely to succeed when they unfold in the dense interaction of the organic system than in the stylized interaction of the mechanistic system.

Our analysis also led us to a deeper appreciation for the role of charisma in professional organizations. This came about because so many issues in professional organizations leave the interpretation process still laden with uncertainty about causation and preferences, so that they can only be resolved by inspiration. Since charisma and transformational leadership are potential sources of inspiration,[47] schools may rise or fall depending on whether they can attract charismatic professionals, develop noncharismatics into charismatics, or institutionalize the charisma of former charismatics.[48]

The third option, the institutionalization of charisma, is of interest because it implies that the decision strategy of inspiration may be susceptible to institutionalization, which in turn would mean that inspiration can be transformed into computation. As Trice and Beyer note, Bill Wilson's charisma, which built Alcoholics Anonymous, has been institutionalized in rituals, traditions, steps, slogans, and assumptions. This institutionalized charisma clarifies issues of causation (alcoholism is a disease) and issues of outcome preference (abstinence), so that diverse people and problems are interpreted with certainty and are handled with a standard routine (work your way through the Twelve Steps to recover from dependence on alcohol).

Inspiration and charisma are not issues that one often associates with the workaday world of schools and teachers. Yet our focus on problems of interpretation faced by professionals suggests that, more often than might be expected, the combination of unclear causation and unclear preferences will force professionals to decide issues using something like inspiration to guide them. This may be one reason why educators appear so receptive to fads, fashions, and novelties. The high-powered rhetoric that often accompanies these innovations may seem to clarify the muddled picture of causation and preference that besets so many of the issues.

The framework we have used throughout this chapter has the advantage that it suggests bases on which to make comparisons among schools. Schools are distinguished by such things as the amount and kind of nonroutine information they process, the extent of their agreement on outcome preferences, and their knowledge of cause–effect relations. To see how such a comparison might be structured, consider the following description taken from Bidwell.

> [I]n elementary classrooms the achievement criteria form a diffuse combination of cognitive and moral standards, emphasizing the "goodness" of the pupil, e.g., his responsiveness and obedience, rather than the specific quality of achievement. These standards provide the teacher with considerable latitude for nurturant interaction with her pupils. . . . But the emphasis in secondary school classrooms is on the quality of achievement, and students are differentially evaluated according to the specific nature of their technical accomplishments. Here

the teacher is more purely the instrumental leader of the classroom group—less nurturant and more distant and universalistic in interaction with students.[49]

While readers may differ on how they interpret the preceding quotation and where they place the emphasis, one way to read it is as asserting that elementary schools interpret inputs into clear outcome standards (the goodness of the pupil), whereas secondary schools interpret inputs into clear cause–effect structures (instrumental leader focuses on technical accomplishments). Using that information alone, we would predict that elementary schools rely more heavily on decision strategies of computation and judgment, whereas secondary schools rely more heavily on decision strategies of computation and compromise. These predictions derive from our attempt to intuit from Bidwell's descriptions what kind of success teaching professionals have when they try to interpret the nonroutine inputs of elementary and secondary students. From that inference, it can then be predicted how the school will function when it makes key decisions.

The final two implications we want to underscore are first, that processing nonroutine information is labor-intensive, and second, that substitutes for leadership provide a means by which organizations can be inched toward an organic, professional form.

If information processing is labor-intensive, organizational properties such as structural looseness, loose coupling, slack, and discussion are instrumental to effectiveness—not symptoms of poor management. In the current vernacular, a "lean, mean" organization cannot handle nonroutine information, because it doesn't have the resources to do so. It can survive if its inputs remain routine and its environment stable, but not if they change.

The implementation of substitutes for leadership seems to be a useful way to move toward more professionalism. In Kerr and Jermeier's original description of this phenomenon, they were interested in the fact that substitutes neutralized leader interventions; they explained why some predictions from leadership theories were not confirmed. We have added the twist that the neutralization of leadership also encourages professional development, collegial interaction, and greater assumption of responsibility.[50]

Clearly, leaders are not unqualified liabilities in professional organizations, especially if they are professionals. The implication of the substitutes argument is that leaders should make their first shot at influence their best shot, because as substitutes take hold, their influence will steadily decrease. As we have tried to show, that steady decrease of influence should be counted as a win for professional development, not a loss.

NOTES

1. Remarks by Mary H. Futrell, President of the National Education Association, at the first national meeting of the Holmes Group in Washington, D.C., as quoted by J. Evangelauf, *Chronicle of Higher Education 33*, February 11, 1987.

2. Janice M. Beyer, "Ideologies, Values, and Decision Making in Organizations," in P. C. Nystrom and William H. Starbuck, eds., *Handbook of Organizational Design*, vol. 2 (New York: Oxford, 1981), pp. 166–202.

3. Linda Smircich and Gareth Morgan, "Leadership: The Management of Meaning," *Journal of Applied Behavioral Science 18*, 1982, pp. 257–273.

4. Meryl R. Louis, "Organizations as Culture-bearing Milieux," in L. R. Pondy, Peter J. Frost, Gareth Morgan, and T. C. Dandridge, eds., *Organizational Symbolism* (Greenwich, Conn.: JAI, 1983), pp. 39–54.

5. Sara Kiesler and Lee Sproull, "Managerial Response to Changing Environments: Perspectives on Problem Sensing from Social Cognition," *Administrative Science Quarterly 17*, 1982, pp. 548–570.

6. Richard L. Daft and Karl E. Weick, "Toward a Model of Organizations as Interpretation Systems," *Academy of Management Review 9*, 1984, pp. 284–295.

7. P. Woodring, "Schoolteaching Cannot Be Considered a Profession as Long as Its Entrance Standards Remain So Low," *Chronicle of Higher Education*, November 12, 1986, p. 48.

8. Morgan W. McCall, Jr., "Leadership and the Professional," *Technical Report Number 17* (Greensboro, N.C.: Center for Creative Leadership, June 1981).

9. Allan C. Filley, Robert J. House, and Steven Kerr, *Managerial Process and Organizational Behavior* (Glenview, Ill.: Scott, Foresman, 1976).

10. Chet Schriesheim, Maryann A. Von Glinow, and Steven Kerr, "Professionals in Bureaucracies: A Structural Alternative," *TIMS Studies in Management Sciences 5*, 1977, pp. 55–69.

11. McCall, op. cit.

12. M. R. Haug, "The Deprofessionalization of Everyone?" *Sociological Focus 8*, August 1975, p. 207.

13. Philip Selznick, *Leadership in Administration* (New York: Harper & Row, 1957), p. 120.

14. Beyer, op. cit., p. 166.

15. Richard H. Hall, "Professionalization and Bureaucratization," *American Sociological Review 33*, 1968, pp. 92–104.

16. Ibid., p. 148.

17. See Steven Kerr, "Integrity in Effective Leadership" (unpublished manuscript, University of Southern California, 1987).

18. H. M. Houston, "Restructuring Secondary Schools," in A. Lieberman, ed., *Building a Professional Culture in Schools* (New York: Teachers College Press, 1987), pp. 1, 15, 20.

19. James G. Miller, *Living Systems* (New York: McGraw-Hill, 1978), p. 12.

20. Kenneth E. Knight and Reuben R. McDaniel, Jr., *Organizations: An Information Systems Perspective* (Belmont, Calif.: Wadsworth, 1979).

21. Ibid., p. 142.

22. W. Richard Scott, *Organizations: Rational, Natural, and Open Systems* (Englewood Cliffs, N.J.: Prentice-Hall, 1981), p. 242.

23. Ibid., p. 222.

24. Alvin Gouldner, "Cosmopolitans and Locals: Towards an Analysis of Latent Social Roles," *Administrative Science Quarterly 2*, 1957, pp. 281–306.

25. Nancy B. Tuma and A. J. Grimes, "A Comparison of Models of Role Orientations of Professionals in a Research-Oriented University," *Administrative Science Quarterly 26*, 1981, pp. 187–206; R. Thornton, "Organizational Involvement and Commitment to Organization and Profession," *Administrative Science Quarterly 15*, 1970, pp. 417–426; Kay M. Bartol, "Professionalism as a Predictor of Organizational Commitment, Role Stress, and Turnover: A Multidimensional Approach," *Academy of Management Journal 22*, 1979, pp. 815–821.

26. Amitai Etzioni, *A Comparative Analysis of Complex Organizations* (New York: Free Press, 1975), p. 305.

27. Edgar H. Schein, *Organizational Psychology*, 3rd ed. (Englewood Cliffs, N.J.: Prentice-Hall, 1980).

28. James D. Thompson, *Organizations in Action* (New York: McGraw-Hill, 1967), pp. 134–138.

29. Ibid., p. 84.

30. Etzioni, op. cit., p. 52.

31. Steven Kerr and John M. Jermier, "Substitutes for Leadership: Their Meaning and Measurement," *Organizational Behavior and Human Performance 22*, 1978, pp. 375–403.

32. J. E. Sheridan, D. J. Vredenburgh, and M. A. Abelson, "Contextual Model of Leadership Influence in Hospital Units," *Academy of Management Journal 27*, 1984, pp. 57–78.

33. Steven Kerr, "Substitutes for Leadership: Some Implications for Organizational Design," *Organization and Administrative Sciences 8*, 1977, pp. 135–146.

34. Aaron Lowin and J. R. Craig, "The Influence of Level of Performance on Managerial Style: An Experimental Object-lesson in the Ambiguity of Correlational Data," *Organizational Behavior and Human Performance 3*, 1968, pp. 440–458.

35. Ibid.

36. Steven Kerr and John W. Slocum, "Controlling the Performance of People in Organizations," in P. C. Nystrom and William H. Starbuck, eds., *Handbook of Organizational Design, Vol. 2* (New York: Oxford, 1981): pp. 116–134.

37. Scott, op. cit., pp. 222–223.

38. Donald Gerwin, "Relationships Between Structure and Technology," in P. C. Nystrom and William H. Starbuck, eds., *Handbook of Organizational Design, Vol. 2* (New York: Oxford, 1981): pp. 9–10.

39. Noel Tichy, "Networks in Organizations," in P. C. Nystrom and William H. Starbuck, eds., *Handbook of Organizational Design*, vol. 2 (New York: Oxford, 1981), p. 233.

40. Ibid., p. 238.

41. T. Burns and G. M. Stalker, *The Management of Innovation* (London: Tavistock, 1961), pp. 122–123.

42. Charles E. Bidwell notes an exception in his "The School as a Formal Organization," in James G. March, ed., *Handbook of Organizations* (Chicago: Rand McNally, 1965), p. 988.

43. Ibid., p. 11.

44. James G. March and Johan P. Olsen, *Ambiguity and Choice in Organizations* (Bergen, Norway: Universitetsförlaget, 1976).

45. Ibid.

46. J. M. Stephens, *The Process of Schooling* (New York: Holt, Rinehart, & Winston, 1967).

47. Noel M. Tichy and May Ann Devanna, *The Transformational Leader* (New York: Wiley, 1986).

48. Harrison M. Trice and Janice H. Beyer, "Charisma and its Routinization in Two Social Movements," in Barry M. Staw and L. L. Cummings, eds., *Research in Organizational Behavior*, vol. 8 (Greenwich, Conn.: JAI, 1986), pp. 113–164.

49. Ibid., pp. 993–994.

50. Ibid.

CHAPTER 17

Career Ladders:
A Good Idea Going Awry

PHILLIP C. SCHLECHTY

Gheens Professional Development Academy

The professionalization of the teaching occupation has emerged as a high priority goal of the education reform agenda. In the view of proponents, career ladder programs are a vehicle that can be used to further this end. Opponents, on the other hand, believe the net result of career ladder programs will be further bureaucratization of teaching, which will ultimately lead to further deterioration in the quality of education delivered to children.

As one who has had considerable experience in designing and implementing career ladder programs, I am convinced that many of the ideas suggested by the label "career ladder" are essential to the professionalization of teaching. For example, I do not see how teaching can be professionalized unless those who teach are provided career options that permit them to continue to grow and develop. Neither do I see how it will be possible to professionalize teaching unless career earning power is greatly enhanced. Conceptually at least, I am thus an advocate of career ladders.

On the other hand, having had considerable experience with the nitty-gritty of implementing career ladder programs, I share the concerns of those who oppose the idea of career ladders. In action, many career ladder programs have tended to become bureaucratic and stifling. Rather than encouraging good teachers to remain in teaching, they have prompted the best teachers to leave the classroom; rather than motivating all teachers, they have rewarded a few and inherently punished many.

In spite of the difficulties inherent in implementing career ladders, however, I remain convinced that persistent movement in some of the directions suggested by the *concept* of career ladders is essential to the professionalization of teaching. As the title of this chapter suggests, I am equally persuaded that career ladder programs are not currently moving in this direction.

What I hope to do in the following pages is to share my observations regarding the reasons career ladders have yet to make the desired contribution to the professionalization of teaching. Based on these observations, I will make a series of recommendations regarding ways in which some of the difficulties experienced in the past can be avoided. I will also suggest additional actions necessary to assure that the inherent promise of the career ladder movement can be realized.

A PRELIMINARY STATEMENT

As the reader is by now aware, this chapter is a personal statement. It represents my views, derived primarily from personal experience with efforts to implement career ladder programs. I have served as a primary leader for the design and early implementation of the Charlotte-Mecklenburg Teacher Career Development Program, which many refer to as a career ladder program, though we resisted the label for several years. I have also worked as a consultant to many other school districts, professional organizations, and state agencies.

It is not my intention to present an implicit criticism of those who have worked, and are now working, to install career ladders in their school systems or in their states. Neither should this chapter be taken as a *mea culpa* statement that I have accepted what some of my critics have long argued—that the concept of career ladders is inherently a bad idea. Rather, I hope the reader will find useful the reflections of a *sociologist* who is also a *reform activist*, committed to the proposition that the key to the improvement of instruction for children is the professionalization of teaching. I hope these reflections will be helpful to those who advocate career ladders as a means of professionalizing teaching. I also urge those who are ready to abandon career ladders, and those who advocate abandonment, to consider again the possibility that the concept does contain some meritorious ideas.

CAREER OPTIONS AND SALARY OPPORTUNITIES

In the typical career ladder program, persons who have arrived at different statuses are expected to do different things or are expected to do the same things better than those below them. In addition, those who occupy different rungs on the career ladder receive different salaries. Career level II teachers, for example, are paid more than career level I teachers.

One of the most profound lessons that can be learned from past experience with career ladders is that the linkage between career options and salary opportunities creates serious difficulties in implementation. Among other things, this linkage leads to goal displacement. Teachers come to view career ladders as means of gaining additional salary rather than increased opportunities for growth and development, increased status, and recognition. Those who are denied quick and easy access to these salary options feel relatively deprived. In response to the social and legal challenges that such feelings of deprivation threaten to generate, those who design career ladders feel compelled to develop elaborate technical systems of evaluation that will "hold up in court," thereby virtually assuring a narrow view of evaluation.

As things now stand, the teaching occupation is not sufficiently mature to undertake reforms where issues of salary are intermingled with issues of status and occupational opportunity. Because the typical career ladder program has intermingled these issues, the result has been goal displacement and a diminution of the potential contribution career options could make to teacher development and motivation.

Goal Displacement

Career ladders can address three issues: (1) salary, (2) teacher status and alternative career options, and (3) performance and performance recognition. Early career ladder efforts, including the Charlotte-Mecklenburg plan and the Tennessee plan, were not as sensitive to the distinctions among these issues as they might have been. The Charlotte-Mecklenburg plan did, however, take these issues into consideration more than many of the state plans. Its initial successes may have been due to this, as well as other reasons such as strong teacher involvement in the initial planning, a heavy up-front commitment to planning, and a conscious commitment to developing teachers as well as to identifying outstanding performers. I am not in a position to comment on the present status of the Charlotte program, since I have had only passing contact with it over the past three years.

The Charlotte plan, like the Tennessee plan, offered salary incentives to persons who moved up the career ladder. Unlike the Tennessee plan, however, the Charlotte program was intentionally designed to develop teachers as professionals. (There is considerable controversy regarding its success in this matter.) Indeed, the Charlotte plan was predicated on the assumption that arriving at career level I would be concurrent with receiving tenure. The granting of tenure would be associated with the school system's assurance that the teacher in question was outstanding—*all* career level teachers were to be outstanding. In the long run, the only teachers who would not be career level I (and thereby not "certified" as outstanding) would be neophytes who were in the process of developing the skills to become outstanding.

The system of granting tenure prior to the career development program was based on negative evidence—that one was not incompetent—rather than affirmative evidence that one was capable of giving outstanding performance over a sustained period of time. In the career ladder program, it was perceived as essential that even experienced teachers go through a period of training and systematic evaluation to develop and affirm their professional qualities. Charlotte required at least one year in training and evaluation before career level I status could be granted. There was no "fast track."

The developmental nature of the Tennessee plan was not as clear. Indeed, the teacher training and staff development components of this plan were initiated almost as afterthoughts. From the outset, it was clear that in Tennessee, as well as in other states such as Kentucky, the primary aim of the career ladder was to legitimize pay for performance. The intent was to select and sort persons on a career ladder hierarchy, based on measurable differences in the quality of performance. In Tennessee, career level II teachers were to be persons who had demonstrated that they were better teachers than those at career level I, and career level III teachers were to be superstars.

In Charlotte, on the other hand, career level II teachers were not viewed as better teachers than those at career level I, but rather as teachers who were willing to undergo additional training and assume responsibility for adult leadership (something like the "lead teacher" notion suggested in the Carnegie report). Those at career level III were not viewed as better teachers than those at career level II, but rather as teachers who had demonstrated the ability and commitment to lead others and who had developed the necessary skills to lead research and development activities, head special school improvement projects, and so on. Furthermore, it was understood (at least initially) that career level II and III teachers would be assigned as full-time classroom teachers if it was decided that such an assignment would make the greatest contribution to the improvement of the overall instructional program. As initially conceptualized, the Charlotte plan was what business refers to as a "skill-based" incentive system, while the Tennessee plan was a "performance-based" plan. (I, for one, was not smart enough at the time to appreciate this difference or its significance.)

In operation, the Tennessee plan and the Charlotte plan confronted similar problems. Though the two systems managed these problems differently, the results illustrate why I am now persuaded that career ladders for professionals cannot realize their potential for professionalizing teaching under present circumstances. For this potential to become reality, career ladders must be unhitched from salary structures, but not from salary opportunities such as those provided by extended employment.

Both the Charlotte and Tennessee programs were motivated in part by the view that substantial across-the-board salary increases were unlikely. There seemed to be little sentiment among the citizenry or legislative leaders to increase teachers' salaries unless some means was found to link pay to performance.

Partly because of this perception, and partly because it simply seemed to make sense, both programs combined career status with salary increases, as have most programs since. Thus, an experienced teacher who opted to get on the career ladder (both plans were voluntary for experienced teachers) and who qualified for career level I could receive a salary supplement above the regular salary schedule. In Charlotte, the supplement was $2000 per year, in Tennessee $1000.

As one advanced up the career ladder, additional supplements were available, as were opportunities for summer employment. (There were many other important differences between the design of the Charlotte and the Tennessee salary structures, but these are not of concern here. For readers who are interested, descriptions are available.[1]) In effect, both plans combined differentiated pay and differentiated staffing— which critics of those policies were quick to point out. Once decision-makers had endorsed these plans—indeed, even before the plans were endorsed—there was considerable pressure to assure that "there would be no quotas," for the idea of quotas would clearly make the program a merit pay plan, which is anathema to many teachers. Furthermore, the link between pay structures and career structures put considerable pressure on program designers to give as many people as possible the opportunity to "get on the career ladder" in the shortest period of time.

Tennessee responded to this pressure by easing entry into career level I, providing a variety of ways to qualify, as well as a fast track (one could reach career level I by passing a test). In Charlotte, a temporary quota was established: 150 candidates were accepted the first year, 250 the second year, and increasing numbers until all experienced teachers who wanted to qualify for career level I status could be accommodated. All experienced teachers were to have the opportunity to qualify (by spending one year in training and evaluation) before any newly hired teacher would advance to career level I status.

In neither case were the results particularly happy. The Tennessee response caused many critics to see career level I as a subterfuge intended to get all teachers a $1000 across-the-board raise. (The only teachers excluded were those who would not go through the bureaucratic hassles required to qualify and the few who could meet one of a smorgasbord of standards.) Minor scandals developed around cheating on tests, and the integrity of the "pay for performance" assumptions of the program were compromised.

In Charlotte, many teachers who were excluded from early opportunities to qualify felt that they were being treated unfairly. Most understood that the system did not have the technical capacity to process 3000 teachers without compromising the qualitative integrity of the program; however, but for the luck of the draw, they rather than their colleagues could be earning $2000 more at an earlier date. (Early access to the Charlotte plan was based on nominations by colleagues, combined with a random drawing system. Such a procedure did little to generate strong commitment from experienced teachers, especially those who had to wait three to five years for the opportunity to qualify.)

Perhaps the biggest problem the linkage between salary opportunities and career options has created concerns evaluation. This linkage has forced those who implement career ladder programs to become almost obsessed with developing evaluation systems that are technically and legally defensible, as opposed to developing formative evaluation systems that truly inform the developmental process.

Developmental evaluation systems are not simply reliable; they are persuasive—those who are evaluated believe the evaluation and are willing to act on it. They are not simply technically and legally defensible; they are politically viable—they will be upheld as just and fair by those constituencies whose support must be maintained if the system is to be viable.[2]

Because of this obsession, tremendous resources have been expended in developing "evaluation instruments" that are research-based. Too little attention has been given to the primary functions of an evaluation system from a developmental perspective: (a) to communicate what is expected, (b) to provide feedback regarding how closely performance is meeting those expectations, and (c) to identify ways of improving performance so that expectations can be more fully realized. Rather than designing evaluation systems aimed at supporting the development of outstanding teaching, the link between salary and career options has caused the evaluation system to be aimed toward "identifying and rewarding outstanding teachers."

Motivation and Morale

Conceptually, incentive systems (of which a career ladder program is one type) are future-oriented—they are intended to encourage future performance. Although the reward one receives is for past performance, the intent of the reward is to signify to the individual that what he or she is doing is valued and honored and to indicate to others the kind of performances that are expected. In incentive systems, people are supposed to know what the system *expects* by what the system *inspects* and *respects*.

In working on the design and implementation of incentive systems, including career ladders, I have come to the conclusion that certain basic principles should guide such efforts.

1. Positive rewards are more powerful incentives for performance than the fear of negative sanctions.
2. Rewards are effective only to the degree that they are attached to some prespecified performance expectations.
3. It is appropriate to reward effort expended as well as the quality of results. (The purpose of a reward system should be to encourage people to do things as well as to do them well.)
4. Persons who meet minimum performance expectations should have access to the reward system as well as those persons who exceed minimum performance expectations; that is, what one is expected to do should be honored.
5. Rewards should be short-term as well as long-term, and sustained high-quality performance should produce substantially greater rewards than should short-term, sporadic performance, regardless of its quality. Continuous performance that meets expectations is assumed to be of more value than is sporadic performance of a heroic nature.
6. The purpose of an incentive system is to improve the productivity of the organization as well as the productivity of individuals who work in that organization.
7. Individuals should have a great deal of control over the degree to which they gain access to the reward system and the degree to which they use it. Furthermore, no person should be denied access to the reward system on any grounds other than energy expended or the quality of results.
8. The incentive system should encourage cooperative action and the pursuit of common goals as well as individual initiative.

The present status of school finance, typical salary structures, and the undifferentiated structure of the teaching occupation create a condition in which the effort to link salary opportunities to a more clearly differentiated occupational structure almost assures that many of these principles will be violated. Until the average teacher's salary is equivalent to the average college graduate's salary, any effort to provide salary rewards to teachers on any basis that is not uniformly accessible to all teachers will cause morale problems. Theories of relative deprivation indicate why this is so. So long as teachers feel that their occupational choice inherently precludes them from equal access to the rewards available to other college graduates, they will resist differentiation among themselves. Persons who share a common sense of relative disadvantage place greater value on the commonality of their disadvantaged status than on meager opportunities for a few of their group to escape that status. Critics of present career ladders are, therefore, partially correct in their view that career ladders will not work until and unless teachers' base salaries are greatly enhanced.

Teacher salaries have improved over the past several years, but not yet to the level suggested to be necessary in the preceding paragraph. Furthermore, it does not seem likely that funds will be made available to meet this standard in the short run. So long as salary opportunities and career options are directly linked, career ladders are as likely to have negative effects on teacher morale and professional development as positive effects. There are several reasons for this.

First, teachers are not likely to be inspired if they perceive that it is only by being outstanding that they can gain access to a salary that is equivalent to that of the average college graduate in their community. Second, the average teacher, the teacher capable of solid though not particularly stellar performance, is not likely to be inspired, because he or she knows that doing his or her best will lead to little additional financial reward. The teacher who is less than solid is not likely to be any more inspired than is now the case, since the prospect of keeping one's job when one is marginal is not inherently any better in a career ladder program than under present circumstances.[3] Finally, the professional ideology of teachers leads many to resent the implication that they would work either harder or smarter if they were paid more. Put bluntly, if we have learned anything from the linkage between salary opportunities and career options, it is that Hertzberg is correct.[4] Money is a dissatisfier and a demotivator—it is not a satisfier or a motivator.

People who feel that they are unfairly treated with regard to salary may not perform as well as they can, but persons who feel that they are fairly treated are not likely to perform better simply because more money is involved. Other positive satisfiers must be used—for example, the opportunities for growth, development, increased status, and recognition implicit in the notion of career options for teachers.

Unfortunately, so long as career options and salary options are linked, the satisfying elements of career options are tainted by the dissatisfying elements of the relative deprivation teachers feel vis-à-vis their present salary. Furthermore, so long as this linkage holds, career opportunities for teachers will be precisely as scarce as are salary opportunities. If career opportunities were separated from salary options, then it would be possible to use career options as a positive incentive without contaminating them with the disincentives inherent in the present teacher salary structure. In making this assertion, I proceed from a number of assumptions, derived partially from theories of motivation and partially from hands-on experience. These assumptions are discussed in the paragraphs that follow.

1. Opportunities for job variety, novelty, and intellectual growth are inherently positive rewards for teachers. Indeed, I have observed that when given the choice between a few extra dollars for their own use and the opportunity to pursue a novel career option, many teachers will choose the latter.

2. Teachers are much more willing to support the notion that access to career opportunities such as becoming a mentor teacher, a team leader, or a curriculum coordinator should be based on a thorough assessment of past performance than they are to accept the proposition that salary differentials should be based on past performance.

3. The value that teachers place on the concept of longevity pay implicitly suggests that teachers believe that sustained high-quality performance should produce substantially greater rewards than short-term sporadic performance, regardless of its nature. Indeed, the argument that teachers make against merit pay and for longevity pay is predicated on the assumption that continuous performance that meets expectations is of more value than is sporadic performance of a heroic nature.[5] Thus, it is not unreasonable to assume that teachers would be willing to accept demonstrated long-term performance of an exemplary nature as a prerequisite to gain access to career options.

4. In the "natural order" of schools, there already exist many career options for teachers, and many more could easily be invented. The problem is that the existing opportunities are not perceived as career options, and access to these opportunities is seldom linked to well-articulated and prespecified performance expectations. For example, it would not take much to view the position of department chair, team leader, chairman of a curriculum study group, beginning teacher mentor, or perhaps assistant principal as a part of a career ladder system. Indeed, all it would take is to link access to such opportunities to demonstrated performance in one's present assignment.

Such an idea is not revolutionary in business, but it is revolutionary in too many schools. Potential career options are frequently wasted by passing them out on an arbitrary, nonpurposeful, or willy-nilly basis. Furthermore, when promotional opportunities are available, such as promotion to department chair, they are likely to be treated as new hires—everybody is interviewed and one is selected. Honest promotions (as I use the term) are those career options that any employee can reasonably expect to have offered at some future date if he or she performs well in a present assignment and continues to grow and develop.

The unfortunate consequence of the condition described above is that a tremendously powerful potential source of motivation for growth and development is wasted. Moreover, in the act of wasting this resource, potential growth opportunities are turned into demotivators. Because committee assignments are not clearly articulated as marks of distinguished status based on assessment of past performance, these assignments become an extra burden to be borne by the overloaded few. Because teachers do not know in what performances they must engage if they wish to be considered for a department chairmanship or a team leader position, the selection of department chairs is often perceived to be nothing more than an ordination by the principal or a perk to be passed out to an administrator's sychophant.

It is clear that if career structures could, for the immediate future at least, be separated from salary structures, it would be possible to use career opportunities to develop a system of positive rewards and incentives that would conform with the principles set forth earlier.

CONDITIONS OF THE WORKPLACE

Another important lesson learned from past efforts in designing and implementing career ladders is that issues of status and career opportunities cannot be addressed without addressing the conditions of the workplace. Status may be granted from on high, but status is acted out in local school buildings. New roles may be invented, but if these roles are to have any effect in local schools, the entire role structure of schools must change to accommodate the new addition. Otherwise, the new role simply becomes another specialized function in an already overstuffed bureaucratic structure.

During the 1960s, there was an effort to develop a pattern of differentiated staffing. Some have argued that career ladders are nothing more than a reincarnation of the differentiated staffing pattern of the 1960s. I disagree. Most of the differentiated staffing patterns of the 1960s identified some teachers as master teachers and implicitly turned these people into quasi-administrators. At least conceptually, most career ladder programs have resisted this impulse. What most career ladder programs have done is to link movement up the career ladder with access to special jobs and assignments within the teaching profession. For example, in Charlotte, it was intended that only career level II and III teachers would be permitted to serve as mentors to beginning teachers. Furthermore, it was expected that career level II and III teachers would be willing to accept transfers to schools where it was judged that their services were most needed—to serve, for example, as department chairs or to head up special projects. In addition, it was assumed that career level II and III teachers could be assigned to serve full-time in regular classrooms if they had special talents that were needed in those particular classrooms.[6]

What has become clear is that too few building administrators and too few faculties were encouraged to think outside the phenomenological box that existing bureaucratic structures imposed on them. In many state plans, for example, it is explicitly assumed that advanced career status would require one to abandon classroom teaching, at least on a part-time basis. It was seldom understood that advanced career status could instead be used to confirm the organization's view that the person in question should be looked to as a moral and intellectual leader on the faculty, whose professional advice is especially valued and whose leadership potential is recognized.

Perhaps the clearest illustration of how the conditions of the workplace affect the possibilities of implementing a career ladder program can be found in the beginning teacher mentor programs that are becoming widespread throughout the country. Though often not as fully elaborated as full-blown career ladder programs, beginning teacher programs contain many of the same troublesome elements that confront those who would design and implement career ladders. First, the beginning teacher position is implicitly assumed to have a status inferior to that of the experienced teacher. Second, the mentor teacher or consulting teacher is assumed to be an exemplar of outstanding teaching practice and to have special skills in advising the neophyte.

To achieve success in implementing such a beginning teacher program, a number of difficulties must be confronted. First, if the role of beginning teacher is special (and I believe it should be), then the expectations for the beginning teacher should also be special, in both qualitative and quantitative terms. Beginning teachers should be expected to undergo more rigorous, more fine-grained, and more frequent evaluations than experienced colleagues. Neophytes should be expected to spend more time in consultation with mentors and other instructors than experienced colleagues and probably to participate in a systematic program of instruction designed to induct them into the teaching occupation. Such expectations obviously mean that beginning teachers should not have the same teaching load as do more senior teachers. It also means that beginning teachers should probably start teaching in schools where the level of professional support is optimal.[7]

However, the conditions suggested above are virtually impossible to meet, because of the rigidities of the workplace and the existing career paths of teachers. In the typical beginning teacher program, the neophyte is expected to carry precisely the same teaching load as more experienced colleagues. Few programs make special provisions for the beginning teacher to observe and consult with others, and almost no program provides special classes or educational experiences for the beginning teacher. Furthermore, the majority of the new teachers in this country begin their teaching experience in schools that have the least prospect of providing them with the technical support and models one would expect if the intent were to make the beginning teacher aware of exemplary teaching practice. Many programs do require that the beginning teacher be observed and counseled on a more regular basis than was typically the case in the past. Unfortunately, the counseling that occurs usually takes place on a hit-or-miss basis, in a "free period" or after school.

Clearly, the underlying assumptions of such programs require a reconceptualization of the role of the beginning teacher and a redesign of the career paths of teachers. The conditions of the workplace and the structure of school organizations would have to be modified to accommodate this reconceptualization. To date, there are few examples of such redesign and restructure. As a result, many state-mandated beginning teacher programs make an already burdensome experience increasingly so.

The problems are compounded by the inability of the typical school work site to adjust to the new expectations that are inherent in the role of mentor. Like beginning teachers, mentors are seldom provided additional time, although some are provided additional money. In those instances where additional time is provided (for example, the Kentucky Beginning Teacher Program), the time is bought through the hiring of substitutes. Many experienced teachers have ambivalent feelings about turning their classes over to a substitute so that they can observe a beginning teacher. Furthermore, at least in large urban school systems, the procuring of a substitute frequently involves bureaucratic hassles.

It has been my observation that beginning teacher programs, as well as career ladder programs, can and do play out well in school buildings where the principal and the staff have already established the conditions that are commonly associated with "effective schools." If, however, the conditions of effective schooling are not already in place, neither career ladders nor beginning teacher programs have much chance of success. In sum, a necessary first step in the installation of a growth-oriented program (either a career ladder or a beginning teacher program) is to create conditions that ensure a healthy workplace. Healthy workplaces are adaptable; they can change to accommodate new roles and support new expectations. Unhealthy workplaces are rigid; they accommodate new roles and expectations at first by isolating them and separating them from the ongoing routines, then ultimately expel them from the system.

HARD S's AND SOFT S's

Most of the public discussion regarding career ladders has given emphasis to what Pascale and Athos refer to as the "hard s's": *strategy, structure,* and *systems.*[8] Decisions regarding whether the career ladder should give emphasis to attracting and retaining new teachers or to motivating experienced teachers are *strategic decisions.* Similarly, a decision to bring teachers onto the career ladder by way of a fast track is a strategic decision aimed at increasing the commitment of experienced teachers to the program by providing them with immediate, tangible rewards. Programs that have eschewed the fast track have made a strategic decision that it was more important to assure the community that the program had qualitative integrity than it was to provide teachers with short-term satisfactions. *Structural decisions* have to do with such matters as how many levels there will be in the career ladder program, whether a beginning teacher program will be treated as an integral part of the career ladder or somehow separated from it, and how salary opportunities will relate to career options. Decisions regarding *systems* concern such things as the rate and frequency of evaluations, the instruments and procedures used in evaluations, and the methods of tracking and accounting for results of these procedures.

Less attention has been given to what Pascale and Athos refer to as the "soft s's"; *staff, style, skills,* and *superordinate goals.* In terms of *staff,* for example, few career ladder programs have given systematic attention to such demographic considerations as the desired age and sex distribution of individuals at various levels of the career structure or the conditions under which it would be likely that the top levels of the structure would become overloaded with persons with a relatively long anticipated future tenure in the system (thereby blocking career mobility to those below them or making the system too expensive to maintain political and economic viability). To my knowledge, the Charlotte-Mecklenburg Program is the only program that made an effort to address such issues.

Skills have to do with the distinctive capabilities that individuals who occupy designated positions need to possess. Most career ladder programs overlook the concept of distinctive skills. Indeed, most career ladder programs assume that people should advance on the career ladder because they are *more* skilled than their colleagues rather than that they possess *distinctive* skills.

Style concerns the ways key managers are to behave in achieving the goals of the program. It also concerns the cultural style of the system in which a program is embedded. For example, one style of developing and implementing a career ladder system would be to assume that most decisions should be made centrally (as in the Tennessee Plan). A different stylistic decision would be to assume that decentralized decisions are more appropriate (as in Utah and, to some extent, Arizona). Other stylistic decisions concern whether the intent of key personnel is to identify failure or to promote and encourage success.

Superordinate goals have to do with the guiding concepts that undergird the program, the values the program is intended to express, and the meanings the program is intended to convey. For example, a career ladder program that is intended to convey that teaching should be an honored profession would be unlikely to adopt the posture that career status should be afforded to the minimally competent. On the other hand, a career ladder program that aims to identify and reward outstanding teachers and weed out the incompetent would be more likely to afford career status to the minimally competent.

The "hard s's" can usually be articulated in bold, easily communicable, and relatively unequivocable terms. The hard s's are not subtle; newspaper reporters find it easy to describe decisions related to the hard s's, and policymakers and politicians find them relatively easy to grasp, understand, and discuss. Thus, there is a strong tendency for policymakers, top-level school leaders, and the lay public to focus attention on the hard s's. Given such a focus from power figures, it is not surprising that those who have designed and implemented career ladder programs have been quite attentive to issues related to the hard s's.

The "soft s's," on the other hand, are subtle; the meanings they suggest are communicated by subtle nuances. For example, the dynamics of demographic variables are not easily grasped by persons who have not been exposed to demographic concepts. The distinctions between such phrases as "the purpose of our program is to identify and reward outstanding teachers" and "the purpose of our program is to develop and maintain outstanding teaching" are sometimes too subtle for the uninitiated to grasp. Many will not understand that an evaluation system that is aimed primarily at identifying incompetents may be counterproductive when the goal is to promote and develop competence. Most important, it is more difficult for action-oriented policymakers to deal with the soft s's, which must be changed through process and dialogue, than the hard s's, which can be changed by administrative fiat or legislative mandate.

If career ladders are ever to be implemented successfully, there is no substitute for clear vision and a long-term view. Structural changes as fundamental as those suggested by career ladders require a fundamental shift in school cultures to accommodate the new forms. Therefore, those who would change the hard s's of school life (systems, structure, and strategy) must first contend with the soft s's (skill, style, superordinate goals, and staff). Indeed, I believe that the main reason the Charlotte-Mecklenburg program enjoyed early success was that the school system already had in place a set of mechanisms to deal with the soft s's. Conversely, I am persuaded that many state level programs ran into early difficulty precisely because few state-level units have such mechanisms available to them.[9]

From the outset, the superintendent of the Charlotte-Mecklenburg schools made it clear that the Career Development Program was intended to make it possible for good teachers who met reasonable stan-

dards to receive career and salary rewards commensurate with their performance. He was equally clear that the career development program
was not a mechanism for getting rid of bad teachers. As he put the
matter, "We already know how to get rid of bad teachers. All we need is
the guts to do it. What we don't know how to do is reward good teachers." Most state-level career development programs, on the other hand,
were never so clear about their purposes. The Tennessee plan started as
a straightforward proposal for merit pay and master teachers. Over
time, through a series of political compromises, the Tennessee Master
Teacher plan emerged as the Tennessee career ladder plan. As a result,
the Tennessee plan implicitly and sometimes explicitly conveys the idea
that career level II teachers are more competent than career level I teachers, and career level III teachers are the most competent of all.[10]

In addition to the superintendent's clear vision of the superordinate
goals of the Charlotte-Mecklenburgh Career Development Program, the
school system had a history of strong commitment to continuing education opportunities for teachers and administrators.[11] Thus, there was already in place a mechanism for dealing with issues related to skill—a
mechanism not typically available in local systems and almost never
available at the state level. Finally, the fact that the Charlotte program
was a local initiative made possible a long-term view of the program.
The board of education was relatively stable, and the board members
frequently indicated a commitment to continuing and refining the program regardless of who the superintendent might be and in spite of
short-term difficulties and controversies.[12]

In sum, the installation of a career ladder program aimed at the professionalization of teaching requires an understanding that such a program involves not only organizational change, but also change in the
fundamental culture of schools. Indeed, career ladders cannot be successfully implemented until the bureaucratic ethos that dominates the
thinking of many policymakers and school executives is replaced by a
professional ethos.

JOBS AND CAREERS

If the future of American education depends on enhancing the career options available to teachers, so that the teaching occupation can
emerge as a full-blown profession, one necessary task is to help potential supporters and present adversaries of this view to understand the
distinction between jobs and careers. Jobs happen at a point in time; careers happen over time. Jobs have descriptions, whereas careers have
trajectories. Jobs have present circumstances; careers have future prospects. It is apparent that many who have designed career ladders do not

understand this themselves, for if they did, they would know that it is not possible to "test" a career ladder in a year or two. Careers do not happen over the course of a year or two; they happen over the course of a lifetime. Careers require—and reward—commitment and staying power as well as competence. Indeed, the way continuing competence is ensured is by providing career rewards for the competent who remain committed.

In the past, occupations like teaching did not need to compete for people who were career-oriented. There was an available supply of competent people (mainly women) who were relatively satisfied to accept a short-term job; in fact, many of them rejected the values implicit in careerism. Teaching has traditionally been organized as a short-term job rather than as a career. Nowadays, teaching, nursing, and similar occupations are in the awkward position of needing to compete with other occupations that are organized not as jobs but as careers. Furthermore, many of these occupations, although they are perceived to be more attractive than teaching, are less attractive, at the entry level at least. The salary and the working conditions of a first-year medical intern or a liberal arts graduate who accepts a position as a management trainee in a Fortune 500 corporation are not dramatically superior to the salary and working conditions of a first-year teacher. Furthermore, as jobs, many of these competing occupations offer entry-level employees little that teaching does not offer. Indeed, it is likely that beginning-level teachers have more decisionmaking autonomy and more status and authority relative to their senior colleagues than do management trainees, interns in teaching hospitals, and junior partners in law firms. The difference, of course, is that the junior partner will become a senior partner, and the job will change as well as the person. Senior partners do not do the same thing that junior partners are expected to do. In teaching, senior teachers are expected to do precisely the same things as junior teachers, except that it is assumed that they will do them better.

Career-oriented occupations are predicated on the assumption that wisdom as well as competence, and insight as well as energy, should be rewarded. Indeed, if sheer technical competence were the basis on which rewards were distributed in career-oriented occupations, it is likely that some entry-level employees would receive more rewards than their superiors. For example, it is not unusual for large corporations in technical fields to assign entry-level engineers the task of developing and implementing training programs for more senior personnel. The assumption is that the recent graduate has more up-to-date knowledge of technical developments than do some of the more senior managers. Senior partners in law firms depend on junior partners to "teach them the law" in a particular case. A senior partner's forte is not fine-grained technical expertise or even the willingness to spend long hours in the library reading the law. A senior partner's contribution is in the area of wisdom and refined judgment, qualities assumed to be gained through years of disciplined experience.

In occupations organized the way teaching is organized, the problem is that there are no positions in the occupation that encourage the exercise of wisdom and sound judgment. This is not to say that there are no wise and judicious teachers, but rather that the role of teacher is so undifferentiated that those who have developed wisdom and mature judgment have little time to exercise these abilities. The job of teacher is defined in such a way that it requires the intensive commitment of a vigorous, technically proficient youngster. Wise, experienced teachers could do different things from inexperienced beginning teachers (not simply the same things better), but the undifferentiated nature of the teaching occupation makes it difficult for them to do so. The occupation, as currently organized, demands that experienced teachers do many things that they once found meaningful and exciting but that they now find demeaning and debilitating. For example, as the high school teaching force has grown older, it has become increasingly difficult to find coaches for many sports. One reason is obvious: Middle-aged people have different values from younger people, and spending hours on a football field may not be as attractive as it once was. Similarly, the intensity that is required to sustain a high level of on-task involvement of students may be initially exhilarating, but even this may wear thin over time. As experience is gained, what was unpredictable for the neophyte becomes predictable, and what was novel and exciting becomes routine and potentially boring.

The critical point is that the teaching occupation must be restructured if it is to provide career incentives for career-oriented people. Teaching cannot compete for the talent it needs unless it is organized as a career rather than as simply a job. The professionalization of teaching requires an occupational structure that encourages rather than discourages careerism.

IMPLICATIONS AND RECOMMENDATIONS

If my analysis is correct, the creation of career ladders is not possible outside the context of a fundamental restructuring of schools and the teaching occupation. It is essential that the salary opportunities of teachers be enhanced at the same time as the career opportunities are enhanced. In the short term, however, it is probably unwise to link career options and salary options too tightly. Arguments regarding differentiated pay spill over into arguments regarding differentiated opportunities. Most teachers want and need career variety and will, I believe, support rather radical departures from the present organization of schools. However, if the price of career variety is too heavy to pay, teachers are likely to band together, like any other relatively deprived group, and give priority to group security rather than incentives for individual attainment and growth. Disaster research indicates that people who feel themselves victims of a common disaster develop fierce loyalties to each other and express particular resentment toward those few whom fate somehow spares.

I believe it is possible to enrich career opportunities to a level that benefits all teachers who choose to participate. Given the present condition of educational finance, it may not be possible to do the same with salary opportunities in the short run. Thus, I have come to the position that the thrust of career ladder programs should be in the school restructuring arguments rather than in the arguments regarding the structure and condition of teacher salary.

NOTES

1. Phillip Schlechty and Anne Joslin, *Planning and Implementing a Teacher Career Development Program: the Charlotte-Mecklenburg, North Carolina Case:* Interim Report on NIE Project G-85-2009, 1986.
2. Ibid.
3. Some will suggest that career ladders do lead to tighter evaluations and thus to a greater likelihood that marginal or inadequate teachers will be dismissed. Perhaps. However, tighter evaluation of marginal teachers is now possible. I cannot imagine why one would go to the trouble to implement a career ladder program simply to get rid of bad teachers. Career ladders are only worth the trouble if they develop and maintain outstanding teaching.
4. Frederick Hertzberg, *Work and the Nature of Man* (New York: World Publishing Co., 1966).
5. Critics will be quick to point out that other interpretations could be given to teachers' preference for longevity-based pay schedules, the least flattering of which is that it is a means by which unions defend the interests of the incompetent. Horror stories aside, I am persuaded that if there are incompetents in the classroom, the failure is with management rather than with the unions. Schools have never been particularly good at developing personnel, and they have been even less adequate in the area of evaluation.
6. Unlike many other career development programs, the Charlotte program did not assume that the career level II teacher was superior to a career level I teacher as a classroom performer. Rather, it was assumed that the career level II teacher was a person willing to make an unusual commitment and develop the special skills and talents that were needed to assure a more effective operation of building-level and system-level functions.
7. Critics will argue that beginning teachers who start in such optimal conditions will have unrealistic expectations and thus be unprepared for the "real world." Given time for a long conversation, I believe I could persuade such critics that they are wrong. Suffice it to say that competent physicians do not undergo their initial preparation in M.A.S.H. units. Rather, the initial induction of all physicians occurs in teaching hospitals, where the level of technical and personnel support is superior.
8. Richard Pascale and Anthony Athos, *The Art of Japanese Management* (New York: Simon & Schuster, 1981).
9. I am not in a position to comment on the present status or level of continuing success of the CMS program, since I have had no real contact with it for nearly three years. Based on my own observations, as well as testimony from many others, I am convinced that in the early stages at least, the CMS program ran into fewer difficulties and was more well received by teachers than most other career ladder programs.
10. These observations are not made in order to cast aspersions on the Tennessee plan

or to lay the basis for invidious and self-serving comparisons between the Charlotte and the Tennessee plans. Both plans have had their problems in implementation; both had, and continue to have, many strengths and virtues. The two plans do have a great deal in common, and those who provided leadership to these two efforts learned much from each other. I have a great deal of personal admiration for Governor Alexander and the courage he showed in providing leadership to break the bonds of tradition in education. Indeed, many of the mistakes that were made in Tennessee, and in Charlotte, could have been avoided if some of the more virulent critics had been a bit more reasonable and thoughtful in their responses.

11. Phillip Schlechty and Anne Joslin, *Leading Cultural Change* (forthcoming).
12. Phillip Schlechty and Anne Joslin, op. cit. (1986) and (forthcoming).

POSTSCRIPT: ASSUMPTIONS AND PRINCIPLES FOR IMPLEMENTING THE CAREER LADDER

Position paper of the Trinity Educational Forum, Trinity University, San Antonio, Texas, 1985.

I. Purpose

The career ladder is a design for promoting excellence in teaching by providing incentives and opportunities for teachers to improve their professional competence. To accomplish this purpose, the career ladder provisions of H.B. 72 are intended to develop a merit pay program for teachers and to enhance the teaching career by differentiating roles and responsibilities as teachers progress professionally. Enhanced professional responsibility is more critical to the bill's spirit and intent than merit pay. The career ladder, for example, is *not* an efficient managerial or financial mechanism for providing merit pay. Easier, simpler, and less expensive means are available for accomplishing only this objective.

II. Working definition

The career ladder is a system for improving teaching and promoting excellence which provides for sharing school responsibilities with teachers and for enhancing their roles as professional partners and school leaders. This system provides that teaching roles be upgraded in challenge and responsibility as increases in professional skill, competency, and commitment warrant. Merit is used as a criterion for enhancing responsibility. Salary increases are allocated to teachers to reflect this additional responsibility:

1. Appraisal determines who is meritorious for advancement.
2. Advancement leads to enhanced leadership role and more responsibility.
3. Leadership and responsibility increases result in salary increases.

III. Assumptions and principles about evaluation of teaching

H.B. 72 provides for the development of a universal appraisal instrument for uniformity in teacher evaluation across the state. This strategy makes sense only if the following provisions are added:

1. No one best method of teaching exists which is appropriate for all purposes, objectives, occasions, students and situa-

tions. Teaching strategies and methods need to reflect differences in teaching intents and situations.

2. Universal appraisal systems have a tendency to focus on the lowest levels of competence which characterize generic teaching fundamentals.

3. It is reasonable to expect that all teachers master and display such fundamentals and a universal appraisal system is a suitable evaluation tool for this purpose.

4. Advancement on the career ladder, however, should require that teachers demonstrate more than universal minimums. It does not make professional sense to continue to use an evaluation system which seeks "higher scores" on the same basic competencies for further advancement.

5. When assessing for advancement to higher career levels, the emphasis should shift from measuring competencies to *judging* professional competence and capabilities. When measuring, instruments are more important than evaluators. When judging, evaluators are more important than instruments.

6. In judgmental evaluation, information is collected from a variety of sources but no one source or none of the sources in combination take the place of judgments by evaluators. Instead, the information gathered is used to shape and inform an opinion—a professional judgment by the evaluator.

7. The use of evaluation teams to sort information gathered from a variety of sources and to make informed professional judgments helps provide validity and reliability.

8. It is important that teachers participate on such teams since they can contribute to making more informed judgments.

9. School districts need to be allowed the flexibility of using teachers from the same campus in collecting information to be used by evaluation teams and in the staffing of evaluation teams.

10. Requiring that teachers demonstrate teaching competence and determining this competence by observing teacher behaviors focuses on only one dimension of several which should comprise the professional appraisal process. Evaluation should include: knowledge about teaching, ability to demonstrate this knowledge by actual teaching under observation, willingness to sustain this ability continuously, and demonstration of a commitment to continuous professional growth.

Corollary assumption: Since the individual teaching context is so critical in conducting valid and meaningful assessments, specifying universal evaluation criteria as a standard for LEAs makes more sense than providing a universal appraisal instrument.

IV. Assumptions about professional rewards

Below are listed typical desires of professional workers. Research reveals that fulfilling these desires results in increased motivation and commitment and subsequently more effective teaching and learning. The career ladder should provide for these desires:

1. Achievement and success at work.
2. Recognition for accomplishments and capabilities (merit salary increases, prizes, praise, status gains, titles, etc.).
3. Interesting, challenging, and important work.
4. Opportunity for personal and professional growth and development.
5. Increased leadership responsibilities.
6. Autonomy to make decisions, being accountable for one's actions.
7. Opportunities for work-related social interaction with other professionals.

V. Assumptions about professional growth within the career ladder
1. The career ladder should provide for a system of mentoring and supervision as new teachers work with more accomplished colleagues. Reason: Teacher education programs are not the end of one's training but the beginning. Professional development is a career process.
2. The career ladder should enhance professional sharing and cooperative relationships among teachers. Reason: Teachers typically work alone. Few role models exist for teachers to emulate, and teachers are often uninformed about the teaching practices and problems of colleagues. Few opportunities for teachers to interact with each other about their work are available. Thus teachers have fewer opportunities to provide help and seek help from each other, to give feedback and get feedback.
3. The career ladder should help promote social interaction among teachers. Reason: Social interaction is a key aspect of the improvement process. Teachers, for example, report increases in satisfaction and teaching effectiveness as supervision increases moderately. Social interaction is also the medium for which recognition is given and received. Further, teachers often report that they learn a great deal from each other and trust each other as sources of new ideas and as sharers of problems they face.

VI. Assumptions about cooperation and teaming
Cooperative professional development should be a key component to the career ladder plan. Cooperative professional development can be described as a process by which two or more teachers agree to work together for their own professional growth. It is within cooperative professional development settings that the concept of master teacher and indeed the career ladder system will likely reach its full realization.

VII. Assumptions about local autonomy
Though common principles, purposes, and assumptions might be adopted, LEAs should be allowed the widest discretion in implementing the career ladder in order to reflect local problems and needs, capitalize on the benefits of friendly competition, and obtain spirited and committed involvement at the local level.

PART V

A POSTSCRIPT ON
SCHOOL IMPROVEMENT

Nearly all of the chapters in this book are based on presentations made at the Southwestern Bell conference on school reform held at Trinity University in San Antonio, Texas, during August of 1987. A symposium was held on the last day of the conference to discuss reactions and point the way in needed directions. Participants included Brackenridge fellows David Plylar and Rose Ellen Ranson, both high school teachers; Ronald Brandt, Executive Editor for the Association for Supervision and Curriculum Development; Rebecca Canning, Vice Chair of the Texas State Board of Education; and Professor John H. Moore of Trinity University. The remarks are summarized in the chapters of Part V.

CHAPTER 18

The Reasons for Reforming Schools

RONALD S. BRANDT

Association for Supervision and Curriculum Development

At the conference in San Antonio that produced this book, some of us gathered to talk about prospects for restructuring schools. Kristine Riemann, a teacher who had been asked to chair the discussion, suggested that we start by seeing if we were in agreement about what needed to be restructured and how. It was already clear, however, that we, and the thousands of other educators we represented, were of different minds.

For example, the principals were nearly unanimous in their distaste for terms like "teacher empowerment," arguing that in the schools they lead, teachers are already active participants in the decisions that most concern them, but that teachers do not want to make the "hard" decisions, such as which staff members to lay off if that should become necessary. Central office staff members were offended by Arthur Wise's suggestion that teachers' salaries could be increased by eliminating middle-level managers, and by a teacher's insistence that everyone in school systems, including administrators, should be required to teach part-time.

None of this is new, of course. In every occupation, workers see things differently from supervisors. In education, the twenty-year metamorphosis of the National Education Association from a cooperative professional alliance into a powerful union run by classroom teachers is perhaps the most visible proof that teachers' independence has been growing steadily for some time. While most administrators consider teachers professional allies rather than enemies, they are nevertheless aware that some versions of "restructuring" involve a redistribution of power.

Will further professionalization of teaching really mean a diminished role for principals and supervisors? In the long run, it may; it will surely involve a redefinition of functions. In the next few years, however, nothing so dramatic is likely to happen. As the principals themselves pointed out, teachers in forward-looking schools already choose textbooks, plan curriculum, and even have a voice in selecting their principals. Most administrators believe that participation by faculty members in these activities is a sign of a healthy organization, and they encourage it. Nevertheless, they sometimes suggest (by phrases like "let them" and "give them") that the degree of teacher discretion is determined not by institutional policy but by the generosity and goodwill of individual administrators. Understandably, autonomy-minded teachers expect much more; they want official recognition of their professional prerogatives.

Other educators attending the conference—professors, state department officials, and association staff members like myself—were challenged by the conference experience to examine their own relationships to classroom teachers. Not that the conference was confrontational in tone—to the contrary, it was scholarly and convivial. There were a few tense moments, though, such as the time a panel moderator invited teachers to respond to a question. When after a few moments of silence a superintendent rose and began saying, "I'm not a teacher but . . . ," he was interrupted by a teacher advocate who shouted, "Then *sit down.* Ever heard of wait time?" The exchange was reasonably good-humored, but its significance did not go unnoticed.

The educators who gathered to hear the presentation of the material printed here, and their fellow educators across the country, face an unavoidable quandary. The nation will need a huge number—perhaps a million or more—new teachers in the decade ahead. It is no longer possible to rely on the fact that opportunities for women, minorities, and the rural poor are limited elsewhere to guarantee a supply of able prospective teachers. This situation is spelled out clearly in the Carnegie Foundation report, *A Nation Prepared,*[1] and in several of the chapters in this book. There is no choice but to compete for prospective employees. Aside from the obvious need to provide salaries not so low as to be "dissatisfiers," school systems must offer teachers working conditions and opportunities for self-realization comparable to those of other attractive occupations.

This does not necessarily mean the debasement of other roles in education; in fact, it may enhance some of them. It does mean creating conditions in which teachers can work productively and with reasonable levels of satisfaction. The alternative, as Arthur Wise predicts, is that teaching will become a less and less desirable occupation, that the quality of people entering it will therefore be lower, and that states and other agencies will respond by adopting evermore detailed regulations in order to control the actions of these poorly qualified people. This, of course, will make the occupation even less attractive, and so on.

This frightening scenario raises questions about the prospects for making education a true profession. My personal view is that professionalism is only partly a matter of technical characteristics, such as having a code of ethics and controlling entrance to the occupation. The prime criterion is the importance of the activity in the eyes of the general public. The main reason professional status is accorded to doctors is that they make judgments on matters of life and death and that they can help sick people get well. When health is at stake, few things seem more important.

If it is true that professional standing depends at least partly on people's perception of the importance of the work, it seems inevitable that teaching will become more highly regarded. In the information society, education is clearly of critical importance. What could be more complex, or more valuable, than developing our greatest resource, the human mind? Increasingly, parents, employers, and governments are coming to recognize that. In the future, parents who can afford it will pay, if they must, for quality education, and they will respect those who provide it. (However, the recent rash of malpractice suits shows that clients no longer regard members of even the established professions with the deference they once did.)

In other words, *some* teachers will probably gain more of the recognition and incentives they want and deserve. The question, in an age of privatism, is whether that will happen within the framework of *public* education, or whether there will eventually emerge a pattern of professional teachers employed in private or semiprivate organizations, while those who work in public bureaucracies will be considered semiprofessionals.

The possibility that the middle class might give up on the public schools, and that government policy might intentionally or unintentionally encourage them to do so, is disturbing to people committed to equal opportunity and to the role of public education in its attainment. That raises the question of what aspects of public education are most in need of reform. Three images of classroom activity may help convey the kind of changes that I consider to be most urgently needed.

The first such image may not qualify as "classroom" learning, because it took place on a dusty street in Maiduguri, Nigeria, where I was teaching as part of a Ford Foundation project in the 1960s. As I was riding in a staff car one Sunday morning, I saw a Muslim teacher whipping his students. Five or six little boys, aged about 9 or 10, were sitting in a row with their wooden slates on their laps and their arms crossed over their heads in a vain effort to shield themselves from their teacher, who walked down the line hitting them with a rope. "Why is he doing that, Issac?" I asked our driver. He chuckled (as an Ibo, he was scornful of what he considered the backward people of the North) and said, "He wants them to learn harder, sir."

Many people have a similar attitude toward American students. Michael Kirst reports that a legislator summed up the goal of the school reform movement in his state as "to make the little buggers work harder." That lawmaker had probably been reading reports of international comparisons, which are a concern to many Americans, not because they consider education the ultimate weapon in economic warfare, but because they sense that American students could be learning much more than they are at present. Unfortunately, young people distracted by television and rock music, whose prime concerns are their cars, their jobs, and members of the opposite sex, cannot easily be coerced by external pressures to learn what they consider uninteresting.

My second image comes from the massive study reported by John Goodlad in *A Place Called School.*[2] In observations of over 1000 classrooms selected to be typical of American schools, Goodlad and his colleagues found that students spent most of their classroom time listening to teachers or completing study sheets of various types. They very rarely engaged in "real" activities and were seldom even asked for evidence or opinion. Instead, the questions they were asked were aimed almost exclusively at getting them to recite the contents of their textbooks. This image of passive, rather boring classroom activity is especially striking when contrasted with the restless, exuberant nature of adolescents and with the way people of all ages learn best: through active exploration of problems they feel a need to solve.

It also contrasts with my third image of teaching, which I remember vividly from a visit to Sioux Falls, South Dakota, a few years ago. As an evaluator for an American studies project, I had the opportunity to visit the classrooms of several excellent teachers to find out how they were using what they had learned at a summer institute. When I called the South Dakota teacher to ask if I could visit her classes on a particular day, she said I was welcome but that I wouldn't see much because her students would be taking a lengthy essay exam that day. She offered to arrange for me to spend an hour with students who had been in her class the year before. Thinking that few high school students remember much about their classes from one year to the next, I reluctantly agreed.

To my amazement, the students described their activities of the year before with great enthusiasm and in animated detail. They explained that they had frequently been expected to choose topics from a list of possibilities posed by the teacher, work in small groups to gather information, and then report to their fellow students in imaginative and interesting ways. They exploded with laughter as they told of a report on South Dakota's first woman senator: one of the boys had dressed in a long skirt and a cotton sun bonnet and portrayed the senator in an imaginary television interview. From the delight those students showed as they recalled that incident, I doubt they will soon forget what they learned that day.

Some teachers may respond defensively, even angrily, to Goodlad's description of typical classrooms. Others may feel the same way about my story of the South Dakota teacher. Goodlad's purpose, however, is not to criticize teachers, and neither is mine. I know there are many other examples of inspired teaching, just as I recognize that there are good reasons (well documented in, for example, Ted Sizer's *Horace's Compromise*[3]) that much teaching in today's schools is routine and unexciting. The point is that there must be more teaching that touches students' emotions and fires their imaginations.

A major goal of the second round of school reform, then, should be to foster the conditions associated with such teaching. The agenda should include two related efforts: (1) to identify carefully the incentives that matter most to the kinds of people who will make the best teachers and (2) to redesign schools so as to provide more of those incentives. Many of the factors affecting the quality of teaching, such as salary policies and state testing programs, are not under educators' direct control. Others are, however, and their importance must not be underestimated. Local administrators can strive to make their schools places in which they themselves would want to teach. The purpose is not to mollify individual teachers, but to create the conditions that will nurture great teaching and, therefore, stimulate learning.

NOTES

1. Carnegie Task Force on Teaching as a Profession, *A Nation Prepared: Teachers for the 21st Century* (Hyattsville, Md.: Carnegie Task Force on Teaching as a Profession, 1986).
2. John I. Goodlad, *A Place Called School* (New York: McGraw-Hill, 1984).
3. Theodore R. Sizer, *Horace's Compromise: The Dilemma of the American High School* (Boston: Houghton Mifflin, 1984).

CHAPTER 19

Postscript to the Conference

REBECCA CANNING

State Board of Education of Texas

The premise of this conference has been that education in the United States must again be reformed, because the first wave of reform was authoritarian, top-down, lacking in the correct content, narrow, and rigid. The second wave—as heralded by this conference—is up for grabs. The first three and a half days of the conference gave the impression that the second wave was restructuring, but then that began to be questioned. Then Michael Kirst suggested that, in fact, students at risk might well be riding the crest of the second wave. I tend to believe that Michael Kirst might be right. Throughout Texas, I see growing from the bottom up a tremendous amount of concern for students at risk.

Nevertheless, the conference assumed that immediate reform is imperative. That assumption was made, not on a review of research regarding the effects of the first wave of reform, but on other sorts of research, accumulated wisdom, and common sense. Thus the title of the conference: "A New Reform Agenda."

The participants have met in a great hall—isolated, out of context, and with the notion that their work can somehow make a difference. Can it? If so, how? What are the next steps?

First, I think change must be perceived and developed in an evolving way—that is, there must be a commitment to ongoing change within a positive, constructive process. It must be acknowledged that reform is not the work of a single piece of legislation, a single event, or a single wave, but rather an ongoing obligation to scrutinize what is going on and attempt to make needed improvements. Any call for new reforms must be based on constructive scrutiny and evaluation of present reforms. There must be an end to adversarial roles and rhetoric, snappy determinations of vast failures, oversimplifications about complex educational systems, and condemnations of the know-nothing noneducators. The content espoused here should be used to create a constructive climate for evolving change.

What is that content?

1. The training for recognition of concrete problems and shared or mutual problem solving
2. An attitude of valuing uncertainty rather than quick fixes and ready action
3. An attitude of positive, mutual respect—the very thing teachers claim they want and in fact deeply deserve

Everyone involved in education must become colleagues in shaping change. This approach is necessary because the context of education is a community—cultural, political, and moral. Democratic decisions that affect the schools must take into consideration factors that have not been mentioned within these great walls but are compelling in the real world, such as the following:

1. Cost and cost effectiveness
2. Political expediency as well as the political process
3. The limitations that do exist with regard to measures, power, institutions, and people
4. The encroachment of technology, questioning the very way education is "delivered"
5. Vouchers, the private sector, and parental choice

Secondly, the core must be defined. Tom Sergiovanni's presentation included an especially nifty notion: the concept of leadership by outrage. It begins with a core of central purpose and content, around which structures may vary, but toward which all who are working in an area should be committed. The leader would encourage an enormous amount of flexibility, individuality of approach, and program variance, but if the core were violated, outrage would bring the school community back to its central purpose.

The core of education should be defined in a simple, elegant, and generic way. Much has been said here about the medical model, and it's interesting to note that the core in medicine may be defined in different ways, with varying implications. Francis Peabody, a physician at the Massachusetts General Hospital, said, "The secret of caring for the patient is caring for the patient," thus combining the science and the art of being a healer. In contrast, the Army Medical Corps defines its core commitment as "To preserve the fighting strength." Clearly, different ramifications for content and structure would surround each of these concepts of the core.

It sounds simple to define a core for public education. Even if the participants here agreed among themselves, the community beyond these walls does not agree on the mission and the implications for action. In terms of organization, for instance, colleague relationships and empowerment for teachers have often been invoked here, but there are those who still believe strongly in an absolute hierarchy of authority. In terms of measurement of content, participants here have spoken of higher-order thinking skills and "real world" learning, but there are people throughout the country who believe that test scores are the only measure of educational productivity. Those test scores often become reduced to bits of information and bits of skills in the two or three primary arenas that get tested—reading, math, and sometimes writing. There is also a lack of agreement with regard to teachers. Whereas this conference has expressed a belief in strong individuals, growing professionals capable of being entrusted with the public confidence within their classrooms, there are those who believe that heavy supervision must be built into the school system. That is nowhere more apparent than in the teacher appraisal systems here in Texas.

To define the core, the whole community must be included. The first reform wave happened in Texas because parents and citizens finally noticed that the schools were graduating illiterate children who added by counting on their fingers. Whether or not educators like it or want it, parents and citizens who pay for the schools, and who have their children there, have a right and an obligation to be involved in decision-making about what constitutes the ultimate purpose of the public education system.

The third step is to build useful strategies for evolving change. These strategies must be the bridges between the high, hard ground of rigor and the daily slog through the swamp. First of all models are needed—currently existing programs that are effective, such as Judy Shulman's *The Mentor Teacher Casebook* and Howard Gardner's Spectrum School, and new models, especially those that emphasize the bottom-up restructuring discussed in these meetings. There is a need for models that enable teachers and administrators to work together in creative new ways to develop programs, as well as ways of disseminating information and learning from one another's models.

A second approach must be through teacher education programs. I like Judy Lanier's statement regarding partnerships between universities and schools. There must be strong, direct, practical links between universities and schools, going beyond the lab schools. Those who are preparing teachers must go out into the schools and get their hands dirty on a regular basis. There is room to question current patterns of preparing teachers within the university system, such as the student teaching arrangement. Peer relationships must be developed with other teacher training institutions. Who is at this conference? Representatives of the good universities—the good people, the effective ones. Who is not here? The other teacher training institutions also need the benefit of the new thinking and progressive possibilities envisioned here, and they need practical help in getting there.

Third, all educational entities need to involve themselves in the planning process. Educators must be proactive instead of reactive in the political and community decisions that are made regarding education. Educators need to take responsibility for constructing rather than criticizing.

The fourth step toward the future is communication building. If this sounds soft, I assure you it is equally important. The structure of the Bell conference has been top-down—diametrically opposed to the structure that has been advocated in the content of the presentations. Participants presented their ideas in the form of papers in a formal setting, despite the fact that the content of those papers advocated broader, grass-roots participation. The way we communicate must be reviewed. How do educators share information with others? By way of esoteric monographs and books? How can the base of communication be broadened beyond a theoretical level so that participants become involved in practical conversations about implementation of change?

A couple of years ago, when our State Board of Education started the process of altering the Standards for the Teaching Profession, I met with the sixty-seven deans of the schools of education at their annual meeting. Those deans had just discovered, to their extreme consternation, that the board on which I serve had the authority to alter the standards for the content of teacher education programs. I asked the group assembled what the basic ingredients, the essential components, of equipping persons to become teachers in a classroom would be. What were the primary concepts? What were the essential skills? I asked for their help in making those definitions. Instead, seething with hostility, they declared, "Look, we have our thirty required hours in place, and who are you to reconsider the content of teacher education in Texas?"

So I went to visit Ted Sizer. We had a wonderful morning talking about teacher education. Then I told him about the deans and asked for his advice. He asked me if I had spotted anyone among that group who was less hostile, and I admitted, "Yes, a few." He went on, "How about less hostile but also people who might look bright?" I answered, "Yes, in fact there were a couple of those as well." (I'm happy to say that John Moore was one of them.) Sizer said, "Go and work with them." So I did.

Whose responsibility is communication anyway? What will the participants do after this conference? What touchstones will they have with each other? Will they become, like the portion of the samples in the New England Journal of Medicine studies, the group that was lost to follow-up? Rudyard Kipling, in describing the old men who were recounting their brave and proud exploits of long ago, had them recall "That night we stormed Valhalla a million years ago." Will this conference be a faded memory like that, or will there be viable, useful follow-up? What to share and do with this experience is in the hands of the participants.

Education needs a constructive climate for creating evolving change, a definition of the core, content that includes models and strategies, and communication. Educators will build the confidence and trust that are now missing; they are colleagues already, brothers on a journey.

CHAPTER 20

A Teacher's Comment

DAVID H. PLYLAR

Harlandale Independent School District, San Antonio, Texas

My favorite character in "The Wizard of Oz" is the scarecrow. He teaches something about empowerment for teachers. The scarecrow travels all the way to the Emerald City and risks his life to help do away with the Wicked Witch of the West. He does all this so that the Wizard will give him a brain. Then, toward the end of the story, the wizard admits that he cannot give the scarecrow what he wants. But, says the wizard, you don't really need a brain anyway; what you need is a diploma! So the wizard hands over the diploma, and miraculously, instantaneously, the scarecrow becomes a raving genius. What happened? The wizard had no brain to give; in fact, the wizard by this point is a self-declared fraud. What he *could* do, however, was to help the scarecrow realize that he has had this power—this genius—all along! The wizard's role is to make the scarecrow see his own potential and power and to legitimize the use of it.

This story carries with it some important messages to those of you who are preparing prospective teachers. Aspiring teachers, like so many scarecrows, will come to your classes with the seeds of assertiveness, efficiency, and power already within them. It is encumbant upon you, as wizards, to raise the level of power consciousness in your students. Then you should help them to understand how this power can be used to achieve good ends.

What would be included in the empowerment curriculum in colleges of education? For starters, teacher preparation courses should deal, in a practical way, with the politics of institutions and group dynamics. Assertiveness training would be helpful, as would the study of mediation strategies. The study of ethics has an important place in such a curriculum as well. For teacher educators with more adventure in their hearts, I recommend teaching such things as applied passive/aggressive behavior and tactical stonewalling of state education agency bureaucrats. A dose of Saul Alinsky wouldn't hurt either. Of course, you will need to give the appropriate caveats about the dangers and pitfalls in the uses of power.

When newly empowered teachers begin to work, they will encounter another set of wizards: principals, superintendents, and assorted bureaucrats. Lee Shulman mentioned the key factor that these wizards play in the process of empowerment: Administrators must put trust in the notion that teachers will use power wisely. This won't be quick or easy; it will be a process for teachers to be allowed to prove their trustworthiness. As school administrators become more trusting, they will be more vulnerable. For this reason, raising this level of trust should be the first priority of administrators if empowerment within the profession is important.

The report that the Brackenridge Forum for the Enhancement of Teaching issued earlier this year indicated that in Texas, and many other states, there is "a bureaucratic system within which students, teachers and administrators become more concerned about doing things right than doing right things." In his presentation, Art Wise pointed out that the system of managing education in this country is the "major culprit in distorting educational outcomes we seek to obtain." His suggested remedy is to reduce the size of the bureaucracy significantly. Kathy Krnavek, one of the Brackenridge Fellows, who heard Art make this remark, said, "I can just see our administrators running around saying, 'Wow! We've got to get rid of ourselves.'" Art provides a simple solution to the problem of bureaucracy—reduce it! Kathy's observation speaks to the fact that people will not accede easily to the idea that their work is superfluous, redundant, or counterproductive.

The central question, then, is how to reduce the bureaucracy and the limitations it imposes without producing an adverse impact on programs or putting large numbers of bureaucrats out of work. Here are some partial answers:

1. Decide that large-scale cutbacks can occur over a period of several years—perhaps throughout one generation. Cuts do not have to be made overnight.
2. Never fill a bureaucrat's position left vacant by retirement or voluntary termination. Rather, identify the absolutely essential tasks, if any, performed by the departed one, and apportion those tasks equitably among the remaining bureaucrats.

3. Never contact the state education agency to clarify laws or regulations. Rather, always interpret these laws and regulations yourself—whenever possible, in a way that avoids adding personnel to your staff.
4. Encourage bureaucrats to return to full-time work as teachers or provide opportunities for split time between teaching and administering.

School management in this country tends to mirror the philosophy of business management. This may explain why so many schools look like malls nowadays, but more importantly why the size of the school bureaucracy has mushroomed. Moreover, American business management has earned a worldwide reputation for being highly inefficient. For example, on average, about 15% of our workforce is classified as managerial—twice as high a percentage as in Japan and Germany.

In closing, I note that in the past three days the participants have found themselves elbow-deep in metaphors. A couple of those metaphors bothered me. Yesterday someone likened superintendents to orchestra conductors, and someone else compared the job to a traffic cop's. I'm not too satisfied with either of these, because they raise the superintendent out of the fray. I would offer a third view of the superintendent, as the lead saxophone player in a jazz band. He or she carries the tune part of the time, but also extemporizes and allows fellow musicians the same freedom. In the end, they make pretty music together by using everyone's skills to the fullest.

CHAPTER 21

A Teacher's Comment

ROSE ELLEN RANSON

Alamo Heights Independent School District, San Antonio, Texas

These comments could have been much more easily formulated if I had delivered them before I entered teaching. When I put on the red shoes and started down the yellow brick road, I could have described the Emerald City, my educational utopia, with glib assurance, uninhibited by any contact with reality. However, a funny thing happened on the road to Oz; there have been many detours and several witches to slay. The abrading effects of experience, while they have left the vision intact, have caused me to question that I know how to reach the destination.

Fortunately, there have been many helpful colleagues along the road, most recently the speakers of the last two days. They have spoken with elegance and erudition, assessing problems and charting possible courses of action. Whatever benefit the conference has had for others, for me it has been an energizing and edifying experience. The speakers have broadened my perspective, legitimized with scholarly research some of my dimly formulated notions, and generated provocative questions. Let me react to one or two issues that have been raised.

It is frequently said that the teaching profession is in dire straits, with many experienced teachers leaving the classroom. Susan Rosenholtz has described the isolation that produces teacher burnout after five or seven years in the classroom. By that time, teachers have taught themselves everything they can, have exhausted their personal resources, and have no sources of renewal. Judith Schwartz says that most of you at the conference began work in a primary or secondary classroom until you moved on to loftier pursuits. I have a suggestion: Come back to the classroom for another three or five years. There is work enough for all, and the benefits will be reciprocal. Researchers can do their own field testing; theorists can verify their ideas in actual situations; teacher educators can demonstrate effective strategies; administrators can directly engage the minds of young people and restore their classroom perspective. Perhaps it is time to restructure the design of an educational career, replacing the present linear model with a cyclical arrangement that periodically returns all educators to classrooms.

The question of involving teachers in decisionmaking has surfaced frequently, described in various terms. The phrase "teacher empowerment" sounds more muscular than the emphasis I would make. I think rather of the intellectual power, the professional judgment that is needed to resolve educational issues in this vast and complex enterprise. Inviting teachers to think seriously about their work certainly involves risks and hazards, and several speakers have described those perils. Shakespeare recognized them when he had Julius Caesar say of Cassius, "He thinks too much; such men are dangerous." Dangerous they are— to preconceived ideas, to established systems, to entrenched regimes. Thinking is risky because it can produce unpredictable, unexpected, and sometimes very wonderful results.

During the last two days I've heard people asking, "Do teachers really want to manage the schools?" and "Do teachers have anything useful to say about educational issues in the schools?" To both of these questions, I think the answer is a ringing "yes and no." Some do and some don't. The 2.2 million teachers in America encompass the entire spectrum of ability. The best are formidably intelligent and immensely talented, people who would make a distinguished contribution to any field of endeavor. The worst are surely an embarrassment to the schools, to themselves, and to their students. However, even though some teachers may prefer not to think about instructional issues, it seems essential that they do so. Teachers *ought* to have something useful to say about subjects such as course content, methods of instruction, and working conditions that promote effective teaching.

The significance and complexity of the task make it imperative that all educators get a chance to think about it. If there is conflict, if there is tension, let them be used constructively. Let the criterion for a decision be, "Is this useful for the education of our students?" My view of instructional decisionmaking is more horizontal than vertical. The chapter by Bacharach and Conley identifies five decision areas that may logically involve teachers; Henry Cotton tells us that his teachers in Colorado are already participating in these ways. Even in Texas, where teachers feel severely limited, there are districts that routinely include teachers in instructional decisions. For example, trustees in one district frequently invite teachers to discuss issues with the board before they make a final decision. On one occasion, a committee of teachers drafted an instructional policy for the district and it was later adopted by the trustees. It is possible to shape a productive educational partnership among trustees, administrators, patrons, teachers—and sometimes even students.

Where do we go from here? Well, next week I return to school, my native habitat, not to emerge until Christmas. The Brackenridge Forum continues with new emphases. This year the members are trying to act on some of the concerns raised in the report—teacher recruitment, teacher education, and a mentoring/induction year for teachers entering the profession. In addition, several of the fellows have initiated projects in their buildings or districts—a mini-forum group in one district, a communication plan in another. Perhaps these seem like small steps, but they are an attempt to translate words into action—or, if you prefer, theory into practice. The yellow brick road is under construction. If, or when, we reach the Emerald City and meet the wizard, we will find, in Pogo's pungent grammar, that "he is us." If our students are to gain authentic rather than symbolic hearts and brains, it will require all educators' collective skill, intellect, and energy—and maybe a little magic as well.

CHAPTER 22

Better Schools for the
Twenty-First Century:
A School Improvement Proposal

JOHN H. MOORE

Trinity University

Public elementary and secondary education in the United States is at a crossroads. The success of educators' efforts to enhance teaching and learning and to improve schooling during the remaining years of this century will have a profound influence on the nation's role as leader of the free world, and the quality of life for Americans in the twenty-first century. Perhaps never before in the history of the republic has the success of this nation and people been linked so inextricably to the quality of education available to young people in the nation's elementary and secondary schools. It has become increasingly clear that the indispensable ingredient to success is a better educated citizenry.

The educational reform movement currently underway grew out of a national debate, begun in the 1950s, related to the quality of public education. While it has been argued that public schools are better now than at any previous time in the nation's history, there has been a growing concern in many quarters that American schools are simply not equipped to provide the quality of education young people will need for productive and fulfilling lives during the next century. Moreover, there is substantial evidence to suggest that the nation's business, civic, and political leadership has little confidence that public schools can teach the basic skills students will need in the future. This loss of confidence, exacerbated by the economic success of the Japanese and Koreans, has generated reform initiatives in virtually every state in the nation. The patterns from state to state are similar, and almost without exception the efforts to reform schools have been related to the following concerns:

1. Increasing standards and expectations
2. Defining and prescribing the content to be taught
3. Extending and improving the quality of time allocated for instruction
4. Improving the leadership in public education
5. Assessing and improving the quality of teaching in the classroom
6. Increasing financial support for the educational enterprise

While the jury is still out as to the overall effectiveness of the reform package, there is general agreement that improvements were needed and action overdue. The initiatives have enjoyed wide public support. Indeed, a number of the reform efforts will improve schooling and, perhaps more importantly, play a role in restoring confidence in public education. In short, the reform movement of the 1980s is well along, but important work lies ahead if fundamental and enduring improvements in teaching, learning, and schooling are to be made.

As the school improvement effort continues, two critical questions might guide thinking and shape the agenda: First, what issues are fundamental to school improvement, and thus worth pursuing? Secondly, how to effect change that will ultimately strengthen public education and better serve the young people of the United States?

The issues discussed and the propositions framed in the preceding chapters of this book will undoubtedly influence the next phase of the school reform movement. The salient themes that pervade the book— enhancing the effectiveness of classroom teachers, reconstituting the role and function of school leaders, and recasting the schools as centers of inquiry—will be the cornerstone of serious school improvement efforts during the next few years. A number of projects are underway, and a variety of settings are suitable for pursuing reform projects. I suggest that one of the most appealing is the arena of teacher education.

The teacher education agenda is broad and features such initiatives as continuing efforts to recruit able candidates for teaching, using forgiveable loans and scholarships provided by the federal and state governments, private foundations and corporations, as well as the colleges and universities. A growing number of states have sponsored public-relations campaigns, modeled after recent armed services recruitment projects, to attract more people to careers in teaching. The next decade will bring significant changes in the way teacher education programs are constituted. Approximately one hundred colleges and universities in the nation have adopted the Holmes Group agenda, which encourages extended preparation programs with more rigorous admission standards, a major in the arts and sciences, a strong clinical component set in the public schools, and more meaningful and effective connections with the public schools, including a much more significant role in teacher education for successful practitioners.

Perhaps the vehicle established to reform teacher education could also be utilized to restructure teaching and schools. If one endorses the proposition that improving education is a school-by-school endeavor, best undertaken by a team of individuals from a variety of institutions working together for better schools, then the teacher education model will be effective. One such model is described in ensuing paragraphs.

THE ALLIANCE FOR BETTER SCHOOLS

The Alliance for Better Schools was organized to bring together related institutions committed to the improvement of public education in San Antonio, Texas. The institutions constituting the initial membership of the alliance are Trinity University, North East Independent School District, San Antonio Independent School District, The Psychological Corporation, and the George W. Brackenridge Foundation. It is anticipated that other institutions will join the alliance as specific school improvement projects are identified, defined, and begun.

Goals and Objectives. The principal goal of the alliance is the improvement of elementary and secondary schooling. At the same time, the alliance will seek to develop school improvement models that may be utilized in other educational settings. A second principal goal is to fashion new, effective partnerships among institutions committed to the improvement of public education.

Professional Development Schools. Four school sites—two elementary and two secondary schools—will be used as laboratories (and as Professional Development Schools) for the alliance. These four schools will be experimental and demonstrational in nature and will serve as magnet schools for faculty who want to work in an environment dedicated to the development and dissemination of best practices in teaching, learning, and schooling. The respective school districts will continue to administer the schools, but alliance members will have ready access to the facilities and programs. The initial focus of the alliance will be twofold: school improvement projects and a five-year teacher education program.

School Improvement Projects. The alliance will undertake a variety of carefully selected school improvement projects. Some of the projects will focus on critical day-to-day issues, while other efforts will be more experimental in nature and explore new and creative proposals for school improvement. Many of the recommendations found in this book will be examined carefully by the Alliance for Better Schools over the next decade.

An Extended Teacher Education Program. The alliance will develop and put into place in the Professional Development Schools a new extended teacher education program. The program will feature a clinical approach, with new roles for public school practitioners as well as university faculty.

The Executive Committee and Forum. The Executive Committee will provide leadership and establish general policy for the Alliance for Better Schools. The membership includes the chief executive officers from the member institutions. The real action, however, is in the Forum.

The Forum consists of representatives from the member institutions, but a majority of its membership consists of classroom teachers from the Professional Development Schools. The Forum, with meetings scheduled in the summer and throughout the academic year, is the vehicle for bringing together the key participants in the alliance on a continuing basis. The members of the Forum will be the primary force for establishing specific goals and objectives for the alliance, designing and implementing various school improvement projects, and assessing the effectiveness of the projects. The membership of the Forum will also oversee the development and implementation, as well as the continuous evaluation, of the five-year teacher education program.

Implementation and Funding. The Alliance for Better Schools was organized during the summer of 1987, and the four Professional Development Schools identified. A significant staff development program will be initiated during the summer of 1988, beginning a long-term effort to improve elementary and secondary education. The member institutions will bear the normal and usual costs of the enterprise, but external funding will be sought to support specific school improvement initiatives.

The Alliance for Better Schools is one of many undertakings across the nation to effect fundamental and lasting change in the way schools are structured and teachers organized for instruction. Perhaps the model will be useful to others engaged in school improvement projects.

Public education is one of our nation's most important institutions. The success of the nation and its people in the next century depends to a large degree on the quality of teaching and learning in the elementary and secondary schools. There will be special "windows of opportunity" to effect needed change from time to time, but the process of school improvement is ongoing. Perhaps the issues and propositions featured in this book will make a contribution to the enhancement of teaching and learning and the improvement of schooling in the United States for the twenty-first century.

INDEX